Corporate Financial Strategy

By Keith Ward

Strategic Management Accounting

Corporate Financial Strategy

2nd edition

Ruth Bender and Keith Ward

AMSTERDAM BOSTON HEIDELBERG LONDON NEW YORK OXFORD
PARIS SAN DIEGO SAN FRANCISCO SINGAPORE SYDNEY TOKYO

Butterworth-Heinemann
An imprint of Elsevier Science
Linacre House, Jordan Hill, Oxford OX2 8DP
200 Wheeler Road, Burlington, MA 01803

First published 1993
Reprinted 1993, 1994, 1995, 1997, 1998, 1999, 2000, 2001
Second edition 2002
Reprinted 2003 (twice)

British Library Cataloguing in Publication Data
Bender, R.
  Corporate financial strategy - 2nd ed.
  1. Corporations - Finance   2. Business planning
  I. Title   II. Ward, Keith
  658.1'5

Library of Congress Cataloguing in Publication Data
A catalogue record for this book is available from the Library of Congress

ISBN 0 7506 4899 6

For information on all Butterworth-Heinemann publications
visit our website at www.bh.com

Typeset by Integra Software Services Pvt. Ltd., Pondicherry, India
www.integra-india.com
Printed and bound in Great Britain by Martins the Printers

Contents

PART 4: TRANSACTIONS AND OPERATING ISSUES

APPENDICES

Preface to second edition

It is now nine years since the first edition was published. In that time there have been many developments in the financial world, and in our own views about financial strategy. Feedback from several generations of MBA students and executives has also guided our thoughts. Accordingly, we believe that this edition is more understandable and more relevant to the needs of students and managers today.

The major changes we have made in this edition include:

- The section on financial theory has been placed in an appendix, so as not to disrupt the flow of the text for the knowledgeable reader. A separate appendix discusses option valuation.
- The discussion of the implication for strategy of a company's share price has been expanded and placed in a separate chapter.
- The order of the book has been revised to create a separate section on Financial Instruments, which sets out the key variables and discusses instruments currently on the market.
- A new section on Transactions and Operating Issues discusses the practicalities of flotations, acquisitions, restructuring and MBOs, as well as placing them in the context of financial strategy. The section also introduces chapters on working capital and on executive compensation, both of which can have a major impact on value.
- The section for Banks and Professional Advisors which was in the first edition has been dropped, although some of that information is included elsewhere in this text.

Throughout, our aim has been to make the book more readable, and more useful to the reader. To this end, all of the case studies have been updated, and more
Working Insights included to illustrate the discussions.

The preface to the first edition thanked Keith's family for all of their support.
In this edition, we extend those thanks to Ruth's family, and in particular to
Alfred Bender, for his constant encouragement.

Ruth Bender
Keith Ward

Preface to first edition

This book has been written as a practical guide to the way in which the appropriate use of financial strategy can add value to the overall corporate strategy used by an organization. Thus the relevant theories of corporate finance are considered but their more important applications in the real world represent the major thrust of the book. The material for the book is based upon many years experience as a practising senior financial manager and corporate finance consultant. This material has been refined and tested by use on advanced MBA courses at Cranfield School of Management and in programmes held for senior managers and corporate finance bankers around the world. Hence a large number of real company case studies are included, together with a wide range of illustrative examples which link the various parts of the theory and try to explain numerically how financial markets really work.

I have made no attempt to reproduce the many existing textbooks on financial theory, although the requisite theories are summarized and explained. The objective is to go much further in placing the theory into a usable context which should enable practising managers to understand more fully the potential value added by the best financial strategy available to them. Indeed the major stimulus to writing this book has been the requests from clients, and participants on seminars and courses, for reading material to consolidate and develop the ideas which I have been presenting. Only you, the reader, can judge if this effort has been worthwhile but the structure of the book has been designed to make it of value even if not read from cover to cover.

Thus Part One consists of an overview of financial strategy and its role within the overall corporate strategy of the business. Part Two considers in much more detail the various components of the financial strategies which are appropriate to each stage of development of the company. This is dealing with organic, internal development, whereas in Part Three the important role of dynamic growth is introduced. In this part of the book, many of the recent innovative financial products are considered from both a conceptual and practical viewpoint. This review highlights how the financial markets have, in several cases, become obsessed with the cleverness of their mathematical ways of financially engineering apparent solutions to 'doing deals'. As a consequence they have forgotten the basic fundamentals of relating the financial return to the risk involved in 'the deal'; many companies are now struggling with the consequences of this sophistication in corporate finance!

Part Four considers the impact of the opposite types of strategies which are involved in consolidating or refocusing the business, possibly before embarking on another period of growth but in a different direction. Thus the leveraged buy-outs and management buy-outs which sometime result are considered, as are the fundamental issues raised both by privatization of nationalized industries and decisions to take existing quoted companies out of the public domain, which represents a more logical use of the term 'privatization'. Part Five concludes the book by looking at financial strategy from the perspective of the externally based, professional financial adviser. This ever-increasing body of bankers, accountants, lawyers and other forms of strategic consultant have an understandably keen interest in the practical implementation of financial strategy by their clients, as considered in the earlier parts of the book. However, the particular interests of advisers also include how they should develop their own competitive strategies, so as to earn 'a more than satisfactory return' themselves. Thus the corporate finance deal-making process is analysed and a detailed analytical model is outlined to enable a sound, comprehensive and tailored strategy to be developed for the particular adviser.

Very deliberately the illustrative examples and real case studies used throughout the book have been analysed using relatively simple mathematics; the simplifying assumptions do not destroy the underlying reasoning behind the analysis. The objective is to convey the conceptual logic behind financial strategy rather than to confuse with spuriously accurate mathematics and excessively complex formulae.

I wish to thank my secretary, Sheila Hart and her colleagues, Marjorie Dawe and Joy Fisher, for typing the manuscript and Natalie Thomas for producing the computer-generated figures. I am also very grateful to my family Angela, Sam and Rob for their support during the writing of this book, however grudgingly given; I hope that their sacrifice has been worthwhlie.

Keith Ward

Putting Financial Strategy in Context

Corporate financial strategy: setting the context

OVERVIEW

The aim of a company is to create value for its shareholders. Although other stakeholders are important, and are discussed in this chapter, the shareholder is the principal stakeholder, and creation of shareholder value the main objective. In order to create this value, the company has to create a competitive advantage to exploit inconsistencies in the markets in which it operates – both its trading environment and its financial environment. In this book we discuss how financial strategy can be used to identify and exploit value-creating opportunities.

In this chapter we define financial strategy as having two components: (1) the raising of funds needed by an organization in the most appropriate manner; and (2) managing the employment of those funds within the organization, including the decision to reinvest or distribute any subsequent profits generated; these are the issues addressed throughout the book.

A two-stage investment model is introduced, and it is noted that 'value' can relate either to the underlying business, or to the value created for the investors; a successful company needs to match the two, and to ensure that its share price reflects the fundamental value of its businesses.

An understanding of corporate value is impossible without addressing the issues of perceived risk and required return. We examine the relationship between these factors; note that different stakeholders may have different risk perceptions; and define 'value' as relating to returns generated in excess of the required return. This latter point means that value is only created by investments generating a positive net present value. Following from this, three metrics of value calculation are introduced; two relating to 'internal' value of the business, and one which shows value to the investor.

Finally in this chapter, we discuss the apparent anomaly in that financial academics show that markets are indifferent to the creative manipulation of accounting results, whereas companies and their advisors seem to spend considerable time and effort doing just that. We discuss what this means for financial strategy.

INTRODUCTION

The main focus of a financial strategy is on the financial aspects of strategic decisions. Inevitably, this implies a close linkage with the interests of shareholders and hence with capital markets. However, a sound financial strategy must, like the best corporate and competitive strategies, take account of all the external and internal stakeholders in the business.

Also, capital market theories and research are mainly concerned at the macro-economic level, whereas financial strategies are specific and tailored to the needs of the individual company and, in some cases, even to the sub-divisions within that company. Therefore the working definition of financial strategy which will be used throughout the book tries to take account of the need to focus on these inter-relationships at the micro level of individual business organizations.

Financial strategy can be defined as having two components. Firstly, it relates to raising the funds needed by an organization in the most appropriate manner. Its second aspect is in managing the employment of those funds within the organization, including the decision to reinvest or distribute any subsequent profits generated by the organization. 'The most appropriate manner' is dictated both by the overall strategy of the organization and the combined weighted requirements of its key stakeholders; but a major objective of the financial strategy should be to add value, which may not always be achieved by attempting to minimize costs. If it is remembered that a major objective for commercial organizations is to develop a sustainable competitive advantage in order to achieve a more than acceptable, risk-adjusted rate of return for these key stakeholders, a logical way to judge the success of a financial strategy is by reference to the contribution made to such an overall objective.

FINANCIAL STRATEGY AND STANDARD FINANCIAL THEORY

Let us state our case immediately – if you are an apostle of the beliefs of modern financial theory, this book is going to upset you. If you firmly believe in the efficient market hypothesis, or consider that the market value of a company really reflects the discounted value of its future cash flows, you're not going to like much of what we have to say. And should you believe implicitly the work of Modigliani and Miller (as an absolute rather than as a guide to theory development) then this is not the book for you.[1]

However, if, as we have, you have pondered why it is that intelligent and well qualified finance directors and their advisors seem to be prepared to spend large amounts of their time and their shareholders' money in devising complex schemes to do things which, according to financial theory, are either completely unproductive or actually counter-productive in terms of increasing shareholder wealth... read on.

There is a large body of research evidence which indicates that financial markets are quite efficient at identifying and allowing for some relatively simple accounting tricks, such as changes in stock valuation or depreciation policies, etc. The research shows that such accounting manoeuvres do not increase company value, as the markets see through them. However, as will be illustrated by the real examples used throughout the book, many reputable companies employ very sophisticated 'creative' accounting presentations to disguise the effects of their presumably widely-understood transactions. A major thrust of this book is therefore to try to bridge this apparently growing gap between the academic theorists, who profess to believe that financial markets are becoming ever more efficient and perfect, and the practising financial managers, who ignore the financial theory and do what they believe works in practice.

A fundamental proposition behind this book is that financial theory fulfils a very useful conceptual role in providing an analytical framework with which to dissect and understand actual, individual corporate finance transactions. It is also a major contention of the book that financial theory is wrong to suggest that shareholder value cannot be significantly improved by the implementation of the most appropriate financial strategy for each particular business. Value, as we shall see, is a function of the relationship between perceived risk and required return. Shareholders, and other key stakeholders, do not all perceive risks in the same way, nor do they have the same desired relationship between risk and return. Thus value can be created in the cracks between the different perceptions, and it is here that financial strategy can blossom.

RISK AND RETURN: A FUNDAMENTAL OF FINANCE

It is a fundamental principle underlying financial theory that investors will demand a return commensurate with the risk characteristics that they perceive in their investment. This is illustrated in Figure 1.1.

The diagram in Figure 1.1 is known colloquially as the 'risk–return line' and shows the required return for any given level of risk. Although the axes are often referred to as 'risk' and 'return', it is important that you understand that

---

1. Having said that, if you have no idea about the concepts discussed in this paragraph, it would be well worth your while to explore them in one of the standard financial text books, for example *Corporate Financial Management*, by Glen Arnold, Prentice Hall (2002).

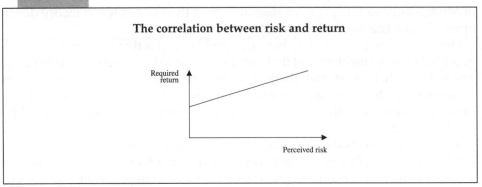

Figure 1.1

The correlation between risk and return

their full descriptions are 'perceived risk' and 'required return'. If I do not understand the full extent of the risks that I am taking on an investment, I may settle for a lower required return than another investor with a better appreciation. Alternatively, a sophisticated investor with a great understanding of the low probability of a particularly adverse outcome may settle for a lower return than a naïve investor who runs scared of the downside. What is important is each investor's *perception* of the risk; it is in the gaps between different perceptions that a tailored financial strategy can often add value.

In a similar fashion the vertical axis in Figure 1.1, often referred to as 'return', is actually *required* return. The very fact that an investment carries a level of risk means that there is no guarantee of its final outcome (risk is generally defined in finance as the volatility of expected outcomes); the graph shows what the investor would need in order to match the market expectations.

FINANCIAL STRATEGY

We must start this section with a disclaimer: this is not a book on competitive strategy. Many excellent tomes discuss that subject, setting out the whys and wherefores of determining and pursuing appropriate strategies. This book is about *corporate financial strategy* and it is in this context that strategy is discussed. However, because we make this distinction, we have to define our terms very clearly, so that you, the reader, are left in no doubt about our purpose.

Consider the representation of a company in Figure 1.2.

To most people, a company is seen as an end in its own right. It serves markets, manufactures product, employs staff, and its strategy should be about selecting the most appropriate markets, production facilities or employees in which to invest. (Throughout the book, the term 'product' will be used to describe both goods and services, and the term 'markets' will be used to cover groups of customers or specific channels of distribution.) Corporate growth and success – often measured in terms of turnover or profit – are what's seen as important, and the business develops a momentum of its own. But Figure 1.2 shows that the investment process does in fact extend over two stages: investors

Figure 1.2

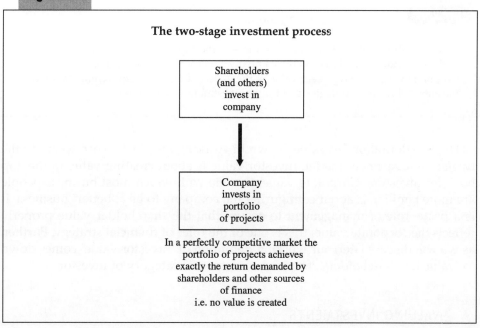

The two-stage investment process

Shareholders
(and others)
invest in
company

Company
invests in
portfolio
of projects

In a perfectly competitive market the
portfolio of projects achieves
exactly the return demanded by
shareholders and other sources
of finance
i.e. no value is created

choose the companies in which they want to invest, and the companies choose how to apply those funds to their activities.

For example, as investors we can choose to invest our funds in the UK or elsewhere in the world. We can opt to put our money into the pharmaceutical sector, or into printing or food production or any other sector we choose. And if we do care to be exposed to UK pharmaceutical companies, we can decide specifically, for example, to buy shares in GlaxoSmithKline or in British Biotechnology. The top process in Figure 1.2 relates to this investor decision.

The lower process shows how the company (acting through its directors' decisions) decides that yes, it does want to be in the pharmaceuticals sector; that it will apply this strategy by developing its own drugs (or perhaps by buying the results of others' research, or perhaps by selling generics); that it will sell in various specific geographical markets but not others, perhaps investing in a dedicated salesforce, etc. The 'projects' referred to in the lower box in Figure 1.2 refer to how the company configures its assets, ranging from how many staff it chooses to employ, through to whether it should develop a new product, acquire a competitor, or move into a different sector.

The energies of most business-people tend to be applied to the lower box, to improving the investment in the project portfolio, to 'making it a better business'. But in corporate financial strategy our aim is different: we are trying to improve matters in the top box, to make it a better investment for shareholders, to create shareholder value.

This leads us to two definitions, one for each of the processes shown in Figure 1.2.

WORKING
1.1

INSIGHT

Definitions of value

Investor value: Reflects the required returns of the capital markets, and is mirrored in the financial value placed on the company's securities by the markets

Corporate value: Is the present value of the expected returns from a combination of the current business strategies and future investment programmes

The two definitions of value shown in Working insight 1.1 correspond to the two-stage investment model. Investor value is about creating value in the 'top box', for investors. Corporate value, the one with which most business-people are more familiar, is about configuring the company to be a 'better' business. It is a prime role of management to ensure that the shareholder value properly reflects the corporate value; this is one of the roles of financial strategy. Further, as we will discuss later, our working definition of 'investor value' comes down to 'value for shareholders', focusing on a specific category of investor.

VALUING INVESTMENTS

Any financial investment can be valued by reference to the present value of the future cash flows which it is expected to generate. Using this well-developed technique, known as discounted cash flow or DCF,[2] the expected future cash flows are converted to their present value equivalents by multiplying them by an appropriate discount factor (an inverse interest rate). It is intuitively obvious that any future cash inflow is not worth as much as the same sum of money received immediately due to the waiting period involved. Even in a theoretical world of certain future cash flows, money has a time value.

However, in the real business world, there is also the risk that these expected future cash flows will not actually be realized. Thus the discount rate used must take into account both the time value of money and the associated risk. Applying such an appropriate discount rate to all the future cash flows makes the resulting present values directly comparable. In other words these present values can be meaningfully added together so as financially to evaluate the total return from any potential investment. This technique can be considered as being equivalent to converting various different foreign currencies into a single common currency, so that the amounts can be meaningfully compared. No-one can directly compare sums of money expressed in US dollars, euros and yen but, once converted into a single currency, their relative values are immediately obvious.

---

2. Readers unfamiliar with the technique will find it fully covered in any of the standard finance textbooks. For a detailed discussion by one of the authors, readers are referred to *Financial Aspects of Marketing* by K. Ward (1989, Heinemann), Chapter 7.

With this simple relative type of comparison, it does not really matter which base currency is used for the calculation. However in most cases there is a need to compare these relative values against a more meaningful external frame of reference; most people achieve this in the case of foreign currencies by converting foreign currencies back into their domestic currency, which is their normal monetary value reference base. The same is true for DCF analysis: techniques (such as compounding to horizon) exist to extrapolate all cash flows forward to the end of the projects and then to compare directly the relative terminal values. The problem is that, even if several associated technical problems are resolved, investors cannot readily interpret and value such future cash summations. However, they can easily compare alternative investments if they are all expressed in today's values. Hence the normal convention is to bring all future

---

WORKING
1.2

INSIGHT

Increasing shareholder value by creating a positive net present value

Investment opportunities:

Project A – Invest £100 000 for 10 years.
Receive £20 000 interest per year.
Repayment of £100 000 at the end of year 10.

Project B – Invest £1 million in a perpetual annuity.
Receive £200 000 interest per year forever.
The investor's minimum return for these types of projects is 20% p.a.
(ignore tax).

Project A

Cash flows		£000s Actual	Discount factor	£000s Present value
Yr 0	Investment outflow	(100)	1	(100)
Yrs 1–10	Interest income	20 p.a.	4.192	83.8
Yr 10	Repayment of principal	100	0.162	16.2
	Net present value			
	(i.e. value created by investment)			£0

Project B

Cash flows		Actual	£000s Discount factor	Present value
Yr 0	Investment outflow	(1000)	1	(1000)
Yrs 1 – ∞	Interest income	200 p.a.	5	1000
	Net present value			
	(i.e. value created by investment)			£0

Both investments merely produce an adequate or a satisfactory return as demanded by the investors – neither produces an excess return which increases shareholder wealth over other alternative investments of similar risk.

cash flows back to today, by calculating their present value equivalents: all these present values are then additive to arrive at the net present value (NPV) for any investment.

Using DCF techniques, a share in a company could be valued as the present value of its expected future dividend stream. To value the entity as a whole, one could discount all of its expected future pre-finance cashflows.

Applying this technique to any investment immediately highlights a key element in increasing shareholder value; shareholder value is increased only if the appropriately discounted present value of the expected future cash flows generated by any investment is greater than the current cost of that investment. It is not good enough merely to generate the 'market' (risk-adjusted) return – we have to exceed it.

Why is it not good enough merely to satisfy shareholders' requirements? The answer to that is that the risk–return line shows what the market requires for a particular level of risk. Any competitor company should deliver that – it's the norm. Providing *value* means being better than the market, otherwise what reason is there for the shareholder to invest in one company rather than another? Merely generating the rate of return required by the investor creates no value at all: it would be the equivalent of paying $100 to receive (immediately) the sum of $100 – value is not destroyed in such a transaction, but there is no real reason for bothering to undertake it. In a zero NPV transaction investors are merely swapping current sums of money for their equivalent in future cash flows. This very obvious but absolutely critical point is numerically illustrated in Working insight 1.2.

CREATING SHAREHOLDER VALUE

In a perfectly competitive market, market forces would dictate that all investments would receive only their risk-adjusted required rates of return. Consequently no shareholder value would be created. Accordingly it stands to reason that shareholder value is only increased by exploiting imperfections in the marketplace.

The greatest imperfections arise in product markets, i.e. the actual marketplaces in which specific products are sold to customers. Therefore, companies can increase shareholder value by creating a sustainable competitive advantage through selecting and implementing an appropriate competitive strategy. For example, barriers to entry into an industry may be created to keep out competitors and thus prevent the rules of perfect competition from applying in that industry. As a result, new companies cannot economically afford to enter the industry even though the financial returns available are above normal levels. This restriction on potential new competition enables the existing players in the industry to enjoy an apparently excessive financial return on their investments. However, in reality, the creation of an effective barrier to entry normally requires substantial additional financial investment; either in very strong branding through heavy marketing expenditure, or in achieving material cost advantages through the development of significant economies of scale, etc. Consequently this apparently excessive financial return can initially be regarded as providing the normal required return on this additional investment. Any remaining excess financial return represents the true 'value added' for shareholders.

More importantly from our point of view, investment can be related to the two-stage process illustrated in Figure 1.2, in which investments in specific product market interfaces form the second stage. Initially a group of investors (shareholders, banks, etc.) invest funds in a company, and the company subsequently invests these funds in a range of specific projects, encompassing individual products in particular markets. The optimum relative mix of these investors in any particular company, the way in which they perceive the risks involved in the investment and the alternative methods of giving them their required financial return can also create a super-normal return and are the principal aspects of financial strategy. Consequently this book concentrates primarily on this first stage of raising the funds required by the business and on the methods of managing these funds within the company. Thus financial strategy is about raising the funds required by the organization in the manner most appropriate to its overall corporate and competitive strategies, and also managing the use of those funds within the organization.

In the theoretical world of perfectly competitive markets, the overall portfolio of projects which makes up each company can only achieve exactly the risk-adjusted return required by the investors in the company. Indeed the modern theory of corporate finance goes further and argues that these investors will not even be financially compensated for any unnecessary risks taken by the company or for any wasted expenditure incurred by its managers. As explained in much more detail in Appendix 1 on financial theory, investors can diversify, and hence reduce, their overall risks by holding an appropriate portfolio of different investments. Thus their dependence upon the financial performance of any single company can be reduced by such diversification strategies. Consequently in an efficient financial market the return received from any such single company investment should be driven only by the specific risk associated with that investment, when considered relative to the total available investment opportunities.

This investor-based view of portfolio management suggests that if companies invest in an inappropriate range of projects which, when combined directly together, compound the overall risk of the business, they will reduce investor value rather than increase it. Sophisticated investors could build their own investment portfolios so as to achieve an equivalent overall return, but without incurring the increased business risk associated with this combined business. Consequently they demand a higher return to compensate for the higher risk, and this is achieved by giving the investment in such a combined business an appropriately lower value. It is not the high risk of any individual project which destroys investor value, as the high risk project should have a correspondingly high required return to offset the risk. However if the overall risk of the portfolio is greater than the sum of its parts, the total portfolio (i.e. the company) will be worth less to an investor.

Interestingly companies which try to reduce risks by investing in a well-diversified range of products can also destroy shareholder value rather than enhance it. If significant costs are incurred by the company (such as the classic conglomerate) in creating and managing such a diversified portfolio of businesses, the investor may be substantially worse off. Intelligent investors can achieve this reduced investment risk at much lower cost by setting up their own, similarly diversified investment portfolio. Consequently in an efficient and rational financial market, they will penalize, rather than reward, companies for incurring these unnecessary management costs which do not add value. Indeed in the real world, with its inherent imperfections, this illustrates the ways in which shareholder value can be created. As shown in Figure 1.3, any strategic move above the risk/return line creates shareholder value, whereas anything which results in a position below the line destroys existing value. Therefore it is not simply a question of increasing return or reducing risk, but of the level of increased return compared to the increased perception of risk, and vice versa.

In Figure 1.3, any strategy which moves below the shareholders' risk–return line will destroy shareholder value. Thus, strategy (A) is obviously value-enhancing, increasing returns by far more than the associated risk profile. Similarly, strategy (B) is obviously value-destroying; although returns have increased, the disproportionate rise in risk moves the value below the line. (For strategy (B), markets might be fooled for a short time by the increase in profits, but as soon as the risk-increasing nature of the strategy changes is realized, share prices will fall.)

Strategy (C) in Figure 1.3 is interesting. Although it is obvious that (C) should add value, as it is an 'above the line' move, many people have difficulty with the concept of a company deliberately reducing profitability and yet still adding value. However, this is a perfectly legitimate, and common, tactic – any time a company buys an insurance policy it is deliberately reducing profits in order to safeguard against risk. A more esoteric example of a decision to follow strategy (C) can be seen in the actions of T&N, a UK-based international company facing huge personal injury claims (estimated at upwards of £350 m) relating to its historic business in the asbestos industry. The company's advisers estimated that the unquantified liability hanging over the company was reducing its market capitalization by up to £1 bn. In order to remove the risk and the market discount, T&N acquired an insurance-based cap on its asbestos liabilities. This reduced profits, but increased its market value.

It should however be noted that there is a potential conflict between the risk/return perceptions of the senior managers of the company and its investors, and that this could cause a conflict in their objectives. The theoretical assumption

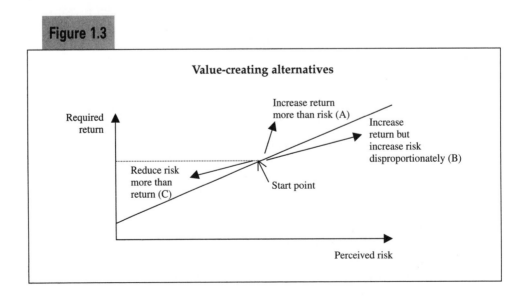

Figure 1.3

Value-creating alternatives

is that everyone has the same perception of risk, but here is a situation where this is most unlikely to be true. As has already been discussed, professionally managed investment institutions can develop sophisticated investment portfolios which substantially diversify their investors' risk away from any particular company. It is much more difficult for the full-time managers within a particular company to diversify their perceived risks, e.g. the risk of losing their jobs, which may be associated with any specific high risk business strategy (particularly if the failure of such a high risk strategy could lead to the total financial collapse of the company). Senior managers can, and often do, attempt to achieve some degree of risk reduction either by implementing a less risky strategy or by diversifying into other areas of operation. As the risk of corporate collapse, or high volatility in profits, etc., is the key driver to this managerially-led diversification strategy, the business is likely to invest in less risky projects or in areas of operation which are counter-cyclical to the current main business focus.

Such a perceived need to reduce overall risk may well become more important to these key managers as they become older, particularly if they have very long periods of employment in a single company. These long-serving managers may only have the normal linear type positive correlation between risk and return at the lower end of the risk spectrum. However, they may demand an almost exponentially increasing return in order to compensate them for taking on what they would otherwise consider as an unacceptably high risk strategy. This is graphically illustrated in Figure 1.4, which also

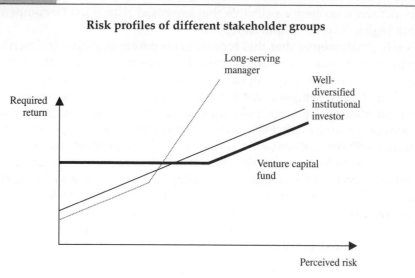

Risk profiles of different stakeholder groups

The well-diversified investor takes a linear view of the risk–return relationship. This contrasts with the long-serving manager, who becomes very risk-averse above a certain level of risk. The venture capital fund demands too high a return to invest in low-risk opportunities, but becomes interested at higher risk levels. Although the venture capital required return could be synchronous with that of other investors, it is shown here as being slightly lower, for illustrative purposes.

shows the well-diversified institutionally based investor, who has a linear risk–return expectation across the whole range of potential investment risks.

A type of investor with yet another different potential perception of risk is also shown in Figure 1.4: the venture capitalist. Venture capitalists can be categorized as investors who are only interested in relatively high risk and high return investments. This is their chosen investment territory, which means that they would consider most large diversified businesses as not being worth their consideration. Thus they demand a relatively high minimum return from any project they take on (represented by the horizontal portion of their line in Figure 1.4). Inevitably this tends to force them to focus on higher risk projects as only these can supply the type of return which they consider acceptable.

In determining a suitable financial and corporate strategy for a business, it is important to understand the drivers of the key stakeholders. A venture capital-backed business run by a risk-averse senior manager may be an uncomfortable place to be, as there will be a clash in their objectives: the minimum return demanded by the venture capitalist may be greater than the return associated with the highest risk project which is acceptable to the manager.

SUSTAINABLE COMPETITIVE ADVANTAGE

The overriding reason for the existence of most commercial organizations is to achieve a more than acceptable return for the investors and other key stake-holders in the business. As demonstrated in Figure 1.1, this return must be assessed in the context of the particular risks associated with any business, as it is a fundamental economic principle that increased risks must be compensated for with higher levels of financial returns.

It is also fundamental that this economic corporate objective is described as achieving a 'more than acceptable' return (i.e. a positive net present value), even though this statement may appear to contradict much of modern financial theory. This theory suggests that it is impossible for investors consistently to achieve an abnormally large risk-adjusted return on their investments. In a perfectly competitive market this is undoubtedly true, as these perfect competition forces will drive down all returns to the 'normal level' required by the market. For example, if the 'market' rate of return is 12 per cent p.a., it is impossible for any specific investment, with a risk profile equivalent to the market, to sustain a different level. (Some of the prerequisite conditions for a perfectly competitive market are that all investors possess exactly the same information about the present, have the same expectations regarding the future, and have exactly the same risk profiles.)

Consequently, if a particular investment were to show a return above the normal market level, these well-informed investors would all try to buy this investment. Inevitably this buying pressure would increase the price of the investment and reduce the rate of return to the normal market level, when it would no longer be exceptionally attractive. Conversely, an investment show-ing a lower than normal return is unattractive, with existing investors looking to sell but other potential investors having no incentive to buy. This will force the price of the investment to fall, until its return has been increased up to the normal market level.

In the real world, it is impossible to find any long-term investment which can truly be regarded as risk-free. (This has been very forcibly demonstrated to many investors in recent years with the dramatic collapse of very large companies and even financial institutions around the world, and the renegotiations of debt repayments by several governments.) Even a completely government-backed security, issued in a financially sound and politically stable economy, can only be regarded as truly risk-free if it is a very short-term investment. Over the longer term, such a government security has risks regarding the relative purchasing power of the funds which are received back at the final maturity of the investment; higher than expected inflation could significantly reduce the real value of these funds. Also such investments normally pay interest during their lifetime, and the total expected return over the life of the investment would have been based on reinvesting these periodic interest receipts at the market rate of return until the final maturity date. If prevailing interest rates decline during the period of the investment, the total funds available on final termination may be lower than originally forecast; such a difference introduces a risk associated with this guaranteed investment.

Much greater uncertainties and risk are inevitable facts of life in the commercial world, where future returns are neither guaranteed nor known with any degree of certainty, and where the competitive situation can change dramatically in a very short period of time. Consequently the ability to manage in such an environment is a critical component of any organization's business strategy, as will be made clear throughout the book. In fact it is true to say that a business can only achieve its desired aim of a 'more than satisfactory return' for its investors by identifying and exploiting imperfections in the markets in which it operates. Thus a major objective of corporate and competitive strategies is to develop a sustainable competitive advantage, which enables the business to achieve and maintain a return in excess of that which would be allowed in a perfectly competitive market. This process is essential to increasing shareholder value, which itself is a key objective for nearly all the large companies, particularly those which are publicly quoted, which today dominate the major economies of the world.

MANAGING AND MEASURING SHAREHOLDER VALUE

Thus far, we have defined shareholder value in terms of the investors' achievement of a positive net present value – a return that more than compensates for the perceived risks. This was illustrated in Figure 1.3 as being an 'above the line' return. In this section we examine three different (but linked) ways of measuring shareholder value, and demonstrate how they might be used in practice to create that value. The three metrics under consideration are:

- Shareholder value analysis
- Economic profit
- Total shareholder return.

SHAREHOLDER VALUE ADDED (SVA)

The Shareholder Value Added (SVA) approach devised by Alfred Rappaport[3] uses discounted cash flow techniques to estimate the value of an investment, discounting forecast cash flows by the cost of capital.

Rappaport stated that the value of a company is dependent on seven drivers of value, as shown in Working insight 1.3.

Management can use their knowledge of current sales levels and forecasts of the first five drivers in order to prepare cash flow forecasts for a suitable period. Such a period would be defined based on the likely period of the company's competitive advantage – driver six. Discounting these at the cost of capital (driver seven) leads to an enterprise value for operations; this can easily be translated into a value for equity. This technique is most effectively applied to individual business units within a company, whose separate values can be cumulated to arrive at the value of a business, or to create alternate scenarios.

Unlike the two metrics discussed below, SVA can be difficult to use as a one-period tool. Positive free cash flow in a period is not necessarily good; negative free cash flow may not be bad. The metric is mainly used for valuation and planning rather than as a periodic measure of performance.

ECONOMIC PROFIT (EP)

Economic profit (sometimes known as 'residual income') is a generic name that covers many of the different variants of profit-based measures of shareholder value. This is the surplus earned by a business in a period after deducting all expenses including the cost of capital. It can be calculated in two ways, as shown in Working insight 1.4.

Economic profit is primarily used for performance measurement. It has the advantage that it teaches managers a great respect for capital – it is no longer seen as 'free' – and encourages them to run their businesses so as to minimize capital employed. In many instances this behavioural change is beneficial to the

---

WORKING
1.3
INSIGHT

The seven drivers of value

1. sales growth
2. operating profit margin
3. cash tax rate
4. incremental investment in capital expenditure
5. investment in working capital
6. time period of competitive advantage
7. cost of capital

---

3. For further information see *Creating Shareholder Value*. Rappaport, The Free Press, 1998.

WORKING
1.4

INSIGHT

Calculation of economic profit

Operating profit after tax	£2400
Capital employed	£20 000
Cost of capital	10%

Calculation 1

Operating profit after tax	2400
less: cost of capital (20 000 @ 10%)	2000
Economic profit	£400

Calculation 2

Economic profit = Capital employed × spread

Spread = Return on Investment less Cost of Capital

(where return on investment represents after tax operating profit as a percentage of opening capital employed)

Economic profit = 20 000 × (12% − 10)% =   £400

business, although some would argue that EP is a single-period measure, and taking it to extremes can lead to capital-starved businesses, limiting growth.

There is of course a relationship between SVA and economic profit. It can be shown that the discounted value of the projected economic profits of a business for the appropriate time period will equate to the SVA. Perhaps more intuitively, whereas SVA shows the value of a business over its lifetime, economic profit shows whether the company is creating value in any single period.

TOTAL SHAREHOLDER RETURN (TSR)

Both SVA and economic profit are 'internal' measures of shareholder value: in terms of the two-decision model introduced in Figure 1.2 they show how well the company is using its competitive strategy to create value from the product-market mix it selects. Total shareholder return (TSR) is an 'external' measure – it looks at the value created for shareholders, the top box in Figure 1.2.

TSR represents the total return to the shareholders in a period: the increase in share price, plus any dividends paid during the period (see Working insight 1.5). This performance measure is very commonly used in directors' long term incentive plans, often calculated over a three year period.

From the point of view of the shareholders, TSR is probably the most accurate measure of value – it shows exactly what they have received from the company in the period. However, as a measure of managers' performance the metric has limitations. Share prices (as we will discuss in depth in Chapter 2) reflect the market's expectations, rather than corporate performance. Adequate performance from a company expected to do poorly might increase share price far more than superb performance from one that was already a market favourite.

Total shareholder return

Share price at 1 January	100p
Share price at 31 December	110p
Capital gain in the year	10p
Dividend paid on 31 December	5p
Total return	15p
Total Shareholder Return (TSR)	15%

A company could be doing well, but be in an out-of-favour sector and thus see its share price fall. Alternately, a poor company could see its price rise for reasons unconnected with underlying performance. When used as a measure of directors' performance, TSR is generally benchmarked relative to similar companies, which helps eliminate some – but by no means all – of these difficulties.

SOME REFLECTIONS ON SHAREHOLDER VALUE

Earlier, we stated that shareholder value should properly reflect corporate value. It is now appropriate to explore that statement in more depth.

Figure 1.5 sets out the dimensions of a company's value in a two-by-two matrix. Assume that you, as a very skilled financier, have calculated the exact price at which the company's shares should trade (perhaps using Rappaport's SVA techniques). This is the *fundamental* value of the share. The *value multiple* on the vertical axis represents the actual market value divided by this fundamental value (MV/FV). If the share is trading at its fundamental value, this will be 1.0.

Figure 1.5

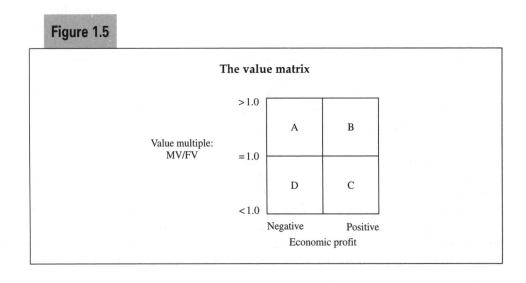

The value matrix

The horizontal axis of the matrix represents economic profit or any similar measure of 'is this a good business?' A positive economic profit implies a business that is doing well; negative economic profit indicates a poor business. (It should be noted that this last definition is quite restrictive as, in practice, a good business might make an economic loss if in any one year it were to invest heavily for the future. However, the principles hold.)

Our company can fall into any of the four segments shown in the matrix, labelled A to D for convenience. So, in which segment do you want to be?

We have asked this question of many different groups of MBA students and executives, with interesting results. Almost invariably the majority of respondents choose to be in segment B, a good company, overvalued by the markets. But there is always a minority that would prefer to be in C, and even the occasional choice of A, or even D. Further questioning reveals that each of the different responses comes about because the respondents have, without consciously realizing it, taken on a different 'persona'.

For a company situated in quadrants A or B, i.e. with a value multiple greater than one, the implication is that the market appears to be over-valuing its shares. The only real issue then becomes: how long can we continue to fool the market? In practice, companies may remain overvalued for many years, but ultimately reality will catch up with them and the share price will fall. So, A or B are good positions to be in if you are about to sell your shares, but probably not otherwise. As managers about to exercise our share options we would like to see the company in B: we could sell the shares quickly, but still remain with a fundamentally good business. As outgoing managers we may have less interest in the strength of the business, so quadrant A would also be a reasonable place – provided that we can escape quickly with our money and reputation intact!

Undervalued companies, with a value multiple of less than one, sit in quadrants C or D. Who would want their company to be undervalued? Well, those same managers who were happy to exercise their share options whilst sitting in quadrant B might be very pleased to be granted those options whilst the company was sitting in C: they could make money on the share options simply by persuading the market to reassess its false view of the company's prospects, causing an automatic share price rise.

There is of course a danger to being in quadrant C or D. The company in C is a takeover target for almost any other company. It is a valuable asset, well-run, and not appreciated by the market. Almost anyone could buy it at this undervalue, and make a profit. The company in D is less attractive: it is an undervalued asset but it is also under-performing. But to a predator in the same industry, who would know what to do to turn it around, it could be an attractive buy. And although as existing shareholders a position in C or D would fail to please us, as prospective shareholders, we might choose to buy into C or D in the hope that they attract a takeover which will return us a swift profit.

There are two key lessons to be learned from an analysis of the value matrix. The first is that the different groups of stakeholders have different interests in the company and its activities, and that these interests may conflict. The shareholders' keen anticipation of a takeover may not be shared by the incumbent management who will lose their jobs. Prospective shareholders seek an under-valued company; existing shareholders want to sell on a high. This stakeholder analysis leads into agency theory, which exposes the different motivations of directors and shareholders. Both stakeholder analysis and agency theory are discussed later in this chapter.

The second key lesson is that in the long term there is only one place to be that is fair to all of the stakeholders, existing and prospective, and that is to be trading at the fundamental value; a company which is fairly valued by the market such that its share price reflects its worth. (We hope that it goes without saying that one would want the company to be on the right hand side of the matrix, in 'good company' territory...)

It is interesting to note that Warren Buffett, the legendary investor who runs Berkshire Hathaway, effectively states this in his 'Owners' Manual' for share-holders. He sets out 14 principles, the 14th of which is that his aim is for shareholders to record a gain/loss in the market value of their investment which is proportionate to the gain or loss in the intrinsic value of the share. Or, to put it another way, that the share price should accurately reflect, as far as possible, the fundamental value of the company.

OTHER STAKEHOLDERS

There are two issues to consider about stakeholders: who are the stakeholders of a company, and why does financial strategy seek to maximize shareholder value rather than the value to any other stakeholder group?

STAKEHOLDER GROUPS

There are many stakeholders who might have an interest in a company's per-formance and may influence its activities, as illustrated in Figure 1.6.

Strategic business decisions are taken in the light of pressures from a wide range of internal and external stakeholders. As financial strategy must always be considered in the context of the overall business strategy, it can be subject to the influences of a wide range of potentially conflicting interests.

The degree of interest in, and influence on, any particular strategic decisions will vary dramatically for each stakeholder group. For example, the current legal position in the UK is that companies can configure their business opera-tions as they choose, opening or closing business units to suit their strategies. However, this is not the case in continental Europe, as the UK retailer Marks & Spencer discovered when in spring 2001 it announced the closure of its Paris shops as a way of saving money whilst the company was struggling. The French workers had significantly more union power and legal rights than their UK counterparts, and the closure was initially blocked.

Another example of stakeholder power came in 1995 when Shell, the global oil company, announced its decision to decommission its Brent Spar oil platform by sinking it in the Atlantic Ocean. Although it ultimately transpired that this disposal option was relatively environmentally friendly, concerted action by the environmental group Greenpeace, supported by boycotts by customers, led

Figure 1.6

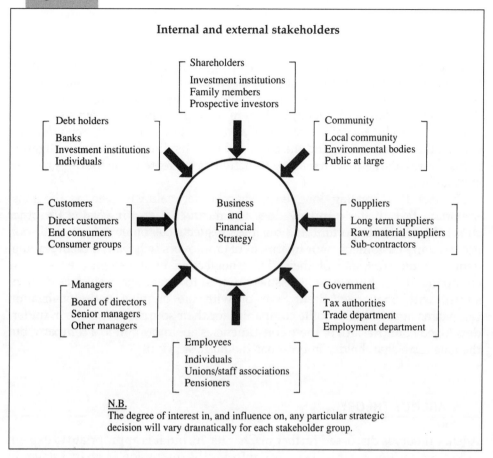

Internal and external stakeholders

Shareholders
Investment institutions
Family members
Prospective investors

Debt holders
Banks
Investment institutions
Individuals

Community
Local community
Environmental bodies
Public at large

Customers
Direct customers
End consumers
Consumer groups

Business
and
Financial
Strategy

Suppliers
Long term suppliers
Raw material suppliers
Sub-contractors

Managers
Board of directors
Senior managers
Other managers

Government
Tax authorities
Trade department
Employment department

Employees
Individuals
Unions/staff associations
Pensioners

N.B.
The degree of interest in, and influence on, any particular strategic
decision will vary dramatically for each stakeholder group.

to a change of strategy on the disposal, and to the rig being towed to Norway for dismantling, a much more expensive option for the company.

The stakeholder relationships between the company and its lenders and shareholders may also change over time. Although the shareholders own the company, lenders often have rights under banking covenants. Accordingly, at times of financial pressure a company might find the lenders rather than the shareholders in the driving seat, dictating its actions. The case study of the Korean semi-conductor company Hynix, set out in Chapter 13, illustrates the impact on a company of conflicting stakeholder interests.

It would be possible to find examples of stakeholder power for each of the groups set out in Figure 1.6. This being the case, why does financial theory (and Anglo-American financial practice) dictate that *shareholder* value is the appropriate corporate aim? There are various responses given to this question, for example that the shareholders are the owners of the company, or that it needs to keep them satisfied in order to protect access to future funds. The answer that we find most persuasive is that the shareholders are the only direct stakeholder group who do not have a contracted relationship with the company.

A supplier of the company will supply product and will receive payment in return. A customer will hand over money and receive the agreed goods or services. Employees know that if they give the specified number of labour hours they will receive an agreed wage at the end of the week or month. Lenders receive interest, governments collect tax. Each of the stakeholders knows what their relationship with the company will produce. Shareholders on the other hand invest their money in the hope of receiving dividends and capital gains, in order to make an above-market return. However, there is no requirement for the directors to declare a dividend, and there is no guarantee that the share price will rise to produce a gain. Accordingly we can state that the shareholders are bearing the ultimate risk, and the company (and its directors) has an obligation to play fair with them by managing its activities to create value for this group of stakeholders.

The fact that creating long term shareholder value is seen as the most important task of the company does not mean that creating value for other stakeholders is unimportant. If a business neglects customer value it will soon not have any customers; poor treatment of employees will lead to them leaving, denuding the company of their skills; neglecting broader concerns such as environmental or human rights issues can lead to consumer protest, as demonstrated with Shell over Brent Spar or with the ongoing anti-globalization campaigns against high profile companies for their sourcing practices in underdeveloped countries. All of these constituencies are important to a company, but the long term shareholder interest has the highest priority.

AGENCY THEORY

Agency theory is discussed further in Chapter 16, but it is appropriate to explain its key propositions at this stage, as it informs the discussion at several stages in this book.

In public companies (although not necessarily in private ones) the directors, who run the business, are different people from the shareholders, who own it. The directors (agents) are meant to run the business for the benefit of the shareholders (principals). However, in practice conflicts of interest are likely to arise, as generally the directors will own few if any of the shares of the company, and so receive their reward (pay) by different means than do the shareholders (dividends and capital gains). This means that directors may not act in the best interests of shareholders at all times. Examples of possible conflicts of interest include:

- payment of excessive salaries or benefits;
- reluctance to undertake high-risk, high net present value projects: if these are successful the shareholders make the gain; if unsuccessful the shareholders will lose only a small part of their diversified portfolios, but the managers may lose their jobs;
- retaining profits rather than paying them out in dividends, to protect the company from any financial risk;
- working less efficiently than the shareholders might desire.

Agency theory suggests that the shareholders should have means to monitor what the directors are doing, or to develop contractual arrangements which encourage mutuality of interest. (Performance-based remuneration contracts, discussed in Chapter 16, are a prime example of this.)

If agency theory is put into operation effectively, it should be impossible for managers to act other than in the best interests of their principals, i.e. the share-holders. These shareholders should utilize their ownership power to force managers to behave in accordance with their wishes. Their ultimate sanction is in their power to sack the management team, either directly or by selling their shares in the company to new owners, who then change the top management.

THE IMPORTANCE OF ACCOUNTING RESULTS

We have established (to our satisfaction at least) that corporate value is created by increasing the discounted value of future cash flows. We could also cite you years of academic research that shows that manipulation of accounting policies is ignored by the market, which sees through the final profit figures to the health of the underlying business. However, we also note that companies and their advisors appear to be obsessed with accounting results and, in particular, earn-ings per share, the profit earned in a year for each ordinary share.

As a significant part of this book discusses how companies can use financial strategy to manipulate earnings per share (eps), we feel obliged to defend our position on this matter. We believe that eps is, in practice, important; our academic colleagues insist that markets ignore accounting practices – who is right? In our defence we cite the recent debate in the US about accounting standards on pooling of interest.

When companies join together, the transaction can be accounted for in one of two ways. Either it is an acquisition, in which one company buys the other; or it is a merger of (more-or-less) equals. These two types of combination are accounted for in different ways. In the UK we refer to 'acquisition accounting' and 'merger accounting'; in the US the terminology used is 'purchase account-ing' and 'pooling of interests' ('pooling').

Broadly speaking, if a transaction is accounted for using purchase accounting, goodwill is created through the acquisition. This goodwill is shown as an asset on the acquirer's balance sheet (normally to be amortized over its useful life). However in a merger, pooling means that the two companies' balance sheets are added together, and no goodwill is created.

In accounting terms, purchase accounting means that return on capital is reduced, relative to the pooling treatment, due to (a) an increase in the capital base of the combination and normally (b) a reduction in its profits due to the amortization of goodwill. The latter point is particularly important, as it will reduce eps. However, this should not impact in any way on the value of the combined company, as there are no cashflow implications (goodwill not currently being tax deductible).

Having said that, US companies have often structured deals specifically in order to obtain the 'benefit' from pooling. Here is a quote from *Business Week* (30 September 1996) on the $7.1 bn acquisition of Duracell by Gillette:

'Making sure that the Duracell deal would immediately add to reported earnings was one of Zeien's [Gillette's CEO] key goals. But to do that, he had to ensure the deal was structured as a stock swap. If Gillette had paid cash for Duracell, which has a low book value but a high market value, the larger company would have absorbed at least $125 m in annual charges for goodwill and depreciation.'

The article goes on to point out that structuring the deal in this way was actually bad news for the Gillette shareholders. Firstly, regulations meant that the company would be unable to buy back its stock for a two year period. More importantly, because the Gillette share price rose significantly on the news of the deal, effectively its shareholders were giving away a large part of the synergy to the Duracell shareholders. (This concept is explained further in Chapter 12 on company acquisitions.) Zeien is quoted as accepting that a cash deal may have been better for his shareholders, but pointed out his belief that 'analysts focus on earnings per share', and the stock price would go down if the company had used purchase accounting.

In September 1999 the US Financial Accounting Standards Board (FASB) issued a Proposed Statement of Financial Accounting Standards: *Business Combinations and Intangible Assets*. This proposed standard announced the intention to force companies to use purchase accounting, and eliminate the use of pooling.

Given that there is no cashflow implication to the accounting change, the reaction to this proposal was interesting.

- The investment community, in particular the large firms such as Morgan Stanley and Goldman Sachs, lobbied US regulators to prevent this change in accounting standards. They stated that the goodwill write offs could deter companies from merging, and would affect US competitiveness in global markets.
- Individual companies also appeared to be affected: it was reported that the timing of the $18bn acquisition of US Bancorp by Firstar was accelerated in order to obtain favourable accounting treatment and avoid the possible end of the pooling of interest provisions. (*Financial Times* 5 October 2000)
- Senators sent an open letter to the FASB to delay the proposed changes to the accounting rules, again citing US competitiveness (specifically in high technology industries) as a concern.

The ultimate effect of this concerted protest was a change in direction by the FASB. As the problem revolved around the profit-reducing write off of goodwill the Board decided that purchased goodwill should no longer be amortized at all. Instead, it should be reviewed for impairment 'when an event or series of events occur indicating that goodwill of a reporting unit might be impaired'. In situations in which the goodwill is not impaired, there is no requirement to amortize it, and so eps will not be reduced. Accordingly, purchase accounting will not reduce profits compared to pooling. (At the time of writing, the final situation on the accounting standard was unresolved.)

Theory tells us that cash flow is what matters in company valuation. However, the reported actions of finance directors and the investment community indicate that it may be some time before we can structure transactions ignoring the effects of eps movements.

CONCLUSION

Value can be looked at from two perspectives: the value of the business and the value to the shareholder. Enhancing the value of the business relates to competitive strategy; positioning the company more effectively in its product-market relationships. However, enhancing the value of the company to the shareholder means not only having a good business, but also managing its share price to reflect that worth.

The company's share price should reflect the risk-adjusted present value of its future returns. Two aspects of this value relationship are within management's control: the future cash flows, and the discount rate used to evaluate them. It is the management of that discount rate, the company's cost of capital, which forms a key part of corporate financial strategy.

Corporate financial strategy is about raising funds in the most appropriate manner, and managing their use to create value. Although financial theory in its purest form might suggest that no advantage can be obtained by changing financial strategy, examples in this book will demonstrate that practitioners, perhaps ignorant of or ignoring the theoretical implications, can create considerable value this way.

What does the share price tell us?

A company's business and financial strategies must operate in tandem to deliver the value demanded by its shareholders. In order to accomplish this, it is useful for its directors and advisors to understand how the shareholders expect to achieve that value; in this chapter we demonstrate these expectations using the P/E ratio.

A company's P/E ratio is the ratio of its current share price to its earnings per share (eps). The ratio is an indicator of the growth that the market expects from the share: a low P/E ratio reflects low growth expectations, and a high P/E implies that the company will need to deliver correspondingly high growth to satisfy those expectations. Thus, although directors often see a high P/E as a 'virility symbol' for their companies, it could instead be looked at as a treadmill – the higher the P/E, the harder they have to work to achieve the implied growth.

Two methods of calculating the growth implicit in a P/E are demonstrated in this chapter. The first uses a simple dividend growth model; the second introduces a more sophisticated model which brings in the concept of 'steady state'.

A company in steady state is one which is neither growing nor reducing in size, and which remains at this constant level to infinity. (As you can see, steady state is an abstract concept, useful in theory but with no place in reality.) Such a company will have a lower cost of equity than a corresponding 'real world' company, as the volatility that comes from growth has been eliminated.

For a company in steady state, the dividend payout ratio will be 100 per cent, as there will be no point in retaining funds for growth. With dividends equivalent to the (unchanging) eps being paid out every year, the shares can be valued as perpetuities by dividing the earnings per share by the steady state cost of equity. This relationship can be re-arranged to derive a 'steady state' P/E, which is almost certainly considerably lower than the P/E at which the company trades. Comparisons between the two can enable the analyst to derive the present value of growth opportunities (PVGO) – the proportion of the current share price which reflects the market's expectations of future growth and development.

The steady state relationship can also be used to show by how much earnings per share needs to be increased in order to achieve the share price growth implicit in the current value.

CALCULATION OF THE PRICE/EARNINGS RATIO

Unsurprisingly, the price/earnings ratio for a company is determined by dividing its current share price by its earnings per share (eps). Thus **price/eps = P/E**. This equation can be rearranged, and so-doing explains, at least partially, a popular misconception about share prices.

If

$$P/E = \text{share price}/eps \tag{1}$$

then

$$\text{Share price} = P/E \times eps \tag{2}$$

So far, there is no problem with this rearrangement. The problem arises when individuals – often with an apparently sophisticated knowledge of finance – assume that this second equation implies a causality: that the share price is a function of P/E and eps rather than P/E being itself a function of the share price.

Why does this matter? Well, if directors believe this causality, they could come to the conclusion that in order to increase the share price, all that needs to be done is to increase the eps. Under this logic, the P/E of the company will remain unchanged, so any increase in eps will translate directly into a higher price. Such reasoning is at least partially to blame for the unnatural focus on earnings per share discussed in Chapter 1. However, as we shall see in this chapter, the P/E is complex and unlikely to remain constant over a period.

WHAT DOES THE PRICE/EARNINGS RATIO MEAN?

A company's price/earnings ratio reflects the market's perceptions of its future eps growth, as illustrated in Figure 2.1.

Figure 2.1 shows two companies. High plc is a company with a high P/E ratio; Low plc, amazingly enough, has a low P/E ratio. At the time of

Figure 2.1

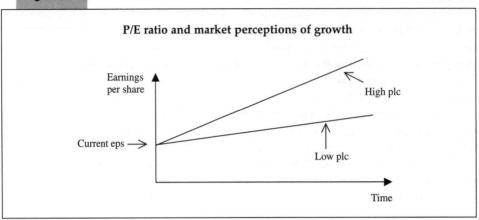

P/E ratio and market perceptions of growth

analysis, both companies have the same level of eps. However, the markets believe that High will grow eps rapidly over a period, and so give it a high P/E rating. They cannot foresee such rapid growth prospects for Low, hence its low multiple.

Before we examine the mathematics behind the illustration in Figure 2.1, it is important to note that the P/E multiple for a company reflects the expected future growth in earnings per share *which is already incorporated into the share price*. Hence the share price will only move due to changes in this expected growth, or if the actual performance shows greater or lower growth than has already been paid for by current investors in the existing share price. Merely achieving some growth in earnings per share is therefore no guarantee of a rising share price; particularly for a high P/E company.

An exposition of some of the key points in financial theory is set out in Appendix 1. However, in order to explain the meaning of the P/E ratio we need at this point to introduce one of the underlying theoretical models, the dividend growth model (DGM).[1] This, very broadly, sets out the shareholders' required return on their investment in terms of the ways in which it is achieved, a mixture of dividend yield and capital gain.

ONE EXPLANATION: USING THE DIVIDEND GROWTH MODEL WITHOUT ALTERATION

The dividend growth model states that

$$K_e = D_1/P + g \tag{3}$$

where K_e is the cost of equity (the shareholders' required return); D_1 is the prospective dividend; P is the current share price; and g is the anticipated dividend growth rate.

---

1. Also known as the dividend discount model and as the Gordon growth model.

Equation 3 states:[2]

Shareholders' required return = dividend yield plus capital growth

Equation 3 can be re-written, to give:

$$P = D_1 \times 1/(K_e - g) \tag{4}$$

We can take the relationship expressed in equation 4 and analyse it in two separate ways. For the first of these, we divide each side of the equation by the prospective earnings per share. Thus:

$$P/eps = D_1/eps \times 1/(K_e - g) \tag{5}$$

The left hand side of this equation, P/eps, is our price/earnings ratio. The right hand side contains two expressions of which one, D_1/eps, represents the prospective payout ratio. Thus, equation 5 states:

$$P/E \text{ ratio} = \text{payout ratio} \times 1/(K_e - g)$$

Given this relationship, an analyst (or indeed, the directors of the company) can feed in estimates of the company's cost of equity (K_e), its prospective dividends and its growth prospects, and determine the P/E ratio at which the company should be trading. Alternately – and often far more significantly – they can analyse the existing P/E ratio (a known number) and payout ratio (a known number) and cost of equity (Appendix 1 explains how to calculate this) to determine what level of growth the market expects. Working insight 2.1 gives an example of such a calculation.

WORKING 2.1 INSIGHT

An estimate of expected growth using the dividend growth model

Expansion plc has a share price of 250 p. Its earnings per share are 10 p, out of which it is expected to pay a dividend of 2 p per share. The cost of equity has been calculated at 10 per cent.

Price/earnings ratio = share price/eps = 250/10 = 25 times

Payout ratio = dividend per share/eps = 2/10 = 20%

Using the equation from (5)

$$P/E = D_1/eps \times 1/(K_e - g)$$
$$25 = 20\% \times 1/(10\% - g)$$
$$g = 9.2\%$$

The directors of Expansion plc now have to determine whether 9.2 per cent compound growth is a target that they can achieve, and how they might be able to attain it. Should they not be able to realize this growth, the share price will fall, and shareholders who bought shares anticipating this growth level will fail to make their required return.

---

2. Yes, we know that this is only an approximation of what the equation states, but it is a useful approximation and serves our purpose well.

One further misconception that follows from equation 5 is that the dividend payout ratio can be used to manipulate the share price. Look again at the equation:

$$P/eps = D_1/eps \times 1/(K_e - g) \tag{5}$$

At first sight, it might appear that the P/E ratio – and thus the share price – could be increased merely by increasing the dividend payout ratio; paying a higher percentage of profits out to the shareholders would have a direct impact on prices. This argument is flawed. The company generates funds which can be used either to pay out dividends or to reinvest in the future growth of the business. If the company were to increase the dividend payout ratio, less funds would be available for reinvestment and so (presumably) future growth would be less than otherwise anticipated. Thus although the function D_1/eps in equation 5 would increase, the denominator $(K_e - g)$ would also increase as g fell. Accordingly, there is not necessarily a simple arithmetical relationship between changes in the dividend payout ratio and changes in the share price.

There are several different methods of demonstrating what the P/E ratio means in terms of corporate growth, and generally they arrive at different answers, depending on the assumptions made. We have set out this simplistic technique as an illustration of what can be done. However, the slightly more sophisticated technique that follows is the one to be used in the rest of this book.

A SECOND EXPLANATION: INTRODUCING 'STEADY STATE'

In Chapter 3 we will introduce a 'lifecycle' model which demonstrates that products move from launch to growth to a mature and ultimately to a decline phase. It shows that at the launch stage the company's sales, profitability and cash generation are all in its future; as the product matures, some of this potential is realized, and so the growth prospects decline. Figure 2.2 sets out the basic S curve on which this is based.

We can use this model in conjunction with a conceptual model of what we call a 'steady state' company. In steady state a company has a growth rate of zero. (It must be emphasized that steady state is a theoretical state; the model is developed in order to build up an argument – in practice there is no such animal

Figure 2.2

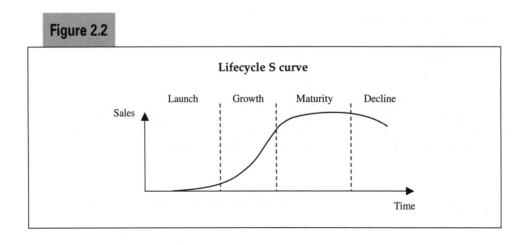

Lifecycle S curve

as a company in steady state, as even mature companies always have an element of growth or decline.)

In order to define steady state we have to make two main assumptions, necessary in order to maintain over time the constant real levels of profit which are essential to the only rational financial definition of 'steady state'. First, depreciation would need to be based on true replacement cost accounting and the annual depreciation expense would have to be reinvested in the business; if this were done the business would be capable of producing the same physical level of output over time. Second, all of the constant real profits achieved after charging this replacement cost depreciation must be paid out as dividends. If any of the profits were reinvested the business should grow, whereas if the dividends paid out were greater than the profits earned the business would get smaller over time; therefore, a 100 per cent dividend pay-out ratio is essential. (Obviously there are some other more general assumptions required such as either the absence of inflation, or the maintenance of real net profit margins and a neutral influence on net working capital.)

The result of these assumptions is that we can determine both a company's P/E and its cost of equity at steady state, as shown in Working insight 2.2. Either of these can be used in a valuation.

As can be seen from Working insight 2.2, for a steady state company the appropriate P/E multiple equals the inverse of the company's cost of equity capital (K_e). *It cannot be emphasized too greatly that this relationship only holds for a steady state company.* For a growth company, the P/E multiple will be greater than this inverse of the cost of equity capital, whereas for a declining company the P/E multiple would be lower, reflecting the expected decline in the future potential stream of earnings and dividends. Hence this very simple relationship provides a very powerful reference base for assessing both the risk profile and the future expectations signalled by any P/E multiple given to a company by the financial markets. It must be remembered that, in reality, the P/E multiple is mathematically calculated by dividing the share price by the current or expected eps, rather than the computation being the other way round; hence it is more correct to say that the share price drives the P/E multiple.

How can this relationship be used to analyse the price–earnings ratio (and thus the share price) of a company? To do this, we have to consider what the risk profile of the company might look like in this mythical steady state.

We know from Chapter 1 that the return required by investors bears a direct relationship to the perceived risk they are taking. Thus investors in high risk companies demand a high return; as risk reduces so does that required return. Risk, to a financier, is the volatility of expected returns: by definition in steady state the results of the company will be stable, so there is less risk. Accordingly, the cost of equity should be lower for a company in steady state than for a growth company. So if we know the current cost of equity, we can establish that the steady state cost of equity, $K_{e_{ss}}$, is lower than this figure.

The steady state cost of equity will be driven, using the Capital Asset Pricing Model described in Appendix 1, by the risk free interest rate, the market premium, and the company's beta:

$$K_e = R_f + \beta \, (R_m - R_f) \tag{10}$$

WORKING
2.2
INSIGHT   **Valuation of a steady state company**

The dividend growth model was set out in equation (4) as:

$P = D_1 \times 1/(K_e - g)$

As shown in Appendix 1, the derivation of this equation is that the share price reflects the discounted value of all future dividends to be received by the shareholder. Compound growth in dividends is forecast at the rate g, and the discount rate applied is the shareholders' cost of equity, K_e.

Thus, the dividend growth model is derived from solving the progression:

$P = \{D_1 \div (1 + K_e)\} + \{D_2 \div (1 + K_e)^2\} + \{D_3 \div (1 + K_e)^3\} + \ldots \{D_t \div (1 + K_e)^t\}$ (6)

But for a steady state company, defined as having zero growth, the dividend stream will be constant. This means that

$D_1 = D_2 = D_3 \ldots = D_t$

Thus the shareholder's income stream is a perpetuity of the dividend payment.

Furthermore, as there is no requirement for reinvestment, the payout ratio will be 100 per cent. Therefore dividends will equal earnings per share. Thus the income stream that the shareholder receives will be a perpetuity of the company's earnings per share.

Thus for a steady state company equation (6) can be simplified to:

$P = eps \div K_e$ (7)

Dividing through by eps gives:

$P/E = 1 \div K_e$ (8)

Again, we emphasize that this relationship only holds at the theoretical point of steady state. Accordingly, we re-write equation 8 as:

$P/E_{ss} = 1 \div K_{e_{ss}}$ (9)

As neither the risk free rate nor the market premium will be affected by a company moving into steady state, the only variable to change will be the company's beta. Accordingly, at steady state, equation 10 may be expressed as:

$K_{e_{ss}} = R_f + \beta_{ss} (R_m - R_f)$ (11)

where β_{ss} must be lower than the company's current beta.

It should be noted that although β_{ss} will be lower than the company's current beta, it will not necessarily be 1.0. A beta of 1.0 implies a company whose risk exactly mirrors that of the market as a whole. Although our steady state company has shed all of its volatility due to growth, it will still reflect the volatility of its industry. For example, a construction company will always reflect the economic cycle even if it is not growing over the cycle; it will inherently have a beta higher than, say, a water company.

Working insight 2.2 sets out the theory behind the steady state model of price earnings ratios. Working insight 2.3 applies this theory to the numbers for Expansion plc.

WORKING
2.3

INSIGHT

**An estimate of expected share price using
the steady state model**

Expansion plc has a share price of 250 p. Its eps are 10 p, out of which it is expected to pay a dividend of 2 p per share. The cost of equity has been calculated at 10 per cent, based on a risk free rate of 4 per cent, a market premium of 5 per cent and a beta of 1.2.

In this example we assume that the industry in which Expansion operates carries an inherent level of risk, such that the steady state beta will be 1.1 (i.e. lower than the current beta but higher than 1.0).

Therefore, using the CAPM per equation (11), the steady state cost of equity will be:

$$K_{e_{ss}} = R_f + \beta_{ss} (R_m - R_f)$$

$$K_{e_{ss}} = 4\% + 1.1 \times 5\%$$
$$= 9.5\%$$

On this basis, the price earnings ratio of the company at steady state will be, per equation (9):

$$P/E_{ss} = 1 \div K_{e_{ss}}$$
$$P/E_{ss} = 1 \div 9.5\%$$
$$= 10.526 \text{ times}$$

(The steady state P/E has been shown to three decimal places solely to facilitate later explanations.)

As explained in Figure 2.1, it is useful to think of the P/E multiple as being a signalling device by current and prospective shareholders (the capital market) to the company, giving a clear indication of their expectations regarding growth in earnings per share. High P/Es indicate high growth expectations; low P/Es indicate an expectation of little growth. These signals can be compared to the signals sent out by the company's managers to the financial markets regarding their own views on future growth prospects, which will be considered further in Chapter 3 and throughout the book.

One of the major problems encountered in the financial strategies of major publicly quoted companies is that senior managers, and especially chief executives and chairpersons, do not seem to accept the inevitability of a declining P/E multiple as their company matures. This overwhelming desire to maintain over time, if not to increase, an already high P/E multiple can become the dominant driver of the corporate and competitive strategy of the business, often leading the company to diversify into new areas of potential growth even though the organization has absolutely no competitive advantage in this new sector.

GROWTH INCLUDED IN THE SHARE PRICE

Consider the mythical steady state company. Its profits are the same year after year; its dividends represent a 100 per cent payout of these profits. A stream of income that is the same year after year into the infinite future is a perpetuity,

---

| WORKING |
| 2.4 |
| INSIGHT |

Steady state value of a company

Let the annual (constant) dividend paid to shareholders be D

Shareholders' cost of capital is K_e

Therefore, the value of the company is D/K_e

---

and its value can be easily calculated. Working insight 2.4 shows the value of a company in steady state.

If we know the value of a company at steady state, we can compare this with the current market value to determine how much growth the market is pricing into the share. The easiest way to explain this is by means of an example, and Working insight 2.5 returns to Expansion plc to illustrate.

The implication of the calculations in Working insight 2.5 is that if Expansion were to announce to the market that the directors see no further prospects of growth and it has become a steady state company, its share price would drop to about 105 p from the current level of 250 p. Thus we can say that 145 p of the current share price, i.e. almost 60 per cent of the value of the share, represents growth anticipated by the market.

This is a fundamental point to appreciate in understanding how shareholder value is created. Most of the share price relates to activities that the company has not yet achieved. Only 40 per cent of Expansion's share price is justified on its current earnings; the rest represents the present value of growth opportunities (PVGO) which the market assumes that the management can generate.

| WORKING |
| 2.5 |
| INSIGHT |

Growth inherent in the share price

Expansion plc has a share price of 250 p and earnings per share of 10 p. Its current cost of equity is 10 per cent, but we have established (Working insight 2.3) that its steady state cost of equity is about 9.5 per cent.

If Expansion were to become overnight a steady state company, the income stream of 10 p per share would continue effectively forever and would be paid out as dividend. Thus the steady state share price of the company, using the perpetuity formula is:

$$P = D/K_e$$
$$= 10/0.095$$
$$= 105.26 \text{ p}$$

Looked at another way, the share price at steady state would be the eps at steady state multiplied by the P/E ratio at steady state:

$$P = eps \times P/E$$
$$= 10 \times 10.526$$
$$= 105.26 \text{ p}$$

Should the management fail to generate growth that meets the market's expectations, the company's value will fall, reflecting the lower growth. Thus although a high P/E ratio, which implies high market expectations of growth, is seen by many as a sign of a strong company, it is also in some ways a curse for management: the more the market believes they can achieve, the faster they have to grow to justify the rating. (Ultimately, of course, most companies fail to meet the ever-increasing market expectations, and the share price is re-based to something more realistic. This makes perfect financial sense, but is understandably traumatic for the management and shareholders at the time.)

PVGO AND GROWTH EXPECTATIONS

The mathematics underlying the growth expectations in share prices can be taken one stage further, to consider the compound annual growth that a company needs to deliver in order to achieve the value for which shareholders have paid by buying its shares.

WORKING
2.6

INSIGHT

**Growth in eps required as the company
falls to steady state**

Expansion plc has a share price of 250 p. Its earnings per share are 10 p, out of which it is expected to pay a dividend of 2 p per share. The current cost of equity has been calculated at 10. The steady state cost of equity is 9.5 per cent, giving a P/E at steady state of 10.5 times.

Shareholders require a return of 10 per cent on their investment. The dividend yield for Expansion is 0.8 per cent ($^2/_{250}$) which implies that they expect a 9.2 per cent per annum cumulative capital gain.
If the P/E multiple were to remain constant over the company's life, a 9.2 per cent per annum capital gain would equate to a growth in eps of 9.2 per cent per annum.

However, if Expansion falls to steady state in 10 years:

Year	share price	=	P/E	×	eps
Year 0	250 p	=	25	×	10 p

	Compound growth of 9.2% per annum		Falls to steady state over 10 years		Year 10 is calculated as the eps required to generate a share price of 603 p at a P/E of 10.5.

| Year 10 | 603 p | = | 10.5 | × | 57.4 p |

Thus, to increase the share price by 9.2 per cent per annum over the period, eps has to grow at a compound rate of 19 per cent.

As a simple illustration, let us look once again at Expansion plc. Let us assume (on a totally arbitrary basis) that the company will reach steady state in 10 years' time. Working insight 2.6 demonstrates the consequences of this.

Working insight 2.6 makes some heroic assumptions about the future for Expansion plc, and draws some interesting conclusions. Let us firstly examine the conclusions.

1. If the P/E ratio of the company is going to fall, the rate of growth in eps must exceed the required rate of growth in the share price.
2. For the share price to reflect a fair value for the company, the directors must understand the high level of eps growth anticipated by the market, and have a strategy in place to achieve this.

The assumptions behind Working insight 2.6 are of course unrealistic. We are assuming that (1) the company will reach steady state; and (2) that it will do so in 10 years. As we have stated earlier, steady state is a concept that does not actually exist, hence assumption (1) is false. And assumption (2) is somewhat arbitrary – see what happens to the required growth if instead you substitute a period of five or 15 years. (A further unrealistic assumption, although one that is slightly more esoteric, is that the required growth in share price remains at 9.2 per cent, which takes no account of either the reduced risk of the company over the period nor changes to its dividend yield over the period. Remember, we're dealing here with illustrative concepts, not facts to be taken literally.)

WORKING
2.7
INSIGHT   **Growth in eps required for a drop in P/E ratio**

If Expansion's P/E of 25 drops to 20 in seven years' time, all other matters remaining the same.

Shareholders require a return of 10 per cent on their investment. The dividend yield for Expansion is 0.8 per cent, which implies that they expect a 9.2 per cent per annum cumulative capital gain.

Year	share price	=	P/E	×	eps
Year 0	250 p	=	25	×	10 p

	Compound growth of 9.2% per annum	Falls to 20 as per assumption	Year 7 is calculated as the eps required to generate a share price of 463 p at a P/E of 20.

| Year 7 | 463 p | = | 20 | × | **23.1 p** |

Thus, to increase the share price by 9.2 per cent per annum over the period, eps has to grow at a compound rate of just under 13 per cent.

If we relax the key assumptions in Working insight 2.6 we can obtain a more realistic analysis. The company will not fall to steady state. However, the logic of a falling P/E still holds. Working insight 2.7 indicates the growth in eps required should the P/E fall to say 20 in seven years' time.

It can thus be seen that any drop in the P/E will have a potentially significant effect on the company's growth requirements over the period.

It must further be remembered that achieving the growth illustrated in Working insight 2.7 is, from the shareholders' point of view, no big deal. Based on Working insight 2.7's assumptions, a shareholder buying today at 250 p *expects* a price of 463 p in seven years' time. Achieving this delivers a return exactly in line with the market which, as we established in Chapter 1, neither adds to or reduces shareholder value. Shareholder value will only be created if the company beats this growth target.

CONCLUSION

A company's share price reflects the market's expectations of its future performance; the higher the share price relative to current earnings (as measured by the P/E ratio), the harder the management will have to work to achieve (or, more importantly, exceed) the growth inherent in the share price. This chapter has illustrated two ways of calculating that required growth: the simple dividend growth model, and the more useful steady state model which will feature throughout the book.

3

Linking corporate and financial strategies

OVERVIEW

In this chapter we discuss financial strategy, including a company's choice of sources of finance and its dividend policy, and relate this to the business risks a company faces. Business risk is the inherent risk associated with the underlying nature of the particular business and the specific competitive strategy that is being implemented. It relates to everything except the risk from the financing structure. Financing risk is about the debt/equity mix.

Debt and equity have different risk profiles for investor and company, and their use has to be balanced to meet the company's particular circumstances. It is inappropriate for a company with high business risk to adopt a financial strategy that involves high financial risk. Similarly, for public companies it is unwise for a low risk business to use mostly equity, which is low risk finance.

A life cycle model is introduced, which considers the risks companies face at the launch, growth, maturity and decline stages. From this we draw up a profile of the suitable financial strategy for each type of company, showing how its financing and its dividend policy should change as it develops.

ASSESSING BUSINESS RISK

As with all the other functional strategies (marketing, operations, personnel, etc.) which are now developed by most companies as essential aspects of their strategic management process, a company's financial strategy must be tailored to the needs of the overall corporate and competitive strategies which are being implemented by the business. If the financial strategy is appropriately designed and properly implemented it can enhance shareholder value but, even more dramatically, when an inappropriate financial strategy is applied the entire business can be placed in jeopardy.

In order to determine what might be appropriate as a financial strategy, it is useful to analyse the business itself in terms of the risks it faces, and to design the financial strategy to complement this analysis. Accordingly, this section commences by considering business risk.

Business risk describes the inherent risk associated with both the underlying nature of the particular business and the specific competitive strategy which is being implemented. Thus a very new, focused, single product, high technology company (such as a business developing a specific aspect of biogenetic engineering or a new style of super-computer) would have a very high intrinsic business risk. At the opposite end of the spectrum is the very well established, highly diversified (both geographically and industrially) conglomerate-style group, which has a relatively low overall business risk. It must be remembered that, of itself, neither a high nor a low business risk is better; as long as the relative level of return matches the level of associated risk, either is acceptable.

The simplest way to consider business risk is that it relates to all of the risks that the company faces, other than those which relate directly to the company's financing decisions. It thus deals with the volatility of the operating cash flows. Such volatility might arise from sources external to the organization, for example: changes in legislation or in fashions or public opinion; the actions of competitors; or the general economic climate. Internal risks also need to be considered, for example: the risks associated with a particular manufacturing process; or the ways in which an organization communicates with its key stakeholders; or its cost structure. Internal risks are often easier to control than external risks, but all potential risks need to be considered.

An embarrassingly simple model for a preliminary analysis of business risk is shown in Figure 3.1

In Figure 3.1 the constituents of profitability are broken down to facilitate analysis. As business risk relates to variability in operating results, it seems reasonable to examine the factors making up these operating results, which takes us back to the basic accounting model: Sales less Costs = Profits. We can then begin to see what affects each of these items for our particular company. For sales, it might be appropriate to examine what affects our selling price and the volumes we sell; or an analysis of products and markets may be more useful; or both may be used. For cost analysis, a preliminary approach may be to determine the 'operating leverage' – the relative level of fixed to variable costs, on the basis that companies with high levels of fixed

Figure 3.1

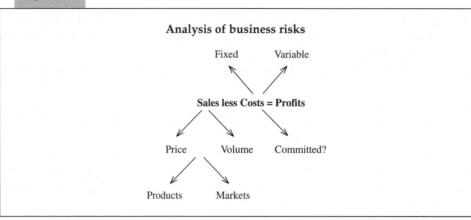

Analysis of business risks

Some examples of issues to consider in analysing business risk

WORKING
3.1

INSIGHT

Demand volatility

- market factors
- changes in tastes
- short product lives
- competitors' actions

Selling price volatility

- market factors
- price wars
- economic conditions
- prices of substitutes and complements
- over-supply (or shortages)

Input cost volatility

- number and strength of suppliers
- efficiency
- relative level of fixed cost
- reliance on commodity markets
- level of committed costs in terms of volume and price

Expense volatility

- reliance on key suppliers
- relative level of fixed cost
- how significant is the level of expenses relative to the size of the business?
- level of committed costs (e.g.leases)

Growth drivers

- ability to develop new products
- ability to find new sites on which to expand
- ability of existing management to take the company to the next stage of development

Other issues to consider

- industry analysis – relative strengths of rivals, suppliers and customers; likelihood of new industry entrants; availability of substitutes
- analysis of political, environmental, social, technological, legal and economic developments that may affect future business
- working capital needs
- exposure to currency risks

Once business risks have been analysed, the company may find it appropriate to develop strategies to mitigate some of its key risks.

costs may have difficulty achieving breakeven if sales fall. The level of committed costs may also be important; a business with a high commitment to forward expenditure is more vulnerable (i.e. riskier) than one with no such commitments.

For each business the specific risk factors will differ. However, Working insight 3.1 illustrates some examples of issues to consider in analysing business risk.

CONSTITUENTS OF FINANCIAL STRATEGY

Business risk was defined as representing the risks to the company's operating results. Financial risk is the risk inherent in the company's choice of financing structure. At this juncture it is worth considering the key decisions to be made in determining a financial strategy, and the associated risks.

Think about the flows of funds through a company.[1] It will use its asset base to generate profits, of which some will be paid out to shareholders as dividends, and the rest will be retained for future growth. Although the level of those profits will depend partly on its operating efficiency, the ultimate level of profit available to shareholders will depend on the interest burden that the company is carrying – which itself depends on the level of debt it takes on. The directors thus have three decisions to make:

1. How large do we want (or need) the asset base to be?
2. How much of the company's finance should be in debt (and therefore how much in equity)? And
3. How much of the profit should be paid out in dividend (and therefore how much should be retained for future growth)?

   These decisions are closely linked. If the directors see attractive growth opportunities, they may wish to retain the funds rather than pay them out in dividend (the practicalities of this action will be discussed in Chapter 10). If they feel obliged to pay out dividends, then the expansion could be financed by increasing the company's debt levels. Should the directors feel that such an action would be unwise, then perhaps they should not increase the asset base at all.

   The three decisions above describe a relatively closed system. There is however a fourth decision for the directors to make:

4. Should we issue new equity?

   Issuing new equity expands the company's funding. If it has a target debt–equity ratio (a practice which appears to be rather more common in academic text books than it is in practice) then increasing the equity base also means that it can take on more debt.

---

1. This explanation is based on work originally published in *Building Value with Capital-Structure Strategies* by H.A. Davis and W.W. Sihler, Financial Executives Research Foundation Inc., 1998.

Putting it very simplistically, these are the only four decisions that need to be taken in financial strategy! (Pedants might argue that a share buyback could be a fifth decision, but we see that merely as the reverse of the 'new equity' decision.)

FINANCIAL RISK

In assessing financial risk, it is essential to decide from which perspective the analysis is being made, as financial risk can be described as two sides of the same coin. This is diagrammatically illustrated with respect to debt and equity funding in Figure 3.2.

It is clear that any commercial lender such as a bank will try to reduce its financial risk by a whole series of actions. These include ensuring that it has priority in terms of both repayment of principal and payment of interest, possibly by taking security over specific assets, and by insisting on covenants in its loan agreements, which can entitle it to demand early and immediate repayment if the financial position of the borrower appears to deteriorate. Clearly these steps transfer a large part of the financial risk to the company, as any breach of the loan agreement conditions (such as failing to pay interest on the due date) can place the continued existence of the company in jeopardy.

Conversely the financial rights of the same company's shareholders are minimal and hence their financial risk is higher. The company has discretion over whether or not to pay a dividend, even if it has sufficient distributable profits, whereas the payment of interest is effectively committed and mandatory. Ordinary shareholders cannot demand from the company the repayment of their investment even if no dividends are paid over a long period; except by placing

Figure 3.2

Financial risk from different perspectives

	Features for Provider (the investor)	Features for User (the company)
Debt	• Interest is contractual • Repayment is contractual • The lender may require security A LOW RISK INSTRUMENT	• Interest must be paid • Repayments must be made • The lender may have the right to repossess assets A HIGH RISK INSTRUMENT
Equity	• Dividends are at the discretion of the company • No requirement to repay the capital A HIGH RISK INSTRUMENT	• Can choose whether to pay dividends • No repayment obligation A LOW RISK INSTRUMENT

the company into liquidation, in which case they are last in the queue and do not receive any distribution until all the company's creditors have been paid in full. They seek a large part of their return in the form of a capital gain in the share price – which is by no means guaranteed to them, even if the company prospers.

Balancing this lack of control and higher level of risk on the part of the shareholders, of course, are the potentially unlimited returns which they can achieve if the share price rises, whereas the lower-risk-taking term lender to the company receives a more guaranteed but much lower maximum return in the form of interest and the repayment of principal.

We deal above with 'plain vanilla' debt and equity. Many years ago, when the authors first became involved in corporate finance, most financing options could quite easily be categorized as either debt or equity; nowadays there is a continuum between secured term lending at one extreme and ordinary, permanent shares at the other. Many of the categories in between are discussed in Chapters 8 and 9 of this book.

For the purposes of this discussion of business and financial risk, our perspective is that of the company raising funding and then investing it. Consequently, although the shareholders' risk associated with investing in equity is quite high, the financial risk of using predominantly equity financing from the company's perspective is much lower than if a high proportion of debt funding is used.

The concept of financial risk can be combined with the business risk profile, in order to develop logical alternative financial strategies for different types of business. These risk profiles combine together to give the overall risk profile for the business in the same manner as all sequential probabilities; i.e. mathematically the individual factors are multiplied together to get the combined result. Therefore combining together a high business risk strategy with a high financial risk strategy (such as would be achieved by funding the start-up bio-tech company with almost all debt financing) gives a very, very high total risk profile: such a company may succeed spectacularly but it is much more likely to fail completely and disappear. Thus, as illustrated in Figure 3.3, this combination of strategies is not a logical, long-term basis for creating a successful business.

However when the differing risk and return profiles of various stakeholders are taken into account, this type of strategy can easily be seen to be potentially very attractive to an entrepreneur style of risk taker. If most of the required funding can be raised in the form of debt, the entrepreneurs have to inject very little of their own money. Yet, if the business turns out to be successful, they will get the vast majority of these upside gains: the return to the lenders of the debt financing being fixed. Whereas if the high risk business fails, as it probably will, they can only lose the small amount of equity which they have injected. From their perspective this appears to be the ultimate combination of 'you take all the risk and we'll take all the return!'.

Unfortunately for these entrepreneurs, lenders do not see this as an acceptable combination of the risk/return relationship. It is now well established that very high business risk enterprises should be funded with equity, which the investors know is potentially at risk (i.e. venture capital). Where it has proved possible to raise large amounts of inappropriate debt capital for such high business risk investments, the fault lies with the lender far more than with the borrower,

Figure 3.3

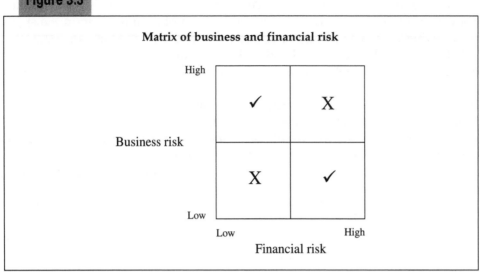

Matrix of business and financial risk

because the lender is committing what can be regarded as the most heinous sin of corporate finance: accepting a debt-type return while taking equity-type risk.

In the opinion of the authors, funding should only be regarded as 'true' debt when there is an alternative way out, i.e. if the lender can still recover the balance outstanding even if the business or project concerned fails to perform as originally expected. Normally this alternative exit route would be provided by realizing the underlying value of certain assets owned by the business or pledged as security for the loan by a guarantor. If no such realizable assets exist, the true risk associated with the funding is that of an equity investor. Hence, if the lenders settle for an interest-based return, they are not matching their real risk profile to the return being achieved. There is nothing wrong in taking on a high risk equity investment, as long as the expected return is commensurately high; otherwise it is a totally unacceptable risk/return relationship.

Referring to Figure 3.3, this means that high business risk companies should use low risk financing, i.e. equity venture capital, and should keep their cost bases as variable and discretionary as possible. This logic is now fairly well understood and accepted by the capital markets, even to the extent that venture capital is primarily provided by a relatively small number of specialist finance organizations. They understand the high business risks involved and aim to manage these risks by demanding a very high level of return on their investment and using portfolio management techniques, which allow for a proportion of their investments failing completely, resulting in a total financial loss.

The greater problems at this very simple level of financial strategy tend to be encountered with the lower business risk companies. In general, business risk tends to reduce as companies mature; not least because the unsuccessful ones tend to fail and cease to exist. For example, the earlier examples of high technology start-up companies have a very high business risk, but the surviving equivalent high-tech start-ups of 100 years or 50 years ago are now the well established major corporations of today, with much lower business risk profiles. Not only does the business risk decline but, as the company matures, the cash flow tends to become heavily positive, having been significantly negative during the development and launch stage. Therefore, if the initial financing has been raised in the most relevant form of equity, the financial structure of this more mature company can easily stay predominantly equity based, due to a lack of need for substantial external funding once the cash flow becomes significantly positive.

Unfortunately for the senior managers of many companies, this has resulted in a disastrous combination of a low business risk strategy and an even lower financial risk; i.e. the bottom left-hand box of Figure 3.3. The common disaster has appeared in the form of a corporate raider or hostile takeover bid for the company, as this incredibly low-risk strategy has led to the company being undervalued by the capital markets. Successful corporate raiders do not often get involved in changing the business strategies of the companies they buy, but they do alter their financial strategies; normally by dramatically increasing the financial risk profile by raising the debt to equity ratio. Thus these highly leveraged takeover deals, which were very popular in the second half of the 1980s, should be focused on relatively mature, low business risk companies with strongly positive cash flows, which would enable the company to service and repay the dramatically increased borrowings. It is interesting to note how many of the subsequent post-deal corporate collapses arose in businesses which did not fit this required profile.

The result of this simple analysis is that there should be an inverse correlation between the business risk of a company and its financial risk profile. Normally the business risk reduces over time as the company's core business matures or it diversifies into other areas and therefore the financial risk should be correspondingly increased. However changes in the external environment or in the internal competitive strategy can lead to quite sudden increases in the level of business risk. When this happens managers may well be advised to restore the overall risk perception for their company by reducing the level of financial risk; such as could be achieved by making an equity rights issue and using the funds raised to repay some of the outstanding debt of the company. Consequently although the most common direction of strategic movement would be from the top left to bottom right of Figure 3.3 – i.e. moving from high to low business risk and from low to high financial risk – it is possible and logical for companies to move in the opposite direction.

PRIVATELY-HELD COMPANIES ARE DIFFERENT

At this point we should point out that although much of what we say in this book is relevant to all companies, the issues raised in the preceding paragraphs need not be applied by the owner/managers of private companies.

In a listed company, as we discussed in Chapter 1, although the shareholders own the company, the directors run it. There is thus a potential agency conflict. Furthermore, most listed companies have tens or hundreds of thousands of shareholders, and it would be impossible for the directors to determine the individual goals of these shareholders, so the generic 'shareholder value' is assumed as the company's target. Added to this is the threat of takeover if a listed company's share price fails to perform.

The situation in a private company is very different. The directors are often the owners, and even if they are not, there is likely to be a strong link between the two. Accordingly, the directors can ask the shareholders directly what they want from the company. The answer may not be 'shareholder value': in many private companies the chief objectives are financial security for the family shareholders, and the creation of a business to pass down to future generations. Accordingly, shareholders in private companies may be reluctant to take on any debt, despite it being an excellent idea in theory, if it means that they could lose sleep over it. And as private companies cannot suffer the threat of a hostile takeover, there is no need for them to follow the prescribed strategy of gearing up a low risk business.

RISK AND THE PRODUCT LIFE CYCLE

In Chapter 2 we briefly introduced the product lifecycle. Here, we expand on it considerably and apply the model in terms of business risk and financial strategy.

All products follow a well-established life cycle in that the trends in sales values, in real terms, are rationally explained by reference to the current stage of development of the product. The basic practical problem associated with the life cycle is that it is much easier to use the technique to explain why sales moved as they did (used as an *ex post* analysis), than it is to use it to predict what sales will be in the future (in an *ex ante* role). However if the life cycle is broken into several stages, as shown in Figure 3.4, it does become possible to understand what the long-term future trend in sales levels might be and to make strategic decisions accordingly.

Figure 3.4

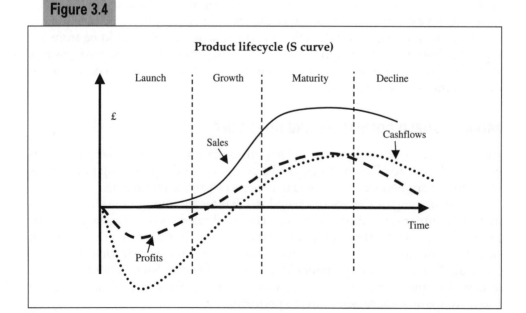

The traditional 'S curve' focuses on the level of sales over the lifecycle. Figure 3.4 also illustrates what the related profits and cash flows profiles could be. In the launch stage, both profit and cashflow are likely to be negative, reflecting the investment made in developing the product and the market. The progression through the lifecycle sees both profit and cashflow becoming positive. (There is little point in starting if this is not likely to happen!) The stage at which each stops being a drain on the organization will depend on the characteristics of the enterprise; in Figure 3.4 it is assumed that capitalization of costs will mean that profits turn the corner sooner than cashflows.

Clearly the initial sales levels during the launch phase of any product will be low; at this stage there is a significant business risk that sales will never increase and may disappear altogether if the product either does not work properly or is not accepted by the market. Should these initial risks be overcome so that the product becomes accepted by the critical mass of the important opinion-forming segment of potential customers, sales levels should start to increase significantly. This period of dramatic sales growth cannot continue forever, as the total demand for any product is finite. Inevitably the increase in sales starts to slow down as all the potential customers for the product come into the market and establish their normal rate of usage for the product. (It must be remembered that, at present, this discussion is concentrating on the demand for the total product and is not considering the relative market shares of competing companies.)

It is very common to find that this period of fast growth in demand attracts a number of late entrants into the market; the apparent risk associated with the product has reduced since it is now accepted by the customers, but the continuing growth indicates an opportunity to make an attractive financial return. Obviously these new entrants will increase the total capacity for the product, but the existing players are also trying to increase their shares of this growing market (the reasons for this strategic thrust are considered later in the chapter). This can cause a significant increase in total industry capacity, even though the demand for the product is starting to stabilize (the problems of accurately forecasting the change-over points in the product life cycle are substantial). As a result many businesses in the industry will have spare new capacity, which can cause fierce price competition until a more stable equilibrium position is established. This overcapacity is diagrammatically shown in Figure 3.5, and the maturity stage of the life cycle cannot be properly started until this position is resolved.

In the maturity stage demand and supply are much more in balance, so that the remaining efficient producers can expect to make stable profits on their substantial sales volumes. Unfortunately, this happy state of affairs eventually ends when demand for the product starts to die away. This can be caused by saturation of the market or by the launch of a better replacement product which rapidly attracts away most of the current mature product's users.

The question of replacement products has generated much debate over the years because, if the initial product is very broadly defined, it can be argued that this 'new' product is a development rather than a replacement. A classical illustration, which also serves to demonstrate the absurdity of taking this argument too far, is the decline of various forms of transportation. Was the

Figure 3.5

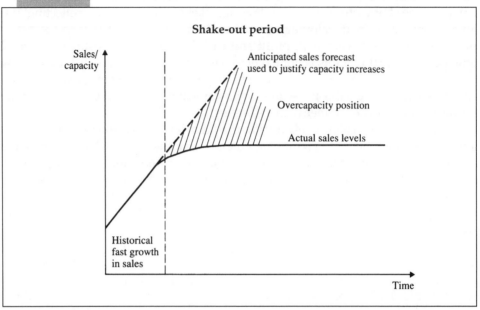

horse-drawn carriage 'product' developed into the automobile, or replaced by it; as both provide personal forms of transport? If the railways had defined their product offering as 'general transportation', the demand for their 'product' would not have declined as dramatically with the advent of aeroplanes, trucks and cars. However, unless their business strategies had been completely altered so that they moved into these newer forms of transport, their share of this still expanding 'transportation' market would have significantly fallen.

A very important element highlighted by the product life cycle is the concept of changes in market share for the competitors in any particular industry. It is quite straightforward to distinguish among the different stages of development in terms of the key strategic thrusts of the business and to relate these to the relative associated business risks at each stage. This can be most easily demonstrated by applying the Boston Consulting Group's portfolio matrix, albeit in a slightly different manner to its traditional use.

THE BOSTON MATRIX

Figure 3.6 shows the product life cycle in a diagrammatic representation developed by the Boston Consulting Group in order to explain the concept of product portfolio management to senior managers of large groups.

The two axes are based on key business success factors identified from the PIMS (profit impact of market strategies) database set up by General Electric and now run by the Strategic Planning Institute. This database holds financial and other performance data on over several thousand business units and provides a good source of comparative information on business performance.

Figure 3.6

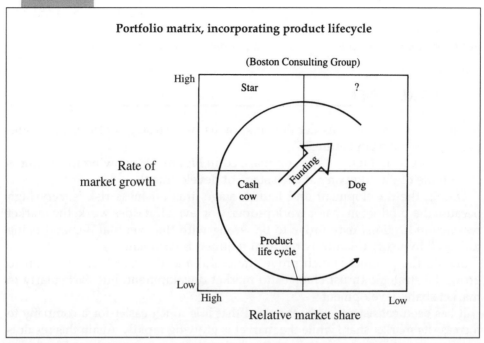

During the 1960s it was generally agreed that two of the three most important determinant factors of business success were relative market share and the rate of growth of the particular markets (the third factor being the level of profitability of the product).

These factors are hardly surprising, but if the product life cycle is added into the discussion they can be related to the key strategic thrusts of the business and to the most appropriate management style, as shown in Figure 3.6. The horizontal axis shows the relative market share of the company, i.e. its share compared to its largest competitor. This relative measure is vitally important because a 20 per cent market share may sound impressive, but if the only competitor has the other 80 per cent market share, the company's competitive position is relatively weak. The vertical axis represents the rate of growth in sales volumes for the market in total, and hence goes from highly positive at the top to significantly negative at the bottom; thus replicating the product life cycle's S curve (this represents a digression from the traditional Boston matrix, which did not include negative growth).

When a company launches a new product into an existing market, it will, by definition, have an initial low share of the market but will normally select a high growth market. (If a new product is launched into an already declining market, the company will start in the bottom right-hand box and stay there; what one of the authors often describes as an example of a 'Wally' strategy.) Its position will, therefore, be in the top right-hand box of the market. The key strategic thrust of the business at this launch stage should clearly be to focus on both research and development and market research for the new product, as the potential success of any new product can be severely curtailed if its entry into the market is so delayed that competitors have become solidly established. Given this strategic focus, the most appropriate management style is entrepreneurial and innovative, in order to stimulate the drive and enthusiasm to create and launch the new product which, quite frequently, requires very substantial obstacles to be overcome.

BUSINESS RISK

In this section we will consider the 'unknowns' at each stage of the product life-cycle, as set out as in Figure 3.7.

The analysis in Figure 3.7 is summarized in Figure 3.8, showing the business risk profile of the company at each stage of development.

During the development and launch stage, this business risk is very high because the product may not work properly or, even if it does work, the market research indications may prove to be wrong with the eventual demand being too small to justify financially the total required investment.

Should the product launch prove successful and the sales volumes start to grow, the strategic thrust changes to market development, but particularly to market share development.

It has been consistently demonstrated that it is much easier for a company to increase its market share while the market is growing rapidly. Again this result is not surprising because even if the particular company grows its sales at 50 per cent per year while the market is expanding at 40 per cent per year, its main competitors would still be expanding their own sales volumes quite rapidly on a year-on-year basis. It is possible that they may not even notice that their market shares are declining or, if they do, they may be capacity or capital constrained from increasing their output sufficiently rapidly to maintain their previous shares. If a similar market share growth objective were set for a mature, very low growth product, the

Figure 3.7

Changes in unknowns over the lifecycle

LAUNCH	GROWTH	MATURITY	DECLINE
• Product risk			
• Market acceptance			
• Market share	• Market share		
• Size of mkt at maturity	• Size of mkt at maturity		
• Length of maturity period	• Length of maturity period	• Length of maturity period	
• Maintenance of mkt share	• Maintenance of mkt share	• Maintenance of mkt share	
• Rate of eventual decline	• Rate of eventual decline	• Rate of eventual decline	• Rate of eventual decline

Figure 3.8

Business risk

Growth	Launch
High	Very high
Maturity	Decline
Medium	Low

competitive response would probably be much more severe, as the increased sales volumes would almost all have to be achieved at the expense of lower sales volumes on the part of competitors. Consequently it is a sound business strategy to try to achieve the maximum desired market share before the market itself reaches its maximum size. This requires a clear focus on market share development, but a leading company in a high growth industry should also invest in ensuring that the market matures at as large a size as is financially justifiable. (Financial expenditure on market development – increasing the size of the overall market, rather than increasing the company's own share of this market – is very difficult to justify if the company has only a small share of the market. If only a 10 per cent share is held by the company, 90 per cent of any general market development expenditure can be argued as being to the benefit of competitors.)

Such a concentrated strategic focus on market development and sales growth requires a shift in management style to 'marketing led' management, where the emphasis is not necessarily on continually changing the product unless that is required to achieve a competitive advantage in the marketplace. Some management teams seem to be capable of operating successfully in both entrepreneurial and marketing-led modes, whereas relatively few have been able to make the required transitions to incorporate the later styles of management. The business risk profile during this rapid growth phase has declined somewhat from the very high level of the launch stage but is still high. The main business risks now relate to the ultimate market share achieved by the company and the length of this period of sustained growth which together dictate the sales volumes which will be achieved during the maturity stage of the life cycle.

As already stated, the sales growth will eventually slow and the product will enter its mature phase.

If the company has been successful in implementing its marketing strategy during the period of rapid growth, it should enter the maturity stage with a very high relative market share of a large total market. This is important because it is during this stage that the company recoups the investments made during the

Figure 3.9

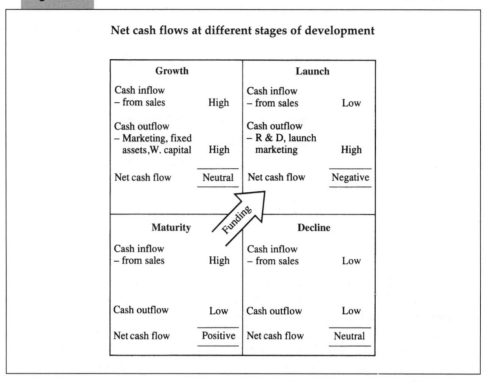

earlier stages. As shown in Figure 3.9, the net cash flows in the launch phase are heavily negative and they are normally reasonably balanced or slightly negative during the high growth stage, depending on the rate of growth and need for additional investment in fixed assets or working capital. Once the rate of growth slows this cash outflow reduces, while the cash produced from sales revenues increases (high sales volumes at a good profit per unit) resulting in a strong positive net cash flow.

During the final decline stage of the life cycle, both cash inflows and outflows are severely reduced, but the net cash flow must be at least neutral as otherwise the product should be culled instantly. (No company should be a net investor on a long-term basis in a dying product.) This overall position often causes management to invest in new growth opportunities, resulting in funding moving in the direction indicated by the arrow in Figure 3.6, from the appropriately named 'cash cow' box to the launch stage. However as is argued later in the chapter such a reinvestment is neither inevitable nor, in many cases, desirable.

Clearly this move into the maturity stage of the life cycle represents a very significant change in the strategic thrust of the business. As previously mentioned, any attempt now to increase significantly market share is likely to be fiercely resisted by competitors, particularly where the cost structure of the industry is substantially fixed and committed on a long-term basis. (In other words, if significant exit barriers from the industry have been erected, there may well be intense competition to maintain market share.)

The most appropriate management style during this phase can be described as 'controller' mode, because the business should be maximizing the return which can be generated over this mature stage of the life cycle. It is important that the business does not switch suddenly from its marketing-led growth strategy to a 'cost-cutting', short-term profit maximization mindset. This type of change could lead to a rapid decline in market share and a dramatic shortening of the period over which high profits and strong positive cash flows can be generated. The key objective is to maintain market share as long as the total market demand justifies the required level of marketing support, but at the same time to look for efficiency gains which can improve the overall return on investment. This fundamental change away from a growth management focus to a profit improvement emphasis is very difficult for many management teams to accept and implement, with the result that many businesses try to grow when market conditions and competitive pressures make this financially very unattractive. If such growth is impossible in their original business, they may turn to a diversification strategy by investing in new product areas.

Once again this move along the product life cycle reduces the level of business risk as, in the maturity stage, the main risk relates to the length of this period of stable sales volumes and high total profit levels. From the economic viewpoint of the shareholder, this cash positive phase is the justification for the initial investment in the development and launch of the product. Indeed financially rational investors would like the company to move as rapidly as possible around the product life cycle until the maturity stage is reached, and then the company should stay in this cash generating phase for as long as possible. Unfortunately the earlier styles of innovation and growth tend to be more attractive to many managers, who can find the appropriate controller style of the maturity phase very boring. (Oddly, shareholders find it far from boring to see increasing profits and cash flows generated year after year!)

In fact, for some groups of managers the declining stage of the product life cycle may be more exciting, as the dominant style now becomes 'cost-cutter' in order to ensure that the cash flows do remain at least neutral. The product is now dying, although the process may take many years and some spin-off ideas may be relaunched as new products in their own right. However, even in the move from the maturity stage to the declining phase, the business risk can still be argued as reducing. The only remaining business risk associated with the product is how long it will take to die. No dramatic positive cash inflows are expected from this phase and, if no further cost savings can be made to keep the cash flow slightly positive or neutral, the product may be closed down by the company before the market demand completely disappears. One major practical problem, caused by the failure to change managers during the progression of a product through its life cycle, is that it is very difficult for the managers who have developed, launched, grown and then maintained a product to accept that it is now time to kill what has become part of their lives (one of the family!). Far too often, products are kept going too long in the vain hope that the market will pick up or that a new way will be found of reducing the associated costs still further.

INVERSE CORRELATION OF FINANCIAL RISK WITH BUSINESS RISK

It is now possible to develop the appropriate financial strategy for each stage of the product life cycle by using the required inverse correlation between business risk and financial risk, which was considered earlier. Since the associated business risk decreases as the product moves through its life cycle, it is logical that the financial risk can be correspondingly increased without creating a completely unacceptable combined risk for the shareholders and other stakeholders in the company. This is illustrated in Figure 3.10 and leads to the obvious question of what impact this changing risk profile has on the financial strategy of the business.

As is clearly illustrated in Figure 3.10, the financial risk profile should be very low during the very high risk stage of product development and launch.[2] Earlier, the relatively low risk nature of equity funding was discussed; it is desirable at this stage to use low risk equity sources of funding and this can be achieved by raising capital from specialist investors who understand the high business risk associated with the company. This funding is properly described as venture capital.

(Unfortunately, many investment funds nowadays describe themselves as doing 'venture capital' when, in reality, they invest in existing, successful

Figure 3.10

Growth *Business risk high* **Financial risk low**	**Launch** *Business risk v. high* **Financial risk very low**
Maturity *Business risk medium* **Financial risk medium**	**Decline** *Business risk low* **Financial risk high**

Financial risk

2. It should be registered that the weighting of these business risks and financial risks is normally by no means equal; for most companies, the importance of the business risk profile is greater than the financial risk element. After all, an unsound business strategy cannot be made successful by clever financing; if the fundamental business is doomed, the best financial strategy can only delay its inevitable collapse.

business rather than green field, start-up companies; they should be more appropriately described as 'development capital' investors or, more broadly, as 'private equity'. In the rest of the book we acknowledge common usage, but try to point out the more appropriate descriptions.)

A sensible venture capital investor will have a portfolio of similarly high risk, start-up investments and will require a very high potential return from each investment made. This type of investment strategy, which is still focused on high risk projects but diversifies the risk of any single project, allows for the quite possible total failure of a start-up business during the very early stages of the product life cycle. As long as a reasonable proportion of the total venture capital portfolio actually delivers the expected high financial returns, the overall return on the portfolio should be satisfactory. In other words the very high return required by the venture capitalist investor is simply caused by the very high business risk associated with this type of investment.

A primary interest of such venture capital investors is how do they get to realize or receive these high returns on their successful investments. As previously explained, the product will eventually become cash positive when it matures but this may be many years away, whereas venture capitalists tend to have a relatively short investment time horizon (the normal period is between three and five years, with a seven-year investment period being the maximum acceptable to many investors). This short-term focus is exacerbated due to their high requirements for financial return, which force them to invest in high risk projects. As businesses successfully develop and mature, their associated business risk tends to reduce and, consequently, so does the level of return which can be expected. Thus staying as an investor until the product is significantly cash positive is a very unattractive proposition for such a venture capitalist.

Hence, identifying a relatively early exit route once the product has been successfully launched onto the market is an important prerequisite of designing a good venture capital investment. The funds to buy-out these venture capital investors will not be available from within the company, as its cash flow during its rapid growth phase will be neutral at best. Therefore new appropriate external sources of funding must be identified to replace the initial launch financing and to provide for the growth of the business during this next stage of the product's development. The business risk associated with the growth stage is still high, so that the ideal financial risk should still be low. This means that the source of this new replacement and growth funding should still be equity. However these equity investors will have a slightly lower risk appetite than the original venture capitalists, and will accordingly demand a lower return on their investment.

The best way of achieving this type of exit route for venture capital initial funding is through the flotation (listing) of the company onto a public stock market, where a much broader range of equity investors can be attracted to buy shares in the company. Such an initial public offering (IPO) is not normally possible for a start-up company as, by definition, the business has no track record which can be used to indicate its existing success or its realistic prospects for the future. (We prefer to draw a veil over the excesses of the stock markets during the internet bubble of the late 1990s,when companies appeared able to defy gravity by floating with little more than a catchy name and an improbable business plan.)

In essence, an investment at this early stage is made on the strength of a product concept, with possibly some prototypes and some market research, and a business plan indicating the future prospects for the successful, eventual product. Such investments are normally only attractive to a small number of specialized, professional investors whereas, once the product is launched and initial sales growth can be demonstrated together with substantial future growth prospects a much larger body of potential investors becomes available to the company.

The changing source of funding is illustrated in Figure 3.11 and this indicates the fundamental change which can occur when the product matures. This maturity stage reduces the associated business risk so that a medium level of financial risk can now be taken on by the company. The cash flow from the product has also turned significantly positive at this time and this combination allows the company to borrow funds rather than only using the equity sources of funding which have been accessed so far in its development. It is also important to consider the business from the perspective of the rational investor, who quite rightly regards this cash positive, mature stage as the most attractive phase of the life cycle. So far equity funding has been injected into the business to develop and launch the product and then to increase both the total market size and the company's share of that market. If more equity funding is required during the maturity stage, this investment starts to look a lot like a financial black hole; money keeps going in, but nothing ever comes out.

Therefore the only logical source of additional equity funding during this maturity stage is for some of the profits being made by the company to be reinvested into the business. It must be remembered not only that these profits

Figure 3.11

Changing sources of funding

Growth	Launch
Business risk high *Financial risk low*	*Business risk v. high* *Financial risk v. low*
Equity **(growth investors)**	**Equity** **(venture capital)**
Maturity	**Decline**
Business risk medium *Financial risk medium*	*Business risk low* *Financial risk high*
Debt and equity **(retained earnings)**	**Debt**

should be substantial in order to justify the investments made earlier in the cycle but also that additional financing can be raised through borrowing money.

This is now practical because the positive cash flow of the business provides the source of servicing the debt (paying the interest) and of repaying the principal. If debt financing is used at the earlier stages of the life cycle, the absence of such positive cash flow means that the repayments can only be made by rolling-over the original loans or by raising equity to repay the debt funding.

This highlights a key issue regarding the use of debt and equity funding; as mentioned earlier, the risk associated with debt funding from the viewpoint of the lender is lower than the equity investors' risk, due to the security taken and legally granted priority on full repayment. (Remember that the risk ranking is reversed when viewed from the perspective of the company, i.e. the user of the funding.) Risk and return are positively correlated, so that the return required on debt funding should always be less than that required on equity financing for the same company; i.e. debt is cheaper for the company. This is completely logical from the company's perspective because, as debt is higher risk funding for the company, the company should demand a cost saving to justify incurring the extra risk.

Therefore, as long as increasing the financial risk through borrowing (increasing the 'leverage' of the company) does not lead to an unacceptable total combined risk, the cheaper debt funding will increase the residual profits achieved by the company. Thus the profits generated by the mature company, which uses some debt financing, will be enhanced and the return on equity will look even better, as less equity is required to fund the business.

This is even more important when the product moves into the decline phase of the life cycle, and it becomes clear that the product is dying. If debt is cheaper than equity, it is financially beneficial to the shareholders to extract their equity investment from the dying business as early as possible by replacing it with debt. Clearly it should not be acceptable to a lender to take on an unacceptable, equity type risk, but it is often quite practical to borrow against the residual value of those assets which are, of necessity, tied up in the business until it is finally liquidated. These funds can then be distributed to shareholders, effectively representing a repayment of capital. In this way the present value of the shareholders' investment is increased, without adversely affecting the position of the lender who is suitably secured on the residual value of the assets (such as land and buildings, some non-specialized plant, cars, debtors and certain other working capital items) and who receives a risk-related rate of interest. Consequently the principal source of funding for the declining business is debt finance with its associated high financial risk, partially offsetting the low business risk associated with this final stage of development.

DEBT PROFILE

In considering the balance between debt and equity in a company's financial strategy, one other issue should be mentioned: of the debt, how much should be borrowed short term and how much long term?

The answer to this question depends, unsurprisingly, on the company's business, its assets and the structure of its operations. Broadly, the company's debt portfolio should attempt to match long term assets with long term finance, and short term assets with short term funding sources. So, the acquisition of a building would best be financed through long term debt (if, indeed, debt is the best solution); additional stocks should be funded using short term facilities such as an overdraft or revolving credit line. However, if a company has permanent working capital, this should be regarded as part of long term needs. (This is discussed further in Chapter 15.)

The advantage to a company of using long term rather than short term debt finance is that once the loan has been agreed, the company can be confident that it cannot be removed.[3] Short term debt needs to be refinanced at regular intervals and, if the company's financial situation has deteriorated or the credit market tightened, this may become a problem.

Exceptions do exist to this broad rule about using long term funding for long term needs. If short term interest rates are considerably lower than long term ones, and the company believes that long term rates will fall, it may be worth using short term finance to start, with the intention of refinancing at a later date, in a more favourable environment. This strategy does, of course, carry obvious risks. The point here is that the *policy* would be for long term debt, the issue is one of *timing*.

A LOGICAL DIVIDEND POLICY

Throughout this discussion on increasing levels of financial risk, the issue of how investors receive their required financial return has been critical. Ordinary shareholders can only receive this return in two ways; either the company pays a dividend or the value of their shares increases so that they can sell and achieve a capital gain. Obviously the total return can take the form of a combination of dividend yield (the actual dividend received divided by the value of the investment) and capital appreciation but, theoretically, the shareholder should be indifferent as to whether the company pays a dividend or not. This is because, if the company does not pay a dividend, the value of the shares should increase to reflect the present value of the future cash flows which should be generated by the reinvestment of these profits which were available to be paid out as dividends. Clearly this argument is based on an assumption regarding the availability of attractive reinvestment opportunities. Such an assumption of an infinite number of attractive reinvestment projects is not relevant if the company is restricted to one product, which progresses through its life cycle.

Hence for the current structured analysis, it is possible to indicate a logical dividend policy for a company at each stage of development, and this is diagrammatically shown in Figure 3.12. During the cash negative launch phase it is completely illogical for shareholders to expect a dividend from the company. They are supplying all the funding and therefore, if the company were to be able to pay a dividend, they would have to increase their investment

---

3. Subject of course to the company continuing to meet its obligations under the loan agreement. This is discussed further in Chapter 8.

Figure 3.12

Dividend policy – payout ratio

Growth	Launch
Business risk high *Financial risk low* *Funding equity*	*Business risk v. high* *Financial risk v. low* *Funding equity*
Nominal dividend payout ratio	**Nil dividend payout ratio**
Maturity	Decline
Business risk medium *Financial risk medium* *Funding debt*	*Business risk low* *Financial risk high* *Funding debt*
High dividend payout ratio	**Total dividend payout ratio**

in order to pay part of it back to themselves! Consequently a nil dividend payout ratio is appropriate for these start-up, venture capital funded businesses; all of the high required return being in the form of capital growth.

There is also a very simple practical restraint on many such companies paying dividends. In order to pay dividends, companies require both cash and distributable profits, e.g. profits after tax generated either in the current year or retained from past years. During the launch phase, the business may be generating accounting losses and therefore may have no distributable profits from which it can declare a dividend.

Even when the company has moved into the high growth stage of the life cycle, the cash flow is still, at best, only neutral and the source of funding is still equity. Thus a high dividend payout policy is still illogical and this is made even more clear when the key strategic thrust at this stage is considered. The business is trying to increase its market share while the market is still growing strongly: a logical investor would want the company to take advantage of these attractive growth opportunities while they exist and this could be constrained if current profits are paid out as dividends. As new investors are being attracted into the company during this stage in order to replace the existing venture capitalists and to finance the rapid growth, it may be necessary to pay a nominal dividend out of the increasing profit stream. However most of the required investor return would still come from capital growth in the value of the shares in the company.

Once the maturity stage of the life cycle is reached, the dividend policy should change for a number of reasons. The cash flow from the business is now strongly positive and debt financing is now a practical and sensible alternative source of funding. Accounting profits should now be high and relatively stable so that a high dividend payout can be properly supported. More fundamentally, it is important that the dividend payout ratio is increased as there will be restricted opportunities for reinvesting the whole of the current profit stream in the existing business. There is a strong possibility of the law of diminishing returns setting in on incremental levels of reinvestment. If a company cannot reinvest funds at the rate of return demanded by its shareholders, it destroys shareholder value by retaining these funds. Consequently, as profitable reinvestment opportunities reduce due to the lack of growth in the now mature business, shareholder value can be maximized by paying out these surplus funds as dividends. Furthermore, as the company matures the opportunities for the shareholders to make a substantial capital gain must be limited, as the high-growth period is in the past. Accordingly, in order to provide shareholder return the dividend yield would be expected to increase, to compensate for the decline in potential capital gain.

This required change in dividend policy represents yet another of the potential conflicts discussed in agency theory (introduced in Chapter 1), because senior managers will normally prefer to retain these surplus funds within the company. These funds provide them with operational flexibility should an attractive opportunity be identified in the future and they also act as a buffer in case there is an unforeseen economic downturn or adverse change in the competitive environment. Neither of these arguments is based on the concept of maximizing shareholder wealth, but is more closely focused on a concept of reducing either managerial risk or accountability.

Inevitably the strong cash flows and high profits will die away as the product starts to decline, yet Figure 3.12 then advocates a total dividend payout ratio. In this context, 'total' means all the free cash flow generated by the business which, during this declining stage, is likely to be in excess of the profit levels reported by the company.

During the maturity phase, the company produces high profits and high net cash flows, out of which it should pay a high proportion as dividend. As illustrated in Working insight 3.2, this dividend yield will represent a substantial proportion of the total return expected by the shareholders, because future prospects for capital growth are now relatively low (profits may increase in future years due to improvements in efficiency levels, etc.). However once the product starts to decline, this future growth becomes negative with the result that the company may not want to reinvest to maintain the existing scale of business. This means that the depreciation expense (which is, of course, a non-cash operating expense charged in arriving at the post-tax profits out of which dividends are paid) may not necessarily be reinvested in replacing the assets which are being used up. This would increase the level of free cash flow generated by the business which could be paid out as dividends to shareholders.

The dividends could be further increased if the residual value of essential assets was raised by borrowing and the cash distributed to shareholders, as mentioned earlier, clearly highlighting that part of the high dividends paid by declining companies really represents a repayment of shareholders' capital.

WORKING
3.2

INSIGHT   **Illustrative example of changes in total shareholder return**
and its component elements

Stage of maturity	Total annual required return (i.e. K_e)		Generated by:		
			Dividend yield	+	Capital growth
Launch	40%	=	0	+	40%
Growth	25%	=	2%	+	23%
Maturity	15%	=	12%	+	3%
Decline	12%	=	18%	−	6%

(These total returns are illustrative only. Tax is ignored, but does not affect the logic of the analysis. However, the different tax positions of various groups of shareholders may make companies in particular stages of maturity more or less attractive to them.)

This changing picture of the dividend payout ratio and its offsetting relationship with expected capital growth in the share value must always be considered in the context of a decreasing overall risk profile for the company as it matures. The reducing risk profile means that investors demand a lower total rate of return; the sort of relationships which can apply between dividend yields and capital growth are illustrated in Working insight 3.2.

THE IMPACT ON THE PRICE/EARNINGS MULTIPLE

It is clear from Working insight 3.2 that the capital growth component of the total expected shareholder return reduces as the product passes through its lifecycle. This is very logical because the future growth prospects for the product start off very high and reduce as these prospects are actually achieved; obviously if the product is unsuccessful, these future growth prospects may be destroyed very quickly, rather than being delivered over time. The development of future growth prospects over the life cycle is illustrated in Figure 3.13, which highlights that the future growth of a mature product is relatively low and that a declining product will experience negative growth in the future.

As discussed in Chapter 2, a company's price/earnings (P/E) ratio bears a direct relationship to its expected future growth prospects: the higher the growth expectations, the higher the P/E. Accordingly, the P/E ratio might be expected to fall over the company's lifecycle. Figure 3.14 shows this.

We can expand upon the analysis in Chapter 2 and thus far in this chapter, to show how a company's earnings per share may need to increase over its lifecycle due to the decreasing P/E ratio. Working insight 3.3 demonstrates the rising levels of eps needed to justify a share price of 100 p.

In Working insight 3.3 the share price does not rise above the initial 100 p paid by the shareholders. Of course, were this to happen in practice the shareholders would be most dissatisfied with the company's performance. This illustrates an

Figure 3.13

Future growth prospects

Growth	Launch
Business risk high *Financial risk low* *Funding equity* *Divd. pay-out nominal* **High growth**	*Business risk v. high* *Financial risk v. low* *Funding equity* *Divd. pay-out nil* **Very high growth**
Maturity	Decline
Business risk medium *Financial risk medium* *Funding debt* *Divd. pay-out high* **Med/low growth**	*Business risk low* *Financial risk high* *Funding debt* *Divd. pay-out total* **Negative growth**

Figure 3.14

Price/Earnings multiple

Growth	Launch
Business risk high *Financial risk low* *Funding equity* *Divd. pay-out nominal* *Growth high* **High P/E**	*Business risk v. high* *Financial risk v. low* *Funding equity* *Divd. pay-out nil* *Growth v. high* **Very high P/E**
Maturity	Decline
Business risk medium *Financial risk medium* *Funding debt* *Divd. pay-out high* *Growth med/low* **Med/low P/E**	*Business risk low* *Financial risk high* *Funding debt* *Divd. pay-out total* *Growth negative* **Low P/E**

WORKING
3.3
INSIGHT   **The inevitability of a reducing P/E multiple**

Stage of maturity	Appropriate P/E multiple	×	Current earnings per share	=	Market price of share
Launch	40	×	2.5 p	=	100 p[1]
Growth	20	×	5 p[2]	=	100 p (base price)
Maturity	10	×	10 p[2]	=	100 p (base price)
Steady state	7	×	14.3 p[2]	=	100 p (base price)
Decline	4	×	12.5 p	=	50 p[3]

(1) The current price of 100 p includes a very high expectation of future growth. In order to support this existing price, the company must deliver over its life cycle the growth in eps indicated as item (2).

(3) As indicated in Working insight 3.2 the share price starts to fall when the product moves into the decline phase, as both the P/E multiple and eps fall.

important point: the very high real growth in eps already included in the share price when a very high P/E multiple is applied to the company. The delivery of this expected growth will not make the share price increase because it has already been discounted (taken account of) in the current share price. The share price will only rise if the company can actually exceed this expected and paid-for rate of growth, or continue to grow at this rate for longer than expected. However in the first three stages of the life cycle it is quite possible for the company to deliver strongly growing eps.

This continued period of rapidly increasing eps is very important from the shareholders' point of view because, as was made clear in Working insight 3.2, during the launch and growth stages almost all of their financial return is generated from capital growth in the value of their share, the company having a very low dividend payout policy at this time. Consequently, generating only that rate of growth in eps which merely maintains the existing share price would be considered a very poor performance by the company. The eps growth during the launch and growth periods should drive up the share price so that an acceptable overall annual rate of return is achieved by the shareholders. This needs to take account both of the declining P/E multiple which will be applied to these earnings as they grow, and of the changing dividend payout ratio which should reduce expectations of future growth as the company matures.

The dramatic impact which this additional requirement for share value growth has on the need to generate eps growth is mathematically illustrated in Working insight 3.4.

Working insight 3.4 builds on the discussion in Chapter 2 about the need for eps to grow at a faster rate than the share price. It shows that for a particular, relatively short life cycle the growth in share price which is required to give shareholders their expected total annual return, including the capital gain element, is itself quite dramatic (e.g. from 100 p to 742 p over the 17-year life cycle period to the steady state stage as shown in column 4). However, due to the declining P/E multiple which is also correctly applied as the product

WORKING
3.4

INSIGHT

Uphill struggle

Stage of maturity	(1) Illustrative length of stage (in years)	(2) Appropriate annual capital gain required through share price (from Working insight 3.2)	(3) Compound factor (based on [column 2]^f)	(4) Required share price at start of each stage (see note)	(5) Future growth related P/E multiple (from Working insight 3.3)	(6) Desired eps by start of each stage
Initial value at time of first external investment – 100p						
Launch	2	40%	1.960	100 p = ↓	40 ×	2.5 p
Growth	5	23%	2.815	196 p = ↓	20 ×	9.8 p
Maturity	10	3%	1.344	552 p = ↓	10 ×	55.2 p
Steady state	N/A	Nil	1	742 p =	7 ×	106 p

Thus in the 17 years that this product takes to reach a steady state position the growth in eps is from 2.5 p to 106 p. If the company were only to achieve the eps of 14.3 p shown in Working insight 3.3 the share price would not increase to the level required by investors.

At the final steady state position, the eps of 106 p will be paid out annually as a dividend. Based on the share price of 742 p this gives a dividend yield of 14.3 per cent. This return represents the full cost of capital to shareholders (consistent with the inverse of the steady state P/E ratio of seven times).

Note to column (4): The required share price at the beginning of each subsequent stage is calculated by multiplying the opening share price for the previous stage by the compound factor required for that stage.

matures, the required increase in eps needed to generate this final share price is even greater (an incredible growth from 2.5 p to 106 p, as shown in column 6).

The underlying assumptions for these illustrations have been deliberately kept consistent so that the scale of the changes can be seen quite clearly as the analysis is made more comprehensive. This enables the overall financial strategy analysis to be completed by adding in the share price of the company over the product life cycle, as is done in Figure 3.15.

This figure shows both the movement in the actual share price over the life cycle and the associated volatility. The share price is obviously the result of multiplying the P/E multiple and the eps level, and its required trend over time depends on the proportion of the total shareholders' return which must be delivered through capital growth. As highlighted in Working insight 3.4 the share price should be increasing during the launch and growth stages, and then stabilizing during maturity, before declining during the product's final phase of its life cycle.

During the very early period of the launch stage, any financial valuation exercise is very speculative as nominal (or even negative) earnings are being

Figure 3.15

<table>
<tr><td colspan="2" align="center">Share price / volatility</td></tr>
<tr>
<td align="center">Growth

Business risk high
Financial risk low
Funding equity
Dividend payout nominal
Growth high
P/E high

Share price growing and volatile</td>
<td align="center">Launch

Business risk very high
Financial risk very low
Funding equity
Dividend payout nil
Growth very high
P/E very high

Share price growing and highly volatile</td>
</tr>
<tr>
<td align="center">Maturity

Business risk medium
Financial risk medium
Funding debt
Dividend payout high
Growth medium/low
P/E medium

Share price stable with limited volatility</td>
<td align="center">Decline

Business risk low
Financial risk high
Funding debt
Dividend payout total
Growth negative
P/E low

Share price declining and volatile</td>
</tr>
</table>

multiplied by the very high P/E multiple which reflects the expectations of strong future growth. As already discussed, this stage of investment is really an area for sophisticated professionals who appreciate the high associated risks and potentially, commensurately high financial returns. The considerable potential for complete business failure or outstanding success results in very high volatility in share prices during this stage of the life cycle.

Once the product moves into the growth phase, this volatility will decline somewhat but will still be high due to the continued expectations of significant future growth in share values/eps, market share, and the total size of the market. Failure of any of these factors (which are of course interlinked) can lead to a rapid decline in share values, while unpredicted favourable developments can create quite spectacular growth in share prices. However, during the maturity stage, when the major element of shareholders' return comes from dividend yield, the share price should become much less volatile. This is because the strong positive cash flow and ability to use debt financing should enable the company to maintain the expected dividend payments even through normal economic cycles, so that the share price is consistently supported by this stable dividend stream. It is also much easier to value this type of income-generating share by reference to equivalent risk-adjusted interest-earning alternative investments; thus prices of high dividend-paying shares tend to move very directly as a result of any changes in interest rates which affect the yields on corporate bonds and other such investments.

This period of relatively low volatility comes to an end as the single product company moves into the final phase of its life cycle because the volatility of the now declining share price increases again. In spite of the reducing business risk, the share price is now controlled by a total dividend payout policy and the investors' view on the length of time for which such payments can be maintained. Consequently small external influences on the rate of decline of the product and its consequent cash generation capability can have very significant impacts on the share value, thus increasing the volatility.

IMPACT OF A DIVERSIFICATION STRATEGY

So far in this chapter consideration has been concentrated on single-product companies as they, and their products, progress through the life cycle. As mentioned earlier and discussed in Chapter 1 the inevitable result of the ultimate decline and death of such companies is not an attractive proposition for the senior managers and some of the other stakeholders. The analysis in this chapter does however highlight that this inevitable liquidation of the company is not necessarily of great concern to the shareholders in the company; although these shareholders are likely to change over time as the relative balance in the form of their financial return between capital gain and dividend yield changes.

(A major reason for such changes in shareholder structures is the different taxation treatments applied both to different shareholder groupings and to the different types of return available to each of these classifications of investors. As usual, these taxation differences create inefficiencies in the way capital markets operate, which is why most theories of finance are based on assumptions of no taxes at all. Major improvements from this point of view have been achieved in several economies around the world during the 1980s by the reduction in corporate taxation rates and the simplification of the related tax systems to reduce some of the main distorting factors.)

Clearly, rational shareholders may be unconcerned about the forthcoming decline and death of any one investment from which they are currently receiving very high dividends (which partially represent a repayment of their invested capital). If they wish to preserve the value of their total investments, they can reinvest this capital repayment in other companies. Indeed it is fairly obvious that rational investors can generate any desired mix of capital gain and dividend yield by investing in a suitable portfolio of companies. Similarly they can create a portfolio with any desired overall risk profile by suitably weighting the different types of available investments. Thus no sensible investor is forced to accept the reducing risk profile and increasing dividend yield which should be offered by a maturing company. A readjustment to the overall portfolio can be made either by reinvesting this increasing income stream in higher risk, higher growth companies or, more rapidly, by actually selling some shares in the now mature business.

The costs of these changes to the investors' portfolios are normally very small and, more importantly, such changes should be easily planned well in advance if the company and the capital markets are using the appropriate signalling procedures. Therefore, from a shareholder's perspective there is no obvious need for a company to implement a diversification strategy when the growth prospects from the original core business reduce due to the product's maturity. However, such corporate strategies of utilizing the strong positive cash flow from the successful, but now mature, core businesses to invest in new higher growth potential products, lie at the very heart of the Boston Matrix shown in Figure 3.6.

As clearly demonstrated in Figure 3.9 the growth and decline stages of the life cycle are both broadly neutral in terms of net cash flow. The strong positive net cash flows of the maturity stage, which are not required for reinvestment in the core business, are therefore often used to fund the launch of other new products, which are at the beginning of their life cycles. Inevitably, over time, such a cross-subsidization reinvestment strategy will create a diversified conglomerate style group which, due to its continued high level of reinvestment, should be considerably bigger than an originally similar, but still focused business which had followed a financial strategy of increasing its dividend pay-out ratio over the same period. The major question is whether shareholder value has been increased or destroyed by the diversification alternative strategy.

In Chapter 1 the key point was emphasized that shareholder value is increased by developing and maintaining a sustainable competitive advantage. It is therefore critical whether the business can develop such a competitive advantage in these new areas of commercial endeavour. Obviously it may be that the new products utilize some technological breakthrough which was developed in the core business, and thus the company is not truly diversifying. Similarly the new areas of investment may build on an existing strength of the business so as to increase the overall competitive advantage held by the company. This can be diagrammatically illustrated by using a variation of the Ansoff matrix, as is shown in Figure 3.16.

If a key competitive strength of the existing business is built on the current product attributes or strong branding which have created very loyal customers, a strategic thrust for continued growth could be based on umbrella branding of new products with comparable attributes. This would utilize the major intangible asset of the company; its loyal customers. Such a customer-based competitive strategy has been implemented by many retailers, highlighted by the development of 'retailer' brands. Alternatively the existing product may have reached maturity in its current markets but other markets may be less fully developed, and so may represent additional growth opportunities. Once again this growth strategy is based on an existing competitive advantage of the business; its ability to manage the launch and growth stages of a product, as demonstrated in its original market. However, if doing this the managers need to be very careful to modify their previous strategy to reflect a different competitive environment.

These growth strategies can be successfully developed from an existing competitive advantage but, as with the case of the growth strategy focused on the original core business, the external business environment must be consistent with the strategy selected. Thus for growth of the core business to be financially successful the product must be at the right stage of development. Similarly, for the customer-led strategy any new products must have similar attributes so that they appeal to existing loyal customers and any umbrella branding is appropriate. For the market development strategy, the dynamics of the new markets must be sufficiently similar to enable the company to make use of its existing competitive advantage developed in its more mature home market; there are many examples

Figure 3.16

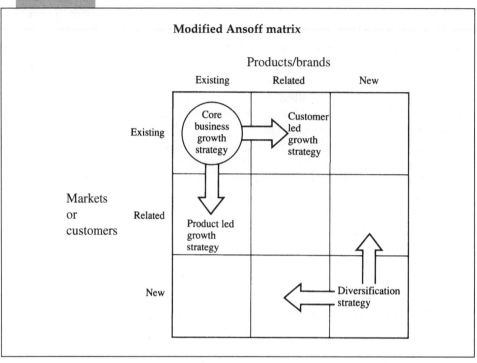

of very expensive failures from this type of product globalization strategy and far fewer examples of success. However Figure 3.16 also shows where genuine diversification strategies fit and why they are most unlikely to create increased shareholder value. Rather than building on existing competitive advantages, diversification goes to the other extreme and can be somewhat cynically described as 'selling products you don't have to people you don't know'.

It is very interesting that most companies regard diversification as a risk reduction exercise. For the shareholder, it is clear that investing in a portfolio of shares spreads, and hence reduces, the risk associated with any one share. However, from the company's perspective, it normally means moving into areas where it has little or no experience and thus there is no particular reason why the company should achieve an above normal rate of return. Of course, if the risk profile is reduced then a lower rate of return may still create shareholder value.

This highlights another major problem with basing a diversification strategy on a successful mature, cash positive business. As was clearly shown in Figure 3.15, the mature stage of the life cycle should have the lowest volatility in share prices. Volatility is a good indicator of risk in assessing any financial investment, as a 'guaranteed' level of return represents a low risk to the investor. Hence, if a company diversifies into launch and growth products, the associated risk will increase from the perception of the investor; thus an increased return will be demanded to compensate for this increased risk. As the company has no significant competitive advantage it may not be possible to deliver such an increased return, with a consequent reduction in shareholder value.

Further it is clearly much more difficult for a diversified company, with businesses at all the different stages of the life cycle, to communicate a clear, focused financial strategy to the financial markets via its dividend policy or its debt-to-equity ratio. Theoretically such a conglomerate should be valued by the financial markets at a minimum of the weighted average P/E multiple of its component businesses; the excess valuation over this minimum representing the value 'created' by the existence of the conglomerate group. In reality the share price of most such groups is at a discount to this theoretical minimum, which explains why so many of these companies have been the target of corporate raiders in recent years. If successful, the raider changes the financial strategy of the group rather than the competitive strategies of the component parts.

APPLICATION INTERNALLY TO THE DIVISIONS OF A GROUP

As the threat of takeover and break-up is potentially on the horizon for many large diversified groups, it is important that this analysis of appropriate financial strategies is applied internally by them to their individual operating divisions. In other words, the target financial return set for each division should be based on an assessment of the associated risk; thus a start-up division would be treated as effectively having venture capital funding, with a consequently high requirement for financial return. Also the form of that financial return would be dictated by the stage of development of the particular business so that cash (dividends paid by the division to head office as the only shareholder) would only be extracted from mature divisions, where the opportunities for reinvestment were less attractive.

The establishment of very clear, specific, tailored financial targets for each division of a large group can greatly help to focus the attention of divisional managers on those objectives which can create the maximum impact on the value of the total group. This would not be achieved if all the divisions tried to maximize short-term profits or cash flow, or even used some form of return on investment as the principal measure of divisional performance. Unfortunately, in many large groups, this level of financial sophistication is still not being applied today. In many, the hurdle rate for financial investments throughout the group is taken to be the weighted average cost of capital for the group and almost all divisions are expected to contribute towards the overall dividends paid out by the group to its shareholders. The almost inevitable result of this type of control system is that the divisions themselves start to develop a portfolio of businesses which are in different stages of development, so that they can then manage their financial resources across their own portfolio!

CONCLUSION

A company's choice of financial strategy – how it chooses to finance its business, and its selection of dividend policies – must relate to its business strategy. High risk businesses should adopt low risk financing structures, primarily equity-based. Similarly, low risk businesses can improve their return to shareholders by taking on debt, increasing their financing risk.

The lifecycle model introduced in this chapter shows how business risk is likely to change as a company develops. It illustrates the business risk profile, from which the appropriate gearing and dividend policy follow logically. It also demonstrates how market perceptions – and thus the share price – are likely to change over time. An understanding of this model informs the discussions in the rest of the book.

3.1   BIOGLAN PHARMA PLC

CASE STUDY

We stated earlier in this chapter that companies can add far more value in pursuing an appropriate business strategy than they can in tailoring their financial strategy. However, we also pointed out that an inappropriate financial strategy can destroy value. An example of such an event occurred whilst we were in the process of writing this book.

Bioglan Pharma is a UK-based speciality pharmaceutical company. Floated in December 1998, the company saw turnover grow from £23 m in 1998 to £101 m in 2001. It is led by its chairman and chief executive, Terry Sadler, owner of some 35 per cent of the shares.

At the end of July 2001 the company announced that it was negotiating the acquisition of a skincare business, which would greatly complement its business strategy. The cost of the acquisition would be £540 m, to be paid in instalments over three years. At the time of the announcement Bioglan shares were trading at over 400 p.

Towards the end of August 2001 there were several further developments. On 23 August it was announced that the company's finance director, who had joined the company only six weeks earlier, was to resign. Bioglan cited 'personality clashes' with Mr Sadler as the reason. The shares fell by over 70 p on this unexpected news. However, more was to come. On 29 August ABN Amro, the company's broker, resigned, and the company's share price fell to just over 200 p.

Press comment suggested that the reason for both of the resignations was a disagreement over the company's proposed strategy for financing the acquisition. Bioglan already had a high ratio of debt to equity (apparently exceeding the already high 61 per cent reported in the January 2001 financial statements). Both the finance director and the broker believed that equity should be used to finance the acquisition, but Mr Sadler was reported to be insisting on debt finance.

As outsiders to the transaction, we can only speculate on the detail behind the press stories. However, this does neatly illustrate our thesis that growth companies should be financed with equity; apparently the outgoing executive and advisor were of this opinion, as, it is reported, were many of the institutional investors. (It is possible that Mr Sadler's 35 per cent holding in the company, which would have been diluted in the event of a large equity issue, was one of his reasons for preferring a debt-funded deal.)

At the time of writing, Goldman Sachs had been appointed to replace ABN Amro, and they were considering the possibility of issuing a convertible bond to finance the deal. Convertibles, a hybrid of debt and equity, are discussed in Chapter 9: they may provide a suitable bridge to meet the stakeholders' differing needs.

It is interesting to note that had Bioglan announced an equity-financed acquisition in July, it would have been able to raise the new capital at round about the then share price of 400 p. The clash over financial strategy means that any future equity issue (or convertibles issue) will be based on the current price, which is of course much lower. A confused financial strategy has had a direct impact on shareholder value.

Sources: Financial Times (various dates); Hydra financial database; Bioglan Pharma financial statements to 31 January 2001.

PART 2

Financial Strategy and the Corporate Lifecycle

4

Start up businesses and venture capital

SUMMARY OF OVERALL MODEL AS APPLIED TO START UP BUSINESSES

The start up stage of the business life cycle clearly represents the highest level of business risk. There are compounding risks associated with whether the new product will work effectively; if it works, whether the product will be accepted by its prospective customers; if it is accepted, whether the market will grow to a sufficient size given the development and launch costs involved; and, even if all this succeeds, whether the company will gain an adequate market share to justify its involvement in the industry.

This high level of business risk means that the associated financial risk should be kept as low as possible during this period. Thus equity funding is most appropriate, but even this equity investment may not be attractive to all potential investors. The high overall risk of the company will attract only those investors who are prepared to undertake such a high risk and they will, consequently, expect a correspondingly high return. This high return will come in the form of capital gains to the investors because the negative cash flow of the business makes it impractical to pay dividends during this start up stage. These issues are illustrated in Working insight 4.1.

WORKING
4.1
INSIGHT

Financial strategy parameters

Start-up businesses

Business risk	Very high
Financial risk	Very low
Source of funding	Venture capital
Dividend policy	Nil payout ratio
Future growth prospects	Very high
Price/earnings multiple	Very high
Current profitability, i.e. eps	Nominal or negative
Share price	Rapidly growing but highly volatile

This dominance of capital gains creates a key concern on the part of the venture capital investors in such high risk businesses. How do they realize the capital gain which is created if the company is successful? They do not wish to be locked in until the business becomes cash positive and can start to pay dividends. Hence buyers need to be found for this equity at its increased value, once the company has proved that the product works and that its market potential makes the investment financially attractive.

It is in the interest of all parties that this exit should take place because venture capitalists normally expect very high rates of return on their investment portfolio. As the total risk of the company reduces over its transition from launch to growth, the returns on new capital will inevitably decline. Accordingly the original venture capitalists may not be interested in several further funding rounds, for which they would have to pay higher and higher prices. Ideally, they want to exit at this point, to realize their gains and to reinvest the proceeds in further high risk investments. This initial funding can be replaced by equity investors who require a lower rate of return, even though they are still primarily interested in investing for capital growth.

Potentially the most attractive exit route for venture capitalists is the subsequent public flotation of the company on a stock exchange. However, it is important that entrepreneurs and venture capitalists understand each others' needs at the start of the investment process: the nightmare for a venture capitalist is to have funds tied up in a successful company for which the owner/directors have no desire to create an exit: until that exit is achieved, the return is not made.[1]

In many cases, a start up business will either be very successful or will fail completely; there may be no middle ground. Thus the venture capitalist's outcome is either very good or very bad. Venture capitalists can diversify their investment

---

1. One way in which the venture capital investors may choose to ensure such an exit is to write a clause into the shareholders' agreement which states that if the company has not floated or been sold or engineered another form of exit within say five years, the venture capitalists are entitled to an increasing percentage of profits each year as a special dividend. This focuses the management's attention on the need to achieve an exit, and at least gives the venture capitalist a running yield while they await exit.

risk by investing in a portfolio of start up businesses, rather than in one company only. This also implies that the very high returns apparently demanded by venture capitalists are really 'promised returns' which are reduced by the probability of zero returns to a still high, but more realistic level of expected return.

INTRODUCTION

It can be strongly argued that it is vitally important for any economy (whether mature or rapidly growing overall) to have a good supply of start up businesses and industries. These are needed to replace the employment prospects and wealth creation power of the current mature and declining industries. A major problem for those economies which industrialized first is how to replace many of these now dying industries, on which the past growth of the economy was based. There have been various attempts by governments to acknowledge this importance and accordingly to encourage investment in new areas by giving tax incentives. Unfortunately, as with most such tax-based economic strategies, the results have seldom been successful in terms of achieving the desired aims.

There is, however, no doubt of the strategic importance of this start up category of business and this is true whether it is a stand-alone company or is created as a division of a larger business. The key issues regarding the appropriate financial strategy are the same; thus in this chapter the stand-alone company will be discussed initially but the impact of the new business being part of a group will also be considered.

VERY HIGH LEVEL OF BUSINESS RISK

The first stage of many start up businesses requires investment in research and development in order to try to identify new product concepts which may be worthy of closer investigation. This is the pre-launch stage of the business, and funding at this stage is often referred to as *seed capital*. Similarly, the product concept might already be in existence, but this first stage will require expenditure on market research to determine whether there is truly a valuable business opportunity.

If the product opportunity still appears financially attractive after these investments have been made, there is normally considerable additional expenditure required for operating facilities (such as production plant for a manufactured good), support facilities, and initial sales and marketing activities before the product can actually be launched. For most products, these early stages of launch and sales development are also periods of net cash outflow. The inflows from sales revenues are not only small but delayed, while the cash outflows still include high levels of one-off launch-associated costs as well as the normal ongoing operating expenses.

Capital invested at this stage, slightly less of a gamble than seed capital but still enormously risky, is known as *start up capital*. Some venture capital companies (and some of their individual counterparts, known as *business angels*) have a preference for investing only at the seed stage, others only invest in start ups. (Still others, who may call themselves venture capitalists, only invest in large, safe deals such as management buyouts or development capital for established companies. These investors provide private equity, but the term 'venture capital' should really be restricted to use in high risk situations. The mechanics of buyout deals, which use very high levels of debt in a relatively low business risk environment, are discussed in Chapter 14.)

Seed and start up funds are invested in the hope of the successful development of the product and the resulting high ultimate net cash inflows when the sales volumes finally mature. Clearly there are very significant business risks associated with this start up strategy. Each subsequent stage is dependent on the successful completion of the earlier stages; hence a decision tree type of financial analysis can be used.

Initially the project is subject to the successful identification of a marketing opportunity in an area where the business believes it either has or can develop a sustainable competitive advantage. This marketing opportunity frequently requires the business to solve some technical problems before it can be exploited. The launch of the product therefore depends on a successful outcome of the research and development activity as well, but even then the existence of the market demand has to be confirmed. In other words the product may work as expected but the expected customers may not materialize to buy it. The size of the ultimate market is also vitally important because the total investment will be financially justified on the cash inflows from these predicted sales. Further it is quite possible that the product and market achieve all that was predicted and more, and yet the company itself is still unsuccessful. This depends upon the level of market share which not only is achieved during the launch phase but also is developed and retained through the growth and maturity stages of the life cycle.

CORRESPONDINGLY HIGH LEVEL OF RETURN?

The compounding sequential risks lead to the conclusion that the start up phase is a very high risk stage of the life cycle; therefore logically a correspondingly high return should be required. This is intuitively self-evident. However, it is not at first sight in accordance with financial theory.

If the rationale of the capital asset pricing model is applied, the increase in return should only be related to the level of market (or systematic) risk incurred by the company; i.e. the degree to which the company's total return is affected by changes in the return of the market. The specific sales opportunity and, particularly, the required solution of a technical problem may be almost completely unrelated to any changes in the overall market, so that their appropriate beta factor would be zero. Only once the company has become established might the ultimate level of sales and the subsequent cash inflows be much more affected by changes in the market as a whole, so that the beta of these later cash flows would be higher. Under the CAPM, the beta drives the required premium return over the risk-free rate, so a CAPM analysis would seem to indicate that the required rate of return could start relatively low but would need to increase over the life of the product; yet this seems counter-intuitive to the trend of business risk.

The argument of the pure theorist is that the undoubtedly very high business risk at the start of the product's life cycle is almost exclusively caused by the unique risk associated with the product. Therefore this can be diversified away by rational investors, who would always incorporate this high risk investment into an efficiently constructed portfolio. This does not mean that the company can only undertake such start up product investments as part of a widely diversified portfolio of products. As has already been discussed, since investors can themselves easily diversify away unique company risk they will not pay extra for companies to do this for them.

The dramatic implication of the CAPM theory is that a start up business does not need to offer significantly enhanced rates of return to investors to compensate for the high business risk because this is mainly unique, diversifiable risk. Yet in practice the returns demanded by investors in new business start ups are significantly higher than for more mature companies; does this represent an inefficiency in the market, a breakdown in the theory, or both?

The answer is no to all the above questions, because the apparently relatively low return expected by these rational diversified investors under the theory would be based on the probability-adjusted expected value of the cash flows of the company.

For a start up business the range of its expected cash flows is going to be very wide, potentially from zero to an extremely high value, due to all of the volatilities discussed earlier. As explained, the high standard deviation (volatility) of these future cash flows can be regarded as being caused primarily by the unique or unsystematic risk of the company, and therefore it does not lead to an increased expected return. The true expected value of the resulting cash flows is going to be depressed however due to the sequential probabilities which need to be applied to each subsequent stage of the project. As illustrated in Working insight 4.2, the investments required in the very early years of the product's development are much more certain than the subsequent cash flows, which depend on the successful conclusion of all the earlier stages; thus the expected values of these later cash flows are significantly affected by the cumulative probability factors which need to be applied.

The application of the (subjective) probability factors results in the less certain cash inflows being reduced in both expected value terms and in present value, not by having an extremely high discount factor applied to them directly, but by being assessed as expected values before being discounted. Clearly the overall effect of the two approaches is similar, because by using probability weighted expected cash flows the unique risk of the investment has already been taken into account so that only the market related risk remains. In Working insight 4.3 net present values are compared if the original cash flow estimates given in Working insight 4.2 are discounted at 35 per cent p.a. (a high risk discount rate) and if the probability adjusted expected cash flows are discounted at 15 per cent (a more normal company cost of capital rate).

From Working insight 4.3 we can see that although the approaches are similar, they give different results. The use of probability-adjusted expected cash flows is greatly to be preferred over the alternative use of a much higher discount rate. It is theoretically more sound, if only for the reason that the discount factor is applied to *all* cash flows, whereas normally it is only the cash

WORKING 4.2

INSIGHT   Use of expected values in start up business cash projections

A new business estimates that the annual expenditures shown below are needed to develop and launch a new product. If successful, the *expected* annual cash inflows are also shown. At the end of each year, the business can review the project and cancel all subsequent expenditures if insufficient progress has been made; therefore probability forecasts of success at each individual stage are also given, together with the appropriate cumulative probabilities.

Years	Forecast annual cash flow (£millions)	Probability of success of previous stage	Cumulative probability factor	Probability-adjusted expected annual cash flow (£millions)
1	(2)	N/A	1	(2)
2	(4)	0.5	0.5	(2)
3	(4)	0.6	0.3	(1.2)
4	(6)	0.8	0.24	(1.44)
5–15	10	0.8	0.192	1.92

Explanation of final column figures:

The expenditure of £4 million in year 2 is dependent on the success of the development activity in year 1. As this success is only a 50 per cent probability, it is not certain that £4 million will be spent in year 2 (while it is certain that £2 million will be spent in year 1); hence the expected value of £2 million (£4 million at a probability of 50 per cent) for year 2. As each successive stage is conditional on the success of *all* the preceding stages, the cumulative probability factor is the product of all these probabilities. Thus there is less than a 20 per cent chance that the £10 million annual cash flow will be received from years 5–15 (note that the expected values of £10 million quoted above are if the project development is successful).

WORKING 4.3

INSIGHT   Comparison of net present value calculations

Year	Probability factor adjusted cash flows			Unadjusted cash flows		
	Expected annual cash flows (£m)	Discount factor @ 15%	Present value	Original annual cash flows (£m)	Discount factor @ 35%	Present value
1	(2)	0.870	(1.74)	(2)	0.741	(1.48)
2	(2)	0.756	(1.51)	(4)	0.549	(2.20)
3	(1.2)	0.658	(0.79)	(4)	0.406	(1.62)
4	(1.44)	0.572	(0.82)	(6)	0.301	(1.81)
5–15	1.92	2.992	5.74	10	0.828	8.28
	Net present value		+0.88	Net present value		+1.17

inflows that are uncertain – costs can often be forecast with reasonable accuracy, but the emergent market is an unknown.

(We should however point out that, as in many similar cases in finance, theoretical soundness tends to lose out to ease and accepted practice. Most companies and investors seem to apply higher discount rates in these situations rather than using probability weighted expected values for the cash flows together with a lower discount rate. Similar examples can be cited of net present value and residual income being conceptually superior to internal rate of return and return on investment respectively, yet in practice the latter methods are more widely used.)

In the example in Working insight 4.3, the 35 per cent rate is arbitrarily applied to all the cash flows including the very early expenditures which are relatively certain (e.g. the £2 million investment in year 1 is guaranteed to be incurred, and the £4 million expenditure in year 2 has a 50 per cent probability). Instead, the use of expected cash flows highlights the rapidly increasing value of the project as a successful outcome becomes progressively more likely.

In Working insight 4.4, the present values under the two methods have been recalculated as if the expenditure in year 1 has now been successfully completed. This now increases significantly the probability of receiving the £10 million cash inflows and therefore the net present value is also increased dramatically, even though the same discount rate of 15 per cent is applied. In order to reflect the higher probability of success under the other method, the risk-related discount rate should be reduced as each stage of the project is completed. Unfortunately in practice it is very difficult to develop meaningful risk measures for such discrete elements within a total business project.

Of course, had the project in Working insight 4.4 shown in year 1 or year 2 that the potential long term outcome was not as good as originally expected, perhaps because the expected market had not materialized or because prices were lower than projected, the project would be terminated. There is no point in continuing with a project that will not increase shareholder value, and managers always have the discretion to change their minds.

(This highlights an interesting aspect of discounted cash flow analysis. The way that we set out forecasts in DCF analysis, and calculate the expected probabilities of success, indicates a static position. It implies that this is what will happen, and ignores the flexibility that a change in circumstances could bring. A relatively new branch of finance, *real options*, considers the value of flexibility and having the option to change plans, or to develop a larger business from an initial pilot study. A full discussion on how real options are used is outside the scope of this book. Interested readers may wish to consult one of the specialist texts in this area.[2])

Returning to our main argument about the required returns on start up investments, this means that in reality venture capital investors should not expect each investment to generate vast returns but each and every investment must promise the potential of very high returns in order to compensate for those that fail completely.

---

2. For example, *Real Options: Managing Strategic Investment in an Uncertain World* by M. Amram and N. Kulatilaka. 1999. Harvard Business School Press.

WORKING
4.4

INSIGHT

Increasing present values as project success becomes more likely

The first investment stage (year one) has now been successfully completed on budget. No other estimates have been changed and the same discount factors have been appropriately applied to the expected remaining future cash flows.

Year	Annual cash flow (£m)	Probability of success of previous stage	Cumulative probability factor	Probability-adjusted expected annual cash flow
1	(4)	N/A	1	(4)
2	(4)	0.6	0.6	(2.4)
3	(6)	0.8	0.48	(2.88)
4–14	10	0.8	0.384	3.84

	Probability factor adjusted cash flows			Unadjusted cash flows		
Year	Expected annual cash flows (£m)	Discount factor @ 15%	Present value	Original annual cash flows (£m)	Discount factor @ 35%	Present value
1	(4)	0.870	(3.48)	(4)	0.741	(2.96)
2	(2.4)	0.756	(1.81)	(4)	0.549	(2.20)
3	(2.88)	0.658	(1.89)	(6)	0.406	(2.44)
4–14	3.84	3.441	13.21	10	1.118	11.18
		Net present value	+6.03		Net present value	+3.58

In order to generate the same net present value as given by the probability-adjusted flows, the discount factor used on the gross expected cash flows would have to be reduced to approximately 30 per cent.

Overall a portfolio of such venture capital investments should produce both an acceptable expected return at the outset and over time. In the example given, the increase in net present value of the successful investment of £2 million in year 1 would balance the cost incurred by another similar scale project which was aborted at the end of year 1 because of lack of success in its development activity.

If a portfolio of similar projects actually achieved the predicted success rates, as it should do if appropriate probability estimates are used, there would be no net increase in the net present value of the portfolio over the life of the projects after writing off the expenditure incurred on all projects, both successful and cancelled, i.e. the portfolio would deliver the original return expected at the outset. However, the net present value of the totally successful projects would increase dramatically as that success became more certain. Unfortunately, in an efficient market it is supposed to be impossible to outperform the market which would clearly be achieved by selecting only that 19.2 per cent of the projects like that in Working insight 4.2 which would actually be successful, rather than investing in a portfolio including more losers than winners.

The conclusions that can be drawn from this analysis are that the very high business risk associated with new start ups is taken into account in the return expected by investors applying the CAPM theory, but not by directly increasing the discount rate to include the unique risk of the company.

On a practical basis, this has very important implications for companies trying to raise start up capital and for venture capital fund managers. The very high rates of return applied by most venture capital fund managers (in the UK a post-tax compound annual rate of return of 40 per cent is quite normal) to evaluate potential start up investments must be applied to the expected cash flows assuming a successful outcome. Much lower beta-driven rates of return must be applied to future cash flows which have been adjusted to reflect the probability weightings of this successful outcome.

It is vitally important that the cash flow projections resulting from the business plans of prospective start ups are compiled in a manner totally consistent with the way in which they will subsequently be valued by the venture capitalist. Unfortunately, it is not uncommon to find entrepreneurs preparing their plans on a very prudent basis and incorporating decision trees and probabilities to produce the adjusted best estimate expected cash flow, and then for this to be discounted by the venture capitalists at their very high, risk inclusive, required rates of return. Not surprisingly the resulting investment valuation does not normally look too appealing to either party.

This argument can be even more important when the start up project is within an existing large group. Most large groups now use increased discount rates to evaluate investment projects which appear to have higher than normal levels of risk. However, this risk assessment normally includes all the aspects of risk associated with the new project, whether these are unique to the project or reflect the systematic risk. More critically, the resulting high, risk inclusive discount rate is often applied to project cash flows which have already been subjected to the application of sequential, cumulative probability factor weightings. Consequently, the major element of the project risk is included in the evaluation twice, and these large groups find it very difficult to approve investments in new products or in any area with higher than normal risk levels.

NEED FOR LOW FINANCIAL RISK

The required inverse correlation of business and financial risk, discussed in Chapter 3, leads to the logical conclusion that start up businesses should be funded by equity, preferably with no debt financing at all. It is important to see if that conclusion is supported by the relevant finance theory. In a perfect market, there is no added value from different capital structures but the effects of taxation and costs of financial distress discussed in Appendix 1 do indicate that capital structure is important to companies.

Merely using these two market imperfections highlights why start up companies cannot gain from the use of debt financing. If having any level of debt in a company increases the risk of default, investors will reduce the value of the investment by at least the expected value of any costs associated with such default or earlier stage of financial distress. Therefore a key factor in assessing the importance of potential financial distress is the relative level of costs which are likely to be incurred in the event of such financial distress. Where the underlying assets of the business are relatively discrete with clearly established, high realizable values the costs of financial distress are likely to be quite low. However, for most start up companies the current investment value is created by the present value of the expected future cash flows which will result from the successful development, launch and growth of the product. Thus the assets underlying the business are intangible, without any easily established discrete realizable values; this means that the costs of financial distress are likely to be very high for a start up business.

The other key component determining the total impact of the risk of default is the likelihood of it occurring. This obviously increases with the relative proportion of debt financing used by the business, but for a start up company the risk can be high if even a small proportion of debt funding is raised. The high risk of complete business failure means that no cash inflows may actually be generated, so that any level of outstanding debt would lead to a state of severe financial distress.

A high probability of occurrence combined with a high cost if it occurs makes the risk premium required for potential financial distress very high; thus making debt financing unattractive from this perspective.

At the other end of the capital structure analysis was the benefit created by the tax shield effect of debt financing. However the start up business may well be making accounting losses or very nominal profits in its early years of operations so that there is no positive impact to be gained from debt financing either.

Quite apart from the issues of risk correlation and financial theory, there is a practical reason why start up businesses should not be financed using debt. Start up companies have a large and growing demand for cashflow. Taking on debt involves making regular cash outgoings to service the interest and repayments; that cash would be better used within the company to drive the growth.

(We should point out that in practice we have known businesses started up on the back of the entrepreneurs' credit cards, due to their inability to convince financiers of the validity of their arguments. Some of these have worked; some have not. Our thesis is that this compounding of risk is not a good idea – not that it never happens.)

NIL DIVIDEND PAYOUT POLICY

This leads to consideration of another aspect of finance theory, regarding the company's dividend policy. In theory, investors should be indifferent as to whether they receive dividends or achieve their return through capital gains; yet the recommended dividend policy for a start up company is to pay no dividends at all.

The cash flow of a newly formed business is normally highly negative and new funds are needed for the investment opportunities available to the company. If debt financing is inappropriate this funding has to be by equity, which means that if investors require a dividend they would have to invest more money into the business to pay for this dividend. In a perfect capital market this would be perfectly acceptable and, indeed, many finance textbooks go to great lengths to demonstrate how it doesn't make any difference to the investors. This is, of course, fairly obvious if there are no taxes and no transaction costs. Unfortunately, in the real world both exist and the transaction costs associated with raising new equity funding are considerable for high risk start up businesses. Not only are the costs high but they are relatively fixed, which means that to raise small amounts of equity is exorbitantly expensive. These costs cover the legal and professional fees charged, where the work involved does not vary in accordance with the amount of money being raised. Hence it is not logical to pay dividends and replace the funding by raising new equity investments.

Further constraints include the tax and legal positions on dividends. Dividends are not a tax deductible expense for the company but are taxable on the investor, so there is a tax penalty involved. Also the company may not legally be able to pay dividends as it must have distributable reserves (principally undistributed post-tax profits) out of which to declare dividends. Many loss-making new businesses will have no such accumulated profits and so cannot legally declare dividends.

VENTURE CAPITAL INVESTORS

The ideal equity investors for start up companies must appreciate the risks involved, including the potential for a total loss of their investment, and must want to receive their financial return in the form of capital gains. These venture capitalists are normally professional investors (including investment managers controlling venture capital funds) who attempt to compensate for the high risks associated with any specific investment by developing a portfolio comprising similarly high risk individual investments. Thus the complete failure of some investments in the portfolio is offset by the outstanding success of other investments made. Indeed, although many such venture capital investors specialize in particular industry sectors, such as information technology or bio-technology, they still hold a portfolio of investments in this sector.

Using the logic developed earlier in this chapter, such a focused portfolio would clearly deserve the beta for the particular industry sector. This should enable a risk-adjusted discount factor to be developed, incorporating the appropriate level of market-related risk premium, but the unique project risks must still be included by the use of probability-weighted expected cash flows. The argument used by many such focused, yet portfolio-diversified venture capital fund managers is that they are confident that the particular industry (say bio-technology) will generate some major new companies in the future, but they are less confident of their ability to pick out these specific companies at this very early stage. Hence by investing in a broad range of the high potential growth companies in this industry, it is hoped that the venture capital fund participates in the success of the few; even at the expense of making many more unsuccessful investments.

Further, contrary to common perceptions, venture capitalists generally act in a risk-averse manner, inasmuch as they manage their risks by limiting their investment portfolios to sectors they understand. Thus certain venture capital firms will only invest in certain sectors – or will not invest in certain sectors. Their industry specialism gives them a greater knowledge of the issues, thus reducing their investment risk. Others will limit their investment portfolio to a particular geographical area, or to a particular size of investment, with which they have experience. Venture capital is about making investments with the potential to generate high returns; it is not about taking unnecessary risks.

There is also an issue that, even for the successful investments, there may be a long time gap between the development of the new technology and the cash-positive maturity stage of the resulting products. This factor proved particularly interesting during the 'dot.com' boom of the late 1990s, during which many 'incubator' firms were formed to invest in and nurture very early stage invest-ment opportunities. These incubators mostly had a fundamental flaw in their own financial strategies: the funds outflow to the investee company occurred immediately; if exits were not possible through the anticipated early flotation the incubator still had to find cashflow to support its own level of expenses. Many of the incubators, including some high profile ones, followed their investee companies into liquidation.

Most venture capitalists have a relatively short investment time horizon (normally three to five years). This is logical as they wish to focus on investing during the high risk start up period of a business; if it succeeds, they want to realize their resulting capital gain and reinvest this in more new start up invest-ments. Therefore, being locked into any particular company, no matter how successful it is, is not an attractive proposition for the investor. It should not be regarded as attractive by the company either, unless the venture capitalist is prepared to accept a reducing level of return as the associated risk is reduced. This is not usually the case, so that it is mutually beneficial to find new equity investors who are willing to buy out the venture capitalists well before the company has become cash positive and dividend paying. This refinancing issue is discussed as part of the transition from start up to growth stage in Chapter 5.

BUSINESS ANGELS

As mentioned earlier, individuals who invest in venture capital opportunities are known as business angels. Often these individuals have made money in their own enterprises and are seeking the excitement and the financial reward of investing in another's business.

Business angel investment is often more informal than that from specialist venture capital companies: the documentation is much simpler, and the deal can be done more quickly due to the individuals being satisfied with doing less due diligence. Angels' decision criteria for investment include having a favourable impression of the management team, a familiarity with the sector, projected financial rewards, and a synergy with their own skills.

Companies which have used angel investment report both good and bad experi-ences with it. On the positive side, angels will often rush in where venture cap-italists fear to tread, and will provide finance for investment opportunities that have been unable to attract it otherwise. They will invest much lower amounts than traditional venture capitalists (which they can afford to do as their fixed costs per deal are much less than those of the venture capital companies). Also, they may be a lot more flexible in their approach, prepared to invest for the longer term, and are able to provide management skills which the entrepreneur may lack. However, the negatives of angel investment include the fact that they rarely have 'deep pockets' and so cannot invest in second and third round financing. Also, individuals who have made money in their own companies may have a 'Midas complex', believing that their judgement is infallible, or may be seeking to 'buy a job' by using a redundancy package to buy into another company.

CORPORATE VENTURING

An alternative to traditional venture capital, or even to angel capital, is to accept funding from a large corporate that is undertaking corporate venturing. Many businesses, such as Cisco and Reuters, have large corporate venturing arms, the aim of which is twofold. Firstly, these companies invest in promising new ventures in order to exploit their ideas, to obtain the benefit of their new technologies and gain an edge on the market (interestingly, the CIA in America apparently also does this, for the same reasons). Secondly, corporate venturing can prove profitable for these companies, in the same way that it provides a good return for professional venture capitalists.

Accepting investment from a corporate venturer can provide useful financial support, and give access to a wide range of useful business contacts. If the venturer has a portfolio of investments, there might also be synergies between the different businesses. If it is in a related industry, there can be a lot of spin-off benefits. And, as with high profile venture capital investors, having a significant investor can add to a company's profile in the business and investment communities.

However, there are three main issues to consider before accepting funding from a corporate venturer.

1. Does each party understand the other's motivation? In particular, it is important to understand whether the venturer is expecting to buy out the investee business once it has developed its products and grown. (In this vein, it is also vital to understand the shareholder agreement with the venturer – often these contain 'first refusal' clauses that can prevent the investee company selling out to another party should the opportunity arise.)
2. Is a reciprocal arrangement planned whereby the venturer will provide business advice and contacts (similar in some ways to an incubator)? If so, does the venturer have a good track record in this area? Often the planned advice and contacts fail to materialize, at least to the extent promised at the start of the deal.
3. How important is the investee business to the venturer? Many companies moved into corporate venturing at the heart of the dot.com boom, only to retreat again once the bubble burst, leaving their investee companies without recourse to the anticipated further funds.

YOUR START UP BUSINESS

Many years of experience in advising entrepreneurs and start up businesses have left us with a desire to pass on some pointers to prospective entrepreneurs.

1. Are you suited to entrepreneurship? Often, middle managers from large companies take a redundancy package and decide to invest it in running their own business. The skills required for this are completely different to those needed in a large company: why are you doing this and do you have what it takes?

2. Minimize the level of fixed costs. As we have mentioned several times, the level of income for a start up is an unknown factor – the expenses are bound to happen. Defer all expenses that you can, and minimize the risk of the business by making as many of those costs as possible into variable rather than fixed costs; this may at times lead to a higher overall price being paid for some services, but it is essential to reduce cash outflows until the pattern of inflows is established.

3. Prepare a detailed cash flow forecast. Integrate this with a forecast profit and loss account and balance sheet, to ensure that it makes sense. (If you do not have the ability to prepare the forecast yourself, use the services of a professional advisor, but make sure that the underlying assumptions are yours, not theirs.)

4.1   WEBVAN – A RISKY START UP

CASE STUDY

Webvan, the online grocery business, was launched in California in 1999, backed by venture capital funds. The company's vision was to revolutionize the grocery business; it intended to take a significant proportion of the US groceries market by offering customers home delivery within an agreed time slot, at prices at or slightly below the price they would pay were they to visit their local supermarkets. As with many internet-based businesses at the time, a key element of the strategy was to obtain first-mover advantage; capturing the potential market before competitors could encroach on it.

Webvan's business plan depended on the use of technology. It used its first $120 million tranche of venture capital to build a state-of-the-art warehouse, and then almost immediately announced plans to roll out the concept across 26 sites around the US. Sophisticated purpose-built software systems were developed, to manage the expected volume of orders and to run the highly automated warehouses. Deliveries were made using fleets of customized vans. To match this investment in the operating side of the business, offices were fitted out to the highest specifications, to attract the top quality people that the company needed.

The huge fixed cost base that the company installed was never matched by the revenues generated. Customers did not take to the Webvan concept. In two years the company burned its way through some $1.2 billion, before filing for Chapter 11 in July 2001.

Webvan incurred unnecessary business risks by investing heavily in infrastructure before its business concept was proven. Contrast this with the online grocery strategy adopted by Tesco, the UK retailer.

Tesco.com was formed to capitalize on the company's strong brand, and to produce another way of servicing customers. The company did not invest in purpose-built warehouses: it used inventory from the shelves of its existing stores, picked from the aisles by its employees. Shopping would be delivered from the stores within a local area, or customers could opt to collect their pre-packed shopping from the store.

The Tesco.com strategy proved successful and the company is now rolling it out throughout the UK, and has commenced operations in a joint venture in the US. By minimizing the fixed costs of the start up, Tesco reduced its business risk until the concept was proven.

5

Growth companies: marketing focused

OVERVIEW

| SUMMARY OF APPROPRIATE SECTION
| OF OVERALL MODEL

Once the new product has been successfully launched into its marketplace, the sales volumes should start to grow rapidly. Not only does this represent a reduction in the overall business risk associated with the product, but it also indicates the need for a modification in the strategic thrust of the company. The key emphasis of the competitive strategy should now be placed on marketing activities in order to ensure both that the total growth of product sales are satisfactory and that the company increases its market share of this expanding sales volume.

These critical issues show that the business risk, although reduced from the start-up stage, is still high during the period of rapid sales growth. Thus the appropriate source of funding must be designed to keep the financial risk profile low, which indicates continued use of equity funding. However, an important aspect of managing the transition from start-up to growth is that the initial venture capitalist investors will be keen to realize their capital gains in order to enable them to reinvest in other new start-up businesses.

Financial strategy parameters

Growth business

Business risk	High
Financial risk	Low
Source of funding	Growth equity investors
Dividend policy	Nominal payout ratio
Future growth prospects	High
Price/earnings multiple	High
Current profitability i.e. eps	Low
Share price	Growing but volatile

This means that new equity investors need to be identified to replace the original venture capital and to provide for any continued funding needs during this period of high growth. The most attractive source of such funding is often from a public flotation of the company.

The higher sales volumes which should now be achieved at quite reasonable profit margins will generate much stronger cash flows than during the start-up stage. However, the company should be investing heavily in both overall market development and market share development activities, as well as requiring investments to keep pace with the increasing levels of operational activity. Consequently, the cash generated by the business is required for reinvestment in the business with the result that the dividend payout ratio will remain very low. This should not be a problem for the new equity investors in the company because they will have been attracted primarily by the prospects of high future growth.

These growth prospects would have been reflected in a high price/earnings multiple applied to the low existing earnings per share of the company when calculating the current share price. As the dividend yield is very small, the bulk of the investors' expected return has to be generated as capital gains, by increases in the share price. This means that the company has to produce substantial growth in earnings per share during this stage of development; this should be achieved by winning a dominant market share in the rapidly growing market. These issues are illustrated in Working insight 5.1.

It is important to realize that it is during these first two stages of the product life cycle that the company has its main opportunities to develop the sustainable competitive advantage which it will utilize during the later, cash positive, maturity stage.

CONTINUING HIGH BUSINESS RISK

This need to develop the sustainable competitive advantage is a good indicator of the level of business risk which is carried over from the start-up stage into this growth phase of the life cycle. For most companies, the major entry barriers to the industry are constructed during the rapid growth period so as to prevent competitors following the company's competitive initiatives once the product's potential has been identified. These barriers can take many forms, such as the development of strong branding (which differentiates the product in the minds of customers), and the early achievement of significant economies of scale or learning curve cost reductions (which establishes a potentially sustainable position as the low cost producer in the industry).

There are obviously significant risks associated with the implementation of each of these competitive strategies and they all require considerable up-front investment by the company, which is financially justified on the expectation of the future long-term growth in the sales of the product. Thus for these companies the level of business risk remains high because these risks must be considered alongside the risks that the anticipated growth in demand will not fully materialize. However, some companies can enter this stage in a more confident position, as their competitive advantage has already been well established during the start-up phase.

A classic example would be in the pharmaceutical industry where a completely new drug would normally have been patented as early as possible. If the subsequent development process, including the essential clinical trials, and the actual product launch are successful, the patent guarantees its owner a finite period of sustainable competitive advantage during which the returns are predominantly governed by the total growth of demand for the product. The substantial contribution of a single product, Zantac, to the Glaxo pharmaceutical group's tremendous financial success during the 1980s and early 1990s clearly highlights this point. The converse to this is, of course, that the development costs of such a new product are immense and the associated risks of failure very high; it simply means that the major risk-taking period is earlier in the life cycle for some industries than others.

Another reason for the business risk of the growth phase to be considered as still being high is that the transition from start-up to growth requires a number of changes to be implemented by the company. Change always implies risk as, if the change is not managed properly, it can lead to a downturn in the future performance of the business. Where the required changes are significant and wide-reaching, the level of increased risk that results is also greater. An obvious area of change is in the strategic thrust of the company. During their start-up periods, most businesses would have concentrated on research and development, either in order to exploit an identified market opportunity or in the hopes of creating one through a technological breakthrough. Even in its latter stages where the product was being prepared for launch, the main emphasis would have been on problem-solving as quickly as possible. Delays in getting the product into the marketplace can prove extremely expensive if, as a consequence, a competitor is able to establish its product first, or if the window of opportunity has simply been closed during the period of delay.

Once the product has been successfully launched, the company should concentrate its efforts on building both the total market and its share of this expanding market. This requires a marketing focus on the part of senior managers rather than the R & D or technology focus which may have been more appropriate during its earlier years. A fundamental change in management focus is not easy to achieve (without changing the managers) and so the scale of the required change is important in terms of the risk associated with this transition. If the company's original product development strategy was very market orientated, the change may not be that great. However, for many very high technology businesses the requirement to focus on the needs of customers rather than solving stimulating intellectual problems has proved very difficult to manage.

As mentioned in the previous chapter, there also needs to be a fundamental change in the investor profile during the transition from start-up to rapid growth style of company. The venture capitalist is the ideal shareholder for the newly formed very high risk company, but, for the reasons already discussed, it is not appropriate for the company to retain this investor base throughout its movement through the growth stage. However, the continuing high business risk associated with most rapidly growing companies means that low risk financing is still appropriate. This requires finding new equity investors who are prepared not only to buy out the original venture capital shareholders but also to provide any funding needed during this period of rapid growth.

These new investors are taking on a lower risk investment than did the venture capitalists, because the product is normally now proven and at least some customers will have accepted the specific product offering of the company. Also the company is now much more substantive than the business plan and product concept which it may have comprised when initial financing was being raised. Hence it is possible to look to raise this new equity funding from a broader potential base of investors, possibly including the 'general public'.

In most countries there are much tighter rules applying to the control of companies which wish to raise funds from the general public; even though, unfortunately, several recent abuses of financial management in major public companies have highlighted that these controls do not always work. The objective of the increased controls is to try to safeguard the less-sophisticated investor and to maintain the confidence of investors in general in the way financial markets are administered. Clearly, if the confidence of investors were undermined they would either cease to invest altogether or would demand significantly increased returns to compensate for their higher risk perceptions. The implications for companies needing to raise equity funding would be very severe in either case. An immediate practical implication of these tighter controls, designed to maintain a high level of investor confidence, is to increase the costs to the companies concerned. These higher costs relate to registration fees (including the costs of being listed on a stock exchange and of having share price information included in major newspapers and other information services): legal and professional costs of raising funding and of maintaining a stock exchange listing; shareholder communication costs (to both existing and prospective shareholders and to all shareholders whether large or small); and the costs of compliance with the rules of the various bodies of which the company becomes a member.

Many of these costs can be minimized if this second phase of equity funding is raised by private placement (without inviting the public to invest in the company) and if the company does not seek a stock exchange listing for its shares. Many private equity institutions have portfolios including pre-IPO companies, which have raised private funding as a second stage of their development prior to flotation. However, these new investors must be prepared, with part of their funds at least, to buy out existing venture capital shareholders: this portion of their investment does not go to the company itself, but into the hands of existing shareholders. The remainder of the investment goes into the company and is used to finance the rapid growth of the business. Thus the major financial return to these new investors will take the form of capital gains on their shares, as in the case of the venture capitalists. Unless these investors are going to stay in the company until it eventually does become mature, cash positive and dividend paying, they too will require other new investors to buy their shares in due course. This is a key problem caused by continuing to use private (i.e. non-public) sources of equity finance; it provides initial funding to the company but it does not create an easy exit route for these investors who wish to sell some shares and realize part of their capital gain.

The best way of achieving this exit is for the company to be quoted on a stock exchange so that prices for its shares are known. Equally importantly, financial traders (market makers) stand ready to buy and sell the shares at all times, thus providing a ready exit route for current shareholders. Flotations are discussed in more detail in Chapter 11. Much of the remainder of this chapter considers financial strategy issues from the perspective of companies already listed on a public stock exchange.

CALCULATING THE COST OF EQUITY

Prospective investors in a newly floated company will compare the return on this company as a potential investment against all their similar existing available opportunities. This means that they will need to assess their required return from the new company and, according to finance theory, this is dictated by the beta factor of the company. The problem is that to calculate the beta, the volatility of the company's return relative to the total market should be measured. It is very difficult to do this for unquoted shares because comparable changes in share price are not readily available. This makes an assessment of the market sensitivity particularly fraught for unquoted high growth companies, where capital growth is a major component of the investors' return. One way round the problem is to try to identify similar companies which are publicly quoted and to use some sort of suitably adjusted average of their beta factors.

However, several problems remain even if such a compromise proves possible. Investors want compensation for the increased risk associated with the future volatility of returns from any company relative to the total market. Measuring actual volatilities, whether specific to the company or proxies using similar companies, gives historic information on betas, which is particularly problematical if the company is changing very rapidly and will continue to do so in the future. This is clearly likely to be the case with many high growth companies, with the result that any such historically based estimate of beta must be treated with extreme caution.

There are statistical techniques which assist in this assessment of risk. Any calculation of the beta from actual data is subject to an estimating range, which can itself be calculated. If it is assumed that the actual measurements are normally distributed about the mean (i.e. the individual measurements are randomly distributed rather than being skewed by some estimating bias or flaw in the method of calculation), it is possible to be 95 per cent confident that the true beta lies within 1.96 standard deviations (in either direction) of the estimated value. (There are also statistical tests to indicate whether the measurements taken generate a statistically valid result and are normally distributed.) This gives a range for the expected value of the beta for any particular company which appears to be helpful, particularly since sophisticated beta calculations are available for the major shares in many stock markets from, for example, interested stockbrokers, investment banks and some business schools. Unfortunately, the standard deviations for most high growth companies are very large, due to the commonly violent swings in returns experienced during the periods used in the calculations. This high level of movement in return should not come as a surprise due to the high level of business risk during this period.

This high level of total business risk now includes an increasing component of market or systematic risk, because most high growth businesses are more affected by changes in external environmental factors than many more mature, well-established companies. Obviously there is still a substantial element of unique risk associated with high growth businesses, relating to the development of the particular product and the marketing success of the company in building its share of the market. This unique risk can be taken into account by using cumulative probability factors to adjust the expected values of the future returns, as explained in Chapter 4, but the higher market-related risk may lead to an increase in the discount rate applied to these adjusted expected cash flows.

WORKING 5.2

INSIGHT   **Estimating costs of capital for high growth companies**

Risk-free debt has an expected return of 3 per cent. The stock market premium is estimated to be 8 per cent and the calculated beta factor for a particular high growth company is 1.5. The standard error for this company is calculated to be 0.25.
  Using the CAPM on the base data gives

$$K_e = R_f + \beta(R_m - R_f)$$
$$= 3\% + 1.5 \times 8\%$$
$$= 15\%$$

However, the standard error means that the 95 per cent confidence limit for the beta factor is given by

$$\text{95 per cent confidence range} = \text{estimated value} + 1.96 \text{ standard errors (say two)}$$
$$= 1.5 \pm 0.5$$
$$= 1 \text{ to } 2$$

Therefore the cost of capital for this company is between

$$K_e = 3\% + 1 \times 8\% = 11\%$$

and

$$K_e = 3\% + 2 \times 8\% = 19\%$$

However, if the estimated beta for a particular high growth company, calculated as indicated above, is 1.5 but the standard deviation is 0.25, the confidence range for the beta factor is between one and two. As illustrated in Working insight 5.2 this can give an estimated cost of capital between 11 per cent and 19 per cent for the company, which is too broad a range to be of much use in assessing the attractiveness of the investment. Many investors appear to rank companies on their expected returns calculated using the arithmetic mean of the factor computations, but with such high ranges this is a somewhat dangerous practice.

REINVESTMENT PROJECTS

Growth companies tend to be developed with full retention of their post-tax profits (i.e. a nil dividend payout ratio on their ordinary shares) and tend to continue to reinvest a high proportion to finance their high growth objectives. Such growth can come from taking on projects with a very similar risk profile to the existing business, or taking on projects with a different risk profile.

If growth is through new projects with a similar risk profile to the existing business, the return on reinvestment must be at least equal to the investors' demanded return on equity if shareholder wealth is to be enhanced not destroyed.

However, many businesses expand in different directions, such that it is not true that all their projects face the same level of risks. A fundamental reinvestment question is therefore whether all reinvestment projects should be expected to make a return greater than the company's cost of capital. It should be immediately clear that this would be illogical; if a project has a lower risk than the average risk of the company, it should be expected to make a lower return. As long as the expected return from the project is greater than its risk-adjusted cost of capital, the project is financially acceptable. If all projects are required to earn more than the company's average cost of capital, the business runs the risk of rejecting many financially attractive, low risk projects while accepting some unattractive higher risk projects. This is clearly illustrated in Figure 5.1.

Unfortunately, this concept is not applied by many leading companies. In many cases the company's cost of capital (which should be related to its overall risk level) is taken as a minimum required rate of return for reinvestment projects, with extra return requirements being added for above average risk projects. This leads to the position shown in Figure 5.2, where low risk investment opportunities are rejected because their return is below the company's cost of capital.

In some leading companies, the use of an average cost of capital as a hurdle is a deliberate strategy rather than being based on ignorance or misunderstanding of the financial theory. One financially very astute chairman of a very large UK-based group justified this strategy because 'our investors would not understand why we should reinvest their money at lower rates of return than they demanded'. In other words this chairman did not believe that the risk profile of the group would be adjusted to reflect its new overall weighting, including the lower risk/lower return projects. (This might indeed be true but, as will be illustrated in examples later in the book, senior managers may well understand the financial theory but often they don't believe it applies to their particular company.)

Figure 5.1

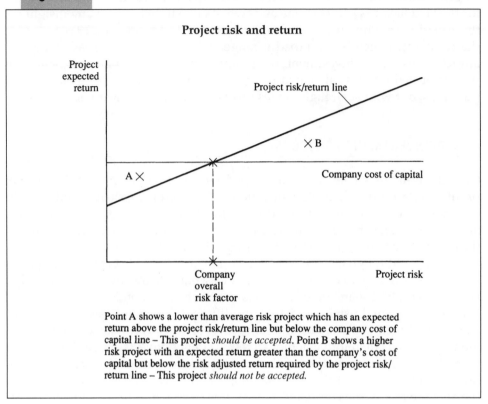

Project risk and return

Point A shows a lower than average risk project which has an expected return above the project risk/return line but below the company cost of capital line – This project *should be accepted*. Point B shows a higher risk project with an expected return greater than the company's cost of capital but below the risk adjusted return required by the project risk/return line – This project *should not be accepted*.

Figure 5.2

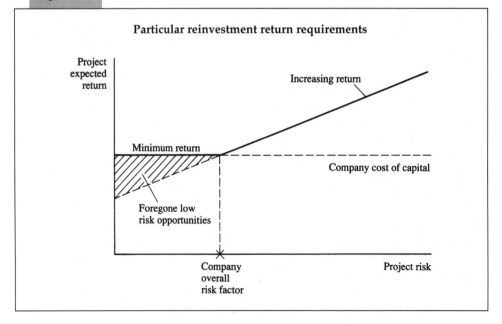

Particular reinvestment return requirements

Unfortunately this group also tried to reflect all of the project associated risk through the discount rate, rather than using probability weighting factors to take account of the unique risk of each project. This latter method leaves only the market-related risk to be reflected in the discount factor applied to these adjusted cash flows. This part of the project risk can be much more logically compared to the company's overall cost of capital, which will be linked to the company's beta. The problem that this causes is that the project beta has to be estimated, which raises all the issues already discussed in respect of the company itself. However there is no way of avoiding assessing the risks associated with an investment project and this method at least forces the company to focus separately on the unique risks of the project (which can be managed or diversified) and the impact of the project on the systematic risk of the company.

For most high growth companies, the dominant source of funding will be equity, as has been discussed. Therefore the company's cost of capital is the cost of equity. However when this reinvestment analysis is applied to more mature businesses, the impact of capital structure also needs to be taken into account. In general the company's weighted average cost of capital is normally used but this is not appropriate if the funding for a particular project should differ from the average of the group, or where this project leads to a change in the group funding strategy. Thus, if a mature group with a relatively high debt:equity ratio is considering a reinvestment project in a new high growth or even start-up area of activity, the project should be regarded as being funded appropriately to its risk profile, i.e. with equity funding rather than using a high proportion of debt.

5.1 | **MARCONI PLC**

CASE STUDY

The GEC group was a UK-based defence and electronics company, which produced strong operating performance from a series of growing and mature businesses. The operating results meant that the business was strongly cash positive. Indeed, during the 1980s and early 1990s GEC was criticized by the markets for the excessive cash holdings the company maintained; well in excess of £2 billion. This cash mountain was not required to fund the company's growth, and the City's view was that it should be returned to shareholders.

In 1996 the management of the company changed, as did its strategy. Over the next few years a number of the company's businesses were sold, including its defence interests. Acquisitions were made to reposition the company in the fast-growing telecoms sector, and GEC was re-named 'Marconi' in 1999 to reflect this.

The serial acquisitions were paid for out of the company's cash pile, and in addition debt was taken on to meet their financing needs. By 2001 the company had net debt of about £3 billion.

Although initially investors approved the change in strategy from a cash-rich low risk defence company to a highly geared telecoms business, changes in market conditions in the telecoms sector led to the collapse of the company's markets, its share price and its credit rating. At the time of writing, Marconi's financial position is still uncertain.

With hindsight, it is apparent that whilst it was wrong for the mature defence businesses to be financed using equity (as will be discussed in Chapter 6), it was also wrong for the high growth telecoms business – with its considerable business risk – to be funded mainly with debt. The Marconi story appears to be a case of total mismatch of business and financial strategies. However, whereas GEC's over-reliance on equity 'merely' irritated its shareholders, Marconi's over-gearing destroyed the value of their investment.

RIGHTS ISSUES – CONCEPTS AND PRACTICE

So far, there has been an implicit assumption that these high growth companies can finance their growth by their Initial Public Offering proceeds, followed by a high retention ratio of existing profit levels. However, even a nil dividend payout policy may not always provide adequate funding to meet the desired growth rates of the business.

Consequently, there may be requirements for additional fund raising exercises from time to time. These should again be in the form of equity because of the continuing high level of business risk. This new equity injection can be raised by an existing publicly quoted company through a direct offer to outside investors of new shares in the company to be issued at the current market price (known not surprisingly as a Secondary Public Offering). An SPO should be made at the full current market price, as otherwise the existing shareholders are giving away a subsidy to these new investors. Once issued, the new shares are indistinguishable from the already issued existing shares and the new total value of the company is simply divided by the new total number of shares in order to arrive at a new price per share; any differential in issue price would therefore represent a wealth transfer from one shareholder to another.

It is not very practical to attempt to issue these new shares at a premium to the existing share price, because a rational new investor would prefer to buy existing shares directly in the market rather than more expensive new ones from the company. Equally it is normally difficult to make a substantial new issue of shares at the prevailing market price; if lots of potential investors wanted shares at this price, there should be substantial buying pressure in the market but, by definition, at the current market price supply and demand are balanced. A significant and sudden increase in the supply of any commodity normally leads to a decline in its price, even if only temporarily.

Thus it is often necessary to consider making the new issue at a discount to the current market price, but to do so would be to rob existing shareholders. This can be avoided if the existing shareholders are given rights to buy these discounted shares in proportion to their existing shareholdings; hence the name 'rights issue'. These issues are normally described by reference to how many new shares can be bought for a number of existing shares owned; e.g. a one for five rights issue means that for every five shares owned the shareholder gets the right (i.e. opportunity) to buy one of the new shares being offered. The company cannot force its existing shareholders to buy any more shares in the company; hence it is granting them an option to buy these new shares. As the new shares are being issued at a lower price than the current market price of the existing shares, this option should have a value and can be sold if the current shareholder does not want to take it up.

These points can be most clearly illustrated by a numerical example and one is given in Working insight 5.3. The rights issue is proposed at a small discount of 10 per cent to the current share price (45 p compared to 50 p), which is quite normal for this type of growth company. It is important to understand what should, in theory, happen and what, in practice, normally does happen as a result of these types of rights issues.

WORKING
5.3

INSIGHT

What price for rights

Satellite Television Audiovisual Recordings plc (STAR) wishes to increase its equity base to fund its exciting product development programme and to finance its continuing high growth rate. It wants to raise over £100 million in new equity through a rights issue. Its existing issued share base of 1000 million 10 p nominal value shares are currently trading at 50 p, giving a market capitalization of £500 million. Current earnings per share are 2.5 p and dividends per share are 0.5 p

The company financial advisers have suggested a rights issue of one for four at 45 p per share, which would raise £112.5 million, excluding issue costs.

Analysis
This company is currently positioned as a growth company because it has a P/E multiple of 20 [50 p ÷ 2.5 p] and a dividend yield of only 1% [0.5 p ÷ 50 p], indicating that existing investors are buying the shares in the expectation of capital growth. This growth expectation seems reasonable as the company is at present retaining 80 per cent of its profits for reinvestment; i.e. 2.0 p out of 2.5 p.

On the announcement of a rights issue, the stock market receives two separate pieces of new information; it is told that the company wishes to raise new equity and it is also told what the company intends to do with that money. The stock market analyses this information and adjusts the share price accordingly,

WORKING
5.4

INSIGHT

Immediate price adjustments on rights issue announcements

STAR plc – one for four rights issue at 45 p per share

	No. of shares (m)		Price (p)		Market Capn. (£m)
Existing position	1000 shares	@	50 p	⇒	500.0
Rights issue (one for four)	250 shares	@	45 p	⇒	112.5
Immediate position – post announcement	1250 shares	⇒	49 p	⇐	612.5

The shareholder is given the right to buy shares at	45 p
The post-rights price of all shares (everything else being equal) should be	49 p
Therefore rights value per right (ignoring the time value of money impact caused by different settlement dates)	4 p

depending on whether it believes that the new issue will lead to substantially enhanced future cash flows, i.e. will the investment have a positive net present value. In other words the information elements of the announcement are separately incorporated into the share price. If the proposed investment looks financially attractive the share price may rise to reflect this new opportunity; if the proposed source of funding, equity, is also considered sensible this may enhance the value still further.

However, initially the company has issued new shares in exchange for an explicit amount of cash. The share price will immediately move to reflect this new situation before then taking into account the longer-term impact of the investment of these funds. This immediate reaction is shown in Working insight 5.4.

It can be seen that the post-rights share price now reflects the weighted average of the original share price and the rights offer price, so that the discount in the rights offer has been spread over all the shares. Thus the share price has fallen slightly but this does not automatically make existing shareholders worse off. They have been given a right to buy a share at 45 p, which will now be worth 49 p when the right is taken up. If they do not wish to invest 45 p more in the company, they can sell the right for 4 p which recoups the 4 p (4×1 p) which they have lost on their existing shareholding. This impact is balanced no matter how large the original shareholding and irrespective of whether the rights are taken up or sold, as shown in Working insight 5.5.

WORKING
5.5

INSIGHT   **Impact of rights issues on substantial shareholders**

STAR plc – alternatives for holder of 100 million shares (i.e. owner of 10 per cent of company)

   This shareholder receives rights to buy 25 million new shares at 45 p and has two alternatives, either take up the rights or sell them.

Take-up rights

Initial investment	100 m	@ 50 p	=	£50.00 m
Pay for rights	25 m	@ 45 p	=	£11.25 m
Shareholder now owns	125 m shares			
but should have an				
investment worth				£61.25 m

If share price moves to 49 p this is true because 125 m shares @ 49 p gives £61.25 m Therefore there is no gain and no loss.

Sell rights

Initial investment	100 m	@ 50 p	=	£50 m
Receive from sale of rights	25 m	@ 4 p	=	£1 m
Leaving a net investment of	100 m	worth		£49 m

This will be true if share price moves to 49 p as it should.

Therefore again, there is no gain and no loss.

It is by no means certain that the share price will move to 49 p, but the final actual price will be affected by the stock market's reaction to the new investment opportunity and by the company's decision to use equity to fund it, as well as any other new information which affects the company or share prices in general. However, any such movement is not caused by the specific details of the rights issue, which produces no gain and no loss whether the rights are taken up or sold.

As it has been shown that the discount on a rights issue confers no advantage or disadvantage to existing shareholders, the terms of a rights issue should make no difference to its attractiveness to the existing shareholders. However, launching a narrow (i.e. small) discount rights issue introduces a risk for the company, in that it may not receive its desired new funding.

A rights issue has to be available for a specified period of time in order for shareholders to decide what to do and to send in their cheques or sell their rights in the market (the normal period is around three weeks). During this period, the rights exercise price is fixed but the share price will fluctuate, so that the gap between the two will change. In the case of a high growth share with a high beta, small movements in the total market can result in larger movements in the particular share price. If the share price rises, the value of the rights offer increases and the rights become more attractive to investors. However, if the share price falls, the converse is true. Should the share price go below the rights offer price there is no reason for anyone to want to buy these new shares (i.e. take up the rights). In the example already given, it would be illogical for an investor to pay 45 p to exercise their rights if the market price of STAR plc's shares had fallen below this level. Equally there is no reason for any outsider to want to buy these rights in order to take them up.

Thus an unexpected fall in the share price could mean that the proposed rights issue would fail, with the result that the company would not receive its desired injection of new equity funding. This could leave the company unable to implement its now publicly stated strategy and so it needs to have an insurance policy. It can remove this risk of funding failure by underwriting the rights issue through a merchant bank or similar institution. (This lead underwriter will normally lay off some of its risk by sub-underwriting smaller parts of the issue with other investment institutions, some of whom will probably already be shareholders in the company making the rights issue.)

An underwriting contract is a guarantee to take up, at the issue price, any of the new shares which are not bought by either existing shareholders or buyers of their rights in the market. Obviously this transfers the risk of any fall in the share price to the underwriters because it is only likely that they will have to buy the shares if the exercise price is below the market value of the shares at the end of the rights offer period. The company has to pay an underwriting premium in order to buy what is really a put option on the underwriters for all the shares, exercisable at the rights offer price. An important driver of option values (discussed in Appendix 2) is the option exercise price (i.e. the rights offer price) relative to the current asset value. Accordingly, the smaller the discount offered on the rights issue, the greater the value of the put option and hence the higher the insurance premium needs to be.

Arranging underwriting provides insurance to the company, but comes at a cost. As we have established that the discount on a rights issue should have no impact on shareholder wealth, this should be an incentive for companies to offer rights issues at much greater discounts; the larger discount would reduce the guarantee costs incurred. This incentive should be dramatically increased because all the analysis and comparisons of actual underwriting fees and their equivalent put option valuations shows that underwriting fees are excessively high; it is therefore a very inefficient market. However, many companies still persist in raising equity funding through narrow discount rights issues, presumably at least partly because 'that is what successful companies do'. (An example of a deep discount rights issue is given in Chapter 7.)

The discussion on the movements in rights values and share prices may have indicated a short-term investment strategy which could be of interest to a high risk speculator. Suppose such a speculator had £196 000 to invest in STAR plc at the time of its rights issue, as is shown in Working insight 5.6; this investment could be made as 400 000 shares at the post rights price of 49 p, or instead the speculator could purchase 4 900 000 short term rights to buy shares.

If the share price is volatile during the period before the rights are actually taken up, these movements will be reflected in the rights value because the exercise price (45 p) of the rights offer is fixed. Thus the increased volume of rights which can be acquired multiplies up the impact of any particular movement in the share price; if this increased impact is the same whether prices go up or down, a similar effect could have been obtained by borrowing funds so as to buy 4.9 million shares (leveraging up the investment). However, the value of

---

WORKING
5.6
INSIGHT

Using rights issues as a leveraged positively skewed speculative investment

STAR plc has offered a one for four rights issue at 45 p compared to its original market price of 50 p. (Post rights weighted average share price should be 49 p.) The rights value should be 4 p per share.

The speculator could invest £196 000 in 400 000 shares of STAR or in buying 4 900 000 rights to STAR shares to be issued at 45 p (*fixed* offer price for rights).

If the share price rises by 10 p during the rights offer period, the value of the rights should also rise 10 p (ignoring the time value of money). However if the share price falls by 10 p, the rights value cannot go below zero; hence the outcome is positively skewed. The higher volume investment in rights multiplies the change in return for the same change in share price in the same way as using borrowed funds increases volatility (i.e. leverages up the return).

		Impact of ± 10 p in share price
Equity investment	400 000 shares	± £40 000
Rights investment	4 900 000 Rights	+ £490 000
		− £196 000

the rights cannot become negative, so the maximum loss is the 4 p purchase price whereas the upside potential is not similarly constrained; thus the return is skewed as well as multiplied. The speculator has really acquired a low valued, short-dated call option on the shares with an exercise price of 45 p.

These option markets in rights issues are actively traded during the offer periods, and arbitrageurs help to ensure the gap between the actual share price and the rights exercise price is always equal to the value of the rights. If this kind of option trading can be done, it may be possible for the underwriters of the rights issue to reduce their risk during the life of their insurance contract. The underwriting risk can, of course, be split into the normal two components, market risk and unique risk. The systematic risk element can be triggered if the whole market collapses during the rights period, with the result that the company exercises its put option and leaves the underwriter sitting on a large capital loss. This risk can be hedged if part of the underwriting premium is used to buy a similarly structured put option, but on the whole market (e.g. the stock market index) rather than on the specific share. If the market does collapse, the gains on this put option will offset the loss on the underwriting contract.

(These examples of the underwriters wanting to hedge their market risk and the speculator wanting to multiply up their potential gain illustrate the critical strengths of option markets and option trading strategies. Players with completely opposite aims and objectives can all be attracted to use options in their different forms as part of their financing and investment strategies.)

There remains the risk that the overall market is stable or goes up, but the share price of the company collapses. It is much more difficult to hedge this risk specifically but it can partly be achieved if a suitably designed portfolio is used as the basis of the option hedge rather than the total market index. This can at least take account of key industry factors or major risk items which may affect the company's share price more violently than the stock market. Of course, in a perfectly efficient market the costs involved in designing the perfect hedge would exactly equal the premium received for undertaking the underwriting contract. Fortunately, life is not that boring as the markets are not that perfectly efficient.

BONUS ISSUES AND SHARE SPLITS

A rights issue can be regarded as a sale of the shares at full price, together with a bonus issue of free shares representing the discount in the rights price. This is mathematically illustrated in Working insight 5.7.

A bonus issue is an issue of shares made from the company's retained profits. Effectively, the retained profits are capitalized, and moved in the balance sheet from the 'reserves' category to the 'share capital' category. Shareholders receive the relevant number of shares (based on their existing shareholdings) for free, leaving them with proportionately the same percentage of the company as they owned previously.

A transaction often compared to a bonus issue is a share split. In a share split the nominal value of each share is proportionately reduced, so that the value of share capital on the balance sheet is unchanged, whereas in the bonus issue the

---

WORKING 5.7

INSIGHT

Rights issues as a sale at full price plus a bonus issue of the discount element

STAR plc

Rights issue of 250 million shares @ 45 p generating	£112.5 m in cash
This cash inflow could have been achieved by selling 225 million shares @ 50 p =	£112.5 m

The remaining 25 million shares therefore represent a free bonus issue distribution to the existing shareholders.

  This idea is not controversial because it is how companies actually account for rights issues. They adjust prior years' figures to take account of this bonus element, as this would otherwise represent dilution in earnings per share due to the increase in the number of issued shares.

---

nominal value of the shares remained the same as reserves were capitalized. Working insight 5.8 illustrates the different transactions.

  As can be seen, in either case there is no cashflow impact to these balance sheet re-arrangements. Bonus issues and share splits should not affect share values because they do not change the expected future cash flows which will be generated by the business. If the number of issued shares is doubled by a bonus issue or split, the price per share should halve. However, this does not always

---

WORKING 5.8

INSIGHT

A bonus issue and a share split

	BonusCo	*SplitCo*
Capital structure prior to transaction		
Share capital		
100 000 shares @ £1 par value	100 000	100 000
Retained profits	250 000	250 000
	350 000	350 000
After a bonus issue of one for four shares:		
Share capital		
125 000 shares @ £1 par value	125 000	
Retained profits	225 000	
	350 000	
After an 1.25 for one share split:		
Share capital		
125 000 shares @ 80 p par value		100 000
Retained profits		250 000
		350 000

seem to happen in practice. Furthermore, companies obviously believe that share splits have some value as they are very common, yet they actually cost the company money in advisers' fees to implement.

There are several explanations suggested for any supposed increase in total market capitalization resulting from a bonus issue or share split:

1. Restriction of future dividends, thus strengthening the balance sheet.
2. A sign of management's confidence in the future.
3. A signal of increased dividends.

The first suggested explanation is that the capitalization of reserves which occurs in a bonus issue (albeit not in a share split) removes the possibility that these reserves can be paid out as dividends and hence reduces the perception of financial risk on the part of lenders to the company. Any value from such a change should be observable through lower interest rates being charged to the company or by a move towards a higher proportion of debt financing; neither has been observed empirically after a bonus issue.

The most popular explanation is that such a move reflects a feeling of confidence on the part of the managers of the company. Therefore a bonus issue or share split may communicate useful information to investors regarding this improved level of confidence which can then get reflected in an increased share price. This can be expressed as, 'successful companies make bonus issues'. (The converse can also be seen in that companies listed on the New York Stock Exchange lose their listing if their share price falls below $1: directors who fear that this might happen undertake share consolidations, which are the opposite of share splits, in order to prevent this happening.)

Another suggestion is that many companies maintain their dividend per share payments after a bonus issue or stock split. Logically, doubling the number of shares should halve the dividend per share. However, often the dividend is reduced by less than 50 per cent. This means that the dividend pay-out ratio is increased unless earnings are expected suddenly to rise following the transaction. (The implication of this explanation is that shareholders prefer dividends to reinvestment by this company, but this is not logical for a high growth company which should be pursuing a high reinvestment strategy.)

Two further arguments are put forward as to why companies undertake share splits. The first relates to companies that encourage employees to hold shares in the business; if the share price rises to too high a level, this may make employee share ownership more difficult, or may discourage them from buying shares.

The final argument that appears particularly relevant to the UK stock market, where companies seem to worry if their share prices are too high in absolute terms, as this might make them less attractive. (Relatively few shares trade on the London Stock Exchange over £10 per share, while in the USA companies trade at more than $100 per share with no detectable decrease in demand.) There is no theoretical logic to this argument because it is the proportionate share of the earnings stream which is important and doubling the physical number of issued shares doesn't change the proportion of the company owned by any individual shareholder. However if the absolute share price is lower, it is supposed to attract more investors to buy shares in the company, thus forcing the price up and increasing the total market capitalization of the company. There is no empirical evidence to support an argument that lower valued shares show greater gains over time which might justify such an investor preference for lower priced shares, but this is a commonly held belief which is acted upon by many publicly quoted companies.

6

Mature companies – to divi or not?

SUMMARY OF APPROPRIATE SECTION OF THE OVERALL MODEL

The end of the growth stage is often marked by some very aggressive price competition among rivals who have been left with considerable excess capacity as the anticipated continued sales growth in the industry fails to materialize. Once the industry has stabilized, the maturity stage of high but relatively stable sales at reasonable profit margins can begin. Clearly, the level of business risk has reduced again as another development phase has now been successfully completed; the company should enter the maturity stage with a good relative market share as a result of its investment in marketing during the growth stage. The critical business risks remaining relate to the duration of this stable, maturity stage and whether the company can maintain its strong market share, on a financially attractive basis, throughout this period.

The strategic emphasis now switches to one of maintaining share and improving efficiency, which can make the transition between growth and maturity quite difficult to manage. However, the reduction in business risk enables the financial risk to be increased through the introduction of debt financing. This is now quite practical because the net cash flow should have turned significantly positive, which

WORKING
6.1
INSIGHT

Financial strategy parameters

Mature businesses

Business risk	Medium
Financial risk	Medium
Source of funding	Retained earnings plus debt
Dividend policy	High payout ratio
Future growth prospects	Medium to low
Price/earnings mutiple	Medium
Current profitability i.e. eps	High
Share price	Stable in real terms with low volatility

enables the debt to be both serviced and repaid. The positive cash flow and ability to use debt funding for reinvestment needs are also important to shareholders as they allow the company to pay much higher dividends. Thus the dividend payout ratio is increased as a proportion of the new high current earnings per share, increasing the absolute dividend payments significantly.

This increased dividend yield is required because the future growth prospects of the business are much lower than in the earlier stages of the life cycle. The lower growth prospects are reflected in a lower P/E ratio, thus shares are given a lower rating by the financial markets, but this does not necessarily lead to a decline in share prices. Earnings per share should be high and increasing slightly, due to efficiency gains, during this stage so that these high eps offset the reducing P/E multiples. The net result should be a much more stable share price, as more of the investors' expected return is now provided through dividend yield rather than the capital gains which dominated the previous stages. These issues are illustrated in Working insight 6.1.

When the reducing business risk and correspondingly required reduction in total expectation of return are added into the equation, it becomes clear that managing this transition requires some clear communication between the company and its investor base.

MANAGING THE TRANSITION TO MATURITY

One of the great problems of the product life cycle is that most management teams do not accept that it is inevitable that their main product will eventually mature and that it should be managed accordingly. Thus companies continue to spend large amounts of money searching desperately for ways to prolong the earlier high rates of growth, even though the financial justifications for such expenditures become increasingly tenuous.

This inevitability of product maturity should, when it arrives, lead to a significant change in managerial focus. The earlier emphasis on growth both in the overall market and in the share of that expanding market should give way to a much greater concentration on profitably maintaining the level of sales which have now been achieved. This means a change in managerial style is desirable because the previous critical success factors are no longer as relevant in a period of much more stable sales volumes. Many management teams find it quite possible to manage the transition from start-up to growth, but relatively few are as successful at moving from the growth stage to the maturity phase of the life cycle. It may therefore be beneficial if key changes are made at senior manager level at an appropriate point in this transition, as this may accelerate the required changes in managerial style.

6.1   MATALAN PLC

CASE STUDY

Matalan is a successful UK retailer of discount clothes and household goods. Founded by John Hargreaves (the current chairman) in the mid 1980s, the company floated on the London Stock Exchange in 1998 and by 2001 had seen its share price rise from 235 p to around 500 p. This growth in the share price reflected the company's rapid growth.

Growth was both organic and by acquisition. By 2001 the company had some 130 large out-of-town stores around the UK. It had also undertaken vertical integration, acquiring the Falmers jeans brand and also the brand and manufacturing business of Lee Cooper, another jeans company.

In spring 2001 Angus Monro, the chief executive who had steered the Company to its success, suddenly left Matalan. Monro had dominated the development and activities of the company over the past few years, and was well regarded in the City.

In Mr Monro's leaving statement he stated that there had been no dispute between himself and the board, nor indeed between himself and the Hargreaves family who still owned over 50 per cent of the company. His leaving statement went on, 'It seemed to me that the difficult job of repositioning the business [i.e. managing the rapid growth] had been done, and I regarded the next few years as more of the same, though not without its challenges. It's a fantastic growth story and an incredibly strong management team'.

However, Press comment suggested that there was a split over the Company's growth strategy, and that although Monro was preparing for a period of slower growth, other senior management figures were taking the view that the Company should be seeking ways to maintain its growth in the medium term and 'develop more aggressively its strategic options'. Indeed, indications were that they were targeting an increase to over 200 stores by 2005, and were anticipating extending the floor-space in existing properties.

From the press reports, it seems likely that Mr Monro took the view that the company had completed its aggressive growth stage and was entering maturity. However, the majority shareholders still desired a high rate of growth. With such a divergence of strategic views, Mr Monro's departure was perhaps inevitable. Future results will show whether the company does in fact continue profitable growth at the desired rate.

The slowdown in sales growth relates to the product life cycle and this needs to be separated from the brand or the company, which often follow their own much longer life cycles. A strong brand may have been developed during the high growth phase of a particular product. If the positioning of the brand was particularly appropriate for the high growth rate being achieved by the product, it may be difficult and/or expensive to try to reposition the brand for the ensuing maturity stage which the product is now entering. It may be more attractive to transfer this brand to another product which is still in, or is just entering, its growth stage where strongly developed brand attributes may be more relevant. This idea of brand transfer is widely practised by several very large consumer goods companies which have a broad range of products which are at very different stages of their life cycles. It is critical that the new product to which the brand name and/or image is transferred has the appropriate characterization to match the brand attributes, but the result can clearly be to extend significantly the economic life of the brand. This can be important, as often the costs of developing a brand from scratch can be very large, so that the original investment decision needs as long a potential life as possible in order to justify the expenditure.

A good example where this tactic can work well is when the product really requires a change in its competitive positioning once it reaches the maturity stage. This can often be where the original competitive strategy was based on differentiation and a significant entry barrier was created by the use of appropriate strong branding. As the market matures, users of the product frequently become more knowledgeable and hence less willing to pay for certain types of differentiation benefit. Alternatively, the increasingly competitive environment (caused possibly by a period of excess capacity at the end of the growth stage) may have forced competitors to improve their quality or incorporate the branded product's previously unique features into their own product, with the result that the brand attributes are no longer as strong as they were. It may be possible and economically sensible for the company to develop a new sustainable competitive advantage by emphasizing the value for money attributes of its product. This would normally require a price reduction as part of the product's repositioning. A corresponding cost saving is needed, part of which may be achieved by no longer incorporating the original brand image into this repositioned product.

The company life cycle can itself be extended by having an appropriate portfolio of products within the business, so that the company can continue to grow even though any particular product has moved into its maturity stage. Some of the issues involved have already been discussed in earlier chapters.

Having mentioned the problems caused by failing to acknowledge a product's move into the maturity stage it is also important to remember that it can be very expensive to assume that a product is mature when in reality it is still growing. A particularly long recession can depress the sales growth of many products to such an extent that companies tend to regard them as now mature, if not already declining. The ensuing upturn in the economy will restore the high growth prospects of many such products and, if the wrong strategy has been implemented, the company may find that it has lost substantial market share in what is now once again a rapidly growing market.

One potential way of avoiding such expensive miscalculations about the stage of development of a product is to consider its market in a progressively segmented manner rather than in total. Thus, for many products it is quite possible to find certain market segments which have definitely matured while other parts are showing all the hallmarks of accelerating growth rates. If these different segments are identified, appropriately tailored competitive strategies can be implemented to maximize the long-term value of the business.

This question of value maximization means that the changes required during this transition from high growth to maturity are not only internal to the company. In the initial stages of the life cycle shareholders expect most of their return to be generated from capital gains as the share price increases over time. These capital gains are produced by the company progressively overcoming many of the factors responsible for the initially very high business risks facing any start-up business. It is also possible that during the growth stage the company may outperform the market's expectations, due either to the higher growth achieved by the product or to the greater market share gained by the particular company. However, once the maturity stage has been reached, these issues have largely been resolved so that the remaining business risks relate to the length of the maturity stage and the levels of profits and cash flows which can be generated during this relatively stable period. This means that the business risk associated with a mature business is reduced to the medium range, which implies that investors should be prepared to accept a lower return than in the earlier higher risk phases of the life cycle.

Such a lower return will only be accepted if the required change in shareholders' expectations is positively managed by the company.

ADDING VALUE THROUGH FINANCIAL STRATEGY

It is once again necessary to consider the components of the remaining business risk and then to relate these components to the level and type of return which should now be offered to the shareholders.

As a company matures, its level of unique risk normally reduces because the cash flows become much more predictable and stable. The proportionate impact of the systematic risk component of the company therefore becomes greater, but the beta factor which drives this level of risk also tends to normalize towards a beta of one, the beta of the markets as a whole. (Note that it may never actually become one, as the market represents an average of all companies, and some companies and industries are inherently more susceptible to market movements than others.) This normalization process is due to the lower growth of the product, which tends to reduce the impact of external environmental changes for companies which had relatively high betas during their growth stages. Conversely, companies with very low betas in the high growth phase (which are very rare) tend to become more responsive to changes affecting the overall market over time.

The demand for the product has now matured. This may have been caused because there are now more replacement products available to customers who were previously locked into the single product, or it may be that customers have eventually simply learned to control their consumption of the product so that demand is no longer increasing. This stable rate of consumption is more likely to be affected by general changes in the economy, as new users are no longer entering the market in large numbers and existing customers are not increasing their rate of usage.

If these factors can be applied to most mature companies, the base cost of equity capital for all such companies will be in a much smaller range than in the earlier stages of development. This smaller range will also be much closer to the expected return on the stock markets as a whole. Thus it is important that the company convinces its shareholders that it does now have a lower risk profile, so that they should accept this lower rate of return without reducing the share price to restore the actual rate of return to the previously higher levels. One obvious way to communicate this lower risk profile is for the company to prove it by delivering less volatile financial results from year to year.

Another major way is to start to change the way in which shareholders expect to receive their return. In the earlier stages, their financial return was achieved by capital gains in the value of their investments but this is less possible once the company has matured. Profits will be less volatile but they cannot be expected to continue to grow dramatically; what future growth can be achieved will come mainly as a result of improvements in efficiency rather than large real increases in sales volumes or values. Indeed these improvements in profitability should become the emphasis of the reinvestments made by the business, whereas in the past most reinvestments would have gone on projects to do with growth in the market or in the share of the market. Now, marketing expenditure is concentrated on maintaining the existing market share, and, by reinvesting the current depreciation expense the company should be able to maintain its productive capacity.

This decline in the need to invest in rapid growth comes at a time of high profitability for the business, with the result that the company, for the first time, is a significant net cash producer. However, these high profits and lack of the earlier tax deferral opportunities (through high levels of capital investment for example) mean that the company is normally now a tax payer. This increases the expected present value of any potential tax shield which could be created by the use of debt financing. Also the assets involved in the business are normally now at their maximum tangible value, with strong stable cash flows being produced from the employment of these assets. This reduces the potential costs of any financial distress which might be created by the use of a level of debt financing which could not be serviced or repaid by the company. The positive cash flows being generated by the business on a relatively stable basis reduce the probability that these lower costs of financial distress would be incurred, because it is now much more likely that the company will be able to pay the interest on any borrowing obligations and to make the principal repayments as required.

Thus the inverse correlation between business risk and financial risk is borne out as the reducing business risk can be offset by increasing the financial risk through raising some debt funding. Such a change in the financial strategy from almost exclusively equity financing to incorporating an increasing proportion of debt funding can add considerable value to the shareholders of a maturing company.

The key is for the company to find a useful way of utilizing this newly acquired access to additional sources of funding, which can further increase the value of the company.

DEVELOPING A DIVIDEND POLICY

The most beneficial application of this increasing cash availability is to start to make higher dividend payments to shareholders. An increasing dividend payout ratio serves several purposes including acting as a very good signalling device to shareholders that future growth prospects are not as exciting as in the past. This will reduce shareholder expectations regarding future growth, but future growth has been the dominant element of the total return to shareholders in the earlier stages of development. This element is now being replaced by an increasing element of dividend yield, which is supported by an increasing dividend payout ratio out of the high stable post-tax profits. Thus the company now has the ability to support a consistent high level of dividends and the cash required to pay these dividends is also readily available from within the company. The reinvestment needs of the business can be met from the lower retention ratio on existing profits supplemented by raising a reasonable proportion of debt funding.

The P/E multiple will reduce as the market reassesses the potential for future growth. However the increasing level of earnings and dividends should maintain the share price at the high levels achieved at the end of the growth stage, as long as the transition is properly managed. If substantial future growth expectations are allowed to be believed by shareholders for too long, the share price may rise too high in the vain hope of this continued growth which cannot be delivered. In almost all such cases the essential reaction of the stock markets when they realize their error is to overreact in the opposite direction, so the share price can often fall significantly when it becomes clear that the expected growth is not going to be delivered. It is by no means uncommon for a company to become a takeover target during such a period of short-term rapid share price collapses caused by badly managing the expectations of the market.

Theoretically there is no difference to the shareholder between the company paying dividends and reinvesting the profits. If the company is reinvesting in positive net present value projects, the share price should increase to reflect the expected increased level of future cash flow which should result from the reinvestment. However, this argument is based on an assumption that a company can always reinvest its profits at a rate of return which is at least equal to the shareholders' expected return on their investment. During the early stages of the product life cycle, the opportunities for financially attractive reinvestment of current profit levels are plentiful. This is due both to the high rate of growth with its resulting need for investment and to the relatively low levels of profits available for reinvestment. With the arrival of the maturity stage the need for reinvestment reduces significantly just as the availability of finance increases substantially.

This means that the company runs a potential risk of retaining profits for which it has no profitable use, which can lead to a declining overall rate of return for the business. Alternatively, the company can start to invest these funds in other areas in the hope of developing new growth opportunities and new sustainable competitive advantages with which to exploit these growth opportunities. These diversification strategies have already been discussed; at this point it is sufficient to say that they normally destroy shareholder value.

The way in which dividend policy can enhance shareholder value can best be illustrated by some simplified numerical examples. In Working insight 6.2 the financial details for STAR plc are given, which indicate that it is currently positioned as a growth company with a relatively low dividend payout ratio. It

WORKING
6.2

INSIGHT   **Star plc – a growth company**

Today's share price of 50 p for Satellite Television Audio Recordings plc (STAR) is supported by an expected 0.5 p dividend to be paid out of expected earnings per share of 2.0 p. It is known that shareholders expect future growth to be maintained at 15 per cent per annum, and that the steady state cost of equity for an equivalent company to STAR is 14.3 per cent per annum. The present dividend policy represents a 25 per cent payout policy.

Using Gordon's dividend growth model:

$$K_e \quad = \quad D_1/P_0 + g$$
$$= \quad 0.5/50 + 15\%$$
$$= \quad 1\% + 15\%$$
$$= \quad 16\%$$

Only 1 per cent of shareholders' requirement for a 16 per cent return is met by the dividend yield; therefore 15 per cent must represent required capital growth.

We can demonstrate in two ways that STAR is seen by the markets as a growth company.

(a) *Present Value of Growth Opportunities*

At steady state, STAR's P/E ratio would be 1/0.143
$$= \quad \text{7 times.}$$
Share price at steady state is 7×2 p
$$=14 \text{ p}$$
Current share price is 50 p
Therefore, 36 p of the current share price represents PVGO – 72 per cent of the price.

(b) *Steady State P/E*

Current P/E is 50/2 = 25 times
Steady state P/E is seven times
Therefore current P/E is considerably greater than steady state P/E, demonstrating the market's growth expectations.

is intended to use Gordon's dividend growth formula (despite its simplifying assumptions, the results in these examples are not misleading and the arithmetic is kept relatively straightforward) to analyse the likely impact on shareholder wealth of possible changes in this dividend policy.

In this example, shareholders expect growth to be maintained at 15 per cent per annum but this expectation is in the knowledge of the current dividend policy of the company. Thus, as shown in Working insight 6.3, the shareholders are basing their growth expectation on the company achieving a return on reinvestment of 20 per cent p.a. in the future. It should be remembered that, in the absence of any additional information, this expected return on reinvestment may be based on the return on equity being achieved by the company.

An important question is whether this rate of retention is adding to shareholder value, or reducing it. In STAR's case, the expected return on reinvestment (20 per cent) is greater than the total return demanded by the shareholder

> **WORKING 6.3**
>
> **INSIGHT**   **Relationship of growth and return on reinvestment**
>
> The rate of internally funded sustainable organic growth is determined by the retention ratio and the return which is achieved on these reinvested funds; so that
>
> g = retention ratio $\times$ return on reinvestment
>
> = [1 − payout ratio] $\times$ return on reinvestment (ROR)
>
> For STAR this gives
>
> $$15\% = \{1 - 0.25\} \times ROR$$
>
> Therefore $ROR = \dfrac{15\%}{0.75} = 20\%$

with the current strategy (16 per cent). It appears to be logical for the company to retain this level of its current profit provided that the directors believe it can achieve 20 per cent return on reinvestment.

However, it may be possible to improve this position by changing the dividend payout ratio. This can most easily be illustrated by considering the position if a nil payout ratio or a 100 per cent payout ratio were adopted. These extremes are used because they each make one element in the formula equal to zero; they are therefore used for arithmetic clarity rather than to advocate that companies should adopt one or other extreme position.

If the company were to switch to a nil payout policy, a rational investor would expect the future rate of growth to increase in order to compensate for forgoing the immediate dividend income. Theoretically the company should be able to reinvest the additional retained profit at the same rate of return but, in the real world, companies do not have an infinite supply of equally attractive investment projects.

Most capital investment budgeting processes select the most attractive projects first and so it is normal to find a law of diminishing returns applying when a company is given an increase in its capital expenditure levels. This may cause a minor reduction in the average rate of return on the reinvestment but it is occasionally found that an increase in available expenditure actually results in an increase in the average rate of return because it enables the company to undertake a particularly attractive project which had previously been rejected due to lack of available funding. (It is again important to remember that in theory such a situation cannot occur because the company should raise new funding in order to undertake all projects which generate an expected return in excess of the company's cost of capital.)

For simplicity an assumption has been made in these examples that the return on reinvestment is unchanged with the movements in dividend policy.

As can be seen in Working insight 6.4, the 100 per cent retention ratio leads to a greater increase in the expected growth rate than the reduction caused by the non-payment of immediate dividends. This means that the total return is increased, unless the share price rises to keep the expected return at its previous level of 16 per cent.

**WORKING
6.4**

INSIGHT   **Star plc – 100 per cent retention ratio**

g =   retention ratio $\times$ return on reinvestment

If no dividends are paid, the retention ratio is 100 per cent

g = $100\% \times ROR$
           = $100\% \times 20\%$
           = 20%

Therefore, using Gordon's dividend growth model:

K_e = $0 + 20\%$
           = 20%

This represents an increase in expected return by shareholders, which was 16 per
cent. This would only be logical if they were to perceive an increased risk due to this
change in financial strategy. Otherwise, the share price should increase to reduce the
return to the normal level of expected returns. With a 100 per cent retention ratio this
cannot be reflected in this simplified formula.

Changes in required rates of return are caused by changes in perceptions of
risk; does changing the dividend payout ratio affect shareholders' risk perceptions? The theory may at first appear to indicate that this should not be so
because if shareholders are indifferent between dividends and capital growth
they should not demand different levels of return if the mix provided by any
company changes. However a high retention rate is only logical for a growth
orientated company and the risk profile of such companies is higher than for
similar but more mature businesses. Hence it could be argued that an increase
in the retention rate should indicate higher future growth expectations and the
greater volatility associated with higher growth may increase the risk perception of investors.

Looked at another way, the shareholders may be more worried about a
company which keeps the vast majority of its current profits when compared
with one which pays a much higher proportion of these profits out as current
dividends. With a high retention policy shareholders are not only backing the
continued success of the current business strategy but are also trusting that the
company's managers can identify and successfully implement financially
attractive new investment projects. Clearly this is less worrying (i.e. risky) if the
new investments are closely related to the existing successful areas of operation
of the company.

The other extreme dividend policy for STAR is to pay out all of its current
profits as dividends. As shown in Working insight 6.5, this means that no future
growth should be expected. Therefore all the return to shareholders comes
through dividend yield, and dividends are likely to stay at their current level.
This potentially places the company in a steady state position, as discussed in
Chapter 2, and the expected steady state return for shareholders in STAR was
already given in Working insight 6.2 as being 14.3 per cent. If this is the new rate

WORKING
6.5

INSIGHT

Impact of a 100 per cent dividend pay-out policy in a growth company

If all current profits are paid out as dividends, the future growth expectation must be zero, thus

g = retention ratio $\times$ return on reinvestment
= {1 − payout ratio} $\times$ return on reinvestment
= (1 − 1) $\times$ ROR
= 0

For STAR plc the maximum sustainable dividend payment is 2.0 p (i.e. the current eps). If the share price stays at 50 p, the shareholder's return is reduced to

$$K_e = \frac{2.0\ p}{50\ p} + 0$$
$$= 4\%$$

but shareholders previously wanted a return of 16 per cent. The company can now be regarded as having moved to a steady-state position (100 per cent pay-out policy) and, as per Working insight 6.2, investors should now expect a 14.3 per cent return. This can only be achieved by a reduction in share price, thus

$$14.3\% = \frac{2.0\ p}{P_1} + 0$$

Therefore

$$P_1 = \frac{2.0\ p}{0.143} = 14\ p \text{ (a reduction of 36 p or 72 per cent)}$$

where P_1 is the share price after announcing the change in dividend policy.

of return expected by shareholders (reflecting their reduced perception of risk due to the higher dividend payout policy as discussed above) this can only be achieved by a fall in the share price to 14 p.

Such a dramatic potential fall should not be surprising for a high growth company because, as noted in Working insight 6.2, 72 per cent of the current share price represents the present value of the future growth opportunities. If the company were to change its dividend policy to a 100 per cent payout ratio, these future growth opportunities would disappear, as would their present value component of the current share price. Thus this reduced potential share price of 14 p for STAR represents the present value of the current earnings stream, without taking into account the future growth opportunities. In practice the stock market makes this adjustment to the share prices of high growth companies which, for whatever reason, are now not expected to produce the previously anticipated growth, irrespective of whether the company acknowledges the change by increasing its dividend payout ratio.

This illustration of the impact of changes in dividend policy for a high growth company can be contrasted with the impacts on a declining business,

WORKING 6.6

INSIGHT   DOG Inc – a declining business

Dear Old Geriatrics Inc. has a share price of 100 p. The company is expected to pay a dividend of 13 p per share out of earnings per share of 16.25 p. Shareholders only expect annual growth of 2 per cent.
   Using Gordon's dividend growth model gives

$$K_e = \frac{D_1}{P_0} + g$$

$$= \frac{13\,p}{100\,p} + 2\%$$

$$= 15\%$$

But

$$g = \text{retention ratio} \times \text{return on reinvestment}$$
$$2\% = 0.2 \times ROR$$

or

$$\text{return on reinvestment} = \frac{2\%}{0.2} = 10\%$$

WORKING 6.7

INSIGHT   Switch to a 100 per cent pay-out ratio in a declining business

If all current profits are paid out, $g = 0$ under Gordon's model. Thus, if the share price is unchanged

$$K_e = \frac{D_1}{P_0} + 0$$

$$K_e = \frac{16.25\,p}{100\,p} = 16.25\%$$

However, shareholders only required 15 per cent rate of return when 20 per cent of profits were being reinvested; if their risk perception has been reduced due to the higher pay-out ratio, the rate of return should also reduce rather than increase. If we were to assume that the expected return stays the same, this would give...

$$P_1 = \frac{D_1}{K_e} = \frac{16.25}{0.15} = 108.33\,p$$

where P_1 is the share price after announcing the change in dividend policy.
   (The logic of maintaining the previous cost of equity capital is that DOG Inc. has been categorized as a declining business, and therefore dividends will not be expected to be maintained at this same level forever; growth will actually be negative in the future!)

WORKING
6.8

INSIGHT   **Increasing the retention ratio in a declining business**

The expected return on reinvestment is assumed to be maintained at 10 per cent. If the retention ratio is increased to 50 per cent, the expected dividend payment reduces to 8.125 p. If we assume that shareholders' required return remains at 15 per cent, this gives:

$$K_e \quad = \quad D_1/P_1 + \text{growth}$$
$$= \quad D_1/P_1 + \{\text{retention ratio} \times \text{return on reinvestment}\}$$

i.e.

$$15\% \quad = \quad 8.125/P_1 + \{0.5 \times 10\%\}$$
$$= \quad 8.125/P_1 + 5\%$$

where P_1 is the share price after the announcement of the change in dividend policy.

$$P_1 \quad = \quad 8.125/10\%$$
$$= \quad 81.25 \text{ p}$$

This represents a decline in the share price of almost 20 per cent

as shown in Working insight 6.6. The expected return on equity for DOG Inc is now dominated by the dividend yield component, which is not surprising considering the 80 per cent payout ratio. However the shareholders are assuming, in their expected growth rate of 2 per cent p.a., that the company's return on reinvestment is only 10 per cent p.a. This is considerably below their required rate of return of 15 per cent, thus giving the impression that the company is destroying shareholder value by retaining even 20 per cent of current profits. If this is so the share price should rise in response to a further increase in the dividend payout ratio. The potential impact of a move to a 100 per cent payout ratio is shown in Working insight 6.7, which indicates a likely rise in share price as the destruction of shareholder value is reversed.

It would be logical to expect that an increase in the retention ratio of this company would lead to a significant decline in share price and the effect of increasing the retention ratio to 50 per cent is shown in Working insight 6.8. The low return on reinvestment means that the growth component is still very low, so that the dividend yield has to be high to compensate. This will only be achieved if the share price falls, as this automatically increases the dividend yield for any given dividend payment. The required reduction in share price signals the greater level of shareholder wealth which is being destroyed by the application of such an inappropriate financial strategy.

These illustrations indicate the importance of the dividend policy during the maturity stage, which is the bridge between high growth and decline for the business. The company should leave the growth stage with a low dividend payout ratio but should enter the decline stage with a 100 per cent payout ratio, or very nearly that level. The rate of transition is governed by the financially attractive reinvestment opportunities available to the company.

7

Declining businesses – a case for euthanasia?

APPLYING THE OVERALL MODEL

Unfortunately, the strong positive cash generation of the maturity stage cannot continue for ever (at least not unless immensely inefficient markets have been created and are maintained to infinity), as the demand for the product will eventually start to die away. As demand fades the cash inflows decline as well. Although during the maturity stage funds were not invested in developing the market or in increasing market share, expenditure was being made to maintain both these factors affecting future sales levels. Once sales demand starts to decline irreversibly, it is no longer sensible to continue spending the same amount on this maintenance type of marketing activity. Thus net cash inflows can be maintained during the early stages of decline by modifying the business strategy appropriately.

Despite this move to decline and the inevitable ultimate death of the product, the associated business risk should be regarded as still reducing from its level in the previous maturity stage. Yet another of the original unknowns, i.e. the length of the maturity stage, has now been resolved and the only major remaining risk is for how long will it make economic sense to allow the business to continue.

This low business risk should be complemented by a relatively high financial risk source of funding. This can be achieved by a combination of a high dividend payout policy and the utilization of debt financing. The reinvestment strategy in a dying business is likely to be low, because the future growth prospects are now negative, and this links very easily to the high dividend payout policy. Indeed dividends paid during this stage can exceed post-tax profits due to the possibility of there being an inadequate financial justification to reinvest depreciation. (Reinvesting depreciation is a normal way of maintaining the scale of the existing business but this may not be logical during the decline stage.) Consequently dividends may equal the total of profits and depreciation, in which case it should be clear that part of the dividend payment really represents a repayment of capital.

This indicates how debt financing can be introduced into a declining business. Although assets may not be replaced as they are fully used up, some funds are inevitably tied up in the business during this period. If these funds are provided by equity investors, they will require a risk-adjusted return on this investment. However, the cost of debt is lower than the cost of equity so that a refinancing operation may enable some of these equity funds to be released by the company prior to its eventual liquidation. Lenders to the company will not want to take on an equity risk for a debt-based return, but they should be willing to lend against the ultimate realizable value of the assets which are locking up shareholders' equity. These borrowings can be paid to shareholders by way of dividend or share repurchase, and again clearly represent a repayment of capital.

The negative growth prospects are translated into a low price/earnings multiple for the shares and, when allied with the declining trend in earnings per share which is experienced during this stage; this now results in a declining share price. However, as long as the shareholders are aware that part of their high dividend payments are effectively repayments of capital, this declining value should not cause undue concern. These issues are illustrated in Working insight 7.1.

WORKING 7.1 INSIGHT

Financial strategy parameters

Declining businesses

Business risk	Low
Financial risk	High
Source of funding	Debt
Dividend policy	Total payout ratio
Future growth prospects	Negative
Price/earnings multiple	Low
Current profitability, i.e. eps	Low and declining
Share price	Declining and increasing in volatility

THE FINAL FINANCIAL STRATEGY

The decline stage of the life cycle should not be regarded as a depressing end to the continuous process of development of business and financial strategies which has gone before. It is important that the financial strategy is reviewed and the appropriate changes are made as the company moves from maturity through to decline. A good example of this analytical review is with regard to the cost structure of the business.

In the launch stage the very high business risk indicated that, as far as possible, costs should be kept variable and long-term financial commitments should be avoided. The high investment requirements of the growth stage usually lead to an increase in the fixed cost base, but the high business risk still means that the proportion of fixed costs should be carefully monitored. It is only when the greater stability of the maturity stage is reached that the business can accept the increased risk associated with a high level of fixed cost. The resulting efficiency gains are important to the continued improvement in operating performance.

When sales volumes start to decline, such a high level of fixed costs would quickly move the company into a severe loss-making position. Therefore it is important that the proportion of fixed costs is reduced, for example by renewing contracts on a short-term or completely variable basis. This represents a reversal of the trend through the earlier stages of the life cycle, and is advocated in spite of the continuing reduction in the business risk profile. It is however completely in accordance with the need to use a much shorter-term timescale for financially evaluating all decisions during this stage.

The major risk associated with a declining business is that sudden relatively small changes in the external business environment can make the business uneconomic, so that immediate closure is forced. If major costs are still of a fixed nature or if new expenditures have been justified over a long future period of continued benefits, the financial impact of such a sudden forced closure can be extremely adverse. The company can effectively hedge itself from some of these adverse consequences by focusing on short-term financial impacts, such as is achieved by using financial payback as a means of justifying expenditures rather than the more sophisticated discounted cash flow techniques.

A similar logic can be used in assessing the economic performance of the business during the decline stage. Return on Investment is the most common accounting technique used by companies for assessing business performance. This compares some measure of periodic profit with the investment required to achieve that profit. Depreciation is normally charged as an expense in calculating the profit; this assumes that the business intends to maintain its asset base by reinvesting the depreciation expense. Once the company moves into decline this may not be a valid assumption. Furthermore, the reducing scale of activity may enable the company to reduce the funds tied up in working capital. This means that the available cash generated from the business may exceed the operating cash flows.

If this increased cash balance is not required by the business, it should be paid out to shareholders: as illustrated in Chapter 6, the potential return on reinvestment in a declining business is often below the shareholders' required rate of return. This creates a high dividend payout ratio which will often exceed 100 per cent, highlighting that part of these dividends are really repayments of capital. As a result, shareholders should not be unduly concerned with a declining share price – as long as they are being compensated with a sufficiently high dividend yield.

This part of the financial strategy is not in conflict with the theory because it is dictated by the declining opportunities for financially attractive reinvestments in the business. However, the reducing business risk has led to the overall financial strategy model of Chapter 3 advocating that the debt funding ratio should be increased during this stage. Theoretically, of course, the debt:equity ratio has no impact on the value of equity but it is generally agreed that there is a positive impact of a tax shield caused by using some debt funding, as well as a negative aspect associated with the costs and likelihood of financial distress.

This argument regarding the overall impact of using debt in any other business depends on the net balance of these offsetting influences. Thus in a mature business, it is possible to add value through borrowings because the positive impact of the tax shield normally outweighs the much smaller adverse consequences of potential financial distress. However, the declining business may be thought less likely to pay corporation taxes due to its reducing profit streams, so that the value of the tax shield may be reduced.

(This may be true for normal operating profits but, in most major economies, corporation taxes are affected by many fiscal factors other than pure accounting profits. For instance, many governments allow companies to claim accelerated depreciation allowances for tax purposes, which create differences between taxable profits and accounting profits. Other regimes have given allowances for additional capital invested in inventories. These fiscal adjustments are normally given as incentives for companies to invest, so they are geared to reduce tax liabilities while the company is growing. It is an inevitable consequence, rather than a devious tax strategy, that these adjustments therefore tend to increase tax payments when a company is running down its investment base. Thus declining companies often face a higher effective rate of tax on their profits which can actually increase the value of a tax shield created by raising some debt financing.)

However, declining companies do not need to raise much funding for reinvestment since it has just been established that they are reducing the net value of their asset base. This debt-carrying capacity can therefore be used to produce cash which is paid out to shareholders sooner rather than later. This is achieved by borrowing against the terminal realizable value of the assets locked into the company. If this capital were not realized now, the shareholders would receive a final capital distribution when the company was eventually wound up. By borrowing against these assets now, it should be possible to increase the present value of the related distribution which can be paid to shareholders using the logic that the cost of debt is always lower than the cost of equity, particularly if the benefit of a tax shield further reduces the cost of debt. This is mathematically illustrated in Working insight 7.2.

The debt funding for a declining business is therefore focused on realizable values of assets and this dramatically reduces the costs associated with future

WORKING
7.2

INSIGHT   **Adding value by borrowing in a declining company**

The terminal value of a particular asset is £100 000 and the company is expected to continue operating for another five years. The shareholders' after tax expected return on equity is 15 per cent p.a. but the company can borrow at an after tax rate of 8 per cent p.a.

The present value to the shareholders of the expected terminal value of the asset is

$$\frac{£\ 100\ 000}{(1.15)^5} \quad \text{or} \quad £\ 49\ 717$$

However, if the company borrowed funds against this terminal value at 8 per cent it could obtain £68 058 now, which could be distributed to its shareholders.

Note: In practice, the lender would want to maintain some buffer to allow for fluctuations in the actual terminal value or date of realization: but there is still an opportunity for significant shareholder value creation.

financial distress. Indeed the structuring of the borrowings will be designed to make it easy for lenders to take possession of and realize the value of their security, when the business no longer has an economically viable use for these assets. Consequently the use of a high level of debt funding in a declining business is not really contradictory to the theory, as long as the theory is sensibly applied.

ALTERNATIVE BUSINESS STRATEGIES TO DELAY OR AVOID DEATH

If the appropriate financial strategy is adopted by the company, the decline stage of the life cycle and the ultimate liquidation of the company are not necessarily injurious to shareholder wealth. However, these events are not normally looked at as neutral or non-threatening by the managers involved in the company. The final phase of the life cycle represents one of the most severe challenges to the concept of agency theory, because it may appear essential to many managers that ways must be found to avoid the final act of winding up the company, even though continuing may not be in the best interests of shareholders.

There are many alternative strategies which are employed by businesses to try to delay or avoid their inevitable deaths, only some of which can be beneficial to the shareholders. One obvious strategy is to diversify into other areas but, if the diversification is left until the core business has moved into its decline stage, it will be very difficult for the company to finance the diversification from a declining cash flow. The lack of shareholder wealth creation from diversification has already been considered.

A potentially more attractive strategy is to examine the main reasons why the company is now in decline. Referring back to the basic Boston matrix, it is clear that a major difference between a cash cow and a dog is the lower market share held by the dog company. This may indicate a possible way of adding value to the business, particularly if it is expected that the decline stage may itself last a long while. If there are a large number of small companies in this market, they all face a slow, lingering, painful unproductive death. However, one of the companies may decide to change the dynamics of the industry by acquiring several of its small competitors. The cost of these acquisitions should not be too great as the companies will be making poor current financial returns and be expecting things to get worse in the future. It is possible that a very small premium over the realizable asset value of each business may secure its purchase.

Once the company has achieved a much more dominant market share, it may be able to improve its overall financial return quite significantly. This could be done simply by rationalizing the total capacity of their group so as to remove capacity from the industry, if this is depressing selling prices. Alternatively the greater market share can be used to change the dynamics of the relative bargaining power with both customers and suppliers; thus increasing the share of the value chain gained by this company. In many cases, the end result is that the company discovers that the industry was not really in decline at all; the companies in the industry were in decline due to the disastrous industry dynamics which had been allowed to develop. Thus, as shown in Figure 7.1, the many small businesses are turned back into the single large cash cow.

If this type of rationalization strategy is successful, it can be argued as demonstrating the synergy benefits of acquisitions which are discussed later in the book.

Figure 7.1

Declining industry transformation strategies (using Boston matrix)

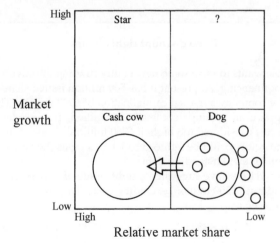

⭘ represents a single company, with size of circle signifying size of company

Note: A single company rationalizes the industry by taking over small competitors until it acquires a dominant share of the market. This dominant share enables it to achieve much greater financial returns than the individual companies could achieve previously.

DEEP DISCOUNT RIGHTS ISSUES

Any attempt to rationalize a very mature or declining industry by a series of acquisitions requires financing to be raised. A logical alternative would be to raise at least some debt, since debt financing is attractive at this latter end of the life cycle. However some equity funding may be considered appropriate and this could be raised via a rights issue to the existing shareholders. (It is most unlikely that the shareholders of the other companies in the industry would find anything other than a full cash offer for their existing shares to be at all attractive; they want to get out of the industry sooner rather than later.) In Chapter 5 the impact of doing a narrow discount rights issue was evaluated and here a similar illustration is used to highlight how a deep discount rights issue works.

The example given in Working insight 7.3 shows a company trying to raise substantial funds which it intends to use to repay some of its excessive outstanding debt. The suggested means of raising new equity is to sell it at a big discount to the existing share price; i.e. a deep discount rights issue. The deep discount simply means that more shares have to be issued to achieve any given fund-raising objectives. Thus in this example the company has to offer a two for one rights issue (i.e. issuing two new shares for each share held) at a price of 25 p. Had the rights exercise price been set at 50 p, a one for one rights issue would have been sufficient; at 100 p, the £250 million could have been raised by selling only 250 million new shares. Remember that any extra shares over this minimum 250 million should therefore be regarded as bonus shares.

WORKING
7.3
INSIGHT   **Deep discount rights issues**

Death Or Glory plc wants to raise some new equity funding in order to repay some of its existing debt financing. At present it has 500 million issued shares trading at £1 each, giving the company a market capitalization of £500 million. This market capitalization supports an existing debt level of £1 billion, giving a debt to market equity of 2:1 which is considered too high; if £250 million of new equity could be raised, this debt to equity could be reduced to 1:1 as long as the new funding was used to repay some of the outstanding debt.

The company's advisers have suggested a rights issue of two for one at 25 p per share which would raise £250 million, excluding costs. The impact of the proposed rights issue can be seen as

500 million issued shares @ £1	⇒	£500 million market capitalization
1000 million new shares @ 25 p	⇒	£250 million rights issue
1500 million total shares ⇒ 50 p	⇐	£750 million new capitalization

The rights value would be 25 p per share (exercise price of 25 p compared to market price at 50 p), so that the gain of 25 p × 2 rights = 50 p compensates for the loss on each existing share of 100 p − 50 p = 50 p, i.e. the two for one rights issue results in no gain and no loss if the share price responds properly.

As discussed in Chapter 5 this means that the terms of the rights issue should not matter, as they cannot make any theoretical difference to the value of the company. However, companies and their advisers obviously believe pricing of rights issues is important, because otherwise they would not spend so much time and money deciding how best to attract investors to subscribe new money.

A large risk associated with the narrow discount rights issue discussed for the growth company in Chapter 5 was that the rights inclusive share price could fall below the exercise price of the rights during the rights offer period. This risk could be hedged but these underwriting costs were described as 'inefficiently high'. If the scale of the discount were increased there might be a lower perceived risk of the rights having no value. In Working insight 7.3, the current share price of £1 is predicted to fall to 50 p because of the deep discount offered and the consequent number of new shares which have to be issued. However, the rights are being offered at an exercise price of 25 p so that the market price has to halve again before the rights have no value. The company may decide not to underwrite the issue or, if underwriting is taken up, the premium charged should be significantly reduced as the risk of the effective put option being exercised by the company is now lower.

(At least, it would be lower if investors behaved totally rationally but there is a great deal of psychology in pricing rights issues. If the market believes that successful growth companies raise new equity through narrow discount rights issues, it tends to accept that a company offering a narrow discount rights issue is successful and has good growth potential. Conversely, if deep discount rights issues are normally made by very mature or declining companies with negative growth prospects, the market may assume that any company making such an issue must have those attributes.)

A key issue is how will investors respond to such an offer. Investors owning 1000 shares in DOG plc receive their notifications of their rights to buy another 2000 shares in the company at the very reduced price of 25 p per share. Even if they like the deep discount, taking up the offer requires them to invest another 50 per cent (£500) on top of the current value of their investment in DOG (£1000). This is a high proportionate increase in investment in one share and for a rational investor this may unbalance the investment portfolio. Other investors may be feeling unhappy about their investment in the company, because, in this example, it is overleveraged and has no positive growth prospects.

There is a strong possibility that many investors may not want to take up their rights. This possibility is increased when the alternative of selling the rights and obtaining cash is added in. Instead of investing an additional £500, the investor with 1000 shares should be able to sell the associated 2000 rights and receive £500 in cash. Of course if the market responds properly, there is no resulting change in value from either course of action but the perception of investors may be different.

If a lot of investors decide to sell their rights, the law of supply and demand means that the rights value will fall. The rights exercise price is fixed so that, if the rights value falls, the share price must also fall by a considerable amount. The decline in share prices closes the gap between it and the rights exercise price, thus making the rights offer look even less attractive than before. Deep discount rights offers have been known to fail when investors simply lost confidence in the company and its shares; not least because the company was offering lots of new shares at 25 p when they are supposed to be worth £1. The danger is that investors start to believe that the £1 share price was wrong and that 25 p is a better reflection of the true value of all the shares.

In addition to being used by declining companies, deep discount rights issues are also of use in company restructuring. Chapter 13 gives illustrations of this.

ADDING VALUE BY REDUCING DEBT RATIOS

Death Or Glory plc is actually raising these new equity funds in order to increase shareholder value by reducing its debt:equity ratio. How this can work is illustrated in Working insights 7.4 and 7.5, which indicate the way in which excessive risk perceptions lead to greater demands for returns, which can drive down investment values.

Normally an increase in the proportion of equity funding would lead to an increase in the weighted average cost of capital (WACC), because the cost of equity is greater than the cost of debt. However, if the existing funding mix contains substantial risk premiums which can be reduced or removed by a change in financial strategy, the overall WACC can actually reduce after the

---

WORKING 7.4 INSIGHT

Reducing risk perceptions and adding value

Death Or Glory plc currently has to pay a premium interest rate of 15 per cent before tax (compared to the normal rate for similar companies of 12 per cent) due to its high debt to equity ratio. Its shareholders' required return is also higher, due to increased perceptions of the risk of financial collapse: thus DOG's cost of equity capital is 20 per cent compared to the 16 per cent demanded from similar companies with normal leverage ratios.

Extracts from DOG's financial data are as follows.

	£m	
Operating profit	337.50	
Less: interest expense	150.00	(£1 billion @ 15%)
Profit before tax	187.50	
Taxation	62.50	
Profit after tax	125.00	
Number of shares	500 million	
Earnings per share	25 pence	
P/E multiple	4 times	
Share price	100 pence	

Note: a P/E multiple of four is applied, as this is slightly below the inverse of the company's cost of equity capital (20 per cent). This reflects the fact that (a) the company is declining rather than at steady state, and (b) there is a risk premium due to the over-gearing.

WORKING
7.5

INSIGHT

Post-rights issue position

If DOG raises £250 million through a rights issue it will be able to reduce both its borrowing cost and its cost of equity. However, the relative proportion of equity in its financial structure will rise, as the new funds are used to repay some of the existing debt. Assuming nothing else changes, the post-rights P&L can be restated as follows.

	£m	
Operating profit	337.50	
Less: interest expense	90.00	(£750 m @ 12%)
Profit before tax	247.50	
Taxation	82.50	
Profit after tax	165.00	
Number of shares	1500 million	(1 billion new share issued)
Earnings per share	11 pence	
P/E multiple	5 times	
Share price	55 pence	

The company's cost of equity has decreased to 16 per cent due to the lower perceived risk of financial collapse. However, as a declining company, the P/E will still be lower than the inverse of the cost of equity. In Working insight 7.4 we reduced the 'steady state' P/E of five by 20 per cent to arrive at four; here we reduce the 'steady state' P/E of 6.25 by a similar proportion, to five times. In practice, the P/E may be slightly higher than this, reflecting a re-rating by the market.

injection of new funding. This would obviously lead to an increase in equity value as discussed in Appendix 1 and highlighted in Working insight 7.5.

If the stock market saw no value added from DOG's rights issue, the post-rights share price should fall from 100 p to 50 p as shown in Working insight 7.3. However, the reductions in both borrowing costs and shareholders' expected returns mean that the share price should move to 55 p rather than to 50 p; thus producing increased value for the existing shareholders due to the reduction in risk premium demanded.

7.1 RECKITT BENCKISER – MANAGING DIVISIONS IN DECLINE

CASE STUDY

Reckitt Benckiser, the Anglo Dutch household products group, made a strategic decision to manage certain of its divisions using a 'decline' strategy. The company had attempted to sell these non core divisions, but prices were not acceptable. Accordingly, it announced that these businesses would be run separately from the rest of the group, with the aim of maximizing total cash return. This releases cash for the group to reinvest in areas in which it can generate better returns.

Source: The *Financial Times* 29 August 2001

Financial Instruments

8

Financial instruments: the building blocks

In previous chapters we established that investors require a return to compensate them for the risk they are taking by making an investment in a company's securities. That return can come from a running yield on their investment, or through a capital gain on the sale of the investment. In this chapter we examine these three building blocks of value – risk, yield and capital gain – and see how they can be used to build a variety of financial instruments. We show how black and white distinctions between 'debt' and 'equity' become blurred as different instruments are designed.

The different ways in which risk can be mitigated are considered, as are the various common forms through which companies provide yield and potential gain to their investors. We note that different companies have different requirements, and these should be matched to the requirements of investor groups in order to design the most efficient financial structure

INTRODUCTION

Investors need to make a return on their money. That return can come from a yield or a capital gain, or both. The amount of return they require depends on the level of risk that they perceive they are taking. Within this simple framework there is a vast panoply of financial instruments that can be created to serve the different needs of companies and their investors.

Throughout this book we have been talking about Debt and Equity. Now is the time to define our terms more carefully. What do we mean by 'debt', and how do we differentiate it from 'equity'? In this chapter we will answer those questions, and explain the building blocks used to create all financial instruments. Chapter 9 will describe some of the more common financial instruments, and discuss how and why they are used.

RISK AND RETURN

It is worth noting that the risk–return continuum provides an overall regulation of what we can do with financial instruments.

For example, if we lend money to a blue chip company (invest in its debt) we can, at the time of writing, obtain a return of about 6 per cent on the investment. When we make the investment the company is contracted to pay us a fixed level of interest at agreed intervals, and to return our money when the debt falls due for repayment. Should the company fail to do this we will have redress to the law, and perhaps have security over its assets; lending to such a company is a relatively low risk activity, and thus we should only expect a relatively low return.

Contrast this with the situation were we to invest in the ordinary shares of the same company. As shareholders we may or may not be paid a dividend, depending on the company's results and the directors' intentions. We may, if the company succeeds in the stock markets, be able to sell the shares for a huge capital gain at some point in the future; but there is no guarantee of this – the company may just 'crash and burn' and we could lose everything in a liquidation.

So, whereas we can reasonably anticipate the returns that we will obtain on the debt investment, there is huge volatility in the expected return from an investment in shares. That volatility of anticipated return is the risk we take, and

Figure 8.1

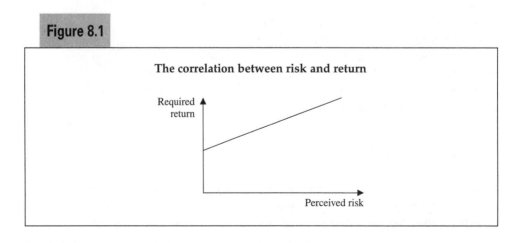

The correlation between risk and return

it is for this that we need to be compensated. If debt pays us 6 per cent, we will demand a much higher return from our shares. (For a discussion of how much extra we might require, see the discussion on the Capital Asset Pricing Model in Appendix 1.)

As discussed in Chapter 1, it is also worth noting that individual investors perceive risk in different ways, and thus demand different levels of return for what is technically the same amount of risk. One of your authors has a very low risk threshold for personal investment, preferring the certainty of a secure retirement to the possible glory of earning millions on speculative investment. This risk/required return profile looks like that shown in Figure 8.2.

However, a venture capitalist may see the risk/return spectrum in an entirely different way. Such an investor is really not interested in low risk investments, as their whole *raison d'etre* is in making high gains on more speculative investments. Their risk profile looks more like that shown in Figure 8.3.

Figure 8.2

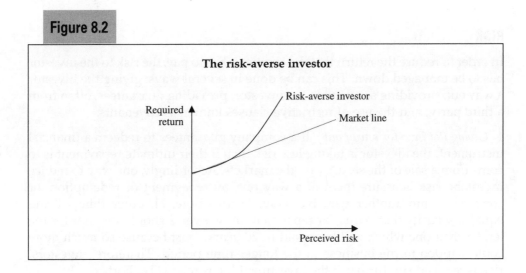

The risk-averse investor

Figure 8.3

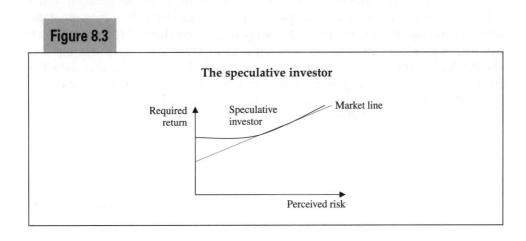

The speculative investor

Knowing that the market includes investors with different appetites for risk, a company can design its financial instruments to suit a particular class of investor. In the next section, we discuss the parameters within which this can take place.

THE BUILDING BLOCKS OF A FINANCIAL INSTRUMENT

As stated above, the return investors require is dependent on their perception of the risk inherent in their investment. That return will comprise some combination of yield and the upside which comes normally from a capital gain. Thus, the three building blocks we can manipulate are:

- Risk
- Yield
- Upside

Each of these is now considered in turn.

RISK

In order to reduce the return that the company has to pay, the risk to the investor has to be managed down. This can be done in several ways: giving the investor a way out; providing security[1] to the investor; providing guarantees, often from a third party; and the use of restrictive clauses known as covenants.

1. *Giving the investor a way out*   If a company guarantees to redeem a financial instrument, the investor is taking less risk than if their ultimate repayment is to come from a sale of the security on the markets. Accordingly, one way to reduce investors' risk is assure them of a way out, by repayment or redemption, or conversion into another valuable asset. Furthermore, all other things being equal, a security that is due for repayment in two years should be safer for the lender than one which will be repaid in 20 years – just because so much more could happen to the business in the longer time period. Therefore, investors' risk is reduced still further if the investment life is relatively short.

2. *Providing security*   The company can provide security to the investor, often referred to as a 'charge' on the company's assets, such that if it fails to meet the terms of the agreement, the investor can protect their downside in some way. For example, a debt may be secured on a property owned by the company; should the borrower fail to pay interest, or to repay the loan on the due date, the lender can seize the charged property and sell it off in order to recover the monies owed. This gives the investor another 'way out' in case the company fails to meet its contracted obligations.

---

1. It should be noted that the term 'security' has two separate meanings. This chapter has so far been discussing securities as a generic term for financial instruments. The term is also used to refer to a mechanism which gives the investors some further means through which they can be repaid if the company defaults, for example, the ability to repossess assets.

Under current UK law, security comes in two flavours – fixed and floating. The difference between them is quite technical, but broadly a fixed charge is one over specific assets such as buildings or fixed plant, and a floating charge is a charge over assets which change on a daily or weekly basis, such as stocks. In a liquidation, the holder of a fixed charge has the higher priority. They can use the proceeds of selling the assets subject to that charge in order to recover their due debts. Holders of floating charges can be repaid from the monies released by selling these assets, but they have a lower priority to the fixed charge holders and to various statutory creditors. However, any type of security puts the lender in a better position than the unsecured creditors.

3. *Providing a third party guarantee*   Investors need to ensure that their downside is limited. However, there is no law that says that the company itself has to provide this assurance. If the company is unable to provide the assurance, it is possible that a third party could do so. For example, a holding company or a major shareholder might agree to guarantee the loan.

4. *Covenants*   Covenants are conditions in a loan contract which protect the lender by stating what the borrower may or may not do. Covenants come in two types – positive covenants and negative covenants.

Positive covenants are loan conditions which state what the borrower must do. For example, the borrowing company must deliver management accounts within a certain period after the month end; must deliver audited annual accounts within a given period; must maintain agreed levels of accounting figures and ratios (such as the level of equity or the working capital ratios).

Negative covenants are clauses which prevent the borrower from undertaking certain actions. For example, negative covenants will prevent directors' remuneration being increased above a pre-agreed level, so that the business loan is not immediately transferred to the directors' benefit. In the same way, there will be covenants preventing large dividends being paid, or setting a maximum level of pay for non-directors. There will also be covenants in place preventing a company from taking further loans, which may have precedence in repayment, unless the lender gives consent. Negative covenants will also prevent the company from spending large amounts on fixed assets that have not been previously agreed with the bank: this ensures that the monies borrowed are spent on the new factory rather than the director's Ferrari!

The main use of covenants is that a breach of the covenant terms can mean that the lender can demand repayment of the loan, even thought its term is not yet due. The ability to demand such repayment is valuable to lenders, to enable them to recover their money before things get worse. However, it should be noted that in some instances lenders will accept a breach of covenants, as they are aware that calling in the loan could result in the company going into liquidation without their being able to realize their money.

YIELD

The yield of a security includes any payment made to the investors during the period for which the investment is outstanding, other than payments which reduce the capital balance. Thus, practical examples include interest on loans and dividends on shares. However, share repurchases or loan redemptions would not be included in yield, as they are capital items.

The yield can be a regular payment, such as contracted quarterly interest, or can be on a more irregular basis, such as an occasional dividend. It can be for a set amount, again such as interest, or at the discretion of the paying company. The fact that a yield is at the discretion of the paying company does not necessarily make it an unpredictable amount – Chapter 10 points out that companies which pay dividends need to maintain a track record of level or increasing payments; this is an example of a discretionary payment which the investor has come to expect.

Yields are often linked to an underlying reference point. For example, interest rates on debt may be fixed rate or floating. Floating rate loans charge interest based on a premium over a reference rate such as LIBOR (London Inter Bank Offered Rate). For example, the contracted interest rate might be set at LIBOR plus a premium of 1 per cent.[2] If LIBOR is 5 per cent, then the interest rate paid on the loan will be 6 per cent; if LIBOR rises to 5.5 per cent, the loan will be charged at 6.5 per cent.

Floating rate interest can reduce risk for the lender, as it ensures that the lender will always receive 'market' rates on the loan. However, it leaves the borrowing company vulnerable to rises in market rates: in the example above, were LIBOR to rise to say 15 per cent (which was the case in the late 1980s), the company would have to pay 16 per cent, which may stretch its cashflow considerably. In order to minimize the borrower's risk in this, interest rate management tools such as caps and collars can be used. The Annex to this chapter set out details of some interest rate management tools.

Yield need not be as predictable as regular interest payments, or dividend payments on a particular trend. One of the authors was involved in designing a capital instrument to finance the construction of a wind farm, in which the main objective was to return as much cash as possible to the shareholders, subject only to bank restrictions. The yield on this instrument was determined as the amount shown as free cash flow (strictly defined) in cash flow forecasts for the wind farm for the following six months; once the banks' requirements were met, all of the free cash was paid out to shareholders.

UPSIDE

The investor obtains an upside from selling the security for an amount greater than was originally invested in it; the upside is the capital gain. The upside can come from various different sources:

a. ultimate sale of the financial instrument to another investor;
b. redemption of the instrument at a premium by the investee company, the premium being paid in cash or in the securities of the investee company;

---

2. The premium would actually be stated as 100 basis points. A basis point is 1/100 of a per cent.

c. redemption at a premium, with a premium denominated in the securities of another company or in another asset.

Each of these is considered below.

a. *Sale of the financial instrument to another investor*   This form of exit is most commonly seen by purchasers of shares listed on a stock exchange. The shares are liquid, in that there are many potential buyers and sellers, and the market sets a price. The holder of the investment can choose to sell at the market price, or can continue to hold the shares in the hope that the price will rise. The difference between the ultimate sales proceeds and the initial amount invested is the capital gain. (This will probably be subject to tax in the hands of the investor, but such taxation is country-specific, may indeed be investor-specific, and is outside the scope of this book.) The company that issued the shares has no interest in this disposal, which is strictly between the buying and selling investors. There is also no guarantee that the disposal price will be greater than the price originally paid for the investment.

b. *Redemption by the investee company at a premium*   Many financial instruments have a defined life, and incorporate a contract to the effect that the company will redeem the instrument at the end of this period. If the agreement is that redemption will take place at par, i.e. with no uplift, then the investor's return comes solely through the yield. However, although the investee company may agree to redeem the security at cost, it is common to agree a redemption premium which gives the investor a capital gain. The premium may be for a fixed amount, or dependent on other factors. An example of a fixed premium might be:

> Company A issues £1 000 000 of a security which will be repurchased in five years' time for £1 200 000.

This gives the investor a capital gain of £200 000 in addition to any yield on the security.

(It is also common for securities which give a repayment premium to carry 'zero interest' as a coupon, with the investor's return being totally rolled up in the final payment.)

Another way of structuring this transaction would be to issue the security at a discount:

> Company B issues a security with a face value of £1 200 000, for £1 000 000. In five years' time the security will be redeemed at face value.

This 'deep discounted bond' achieves the same effect for the investor as in Company A, but may lead to a favourable tax treatment for the issuer.

Instead of a fixed premium, the ultimate amount of capital gain may be unknown when the investment is made. For example:

> Company C issues a security for £1 000 000. In five years' time the £1 000 000 will be repaid and, in addition, the investor will receive shares representing 2 per cent of the equity of Company C.

Here, the value of the upside (known as an 'equity kicker') is dependent on the value of Company C's equity in five years' time; the investor is taking the risk that Company C will perform well, and the potential upside will indeed be valuable. The deal could also have been structured in a different way, as follows.

> Company D issues a security for £1 000 000. In five years' time the investor has the option either of receiving £1 000 000 cash in redemption of the security, or of receiving 200 000 of Company D's shares.

In this example, the investor obvious expects that 200 000 of Company D's shares will be valued at more than £1 000 000 in five years' time – ie that the share price will exceed £5 per share. If the share price is higher than £5, the investor will obtain the capital gain by converting the security into shares in Company D. If Company D has not performed well, the investor will instead ask for the £1 000 000 in cash.

c. *Redemption by the investee company with a premium in securities of another company or in another asset*   Yet another way to obtain the capital uplift would be to enter into an agreement that gave the investor rights over another company's securities. This can be illustrated using an example.

> Company E issues a security for £1 000 000. In five years' time, the investor can either redeem the security for £1 000 000 cash, or can exchange it for 100 000 shares in Company F. As in the case of Company D, the investor is gambling on a share price rise, this time it is the price of Company F that is critical.

Normally, if the capital upside is structured to come from the shares of a third company, there will be a link between the issuing company and the third party. For example, Company F might be a spun-out subsidiary of Company E, or maybe Company E holds shares in Company F as part of a trade investment which it seeks, long term, to reduce. Similarly, there is no reason why the upside should not come from the proceeds of sale of another asset, for example a business property. The key point is that the issuing company should be able to deliver to its investors the asset(s) providing the upside at the time they are required.

DEFINING 'DEBT' AND 'EQUITY'

Now that the basics have been explored, we are ready to look at the two fundamental financial instruments – debt and equity. How do these compare on our three headings?

Debt is a low risk instrument from the lender's point of view (although, of course, it is high risk to the borrower). A contract is entered into which specifies how long the monies will be outstanding, and schedules their repayments; legally, the lender is a creditor of the company. The agreement also states what interest (the yield) is to be paid, and how. The lender's downside is often protected by taking security over specified assets of the borrower. Further

Figure 8.4

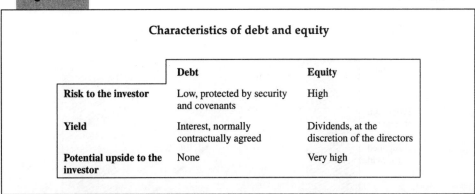

Characteristics of debt and equity

	Debt	Equity
Risk to the investor	Low, protected by security and covenants	High
Yield	Interest, normally contractually agreed	Dividends, at the discretion of the directors
Potential upside to the investor	None	Very high

downside protection may be obtained through the use of covenants – loan clauses which state clearly what the borrower may and may not do while the loan is in place. During the term of the loan repayments are made, to the agreed schedule, which fully repay the capital balance. There is no upside for the lender; the return comes only by way of yield.

Contrast that with equity, in the form of ordinary shares. This is permanent capital for the company. The investor puts money into the company with no guarantee of any return at all. The yield comes, if it comes at all, at the directors' discretion, dependent on the levels of cash and profit, and the company's future investment needs. If the company does well, there may be an upside, in that the shares can be sold at a profit. However, there is no guarantee that the company will do well, or its value will be recognized by the market. This is a high risk investment.

Figure 8.4 summarizes the characteristics of debt and equity.

To give an example: in 1976 the sales revenue of Microsoft exceeded $1 million for the first time. If your authors had at that time lent $5000 to the fledgling Microsoft, we would have handed over the money, received interest for a few years, and then been repaid our $5000. If instead we had invested $5000 of private equity in Microsoft stock...we would not have needed to work so hard for the royalties on this book!

MANIPULATING THE BUILDING BLOCKS

We have established that the financial instrument must offer investors a return commensurate with the risk they perceive, and that such return will be derived from a yield and/or a capital gain. From these basic concepts, two important ideas can be developed:

1. The expected return on a financial instrument must be consistent with the investor's perceived risk.

   Therefore, target instruments at categories of investor who will understand the risks involved, and not charge a premium for their lack of understanding.

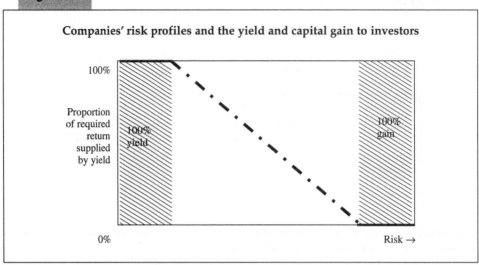

Companies' risk profiles and the yield and capital gain to investors

2. The return will come from yield and upside.

Therefore, an instrument with very high yield would be expected to provide little or no upside, and investors agreeing to receive no yield would anticipate the possibility of a high capital gain.

One final point is worth noting. We established in Chapter 3 that companies in the launch and growth stages of the lifecycle should be financed mostly with equity; those in later stages can afford debt financing. The reasons behind this financial strategy relate to the business risk of the different stages, and to the companies' requirements for funding for growth. These arguments can be extended to consider the different types of financial instrument that a company may wish to use.

Figure 8.5 illustrates the yield/gain continuum of possibilities for providing return to investors. On the left hand side of Figure 8.5, investors receive a return from yield only. This is appropriate when business risks are low. As business risk increases (and, generally, the need for funds for growth also increases) it becomes advisable to provide the return less by yield and more as capital growth. At the extreme right hand side of Figure 8.5, high risk companies use instruments with no yield at all.

Chapter 9 discusses various different types of financial instrument on the market, and shows how these rules are met in practice

ANNEX: INTEREST RATE MANAGEMENT TOOLS

Interest rate management tools are used to lower the financing risk for companies which have borrowed at a floating rate. Floating rate loans bear interest based on a reference rate plus a premium. If the reference rate falls, the company will pay less interest. However, unexpected increases in market interest rates could lead to the company having to pay a much larger than anticipated charge:[3] the interest rate management tools can help protect against this.

REFERENCE RATES

In the UK, and many other jurisdictions, the reference rate most commonly used is LIBOR (London Inter Bank Offered Rate – the rate at which banks lend to each other in London.) The equivalent rate for the 12 countries within Economic and Monetary Union is EURIBOR.

There are several different types of LIBOR, representing money being lent for varying periods. The rates most commonly used as reference points for floating rate debt are three month LIBOR and six month LIBOR. A rate for LIBOR is set every working day by the financial markets, and it will vary depending on supply and demand and market conditions.

As an example, CapCo might borrow say £1m for two years at a rate of three month LIBOR plus 2 per cent (200 basis points). On the first day of the loan, three month LIBOR might be 5 per cent; this means that CapCo will pay interest at 7 per cent (5% + 2%) for three months. At the end of the three months, the new rate for three month LIBOR would be used to set the rate of interest due for the next three month period. If six month LIBOR had been used as the reference rate, CapCo's interest would have remained at that level for six months.

CAPS, FLOORS AND COLLARS

CapCo may be comfortable borrowing when LIBOR is 5 per cent, and may be relaxed about LIBOR rising to say 9 per cent. However, at levels above that there may be problems in meeting interest payments. In order to protect its position, the company can buy an interest rate *cap*. This is in effect an insurance policy that prevents the company having to pay interest at more than a given rate.

For example, Barland Bank has lent CapCo £1 m for two years at three month LIBOR plus 2 per cent. Three month LIBOR is currently 5 per cent. The company wishes to ensure that even if LIBOR rises above 9 per cent, it will not have to pay any more than a total of 11 per cent on its loan (i.e. 9% + 2%). Accordingly, it can buy a LIBOR cap at 9 per cent.

There are several points to note about buying the cap. Firstly, the cap need not be acquired from Barland Bank, who provided the loan. In fact, Barland need not even know about the existence of the cap – CapCo has in fact bought it from ScotWest bank, and it is a separate financial transaction to the loan. This leads to the second point: technically, having a cap does not prevent the company having to pay high interest rates to its lender – it just means that it can offset this

---

3. If market interest rates rise, the company could face a 'double whammy'. Not only will the company's interest charge increase, but the economic factors behind the rate rise may lead to depressed sales, low profits and cashflow problems. Alas, the interest rate management tools only deal with the interest charge – the rest is still management's problem.

extra interest by the receipts from the bank which sold it the cap. So, if LIBOR were to rise to 12 per cent, CapCo would have to pay Barland interest at 14 per cent, but would receive interest back from ScotWest amounting to 3 per cent, leaving it paying a net 11 per cent. And the third point to note is that although the loan is for £1 m, the cap could be for less than that amount, or more, if CapCo wishes to speculate on interest rates!

Acquiring the cap will cost CapCo an up-front payment, the level of which depends on the rate capped, and the time for which it is needed. For example, if our company wanted to cap LIBOR at 6 per cent, it would be a great deal more expensive than capping at 9 per cent; similarly, a six month cap would be cheaper to buy than a two year cap.

Should CapCo wish to avoid paying for its cap, it could enter into a transaction to sell a *floor* to a bank. Just as buying a cap means that the company's interest rate will never move above a certain amount, selling a floor means that even if market rates fall the company will not be able to take full advantage of it. So CapCo might sell ScotWest (or another bank) a LIBOR floor at 4 per cent. This would mean that should LIBOR fall to say 3 per cent, CapCo would be paying Barland interest on its loan at 5 per cent (3% + 2%) but would also be paying 1 per cent (4% − 3%) to ScotWest which owns the floor.

The purchase of a cap and a floor together is known as a *collar*. If terms are set properly, the amount that the company would have had to pay for purchasing the cap can be exactly offset by the amount the bank is paying it for the floor. This is known, unsurprisingly, as a *zero cost collar*.

SWAPS

Another type of interest rate management tool is an interest rate swap. Here, a company which has borrowed at a floating rate agrees to swap interest rate payments with a counter-party which has borrowed at a fixed rate. There may be several reasons for doing this – perhaps our company cannot borrow floating rate in the market, or perhaps the other company is changing its financing strategy and wants to move out of fixed interest. But generally, swaps are done because both parties can make money on them – this is because of the theory of comparative advantage.

The theory of comparative advantage argues that two parties can benefit from trading, even when one of them is more efficient in all cases than the other. In terms of interest rate management, it is most easily explained by an example.

SwapCo can borrow in the markets at 8 per cent fixed rate, or at LIBOR + 2 per cent. FixCo can borrow at 6 per cent fixed rate, or at LIBOR + 1.5 per cent. It can be seen that FixCo has the advantage on both types of borrowing:

	Fixed rate	Floating
SwapCo	8%	LIBOR + 2%
FixCo	6%	LIBOR + 1.5%
FixCo's comparative advantage	2%	0.5%

Each company wants to borrow £1 m. SwapCo would like fixed rate funds, and FixCo would like floating rate funds. If each of them were to borrow the types of funds they wanted, the total rate they would pay would be LIBOR plus 9.5 per cent. However, if SwapCo were to borrow floating rate and FixCo at a fixed rate, the total they paid would be LIBOR plus 8 per cent. It is thus worthwhile for them to borrow at the combined lower rate, and then to swap payments.

So, SwapCo will borrow £1 m at a floating rate, paying LIBOR plus 2 per cent. FixCo will borrow £1 m at 6 per cent fixed. Then the swap agreement will ensure that SwapCo makes the payments at 6 per cent fixed, and FixCo pays at LIBOR plus 2 per cent. The overall saving of 1.5 per cent can be split between the two, and used to reduce FixCo's payment to (at most) the LIBOR plus 1.5 per cent that it would have paid on its own.

Types of financial instrument

As discussed in Chapter 8, financial instruments can be constructed from any commercially acceptable combination of risk protection, yield and upside potential. Thus, companies can select potentially a wide variety of financial instruments to meet their exact needs, and those of their investors.

In this chapter we examine the factors affecting the choice of financial instrument, and discuss the characteristics of some of the commonly used financial instruments. We show that the distinction between 'debt' and 'equity' is blurred, and that there is in fact a continuum of financial instruments which have debt-like and equity-like characteristics. Option theory can be used to identify in any situation which instrument has preferential claims over others; this is perhaps the best way to define 'debt'.

WHAT DO COMPANIES NEED?

As set out in Chapter 3, the basic tenet of sound financial strategy is that the company should match its financing risk to its level of business risk. Companies with a high level of business risk should try to ensure that they do not add to the volatility of their results by taking on financial risk. Similarly, companies with a low business risk will find it worthwhile to use financial instruments that increase their risk profile but reduce their average cost of capital.

Chapter 8 looked at the risk of financial instruments from the point of view of the investor, and stated that debt was relatively low risk, and equity high risk. For the company, of course, the risk relationship is reversed. Borrowing is a high risk activity for companies, as they have to find the resources to make interest payments and repay the principal. Equity is low risk finance for a company as it is permanent, the shareholders having no contractual right to payments from the company.

In addition to the fundamental business risk–financial risk relationship, companies structuring long term financial instruments should concern themselves with two other variables: cash and profits.

Companies which are cash-constrained are best served by using financial instruments that do not demand any significant outflows of cash, at least in the short term. Growing companies, needing their resources to fund expansion, do not wish to pay out such resources to repay their lenders; they are better off with equity, or with an instrument that delays payouts. However, companies which are generating significant cash flows may be able to use debt, knowing that they have the means to repay it.

The profit impact of the financial instrument is a somewhat different matter. Although we have already established that shareholder value has only an indirect link to current profit, the effect on profits (and in particular eps) will also need to be considered by companies in their financing structure, as it might impact on the market's perception of them. Profit reduction due to interest payments may lead companies away from the use of debt, or towards an instrument that dilutes profits in the longer term but not the short term.

DIFFERENTIATING FINANCIAL INSTRUMENTS USING OPTION THEORY

Shortly, we will introduce a model of the continuum of financial products, ranking each in order on the risk–return continuum. Before we do that, this section discusses option theory as a method of making these rankings. (Option theory is discussed more fully in Appendix 2.)

The right to buy something is known as a call option; the right to sell is a put option. These concepts can be helpful in trying to distinguish between different classes of debt and equity sources of funding, provided we have a clear understanding of the relative rights and responsibilities of each party providing finance to a company.

It is generally accepted that in a company with outstanding debt, the equity of a company can be regarded as a call option on the assets of the business, at an exercise price equal to the value of the outstanding debt. This is because if the shareholders want to maintain control of the business, they must ensure that the debt obligations are met, otherwise the debt holders will exercise their rights as creditors of the company, and (by appointing a receiver or liquidator) take control of the assets. Thus the repayment of the debt is the amount to be paid to take control of the unencumbered assets of the company.

An alternate way of looking at this is that the shareholders could be seen as holding a put option on the company's assets to the debt holders. Thus, if the gross value of the company exceeds the value of debt, the shareholders will exercise their call option, repaying the debt and regaining control. Should the gross value of the company be less than the value of debt, shareholders can utilize their put option and let the creditors take control of the assets, walking away from the business. (Of course, this only works in situations where the shareholders have limited liability.)

How does this help us to clarify the graduations from debt to equity? It certainly helps to rank the order of priority of these different types of funding, because it focuses attention on which parties have options. However, you will see when we reach the next section that in practice there is a whole series of options held by each type of financial instrument over its neighbours.

The discussion on methods of risk protection in Chapter 8 suggested that the primary method of protecting the downside is that the instrument should have another way out. This is a good place to start in defining debt: debt has another way out. If the business fails to meet its contractual obligations, the lender can realize the security charged in its favour. Thus, we could say that the lender has a call option on some of the company's assets, which they can exercise if redemption is in doubt: the lender has the right, but not the obligation, to call in the receivers.

In ranking financial instruments, the types of option in existence – and who has the right to exercise them – are important in determining priority. In the example above, the shareholders always have the option not to repay the debt. Normally, the lenders' call option on the assets is only of value if there are sufficiently restrictive covenants surrounding the loan that the lender can act to recover the monies before the value of his/her security has been damaged. If the lender has minimal covenants in place, such that she/he can only act once the company has defaulted, then the option is worth a lot less than one which could be exercised at an earlier stage, as the assets might already have lost much of their value.

Lenders should also try to protect themselves against the subsequent creation of superior options to their own. They should have covenants in place to prevent the exercise of call options by lenders with a position that should be subordinated to their own. (For example, using terms that will be defined in the next section, one would not expect the lender of junior debt to be able to call in the receivers of a company if the holders of senior debt did not so wish.)

TRADABLE FINANCIAL INSTRUMENTS

One further point to be noted about financial instruments is that they can be the subject of a private transaction, or can be traded on public markets. For example, a company could borrow directly from its bank, or could raise bonds on the markets. From the lender's point of view, publicly traded debt has the advantage that it gives another way out – the lender can sell the debt before it falls due, releasing the capital for other uses.

If the debt is publicly tradable, it is important to realize that the lender may be able to make a capital gain (or a capital loss) on selling it. The value of traded debt fluctuates depending on its coupon (interest rate based on the nominal amount of the principal) and market rates. Thus, with the very low interest rates prevailing at the time of writing, a debt instrument issued several years ago with a coupon on 10 per cent will probably trade at greater than £100 per £100 nominal value. (Chapter 1 explored this in more detail.) Of course, by the time the debt falls due, the instrument should be trading at exactly £100 per £100, as that is what the investor will be getting (unless of course there is a possibility of default, in which case the debt will trade at a discount to reflect this).

The fact that a debt is publicly traded may make little difference to the borrowing company, which still has to service the interest and repayments. However, it does give the directors the flexibility of being able to re-purchase the debt in the market, and cancel it. For example, in early September 2001 Colt Telecom paid some £68 m to buy back £115 m of its bonds, which were trading at a discount to face value. This effectively reduced net debt by £47 m: a useful action at a time when Colt, like most European telecom companies, was facing market unease about its significant debt burden. The company's director of investor relations was quoted in the *Financial Times* as stating, '...it's a bit like someone standing on a street corner selling £1 coins for 60 p...It's madness not to buy them'.

THE CONTINUUM OF MODERN FINANCIAL PRODUCTS

Financial instruments can be created with any combination of risk-protection, yield and potential gain. It is useful to be able to set them out on a continuum, showing which are the riskier (for the investor) and how the potential returns

Figure 9.1

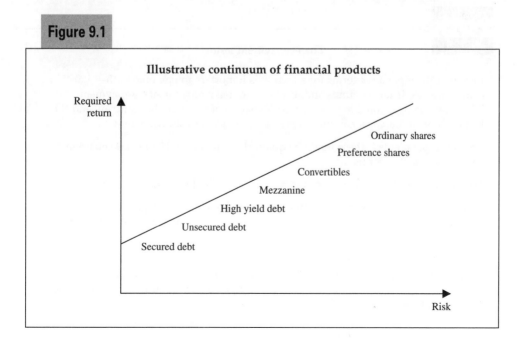

Illustrative continuum of financial products

might change. If this is done, companies have a framework from which they can begin to determine how they should finance themselves.

The continuum set out in Figure 9.1 runs from secured debt as the safest instrument (for the investor) up to ordinary share capital as the riskiest. Other securities are shown at points on the risk–return continuum between these two extremes. It should be pointed out that not all of the securities discussed in this chapter are included, and that the positioning of the securities on the risk–return line is inevitably somewhat arbitrary. The actual risk–return position of any security will depend on the specific terms of the contract under which it is written. Thus, although it is possible to state that high yield bonds (junk bonds) are riskier than senior debt and will provide a greater potential return, it is not possible in all cases to say whether high yield bonds are riskier than mezzanine, or vice versa. The chart should be read with a certain degree of flexibility, and an appreciation that the terms of each individual transaction are vital to an understanding of who has what options over which assets, and so which security is taking the greater risk.

Set out below are brief descriptions of some common securities and how they are used.

SECURED DEBT

Downside protection: charge over assets; covenants
Yield: interest
Upside potential: none

Secured debt is a loan made to the company on the strength of good security, with a registered charge being taken over certain assets (or all of the assets) of

---

WORKING
9.1
INSIGHT

Loan repayment terms

In setting the repayment terms for a loan, it is important to pay note to the company's needs for the funds and its ability to make repayments. Repayment schedules can be tailored to meet any combination of needs of the company and the lender. Some of the most common types of repayment are shown below.

Regular repayments: these might be quarterly or monthly. The loan is repaid in equal instalments over its life.

Bullet repayment: the whole loan is repaid in one 'bullet' at the end of its life.

Balloon repayment: repayments in early years are relatively small. In later years of the loan the repayments might grow, but the main quantum of the loan is repaid at the end.

Capital holiday: if the company is going to be unable to make loan repayments in early years, it might be sensible to allow for a repayments holiday for say the first two years of the loan. Repayments after that might be by regular instalments, or by way of a balloon.

the company. Strong covenants would be in place to ensure that the company could not misuse the monies advanced, and to ensure that the lender would have advance warning of any decline in the company's position. The loan agreement would set out details of the amount of the loan, and the repayment terms (see Working insight 9.1). As the loan is relatively low risk, it should carry a relatively low rate of interest. Accordingly, companies that can afford to borrow (mature businesses with good cash flow and strong asset backing) would make use of this type of instrument.

A company may borrow different tranches of secured debt carrying different conditions. Debt with the strongest claims on the company would be known as 'senior debt'. From this, we can determine that securities known as 'junior debt' will have much weaker claims on the company, and will charge a higher rate of interest to compensate for their greater risk.

LEASING

Downside protection: ownership of assets; covenants
Yield: interest
Upside potential: none

Leasing is a form of secured debt, with the lending being made against a specific asset. Normally, the lease contract is entered into at the same time as the asset is acquired. The lessor retains legal ownership of the asset, and can reclaim it if lease payments are not met. In accounting terms, the leased asset is shown as a fixed asset of the company, and the lease liability under current and long term liabilities.[1]

Hire purchase is another type of lease contract. The main difference between hire purchase and a finance lease is that under hire purchase the assets technically belong to the borrowing company, whereas leased assets belong to the lessor. There can be great tax benefits in leasing assets, as the lessor company may be able to use the tax allowances relating to the assets, and so pass on a reduced finance charge.

Companies can also raise lease finance on assets that they already own. Such transactions, often known as 'sale and leaseback', often (but not always) relate to property. A company will sell its property to a finance company in order to obtain a lump sum payment, and then will lease back the premises so that it can continue using them. The amount of the lump sum payment will depend partly on the value of the premises, but also on the credit status of the borrowing company and the agreed ongoing rent: a company that is prepared to pay a high rent will be able to obtain a larger lump sum than one which wants to minimize future rental payments.

---

1. The type of lease described is a 'finance lease'. Leases which relate to the short term rental of an asset may be classified, at the time of writing, as 'operating leases'. Assets held under operating leases do not, at the time of writing, have to be capitalized on the balance sheet. However, it appears possible that this accounting treatment will be changed. It should of course be remembered that the accounting treatment has no impact on the shareholder value of the company, merely on the reported profits.

SECURITIZATION

Downside protection: charge over assets; may be guarantees
Yield: interest
Upside potential: none

Securitization is used by companies that have a strong and predictable income stream on which to 'securitize' a loan. Effectively, the company sells the future income stream to a financier in exchange for a lump sum payment. Although the company itself may not be very creditworthy, its income stream is, and so the lending is based on this.

Securitization has been around since the 1970s, when the US Government National Mortgage Association, a government organization responsible for purchasing mortgages from mortgage originators, issued its 'Ginnie Maes' as the first mortgage-backed securities. Although each individual mortgage carries a given chance of non-repayment, by putting together a package of mortgages carrying the same level of credit risk, the portfolio carries a lower default risk, and so is more valuable to the purchaser.

Securitization has several advantages to the company.

- It can lead to a lower cost of funds. If the company itself has a poor credit rating, the asset-backed debt may have a much higher one.
- Securitized debt is an off balance sheet transaction, and so can reduce the company's balance sheet gearing.
- Because the lenders have the securitized assets they do not need covenants from the company, which gives management more freedom in running the business.

Many different types of assets produce an income stream that can be securitized. Examples of securitization include: mortgages; commercial and other loans; credit card receivables; commercial leases; car loans; trade debtors; and licence payments. Possibly one of the most unusual securitizations, a pioneer of its time, was the 'Bowie Bond', securitized in 1997 on the future royalties of the albums of the singer David Bowie.

The cash flows of a securitization are shown in Figure 9.2.

The company transfers the assets to be securitized into a Special Purpose Vehicle (which may be a company or a trust, depending, *inter alia*, on the tax regime). Investors make a loan to the SPV based on the income stream which will accrue to it: in Figure 9.2 this is the interest and principal repayments over the lives of the loans. The originating company receives a lump sum from the asset sale, plus a regular fee for ongoing management of the asset portfolio on behalf of the SPV.

If the security of the asset stream is not considered to be good enough, the company (or a third party such as a bank) may enhance the credit status of the SPV. This credit enhancement works by ring-fencing the risks, and putting them to the appropriate party. The key determinants of the credit rating are:

- Assets type, and likelihood of risk of default.
- Cash flow – so that bondholders can get their regular cash for interest. When cash flows are less than 100 per cent certain the credit enhancement can take the form of an escrow account to cover temporary shortfalls.

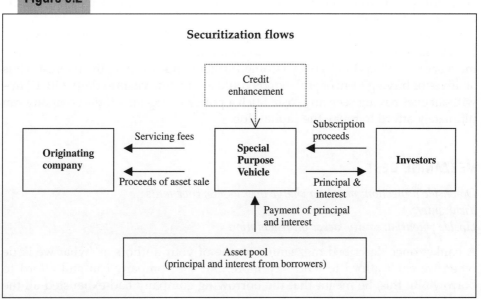

Securitization flows

UNSECURED DEBT

Downside protection: may be covenants
Yield: interest
Upside potential: none

Unsecured loans bear interest at a higher rate than secured debt, to compensate the lender for the greater risk.

HIGH YIELD DEBT

Downside protection: may be a charge over assets; may be covenants
Yield: interest
Upside potential: none

Higher yield debt used to be known as 'junk bonds'. This is sub-investment grade debt, issued with a rating of below BBB- (Standard and Poor's rating) or Baa (Moody's rating).

The concept of junk bonds was invented by the financier Michael Milken. Milken's research indicated that smaller non-investment grade companies had, relatively, no worse a failure or default rate than larger, better known companies. From this, he determined that it might be possible to develop attractive marketable bonds for those companies which offered a slight premium to bond investors, to compensate for the perceived risk.

Junk bonds were a very popular source of company finance in the 1980s. However, in the recessions of the early 1990s there were a lot of defaults, and the instrument became less attractive. Perhaps this was the cause of the change of name from 'junk' to 'high yield'! The bonds came back into fashion in the 1990s, as investors sought instruments that gave a high yield. However, the yields are very susceptible to changes in economic and market conditions, which affect the likelihood of default.

It should be pointed out that many junk bonds, although nominally giving a high yield to investors, in fact gave no cash return at all. These bonds paid their interest out in kind (PIK), i.e. by issuing further bonds to cover the interest. Thus an investor buying £1 m of junk bonds could after a few years end up with £2 m – without ever having seen any cash! Such a policy works only if the company can ultimately afford to repay the capital due.

MEZZANINE DEBT

Downside protection: may be a charge over assets; covenants
Yield: interest
Upside potential: equity kicker on redemption

A banker once described mezzanine to one of your authors as 'what we issue when we can't afford to lend any more, but the company can still afford to borrow'. By this, he meant that the borrowing company had exhausted all the 'good' security, and its financial gearing ratios were higher than a risk-averse lender would live with comfortably, but it was accepted that the company's cash flow and growth prospects merited further borrowing.

Mezzanine might carry covenants, although these might not be very useful, as they would not take precedence over senior covenants.[2] Accordingly, mezzanine debt is higher risk than senior borrowing, and thus attracts a higher return. As it would normally be infeasible for the loan to carry a rate of interest high enough to compensate for the lender's risk, in addition to the interest a mezzanine loan will often carry *warrants* (see below). Thus the return on mezzanine will be a mixture of interest yield and potential capital gain.

An example of a mezzanine loan is as follows. MezzCo wishes to borrow £10 m for seven years, and has exhausted all of its 'normal' debt capacity. A specialist mezzanine provider (which might be a finance house that writes only mezzanine, or could be the mezzanine arm of a clearing bank) will lend the money. The deal is structured such that the loan bears interest at, say, LIBOR plus 3 per cent over the life of the loan. At the end of the seven years the full loan will be repaid, and the lender will also have warrants giving the right to buy say 2 per cent of the company's share capital, at say 1 p per share. This gives the lender a running yield, and enhances the return with the possibility of a capital gain on redemption.

Mezzanine is a private transaction rather than one which is traded on the financial markets.

---

2. One of your authors managed an investment in a mezzanine loan to a company which had been in breach of the mezzanine covenants for two years. However, the senior loan covenants had not been breached, and so the mezzanine lenders were powerless to enforce their position. They merely noted in the files, on a monthly basis, that the covenants were in breach!

SUBORDINATED DEBT

Downside protection: probably none
Yield: interest
Upside potential: none

As its name implies, this debt is subordinated to the claims of other creditors. Because it is riskier, it might carry a higher interest rate. However, subordinated debt is often lent by the owners of the business, or the previous owners, in which case the coupon is unlikely to reflect the commercial risk.

CONVERTIBLE DEBT

Downside protection: may be a charge over assets; may be covenants
Yield: interest
Upside potential: opportunity to convert into equity

This is debt which is convertible into equity (generally ordinary shares). The advantage of this to the lender is that there is a chance to participate in the share capital of the company, and so to make a capital gain. Because of this, the interest rate on convertibles is lower than that on non-convertible debt. (Companies may also issue convertible preference shares – see below.)

To give an example of convertible debt, consider ConCo. ConCo is currently trading at a share price of £1 per share. The directors wish to raise £10 m capital, and have considered their alternatives: issue new equity, raise debt, or issue a convertible. They are reluctant to issue new equity, as they can foresee the share price rising considerably in the near term, and feel that issuing equity now, at only £1, would be an unnecessary dilution for their existing shareholders. Furthermore, they realize that issuing £10 m of equity now would substantially change the voting structure of the company's shares, and they would like to maintain their controlling position for as long as possible.

ConCo has also considered issuing straight debt. The problem with this is that the company's existing lenders would not permit further senior debt to be issued, as this would damage their own position. Anyway, ConCo is already paying out large sums in quarterly interest charges, and taking on further debt would only exacerbate that cash outflow from the company.

Accordingly, ConCo determines that it will issue convertible debt. The terms of the debt are as follows:

> Outstanding for 10 years.
> Carries interest at LIBOR plus 1 per cent.
> Carries conversion rights into ordinary shares at £2 per share.

This means that the holders of the debt will earn a running yield of LIBOR plus 1 per cent (not a large amount, considering the risk they must be taking) over the 10 years of the loan. At the end of the 10 years, they have a call option – the choice either to be repaid their £10 m, or to convert it into shares in ConCo at £2: 5 million shares. Obviously, the lenders hope that shares in ConCo will be trading at considerably more than £2 in 10 years' time. If the shares are trading at, say, £3, the lenders will undertake the conversion, and can immediately sell their five million shares for £15 m, making a capital gain of £5 m. The capital gain boosts the return by the annual equivalent of just over 4 per cent per year – which should give an overall return more commensurate with the risk being taken.

From the issuing company's point of view, convertibles have many advantages, as follows.

- Issuing convertibles rather than equity avoids issuing shares at the current price. This avoids the immediate dilution of eps, and also retains voting rights in their existing proportions for a while longer.
- Issuing convertibles rather than equity means that the eventual issue of equity (the conversion) will take place at a higher share price in the future, benefiting existing shareholders as it will dilute them less.
- Issuing convertibles instead of debt means that the ongoing servicing of the instrument (interest payments) is lower, thus conserving the company's cash resources and improving its reported profitability.
- Convertibles represent self liquidating debt, in that – if all goes according to plan – the debt will never need to be repaid but will be converted into equity instead, thus preserving resources in the company.

(The last point, concerning self-liquidating debt, led to companies treating convertibles as equity in their balance sheets when the instruments first became common, in the 1980s. The view taken was that as the capital would never need to be repaid, it was equity rather than debt. However, the accounting standards bodies have taken a different view, arguing, very reasonably, that there is a potential liability unless and until the conversion option is selected. Accordingly, the instruments are now shown on companies' balance sheets as debt, and the ultimate dilution should they be converted is noted.)

These features make the use of convertibles very attractive to growth companies, which would normally use equity financing, but can leverage it a bit with convertibles. However, when issuing convertibles it is important to consider the likely future trends in the company's share price.

Convertibles seem at first sight to give the best of both worlds – they free the company from having to sell equity cheaply, and they give the lender some downside protection so that even if the share price does not rise, the investment can still be repaid. There is of course a catch – in finance there is no free lunch. If ConCo's shares are still trading at £1 in ten years' time, then the convertibles will not be converted. In this case, the lender will have effectively lent the money to the company at LIBOR plus 1per cent – a return that in no way reflects the risk she/he has taken. Furthermore, if the shares are only trading at £1 in ten years' time, it implies that the company is not trading to expectations; indeed, it could be facing trading problems. Having to repay £10 m unexpectedly (because it was assumed that the holders would convert rather than ask for repayment) might be very difficult.

For example, *The Economist* (1 July 2000) reported that many of the internet companies such as Amazon.com had issued convertible bonds at a time when their share prices were high and expected to rise further. The collapse of the dot.com boom has led to a situation in which (at the time of writing) the shares are performing far below the convertibles' strike prices, effectively rendering the call option worthless unless the share prices recover. If share prices do not recover, the cash call for eventual repayment of these debts could well drive the remaining dot.coms into financial distress.

Appendix 2 explains how convertibles are valued and structured.

EXCHANGEABLE BONDS

Downside protection: may be charge over assets, may be covenants
Yield: interest
Upside potential: opportunity to convert into the equity of another company

Exchangeables are very similar to convertibles, in that the lender has the right to repayment or to convert into another asset. The difference is that the assets into which conversion is offered are not the securities of the company issuing the bonds, but the assets of a related company.

For example, in 2001 France Telecom issued a bond that could be converted into shares in Orange, its subsidiary which was about to be re-listed. At about the same time, Hutchinson Whampoa sold bonds exchangeable into Vodafone stock (which it held). One advantage to the issuing company is the ability to offer upside on the financial instrument. Furthermore, at the time of these transactions the worldwide prices of telecoms stock were depressed, and so the issuing companies did not wish to raise funds by selling off the underlying assets themselves, as they preferred to be able to retain at least part of the potential upside.

PREFERENCE SHARES

Downside protection: minimal
Yield: fixed dividend
Upside potential: none

Preference shares are known as 'non equity' shares – they do not give a right of ownership of the company and do not normally give a capital gain. Their main feature is that they carry a fixed dividend, which takes precedence over the dividend paid on ordinary shares. The dividend is often cumulative: if it is unpaid in any year, the arrears are carried over to be paid in future years. Although the shares do not normally carry votes, it is often the case that they will carry a vote if, and for as long as, their dividend is in arrears.

The 'preference' in the title also refers to the fact that in a winding-up these shares get paid out before the ordinary shares. (This gives a marginal reduction in risk compared to the ordinary shares, but nothing to get excited about.)

Preference shares may be redeemable at the direction of the company, in which case the redemption is normally at par: as stated above, there is no right to a capital gain. However, preference shareholders may be able to make a capital gain if the shares are traded on the market, and market interest rates have changed significantly since the shares were issued. For example, a £1 12 per cent preference share carries an annual dividend of 12 p. If market rates reduce to 6 per cent, the value of the share in the market could rise to £2.

ORDINARY SHARES

Downside protection: none
Yield: dividends
Upside potential: unlimited

The holders of the ordinary shares are the ultimate owners of the company. They are entitled to all of the profits (after the other sources of finance have received their interest or dividends). This is the true risk capital of the company. In the event of a liquidation, the ordinary shareholders are the last to be paid out.

WARRANTS

Downside protection: none
Yield: none
Upside potential: opportunity to acquire the company's equity

Warrants are financial instruments issued by a company in its own shares. Ownership of a warrant gives the holder the right to acquire shares in the company on or after a certain date, at a certain price (which, it is hoped, will be less than the then market price). In this, they are similar to call options.

OPTIONS

Downside protection: none
Yield: none
Upside potential: opportunity to acquire the company's equity (call option) or to sell it (put option)

As explained in Appendix 2, an option gives the holder the right to do something, but not the obligation to do it. The buyer of options may do so to hedge against a risk, or to speculate. The seller of options is taking a significant risk, as the price of the underlying assets may move out of line with expectations. The difference between options and warrants is that whereas warrants are issued by the company in question, any third party can write options over any company's securities.

CONCLUSION

In the beginning there were 'debt' and 'equity'. However, the capital markets have long since diversified their financial instruments, and the continuum shown in Figure 9.1 illustrates that there are many choices in financing a company. When selecting or evaluating a source of finance there are several important things to remember:

• Keep it simple. If it is possible to structure the deal using 'plain vanilla' debt or equity, this is probably the best thing to do. Generally, fancy financial structures mostly benefit the investment banks who sell them (or the academics who write about them).

- The financial instrument chosen should have a risk profile to complement the company's business risk profile. Companies with low business risk can afford to take on high risk debt instruments, to lower their average cost of capital. High risk companies are best to stick to equity instruments.
- Cash requirements and profitability will also affect the choice of instrument.
- Once you have seen the continuum in action, you will realize that there is no such thing as 'gearing'. The gearing of a company is the relationship between its debt and its equity; the continuum shows that there are few absolutes, but a lot of grey areas. When calculating gearing, always do it from the point of view of a particular security: other securities to the left of it in the continuum count as 'debt' as far as it is concerned, as they have better rights against the company's assets. Securities to the right on the continuum line have lesser rights, and can be treated as equity.

10

Dividends and buybacks

In Part 2 of this book we examined the various dividend strategies appropriate for companies at different stages in the lifecycle. In this chapter we bring together those thoughts on dividend strategy, and supplement them with consideration of alternatives to dividends, such as share repurchases or buybacks. We also examine some of the theories behind dividend payment.

SUMMARY OF THE DIVIDEND COMPONENT OF THE OVERALL MODEL

We have established that the payment of dividends is constrained by two main factors: ability to afford the cash outflow from the company, and existence of distributable profits. In terms of the financial model developed in Chapter 3, this translates into dividend strategy as shown in Working insight 10.1.

SOME THOUGHTS ON WHY COMPANIES PAY DIVIDENDS

Appendix 1 shows how Modigliani and Miller took the view that, in the perfect world in which their theories were developed, dividends are an irrelevance. Paying dividends reduces the overall size of the company, thus decreasing the value per share in direct proportion to the dividends

WORKING
10.1
INSIGHT

Dividend strategy and the lifecycle model

	Cash availability	Profit availability	Dividend policy
Launch	No spare cash available. All cash is needed for investment in developing the business.	None. Probably making losses.	Nil dividend payout.
Growth	Cash is needed for development and investment in growing market share	May be profitable.	Nil dividend payout is preferable. However, new shareholders might prefer a nominal payout.
Maturity	The company is now cash positive and has less opportunities to invest in profitable growth	Profitable.	A medium to high dividend payout is preferred.
Decline	The company is cash positive, with no reinvestment potential.	May be profitable.	Full payout of available cash as dividend, even in excess of current profits.

received. Shareholders could choose to sell shares in order to realize funds, and do not need the declaration of a dividend to facilitate this.

However, Modigliani and Miller based their work on a world in which both taxes and transaction costs were ignored. In the real world, dividends are not irrelevant. Before we look at the ways in which they are paid, let us consider just some of the reasons advanced by academics and practitioners as to why they are paid in the way they are.

An argument has been advanced that companies' dividend policies are influenced considerably by the tax systems – both corporate and personal – under which they operate. This seems plausible, in that shareholders might prefer to receive capital gains, taxed at a low rate, rather than dividends which are taxed highly. Furthermore, investors can choose when to trigger a capital gain by selling shares; they do not have a choice about paying tax on dividends so this too is an argument in favour of dividend policies being influenced by tax issues. However, research provides only moderate support for this as a stand-alone theory: for example, if this were truly the case companies in regimes which tax dividends more highly than gains (for example the USA) would never pay dividends: this is not the case.

A case is also made for dividends as a manifestation of agency theory. If a company has surplus cash, the management effectively has three choices as to how to deal with this: it can invest it in positive net present value projects (in which case, the cash is not really surplus); it can waste it on negative net present value projects; or it can distribute it back to the shareholders. Companies that sit on mountains of cash tend to make the investing community quite nervous, as there is always the danger that it will be mis-used. Therefore, giving it to the shareholders as a dividend is seen as a positive sign of good corporate governance. If surplus cash is repaid, then when the directors need additional funding in order to invest in new projects there is an automatic vetting mechanism, in that either lenders or shareholders will have to be convinced of the power of their investment proposal.

Perhaps the strongest argument about how companies pay dividends, and one that relates directly to the theories propounded in this book, is that dividends are seen as a signalling mechanism to the market. Here, changes in dividend levels are seen as far more important than the actual dividends themselves. It is undoubtedly true that changes in dividends carry a signalling effect – any cursory reading of the financial press for a few weeks will demonstrate this. However, as Working insight 10.2 illustrates, reading those signals may be somewhat complex.

WORKING
10.2
INSIGHT

What does a dividend change signal?

Interpretation	Increase the dividend level	Decrease the dividend level
Good news	The company is prospering, and we can afford to pay out more of our profits without damaging our prospects.	The company has changed its strategy and the directors see these very profitable investment opportunities, which will provide more share holder value than will mere payment of dividends.
Bad news	The directors have run out of ideas for profitable growth.	Profits and cash flow are way down, and the company is facing trouble for the foreseeable future.
	The model suggested in this book indicates that increasing the dividend level could be seen as a signal of advancing one stage in the lifecycle.	*The model suggested in this book indicates that decreasing the dividend level could be seen as a signal of moving back one stage in the lifecycle.*

10.1 ICI AND THE REDUCING DIVIDEND

CASE STUDY

In November 2000 ICI, the UK chemicals company, announced that its dividend for 2001 would be cut by about 50 per cent. The company's share price rose by about 10 per cent in the week following the announcement. This contrasted markedly with the last time ICI had announced a dividend cut, in 1981. At that time the investment community was traumatized, and the whole market – not just ICI – fell sharply.

So, what changed?

In 1981 ICI was seen as the 'bellwether' of British industry. A mature chemicals company, sentiment was such that if times were hard enough for ICI to have to conserve cash by cutting its dividend, industry must be in a perilous situation.

In 1997 ICI began its transformation from a commodity bulk chemicals company to a speciality products and paints company. This was seen as a fast growing market, with considerable potential. The transformation was complete by 2000, and the announcement of the dividend cut was accompanied by a letter from the Chairman to each shareholder, setting out the very positive reasons for the reduction in dividend.

The letter stated that the directors believed more value would be created for shareholders by reinvestment in this profitable area than by paying dividends; and that such reinvestment would drive future growth in dividends. As can be seen from the increase in the share price; the company's signals were believed and the dividend cut was seen as a positive move for the future.

As the ICI case shows, because the signalling effect of dividends is so important it is essential that dividend changes are accompanied by a clear investor relations exercise to explain the benefits / limit the damage.

Generally, boards are reluctant to change their dividend policy without good cause. Because of this, companies rarely change dividends exactly in line with changes in profits: one bad year could lead to a fall in dividends, with disastrous results for market sentiment. Instead, they appear to 'smooth' dividend payments, aiming for a continuing upward trend, which can be maintained over an economic cycle. Working insight 10.3 demonstrates how this might work.

WORKING 10.3 INSIGHT

Smoothing dividends over a period.

The directors of DivCo plc believe the company to be in its mature stage, and ideally would like to pay out 50 per cent (no more) of annual profits as dividends to shareholders. However, the company's business model includes taking on large contracts, the profits of which can fall either side of a year end, significantly affecting year-on-year profitability. The dividend paid in Year 0 was £35 m. The following tables demonstrate (a) a 50 per cent payout ratio and (b) a smoothed dividend policy.

	Year 1	Year 2	Year 3	Year 4	Year 5
Profit after tax £ m	100	120	110	150	130
Dividends using a 50 per cent payout ratio	50	60	55	75	65
Smoothed dividend policy	40	46	53	61	70

The smoothed dividend policy illustrated in Working insight 10.3 reflects merely increasing annual dividends by 15 per cent each year, a figure which management believes will be well covered by forecast profits for the next few years. In Year 5 this leads to a dividend payout which reduces dividend cover below two times: this continued increase in dividend payments would (they hope) be seen by the financial markets as a signal of their continued confidence in the company's prospects, and their belief that the fall in profits in Year 5 was a 'blip' in a growing trend.

(The smoothed dividend policy in Working insight 10.3 was determined on a totally arbitrary basis by the authors. In Appendix 1 we discuss the research of Lintner in 1956, who concluded that companies actually apply an adjustment factor to their target payout ratio each year, to allow for such smoothing. Lintner's work was ground-breaking in its time, and a useful development of theory. However, your authors' practical experience with finance directors and boards indicates that the dividend decision is often made on pretty unscientific ground – the main criterion being 'a bit more than last year'!)

STOCK DIVIDENDS

There is another way of paying dividends, in which the company declares a dividend but does not actually pay out any cash. This is normally known as a stock dividend or scrip dividend, and has increased in popularity in the UK in recent years with many companies now giving their shareholders the option to take their dividends either in cash or in the form of new shares.

In the UK at the time of writing, there is no tax advantage for individuals to receive dividends as scrip dividends or in cash. Both are taxable. However, there is an advantage in scrip dividends for the corporate shareholder, as the dividend is not charged to tax.

When shareholders are offered stock dividends, it is always possible for those investors who want to receive cash to sell these new shares in the markets to realize the cash equivalent of their dividend. This is the same argument as used in theory to justify indifference of shareholders to the dividend policy of the company.

One perceived advantage of the stock dividend is that it enables shareholders to increase their holdings without incurring dealing costs. (This, of course, is only valid if some of the shareholders sell their shares, or elect to receive a cash dividend; otherwise, all that happens is each shareholder's absolute holding increases, but their percentage holdings remain the same.) Theoretically a straightforward stock dividend is the same as a bonus share issue; the company is simply capitalizing part of its distributable profits in order to issue new free shares. If the shareholder can choose between a cash dividend and being given more shares, the alternative stock dividend can be seen as a rights issue, with the exercise price being the total dividend divided by the number of shares offered.

A company declaring a stock dividend is effectively retaining the cash in the business for reinvestment. The critical question for shareholders therefore is whether the expected return on that increased reinvestment is financially attractive, so that it increases the total value of the company. From this perspective it can be seen that the declaration of a stock dividend is completely irrelevant – no cash is leaving the company. If stock dividends do not affect the company's reinvestment strategy, they are not part of the real dividend policy of the company.

SHARE REPURCHASES (BUYBACKS)

Paying dividends is a logical way of distributing cash to investors if that cash is no longer required by the company. However another way of effectively achieving the same aim is for the company to repurchase some of its own shares using its excess cash to finance the purchase. In the USA companies have always been able to buy back their own shares and they can continue to hold them; the accounting presentation is to classify them as 'treasury stock' on the published balance sheet, where they are deducted from the total value of issued shares. If the USA company holds its own shares as treasury stock, it can resell them in the market at a later date. Thus a company can make a profit out of trading in itself.

At the time of writing, although UK companies are allowed to repurchase their own shares (subject to safeguarding the position of creditors) the practice of holding these shares for later re-issue is not permitted, and the repurchased shares must be cancelled by the company so that they cease to exist. (The UK Department of Trade and Industry is currently reviewing the legal position on 'treasury stock', as companies have argued that having a facility similar to the US position would give them more flexibility in capital-raising, and lower their costs.)

The current position in continental Europe varies by country. Some countries allow share repurchase, others still do not permit it, or impose severe tax penalties if it is undertaken. Such tax penalties differ from the US situation, where buybacks have a tax advantage over dividend payment, or the UK situation, which is broadly neutral between buybacks and dividends.

When looked at in terms of the real impact, a share repurchase scheme should be regarded as a one-off discretionary dividend offer to shareholders. Thus, as shown arithmetically in Working insight 10.4, if all shareholders accept the repurchase offer pro-rata to their shareholdings, they will own the same proportion of the company after the repurchase but will have received a cash payment from the company. This sounds remarkably like a dividend payment! If any particular shareholders do not want to receive cash at this time, they do not need to sell any of their shares. Their proportionate shareholdings will increase to compensate for the non-receipt of the cash payment: whether the compensation is inadequate or excessive depends on the reaction of the share price to the news of the repurchase.

The market reaction to the repurchase should be conditioned by the appropriate dividend policy for the company and whether this repurchase can be logically explained in this context. For example, if a mature company disposes of one of its business units it may have no need of the large cash balance it receives as a result. It could pay this cash out as a dividend but this level of dividend would be unsustainable in the future. Confusion among shareholders could be avoided by clear communication of the extra payment as a bonus, one-off dividend, stating the source of the cash inflow.

WORKING
10.4
INSIGHT

**Repurchase of shares: impact if taken up
pro-rata by existing shareholders**

Cash Rich Holdings plc has £100 million in surplus cash on its balance sheet. It currently has 500 million shares trading at a market price of £2 each. Rather than declaring a higher dividend, it announces that it intends to purchase 10 per cent of its existing shares in the market at £2 per share. If all shareholders accept the offer pro-rata to their current shareholdings, nothing will change after the event.

For the holders of 10 million shares before the deal they would sell one million shares and receive £2 million in cash. After the repurchase, they own nine million shares but this represents the same 2 per cent of the company which they owned before the deal, i.e.

$$\frac{9 \text{ million}}{450 \text{ million}} = \frac{10 \text{ million}}{500 \text{ million}}$$

Alternatively the company could use the cash to repurchase some of its own shares in the market, thus indirectly paying a bonus dividend to those of its shareholders who choose to sell shares at this time. There is an accounting impact of repurchasing shares which can make it appear more attractive to some companies than the straightforward higher dividend payment. This is that share repurchase can be used to increase earnings per share, whereas they will actually be reduced by the higher dividend payment.[1] As illustrated in Working insight 10.5 this increase is achieved for companies with relatively low P/E multiples, which tend to be mature cash positive businesses where high dividend payout ratios are appropriate.

In a perfectly efficient market, the share price should not be affected merely by changes in earnings per share unless these changes reflect real alterations in future cash flow. The distribution of cash now, whether in the form of dividends or share repurchase, should have the same impact on the company's future cash generation capability; this assumes that there are no differences in the tax treatment of the two cash distributions. Consequently the total value of the company should be the same, which leads to a difference in share price since after the share repurchase there are less issued shares remaining. This difference in share price means that the P/E multiple applied to the company should still be the same in both cases as is shown in Working insight 10.6.

It is quite possible to generalize the conditions under which share repurchases will increase earnings per share, as is explained in Working insight 10.7 but, as mentioned above, this should theoretically have no impact on the share price.

---

1. The higher dividend payment will reduce the company's cash resources; if nothing else, profits will be reduced because the company is not earning interest on its deposits.

WORKING
10.5

INSIGHT   **Impact of share repurchases on earnings per share**

Extracts of the latest profit and loss account of Mega Cash Holdings plc are

	£ millions
Operating profit	120
Interest income	30
Profit before tax	150
Taxation	50
Profit after tax	100
Dividends paid	50
Retained profits	50

The company has 500 million issued shares, so that the earnings per share are 20 p (profit after tax of £100 million divided by 500 million shares). The current share price is £2, representing a P/E multiple of 10. The interest income of £30 million is generated by the investment of a cash mountain totalling £400 million at a pre-tax interest rate of 7.5 per cent.

The company wishes to assess the impact on eps of using the cash mountain either to pay a one-off extra dividend or to repurchase 200 million shares (no change in share price is assumed as a result of the share repurchase and operating income and effective tax rates are kept the same).

	Impact of dividend	**Impact of share buy-back**
Operating profit	120	120
Taxation	40	40
Profit after tax	80	80
Dividends	440	40
Retained profit	(360)	40
Earnings per share	16 p	26.67 p
No. of shares	500 m	300 m

Note: The use of the cash mountain removes the interest income from the profit and loss account thus reducing eps in the dividend payment case.

The 'rule' on the eps impact of buybacks set out in Working insight 10.7 is illustrated in Working insight 10.8

Over the last decade, stock repurchases have become more popular with companies. One reason for this is that previously they were illegal or tax-inefficient in many countries: now these restrictions have been lifted. But many other reasons have been given for the explosion in companies buying back their own shares rather than paying dividends. Working insight 10.9 sets out many of these, some of which appear to have more face validity than others.

In Working insight 10.9, one of the reasons often declared for undertaking share buybacks rather than declaring dividends is that buybacks are more flexible than dividends and do not give rise to a shareholder expectation of future activity. Two such examples are shown in case study 10.2.

WORKING
10.6

INSIGHT

**Impact of share repurchases on share price
and price/earnings multiple**

It is assumed that the original market capitalization (£1 billion) of Mega Cash Holdings plc valued the cash mountain at its face value of £400 million. This implies that the after-tax trading profits of the company of £80 million are capitalized at a P/E multiple of 7.5; so that

PAT (exc. interest income)	£80 m
multiplied at implied P/E of	7.5
gives market value of	£600 m
plus face value of cash	£400 m
Market capitalization of company	£1000 m

After the cash distribution, this market capitalization should therefore fall to £600 million (ignoring the tax impacts).

	Dividend distribution	Share repurchase
Market capitalization	£600 million	£600 million
Issued shares	500 million	300 million
Resulting share price	£1.20*	£2.00
eps (from Working insight 10.5)	16 p	26.67 p
P/E multiple	7.5	7.5

Note: The share price falls after the dividend payment, because this cash payment represents 80 p per share (ignoring the tax impact).

WORKING
10.7

INSIGHT
Assessing the impact of share repurchase on EPS.

Let N = number of shares in issue
n = number to be repurchased
p = price of shares to be bought
K_d = bank interest rate on money borrowed (or not earned) for repurchase
t = tax rate (corporate)
PAT = profits after tax before the share repurchase

Then,
$eps = PAT/N$

and after the buyback
new $eps = [PAT - npK_d(1 - t)]/(N - n)$

If eps is to be enhanced by the transaction, eps < new eps
i.e.
$$PAT/N < [PAT - npK_d(1 - t)]/(N - n) \qquad (1)$$

Equation 1 can be simplified down to:

$PAT > NpK_d(1 - t)$
$PAT/N > pK_d(1 - t)$

Working insight 10.7 contd

i.e. $eps > pK_d(1 - t)$ (2)

i.e. share price paid for the repurchase, $p < eps/K_d(1 - t)$ (3)

If the share price paid is greater than this, eps will be diluted; if the price paid is less than calculated by (3), eps will be enhanced.

Restating equation 3 we can see that at equilibrium (i.e. where new and old eps are the same)

eps = share price paid $\times$ after-tax cost of debt

This shows that eps is reduced by interest on the amount borrowed for the repurchase. So if interest rates are high, or the price paid is high, eps may not be boosted.

BUT – if the directors believe that profit is going to rise in the future, it will be worth the eps effect as eps will rise even more for the fewer shares that are left.

This is the same as:

$p/eps < 1/K_d(1 - t)$ (4)

Eps will be enhanced if the P/E multiple of the company is less than the inverse of the post tax opportunity cost of funding used to repurchase the shares.

WORKING
10.8
INSIGHT   **Impact of share repurchase on earnings per share**

In Working insight 10.5 we showed the impact of a buyback on Mega Cash Holdings. Mega was receiving interest on its cash mountain of 7.5 per cent before tax, 5 per cent after tax. Its shares were trading on a P/E of 10 times.

Using equation (4) derived in Working insight 10.7, the share repurchase will increase eps provided that the P/E multiple of the buyback is less than the inverse of the post-tax opportunity cost of funding used to repurchase the shares, i.e.

$P/E < 1/K_d(1 - t)$

For Mega, the buyback was done at the then current market value, i.e. at a P/E of 10 times. Provided that the post-tax cost of funds was less than 10 per cent, the buyback will enhance eps. As shown in Working insight 10.5, the buyback did indeed have this effect.

In the unlikely event that the company had used its surplus £400 million to buy back 100 million shares at £4, a P/E of 20 times (the inverse of the 5 per cent debt cost), there would have been no impact on eps, as shown below.

	Before £ million	After £ million
Operating profit	120	120
Interest income	30	0
Profit before tax	150	120
Tax	50	40
Profit after tax	100	80
Number of shares	500 m	400 m
Earnings per share	20 pence	20 pence

Reasons for companies to repurchase their own shares

Reasons which apply only to share repurchases
- To increase earnings per share (as demonstrated in Working insight 10.7).
- To strengthen management incentives by reducing the number of outstanding shares so that management ends up with a higher percentage of the company. (Note: this obviously can lead to agency conflicts.)
- Buybacks are considered to be more flexible than dividends, as they are seen as one-offs and do not reflect trend. (But see note below.)
- To buy out 'weaker' shareholders who may otherwise sell to a hostile bidder. (Again, note the potential agency conflict.)
- To give shareholders a choice of how to take their return.
- To offset eps dilution from the exercise of share options.

Reasons which would apply equally to dividend payments
- To improve management's business focus by limiting their opportunities to invest in non-core or value-reducing projects.
- To reduce the cost of capital.

10.2   SHARE BUYBACKS

CASE STUDY

1. Microsoft

Microsoft, a company which is both profitable and cash generative, does not pay dividends to its shareholders. Nor does it have a formal stock repurchase plan. However, since its flotation in 1986 it has frequently bought back shares from its shareholders. These buybacks are at irregular intervals and for differing amounts (a predictable buyback programme would attract attention from the Internal Revenue Service, and may lead the transactions to be treated as dividends for tax purposes). However, a Microsoft shareholder could have received a significant cash return from participating in the buybacks as and when they occurred.

2. UK Former Building Societies

Following their privatization (de-mutualization) many of the UK's former building societies, now banks, were over-capitalized, having too high a capital adequacy ratio and far more funds than they could use in their business. This made the markets nervous: often, companies sitting on a cash pile choose to spend it unwisely; even if they don't, shareholder value is not created when companies merely invest cash on the money markets.

Three of the larger banks chose to give at least part of the surplus cash – almost £2 billion in total – back to the shareholders. Halifax did this by way of a £1.5 billion share buyback; Alliance and Leicester also chose the buyback option; and Woolwich used the alternative of a special dividend together with a buyback.

DO BUYBACKS ADD VALUE?

Given that share buybacks appear to be on the increase, what is the market impact of a company's announcement that it is about to undertake such a transaction? Well, as with dividends the signalling effect may vary. Generally, markets seem in favour of buybacks, as they eliminate the 'slack' for directors, and often the company's share price rises disproportionately. However, as with dividend increases, if the market believes that the directors are proposing a buyback because they have run out of investment ideas, the negative impact could damage sentiment about the company's future.

(What is interesting about this is that many companies appear to announce share buybacks without actually undertaking them. This way they get the flexibility of financial choice, and benefit of the positive market sentiment without all the messiness of losing control of the company's funds!)

Of course, in the final analysis share buybacks only add value for the shareholders if they can be achieved at a buying price below the fundamental value of the company. Buying back shares which are over-priced by the market – however it affects the eps or market sentiment – is not a value-enhancing strategy.

THE MECHANICS OF A BUYBACK

The practicalities of repurchasing shares are more complex than those for declaring a dividend (which means of course that significant fees may be paid to merchant banks and advisers, in turn implying that the company has to be very certain that this is a route it wishes to follow). The regulations will differ in each country: in this book we describe only the current UK situation.

The buyback decision, because of its 'one-off' nature, is more complicated than the dividend decision. As we have stated, with dividends the question to ask is generally 'how much more than last year should we pay?'. With buybacks the two key issues to be addressed are:

1. How much can the company afford to repurchase? Issues to consider are whether or not there is surplus cash in the business; the impact on the company's debt:equity ratio of a buyback; and whether available reserves will permit the desired level of buyback.
2. Is it the intention to give all shareholders an equal chance of selling their shares to the company? This will impact the method by which the buyback is undertaken, as discussed below.

METHODS OF REPURCHASE OF SHARES

In the UK, provided that a company has met with legal requirements such as having sufficient reserves and obtaining shareholder approval for the transaction, there are two main ways in which it can repurchase its shares: buying them on the stock market, and a tender offer. The former is the most common method: buying shares on the market is relatively quick and straightforward, and the company can choose when to make the purchase.[2] For repurchases of relatively small amount of shares – say 2 per cent–3 per cent of the outstanding capital – this is an effective way to proceed.

2. Logically, companies would only buy back their shares on the market if they believed that the shares were undervalued. That would mean that shareholders who wished to stay with the company would benefit, and those who thought the current price fair would be able to exit. However, as most listed company directors seem permanently to regard the market as underpricing their shares (even at the height of a boom) this analysis may be overly academic.

If the company wishes to buy back a higher volume of its shares, or if it wishes to make an offer to all of its shareholders, not just those who are active in the stock market, then a tender offer is better. Current Stock Exchange rules in the UK demand that a tender offer be made if more than 15 per cent of the outstanding capital is being repurchased. In a tender offer the directors state a price at which they will repurchase the shares, and advertise this widely to shareholders. In many ways the process is the same as that for issuing shares on a market.

CONCLUSION

Companies can in some circumstances create value for shareholders by returning money to them. They may choose to return cash to shareholders in two main ways – by paying dividends or by entering into share buyback arrangements. Although in many instances the position for the shareholder is the same – she/he receives a cash payment – the signalling effect by the company can be very different, as can the impact on its financial results. Accordingly, the decision as to how to give the shareholders their return is one that is closely linked to the company's position and future strategy.

Transactions and Operating Issues

11

Floating a company

There are two reasons why a company might choose to float its shares on a recognized stock exchange – cash in and cash out. A cash in float is done by growth companies which seek funding; in a cash out float existing shareholders take the opportunity to sell their shares, and the company does not necessarily raise further finance. It is important that the company makes its strategy clear to the financial markets, as the exercise of flotation is as much about presentation and marketing as it is about financial strategy.

Flotation is a costly and time-consuming exercise. Shareholders and boards who are considering listing their companies have to consider carefully why they wish to do so, and the benefits they expect from the process. They also have to consider which stock market(s) are appropriate for their business, and whether they meet the requirements of those markets.

The burdens of being a listed company persuade some shareholders and boards that listing is no longer appropriate, and many companies choose to delist from their markets. This frees them from much regulation and public account-ability and, for many small companies, has little downside.

INTRODUCTION

In Chapter 5 we discussed how flotation on a recognized stock market may be an appropriate strategy for growth companies seeking to raise capital and provide an exit for their venture capital investors. This chapter addresses in more detail the reasons why a company might float (or, indeed, de-list its shares), and the mechanisms by which it can do so.

The first point to note is that the flotation process is not really a 'finance' issue. Although the decision as to whether listing is appropriate is one that should be driven by financiers (based ultimately on the company's corporate strategy), the actual process of listing is a marketing issue. Back in Figure 1.2 in this book we stated that investment is a two-stage process: investors invest in the company; the company invests in projects. Arranging the sale of the company's products to its target market is widely accepted as an issue for marketers, who advise on the most appropriate positioning and methods of sale. Similarly, arranging the sale of the company's shares to its target market of investors is also a marketing issue: much of what follows will make more sense if you keep this in mind.

ISSUES TO BE ADDRESSED PRIOR TO LISTING

Several issues need to be considered before the IPO (initial public offering) can actually take place. These are:

1. What is our reason for going public?
2. What is our target market?
3. Are we suitable for listing on this market?
4. What method will we employ for the listing?

Each of these considerations will be addressed in turn.

WHY GO PUBLIC?

The two fundamental reasons why a company might seek a listing can be categorized as 'cash in' and 'cash out'. To expand on this, a cash in float is one which is done for the purpose of raising funds for the company's continued expansion. By definition, cash in floats are for growth companies, which issue new shares to obtain the funds they need. In a cash out float, the main purpose of the listing is to obtain an exit for some of the existing shareholders, rather than to raise new money. In such a float, no new shares are issued, instead the existing shareholders sell all or part of their holdings to the new shareholders. Such a flotation would be appropriate for a more mature company. Figure 11.1 illustrates the characteristics of the two types of float.

As stated earlier, a flotation is a marketing exercise, and it is important that the marketing message is clear, so that 'customers' are not confused. A cash in float signals to the market that the company is seeking growth; this is likely to be confirmed in the explanation in its prospectus of its proposed dividend policy. A cash out float is more appropriate for mature companies, which are likely to pay higher dividends and will attract a different type of investor.

A mixed message sends the wrong signals to the market. One of the authors was asked a few years ago to advise on financial strategy for a growing, profitable software company. The owner/director, who was a key employee of the company and had overseen all of its development to date, wanted to float the company, realize his investment and then 'go off to the Bahamas to play golf'.

Figure 11.1

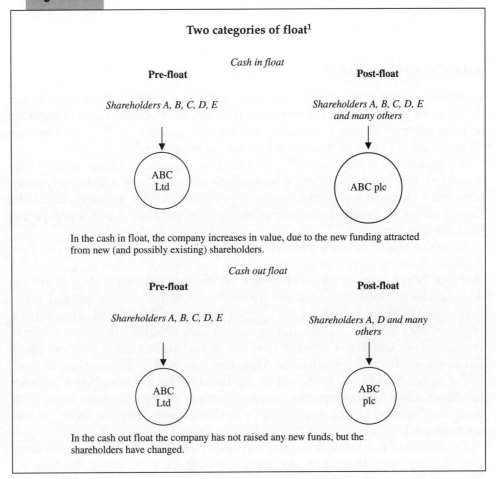

Two categories of float[1]

Cash in float

Pre-float   **Post-float**

Shareholders A, B, C, D, E   Shareholders A, B, C, D, E
                                                    and many others

ABC
Ltd

ABC plc

In the cash in float, the company increases in value, due to the new funding attracted from new (and possibly existing) shareholders.

Cash out float

Pre-float   **Post-float**

Shareholders A, B, C, D, E   Shareholders A, D and many
                                                    others

ABC
Ltd

ABC
plc

In the cash out float the company has not raised any new funds, but the shareholders have changed.

Sadly, he had to be advised that the market was unlikely to accept this as a value proposition – for key personnel to bail out of what was obviously positioned competitively as a growth company was going to invoke a certain level of 'cognitive dissonance' amongst prospective shareholders; to put it bluntly, who would buy the shares if he had so little faith that he was selling out?!

Other, secondary reasons why a company might choose to go public include the desire to have shares which can act as a currency in acquisitions (as discussed in Chapter 12); the wish for future financial flexibility (a listed company tends to have more financing options than an unlisted one); and the desire for prestige, for either the company or the directors. (It goes without saying that your authors think very little of this last reason, but we do acknowledge that flotations are sometimes inspired because 'so-and-so at the golf club did one'.)

---

1. For convenience, the pre-listing company is referred to as 'Ltd' (limited) and the post-listing company is referred to as 'plc' (public limited company). It should be noted that under UK company law it is possible for a company to be a plc without being listed on a stock exchange.

Having a listing is also useful for companies that have issued, or wish to issue, shares or share options to their management and employees; the public quotation gives the staff a benchmark price, and provides an easy way for them to sell the shares in due course.

WHICH TARGET MARKET?

Companies will target potential investment markets in much the same manner that they target markets for their products. There are two key issues to consider in determining the target market: what type of investor is likely to buy our shares?; and which stock market is best suited to our needs?

As regards the type of investor, the issue has been highlighted many times already in this book. Investors who seek dividend income are unlikely to be attracted to growth companies which retain most of their earnings. Similarly, those looking for a capital gain are not going to be persuaded by the prospectus for a mature company.

As to the choice of stock market on which to float, this is a more complex decision. There is now a wealth of markets from which to choose. In the USA there is NYSE (the New York Stock Exchange) or NASDAQ (National Association of Securities Dealers Automated Quotations) or several other exchanges. In Europe there are the various bourses of the individual countries, or NASDAQ Europe, or smaller specialist markets like the Neuer Markt in Germany. The UK currently has its main market, the London Stock Exchange (LSE) and its offshoot AIM, the Alternative Investment Market. LSE also has TechMark, launched at the heart of the dot.com boom in order to attract high-tech companies. And of course other countries each have their own markets, whose operations and investors may be more or less sophisticated.

The choice of market and country depends partly on the prestige and liquidity of the particular market and partly on what the company does. Rational investors know that the market capitalization of a company should represent the discounted value of its future cash flows. However it is a fact that, at the time of writing (and indeed, as far back as we can remember), technology companies are more highly valued on NASDAQ than on NYSE or LSE. Investors may tend to prefer dealing in certain markets, and they perceive less risk in industries with which they are familiar: hence a rational explanation is that NASDAQ investors, accustomed to technology shares, assign them a lower risk level and thus a higher value.

Investors are also comfortable with companies whose names they know: accordingly it might be foolish for a company with no trading presence in the USA to list its shares there. It would be unlikely to receive much press coverage or analyst attention, and so could flounder in the backwaters of the market. Similarly, companies which have a large trading presence in another country often choose to have a secondary listing on one of that country's markets; increasing their name-awareness in their product market by obtaining exposure in the capital markets.

Finally there is the issue of size. Size, to coin a phrase, matters. Although the listing regulations for the LSE state that companies with a market capitalization as low as £700 000 can list on this market, they would be foolish so to do. A glance at today's financial press shows that the LSE includes two or three companies capitalized at over £100 billion each, dozens of other companies capitalized at well over £1 billion and scores that come in at over the £100 million mark. Amongst these giants, how much attention are analysts and investors likely to pay to a 'minnow'? (This issue is picked up again at the end of this chapter, when we look at reasons why companies de-list from a market.) Thus, although it might be painful to the directors' ego, it is probably more useful to be a medium-sized company on a small exchange than to be a tiny company on a large one.

ARE WE SUITABLE FOR LISTING ON THIS MARKET?

Each particular stock market has its own regulations, which companies have to meet in order to obtain an initial listing, and to comply with on a continuous basis in order to maintain it. As those rules differ between markets, and change frequently, little purpose is served by setting out the current versions in this book. However, Working insight 11.1 sets out some of the considerations that a company may need to address.

Beyond the regulatory influences, there are certain characteristics of a company that is suitable for flotation, and again we come back to marketing. The company is more likely to have a successful float if it can show a growing profit trend: an indication of future prospects. Directors with a strong personal track record of business success are another factor in its favour. Also, investors will be more comfortable with buying shares if they know that the business of the company is not in any way mingled with the separate interests of the directors. (For many private companies, directors'/shareholders' and company's interests are seen as one and the same thing, which means that a certain amount of 'pre float grooming' needs to take place, to tidy up the balance sheet and remove the villa in Spain and the daughter's horses!) And it goes without saying (and indeed is generally a Stock Exchange requirement) that the company's accounting systems will be in order, and its internal controls will be sufficient.

WORKING
11.1
INSIGHT   **Possible regulatory requirements for a listing**

- Accounts with unqualified audit reports have been published for a certain number of years prior to the float.
- The company has a substantial business, with a trading record. (This requirement is often waived for high-technology companies.)
- The directors are suitable people to be running a publicly quoted company.
- The company is not controlled by any shareholder with a conflicting interest.
- At least x per cent of the company's shares will be in public hands after the float.
- A minimum post float market capitalization level is to be expected.

METHODS OF GOING PUBLIC

Having selected the market and groomed the company for its float, the final consideration is the method of flotation. Very briefly, there are three possible methods of flotation: an offer for sale, a placing and an introduction.

In an offer for sale, which is by far the most expensive way to float a company, the sponsor (see later in this chapter) will offer shares widely to both private and institutional investors, generally at a fixed price. The prospectus will be carried as an advertisement in the national press, adding to the complexity and costs of the issue.

Placings are a cheaper means of listing, and are by far the most popular choice amongst companies and their advisors. The shares are offered to a selected number of institutional investors, with whom normally the sponsor has (or would like) a business relationship.[2] This can result in a relatively narrow investor base for the company, but this may not in itself be seen as a disadvantage – the cost of communicating with a wide retail investor base is considerable.

Finally, one occasionally sees a company coming to the market by way of an introduction. This takes place when a company's shares are already widely held, and it has no need to raise further capital. The introduction is a means of enabling the shares to be traded on an exchange, to the benefit of the existing shareholders who may otherwise have difficulty selling them.

THE LISTING PROCESS

As with regulatory requirements, the listing process will differ by stock market. What follows is a broad description of the key parties, and the documentation that will be produced.

The first thing to note is that listing is not cheap. There are many documents, and many advisers, and costs mount rapidly. The company will need to prepare a prospectus (otherwise known as listing particulars), sample contents of which are illustrated in Working insight 11.2. It will need to produce (although not for publication) cash flow forecasts to be verified by reporting accountants, confirming its ability to survive on the funds to be raised. Those accountants will also produce a due diligence report, again not for publication, addressed to the company and its sponsors, confirming the company's financial and trading position and reviewing in detail its governance and internal control systems. A report on its prior years' audited results will also be prepared, to be included in the listing particulars. And then there are investor presentations, press releases and a wealth of legal documents.

---

2. At the time of writing, various US investment banks are under investigation for allegedly offering 'hot' shares to their favoured clients and thus depriving other shareholders of the ability to obtain them. This book is being compiled at the end of the dot.com boom, when the possibility of global recession looms. It is a source of fascination to the authors that investors can both cry 'foul' that they were unable to buy as many shares as they wished, and at the same time complain bitterly about the huge falls in share prices that have been experienced!

WORKING
11.2

INSIGHT   **Illustrative contents of listing particulars**

- Details of the shares to be issued, and full details of the share capital of the company, including the rights of different types of share.
- Information about the business of the company, its performance, and the markets in which it trades.
- Information about the directors and key personnel.
- Confirmation that the company will have sufficient funds in the foreseeable future.
- Information about any unusual contracts entered into by the company of which shareholders should be aware.
- Details of any ongoing or potential litigation.
- An indication of the company's dividend policy after flotation.
- Accountants' report on previous years' financial results.
- Anything else that might be of interest to the potential shareholders.

Preparing and reviewing this mass of documentation, and actually getting the company onto the market, involves many different parties. Working insight 11.3 sets out brief details of these protagonists and their roles in the drama.

An obviously important consideration in the flotation process is the price at which the shares are listed. It would be nice to be able to tell you that the company's advisers consider in detail its projected cash flows out into the future, and discount them at a cost of capital to arrive at a valuation. Nice, but alas untrue. Although valuation on fundamentals does undoubtedly take place, much of the art of pricing flotations depends on finding a suitable comparator share and using its price earnings multiple as a benchmark. Market multiples have far more significance in the process than academic purists would care to admit. Similarly, the absolute value of the shares plays its part: the authors have seen at least one flotation before which the company did a one for one share split in order to double the number of shares, halving the potential share price so that it would not seem excessive when compared to its nearest comparator!

On the subject of pricing, what does 'good' look like in a float? When Company X's shares are listed at 100 p and immediately climb to 200 p in the first few hours, is that good? When Company Y's shares float at 100 p and fall to 50 p by the end of the first day, is that good? The answer to both of those questions is 'no'.

If the share rises greatly in price in the first few hours or days of trading, the implication is that the advisers have got the price wrong. The shareholders who bought into Company X on the listing have made a 100 per cent profit; they are happy. But the company could have issued half as many shares and raised the same amount of cash, so it has unfairly diluted its existing shareholders by issuing shares at an undervalue. Or it could have raised twice as much money by issuing the same number of shares. As for Company Y, its new shareholders no doubt feel bitter about 'being conned out of their money by an over-priced

WORKING
11.3
INSIGHT

Who's who in a flotation

Sponsor

Often a merchant bank or stockbroker. They project-manage the issue and advise on all aspects. They effectively (but not necessarily legally) share responsibility with the directors for the contents of the listing particulars.

Broker

Will advise on the ultimate offer price. May also act as a liaison between the company and the Stock Exchange. May arrange the underwriting.

(Often the same company will provide sponsor and broking services.)

Underwriters

The main underwriter guarantees (for a substantial fee) that the company will be able to sell its shares, as they will take them should the issue not be popular in the market. (Effectively, the underwriter sells the company a put option on the shares.) This risk is laid off to sub-underwriters (who receive a large part of that fee).

Reporting accountants

Prepare the accountants' report on prior years' results. Review the company's cash flow forecasts. Carry out due diligence on behalf of the sponsor.

Solicitors

Solicitors to the sponsor and solicitors to the company (normally separate firms). Review all legal documentation and ensure compliance with relevant regulations.

Public relations firm

Promote the company within the City prior to and post float.

Registrars

Responsible for sending out the share certificates and managing the share register.

Receiving bankers

To whom the payment for shares is sent.

Security printers

Prepare many drafts of the extensive documentation required for a listing, to tight deadlines.

---

issue'. The company has obtained the funds it sought, and has created value for any exiting shareholders, but at the expense of its future goodwill in the investment community. Next time it tries to raise capital, investors will remember this debacle and be suspicious.

In a 'good' float the shares are priced at about 10 per cent less than where the advisers expect the closing price to be at the end of day 1. Such a discount – which is easier to describe than to manage (see case study 11.1) – enables the new investors to feel mildly content with their investment, whilst providing reasonable value to existing shareholders.

A further issue to consider about the flotation process is the time it takes. Were you to look at the promotional documentation issued by many of the leading

11.1	PRACTICAL EXAMPLES OF THE DIFFICULTIES OF PRICING IPOS

CASE STUDY

Orange

When France Telecom was considering floating Orange, its subsidiary, it was advised that the company was worth between €70 bn and €80 bn. However, a few weeks later changes in market conditions meant that advisors changed their views, and the pricing was set to raise between €55 bn and €65 bn. The price was cut by a further €10 bn just before the IPO, to ensure that the float would be a success. However, although the share price fell on its debut, the company then out-performed its sector.

Woolworths

When Kingfisher floated its Woolworths subsidiary in August 2001, original expectations had been for a value of £550 million. Investors and advisers then reduced their expectations considerably, and the IPO went ahead at the substantially lower price of £350 million. The market capitalization rose to £475 million on the first day of trading.

stock exchanges, they set out an illustrative timetable for flotation that starts with appointing advisers and ends some four or five months later on 'impact day' when the shares are quoted on the market. In practice, the listing process can take a lot longer than that. Indeed, if advisers think it desirable for the company to engage in pre-float grooming, tidying up its balance sheet and capital structure and ensuring a steady trend in profit growth, the process can take several years.

IS IT WORTH IT?

The first section of this chapter set out the advantages of listing for a company. Having set out the complex decisions and processes involved the question has to be asked 'why would you want to float: is it worth it?'. Certainly, for growing companies seeking access to a new and extensive source of funding, flotation is an excellent way to proceed. But a note of caution should also be exercised. In this section we set out some of the reasons *not* to seek a public listing.

1. Flotation involves a lot of time and cost, as discussed earlier. More significantly, during the period when the company is preparing for flotation its senior management will be unable to focus on the business itself. Their time will be taken up in endless meetings, and in making the rounds of the investing institutions to pitch to their prospective 'customers'. Unless this is carefully planned, the company's business can suffer during this period.
2. As the CEO or chairman of a listed company, less of your time is spent on running the business, even post float, as a considerable proportion of your time will be involved in dealing with investors and analysts. The larger the company, the more investor attention it attracts and the greater this time.

3. For both the company and its directors, flotation involves a heightened public awareness of what they are doing. Directors of listed companies become public figures; often, even their private lives are reported upon by the press. For the company, results and strategies are analysed in close detail, often critically, by commentators who may have only a scant understanding of the industry dynamics.

4. Corporate governance requirements on listed companies are considerable, and independently-minded executives may feel that they interfere with the smooth running of the business.

5. Many directors take the position that the City has a short term view. This is why they focus on manipulating earnings per share in quarterly or half-yearly results; they claim that the market would not understand the long term implications of a strategy that decreased short term profitability.[3]

6. Once listed, the company may become vulnerable to a hostile takeover. (Takeovers, hostile and otherwise, are discussed in Chapter 12.)

7. Once listed, the company becomes far more susceptible to market conditions, and may see its market capitalization fall through no fault of its own. This is discussed further in the next section.

Given this list, the directors and shareholders have to decide whether they really want a listing, or whether their objectives could be achieved in another way. (The shareholders also have to make another decision: given that they choose to obtain a listing, are the current directors the people they want to present to the City, or is a change in management appropriate at this stage? In family-dominated companies this can be a particularly problematic issue.)

DE-LISTING

We have considered in detail how and why a company might list its shares. However, in recent years many directors of listed companies have chosen to de-list their shares, taking their companies private. Occasionally this is done because the company has fallen foul of the rules of its exchange, for example companies on NYSE whose share price falls below $1 for a period. More often, the privatization is voluntary, and the logic behind this action will now be considered.

A key reason for companies being taken private is that the directors believe, often correctly, that the market is under-valuing them. In the current (at the time of writing) investment climate this is particularly true of smaller companies. It was mentioned earlier that most of the attention of analysts and investors is concentrated on the larger companies – for example the FTSE 100

---

3. Although there is certainly some truth to this, the City's short termism is perhaps more discussed than evidenced. For example, were GlaxoSmithKline, one of the world's largest pharmaceutical companies, to announce that next year it is slashing investment in research and development, profits would rise but the share price would plummet as investors immediately realized the impact on long term cashflows and value.

and the FTSE 250, which together comprise the 350 largest companies (by market capitalization) in the LSE. The LSE contains almost 2000 listed companies: therefore a lot of these are relatively neglected.

There is little liquidity in smaller company shares, for two reasons. Firstly, few investors wish to buy them because they are unknown, which means that not only do they not register on the radar as potential investments, but also that they are perceived as risky because fewer analysts report on them so less information is available. Secondly, as a practical issue, many large financial institutions will have a minimum dealing size of upwards of several hundred thousand pounds – such institutions would be unable to buy or sell a stake in a small company without significantly moving the share price. And, of course, such extreme movements in the share price, quite apart from acting to nullify any potential profit on the transaction, will lead to additional volatility in the share price, possibly increasing its beta, and thus establishing it further as a risky stock.

In such circumstances, directors often decide that it would be in their and the company's best interests if it were taken private. If the company was originally floated as a 'cash out' float, then the financing for this should be easy to arrange, as mature companies tend to have strong cashflows against which the company could raise debt.

Similarly, for a company that floated to raise cash and which has since become mature, there is now an ability to raise debt funding and the added incentive that the original reason for the float – to raise cash for growth – is superseded, so there is no further advantage to a listing. Even if the directors still believe the company to be in its growth stage, if its shares are rated poorly there is no further opportunity to raise additional capital at a sensible price (i.e. one which does not greatly dilute existing shareholders), and so the reasons for being listed have disappeared.

Another reason why a poorly-rated company may wish to go private is a fear of takeover, particularly if it is apparently a well-performing company in an out-of-favour sector, as were many small engineering companies at the height of the dot.com boom. Although hostile takeovers are, as discussed in the following chapter, generally hostile to the directors rather than the shareholders (another example of agency theory), for many smaller companies these parties overlap significantly, and the individuals concerned may decide that it is in their own best interests to privatize.

The agency issue between directors and shareholders raises another concern. Directors are meant to act in the best interests of the shareholders over whose interests they are stewards. However, if the executive directors of a company make a bid to take it private, their interests diverge from those of the non-director shareholders. Because of this in many jurisdictions, the UK being one, there is a requirement that the non executives play an active role in such privatizations, taking independent advice in order to inform the shareholders whether the bid is reasonable at an acceptable price.

Even if the company's shares are not under-performing, the directors may decide that privatization is a preferable option. This is often because they feel that the market is too short termist, and is restricting the company's long term growth opportunities. Or they might feel that the public scrutiny of their own performance is unacceptable, and wish to regain the independence of action that they had as executives in a privately-held business.

Of course, de-listing a company is carried out more easily when the directors still own a substantial shareholding. This means that (a) the vote in favour of de-listing is more certain to be passed, and (b) less cash needs to be found to finance the deal, as less shares are in 'public' hands needing to be bought out. But it does occasionally happen that a management buyin team (see Chapter 14) makes an offer to take private a listed company, often against the wishes of the existing management. This might happen in circumstances where the market is under-valuing a good company. The bidding management can see the possibility of running the company privately for a few years, then re-floating it at a more propitious time.

12

Acquisitions, mergers and selling a business

If research indicates that most acquisitions fail, why do companies undertake them? The most appropriate reason for undertaking acquisitions is to add value to the company, by enhancing its competitive advantage. In evaluating potential transactions, the seven drivers of value can be used as a way to determine if such value-enhancement – often referred to as 'synergy' – stands up to scrutiny. The calculations underlying this analysis are vital to determine the ultimate value of the business combination to the bidder's shareholders, but bidders must remember that the value determined is not the same as the amount to be paid for the target; many bidders overpay, and effectively give away the synergies to the target's shareholders.

Listed companies have the choice of financing their acquisitions by offering their own equity to the target shareholders as an alternative to a cash offer. Both sets of shareholders need to evaluate whether a share-based or cash-based bid will be appropriate. Issues to consider in this evaluation include the relative valuations of the two companies, the potential for the bid to create value, the desire of the bidder's management to retain control, and the financial strategy of the bidder. Lesser considerations include the impact that the financing of the transaction will have on the bidder's reported financial results, and, in particular, on its earnings per share.

Acquisitions are sometimes structured as earn outs, whereby the manager/shareholders of the target company agree to stay with the company for a period post-sale, and their consideration for the sale depends in part on the target's performance in that period. Such a deal structure has both advantages and disadvantages for each party, but invariably makes the transaction more complex.

Finally, we consider company disposals, and examine defence strategies that can be used to deflect hostile bids, whilst pointing out that such strategies are not always used in the best interests of shareholders.

INTRODUCTION

We established in the first part of this book that companies need to grow in order to generate capital gains for their shareholders and to justify the growth value already priced into their shares. There are two main ways in which this growth can be obtained: organically, and by acquisition. Organic growth is often less risky, but it can be difficult for larger companies; doubling in size is simpler for a company with £10 m turnover than for one turning over £1 billion. Accordingly, many companies look to acquisitions or mergers as a means to obtain the appropriate growth within the required time frame.

We tend in finance to refer to 'acquisitions and mergers'. In an acquisition, one company (often, but not always, the larger) purchases the other. A merger is more of a meeting of equals; two companies of approximately the same size come together to form one new venture. In practice, it is sometimes difficult to differentiate the two types of transaction as, for accounting reasons (see the discussion in Chapter 1 on 'pooling') companies have incentives to present a deal as a merger when in fact it turns out to have been an acquisition. Accordingly, in this chapter the term 'acquisition' is used to cover both types of transaction.

WHY MAKE AN ACQUISITION?

Academic research shows that most acquisitions fail, in that they do not meet the original expectations of the acquiring party. Although such research can be vulnerable to mis-interpretation (it is difficult to evaluate the aims and outcomes of transactions assessed from a distance) its results are widely disseminated in the popular and business press, and so must be known by most CEOs and finance directors. Nevertheless, acquisition activity is widespread, and not all of it can be driven by a desire to provide large fees to investment banks. So, why make an acquisition?

In the authors' opinion, reasons for acquisition activity fall into two camps – good reasons and bad reasons. The over-riding 'good' reason is the creation of shareholder value; we have, after all, established this as the key corporate objective. More specifically, the good reasons can be analysed as follows:

1. To support value-creating growth that cannot be achieved organically.
2. To complement the business strategy by filling gaps in product range, market segments, geographic territories, technological know-how, etc. And possibly
3. To prevent a competitor from making the acquisition.

We will come back to reasons one and two shortly. However, at this point we have to admit that we do have some doubts about this third reason. On balance, we have included it under 'goods' rather than 'bads' on the basis that allowing a competitor to expand could in some circumstances lead to an erosion of one's own competitive position, thus destroying value in the future. Therefore, making an acquisition to prevent this – provided that the overall effect is value-enhancing – is a legitimate strategy.

The bad reasons for acquisitions, of which there are alas many practical examples, are:

4. To show better financial results (e.g. to increase eps, whether or not this increases shareholder value); and
5. Managerial utility (a polite way of saying 'it's much more fun to buy companies than it is to run them successfully, so that's what we're going to do!').

On the basis that we seek to inculcate good habits in our readers, we intend to ignore the 'bad' acquisition reasons from now on, and to focus on the good ones. And these can all be summarized in a term often used in describing mergers and acquisitions: 'Synergy'.

Almost every acquisition we have ever seen or been involved in has been praised (by the protagonists) for the synergy created. In fact, the term is used so often that it is probably illegal to do a deal without mentioning it! But in the context of acquisition, what exactly does it mean?

The common shorthand used to explain synergy is '2 + 2 = 5', i.e. if we put these two parts together the subsequent whole is worth considerably more than its components. However, this is the sort of woolly terminology that can be used to justify any deal, so let's see what we can do to strengthen our understanding of the concept.

In terms of competitive strategy, synergy can be described as either the creation of a sustainable competitive advantage or at least the removal of a previous competitive disadvantage. The achievement of significant economies of scale or gaining much greater control over channels of distribution or sources of supply may enable the enlarged business to improve its financial return. In these cases the financial justification for the acquisition should be that it would be much more expensive and/or more risky to try to achieve the same improvement in financial return by organic development of the business.

An even tighter definition of synergy can be obtained by referring back to Rappaport's seven drivers of value, discussed in Chapter 1. Rappaport stated that shareholder value can be calculated based on the following drivers:

1. sales growth
2. operating profit margin
3. cash tax rate
4. incremental investment in capital expenditure

> **WORKING 12.1**
>
> **INSIGHT**
>
> ### Synergy checklist
>
> 1. Does this deal increase sales growth (for example, by expanding distribution networks or product lines)? Over what period and by how much?
> 2. Does it increase the operating profit margin (for example, by eliminating cost duplication, creating economies of scale, or transferring best practice from one company to the other)? Over what period and by how much?
> 3. Does this deal reduce our effective tax rate (for example by locating profits in a more tax-efficient part of the world)? Over what period and by how much?
> 4. Does the deal mean that we can save on capital expenditure (for example by merging manufacturing facilities to improve utilization, or by getting rid of one of the head offices)? Over what period and by how much?
> 5. Does the deal lead to better working capital management (for example by pooling stocks, or transferring best practice in debtor management)? Over what period and by how much?
> 6. Does the deal extend our competitive advantage period (for example, by extending the brand franchise)? Over what period and by how much?
> 7. Does the deal reduce our cost of capital? Why? (If both companies have the appropriate capital structure already in place, then their combination should not make a difference.)

5. investment in working capital
6. time period of competitive advantage
7. cost of capital

This listing can be used as a checklist for identifying synergies, as set out in Working insight 12.1.

Using the checklist set out in Working insight 12.1 provides a way to quantify the potential synergies from an acquisition. It takes away the 'wishful thinking' element of the deal, and sets out clear post integration targets. It can also be taken a stage further: as well as asking 'Over what period and by how much?' one could add 'And whose responsibility is it to achieve this?'. If more deals were subject to this kind of analytical rigour, less deals might be done!

Evaluation of the potential deal synergies leads us conveniently to the next section: how should the deal be valued?

HOW MUCH TO PAY?

It is often said that acquirers overpay for deals. Certainly, an analysis of where value lies in an acquisition will lead the researcher to conclude that in general the vendor shareholders obtain a better deal than the acquiring shareholders. But the 'overpay' proposition tends to be made on the basis of prices paid for acquisitions of listed companies – these are often at a premium of 30 per cent or more over the target's pre-bid share price.

To assume that an acquirer is overpaying merely because the bid price is greater than the pre-existing share price is a fallacy. There are two reasons for this.

Firstly, it is a misconception to assume that the market capitalization of a company (the current share price multiplied by the number of outstanding shares) represents the value of that company. It doesn't. The current share price for any company represents the price at which most shareholders were not persuaded to sell their shares. Only a small proportion of any company's capital changes hands on any day, and the quoted price is merely the price of the latest transaction. If this were an over-value, it presumably would persuade most rational investors to sell out. Even if the quoted share price exactly equalled the 'fair' price, it is reasonable to assume that more shareholders would sell (assuming that shareholders' expectations of future performance are distributed normally around the mean of 'fair' price). Thus the market capitalization is generally perceived as an undervalue, and shareholders need to be offered a premium to persuade them to sell.

Secondly, shareholders understand markets. A bidder for the whole of a company's share capital is creating a situation in which demand exceeds supply; the share price obviously goes up to reflect this. And the shareholders realize that acquiring 100 per cent of the company puts the acquirer in a far more powerful, and valuable, position than an investor acquiring a small stake: accordingly they make the bidding company pay for this value.

The issue for the bidder is to ensure that the amount paid for the business does not exceed the value it will generate. Here is where the analysis of synergies from Working insight 12.1 can be used. Figure 12.1 illustrates how value is added in a deal.

The value diagram in Figure 12.1 starts on the left hand side of the page with the value of the company to the vendor. This may be the market capitalization, but a bidder would be better to undertake an analysis of value under the target company's existing strategy and management. From this point the bidder can add in the value created by each of the identified synergies; the seven broad drivers included in Working insight 12.1 may be broken down at this stage, to identify, for example, how much value will come from better procurement practices, how much will come from elimination of duplicate expenses, or how much will be

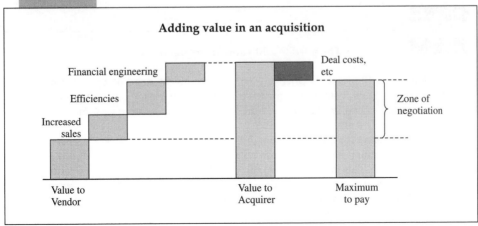

Figure 12.1

Adding value in an acquisition

generated from manufacturing efficiencies. (Often, the detailed due diligence carried out pre-acquisition will give indications of the potential synergies and the realism behind the initial bid assumptions.) For illustration, Figure 12.1 includes only three types of synergy. Adding those to the base value leads us to the target's potential value to the acquirer. However, this is not the amount that should be paid for the target business. Merchant banks and lawyers do not come cheap, and substantial deal costs may be incurred before the transaction is complete, thus reducing the deal's potential value. Similarly, reorganization costs such as redundancies need to be considered. The sum that remains is an indication to the bidder of the maximum amount that they should be prepared to pay for the target company.

This is where things often go wrong. The bidding team, with this 'maximum amount' fixed in their minds, are often prepared to pay up to this amount. This has the effect of giving to the vendor shareholders the benefit of all of the synergies that the company intends to generate – before it has even started. In other words, paying the maximum value for the target company represents a transaction at a net present value of zero: a fun exercise for management, but hardly a value-enhancing strategy. The price paid will probably be greater than the vendor's value, but should be significantly less than the bidder's maximum.

If the value to the vendor is higher than that to the potential bidder, then (unless vendor or bidder is particularly stupid) the deal will not proceed. Similarly in a competitive bidding situation, it is logical (but again not always true) that the bidder who can create the most value is the one who will win the deal.

It can be difficult to add value in an acquisition. Acquisitions raise shareholders' expectations. After all, as shareholders in Company P we can go out and buy shares in Company Q. So if Company P itself chooses to buy Company Q it must be expecting to add some value that we as individual investors could not create. Furthermore, an acquisition premium will almost certainly have been paid – so Company P has paid more for Q than we would have ourselves. And finally, we must remember that the share price of both companies undoubtedly has a PVGO element, with future growth already priced into the shares. Thus if the acquisition is to create value, the combined organization has to outperform the growth already included in its share price. Working insight 12.2 illustrates this.

WORKING
12.2
INSIGHT   **The need to add value in acquisitions**

Target has eps of 10 p, a share price of 200 p and pays a dividend of 2 p per share. Its cost of equity is 11 per cent, which means that, with a dividend yield of 1 per cent, investors are expecting growth in the share price of 10 per cent per annum. Such expectations imply a share price of 322 p in five years' time.

Bidder buys Target for 250 p per share. Assuming the same cost of capital and dividend yield, annual growth of 10 per cent means that a share price of 403 p is required by year 5. This implies eps growth (assuming no change in the P/E ratio) of 15 per cent per annum. Unless Bidder can increase Target's growth rate by an additional 5 per cent per year, it is destroying value for its shareholders.

HOW DO WE FINANCE THE DEAL?

Deals can be financed by an exchange of shares, or through some form of cash. In an exchange of shares, the shareholders of the target company exchange their shares in Target for shares in Bidder. A cash deal involves Bidder paying cash (from its existing resources, or financed through raising debt or by issuing new shares on the market) to the Target shareholders. Thus a share exchange adds the Target shareholders to the shareholder base of Bidder; a cash bid means that Target shareholders do not participate in the future of the combined company.

Deal finance can be considered in two separate ways: we can look at value-enhancing strategies, and we can consider eps-enhancing strategies. Naturally, your authors believe strongly in the former, but a jaundiced view of the markets indicates that many companies put enhancement of eps above shareholder value, so this is where we will start.

FINANCING ACQUISITIONS USING EPS-ENHANCING STRATEGIES

If the acquisition finance is to be structured so as to enhance eps, there are two 'rules' to note:

1. If the Bidder P/E is higher than the Target P/E, using equity to finance the deal will increase eps; if Bidder P/E is less than Target P/E then using equity will dilute eps.
2. If the company's post-tax interest rate is lower than the inverse of the Target P/E ratio, then using debt will enhance eps; if the interest rate exceeds the inverse of Target P/E, then using debt will dilute eps.

These two 'rules' will now be explained.

Working insight 12.3 sets out an example of how the first of these rules works in practice.

Working insight 12.3 illustrates the fallacy of basing deal assessment on whether or not it is immediately eps-enhancing. The Bidder/Target combination is 'bad' because it dilutes eps; the Target/Bidder combination is 'good'. In either case the same assets have been combined – it's just a matter of arithmetic. (The Annex to this chapter sets out a mathematical proof of why this is so.)

The other 'rule' to enhance eps related to debt financing. Working insight 12.4 sets out why this works.

FINANCING ACQUISITIONS USING VALUE-ENHANCING STRATEGIES

As stated earlier, acquisitions can be undertaken by offering the target shareholders shares in the bidding company (an acquisition for shares) or offering them cash. The choice of financing methods will depend at least partly on the business risk of the bidder and, if appropriate, the target company. The bidding company should not upset its long term financial strategy without good cause.

It is important to note that although an acquisition for shares involves issuing new equity, an acquisition for cash need not be financed by raising debt. The bidding company could issue shares in the market and use the proceeds of the

WORKING 12.3

INSIGHT

Relationship between bidder and target P/E and eps dilution

Bidder plc is acquiring Target plc. Each company has 1000 shares in issue, and is trading at £10 per share. For convenience, assume that each company could be bought for its market capitalization (£10 000) by issuing shares at the existing share price. (These assumptions can be relaxed without invalidating the principles shown, but they make the case easier to explain.)

	Bidder	Target
Profit after tax	£1000	£500
Earnings per share	£1	£0.5
Share price	£10	£10
P/E ratio	10	20

1. Bidder to buy Target at £10 000, issuing 1000 new shares.

Revised share capital of Bidder	2000
Combined after-tax profits	£1500
Revised eps	£0.75

If Bidder, a low P/E company, buys Target, a higher P/E company for shares, the eps is diluted from £1 to 75 p. Financial markets may see this as 'bad'.

2. However, what if instead Target were to buy Bidder, issuing 1000 new shares so to do?

Revised share capital of Target	2000
Combined after-tax profits	£1500
Revised eps	£0.75

Thus the combination of Target/Bidder has increased eps from 50 p to 75 p – obviously a good deal!

In practice of course, judgement as to whether it is a good or bad deal should lie only with an assessment of whether shareholder value is increased, not the impact on earnings per share.

WORKING 12.4

INSIGHT

Using debt finance to enhance eps

Target has post-tax earnings of £500 and is being acquired for £10 000. Bidder can borrow at 6.25 per cent and pays tax at the rate of 20 per cent which reduces its cost of debt to an after-tax 5 per cent.

Bidder is buying profits after tax of £500.
The cost of financing the acquisition by debt is £10 000 @ 5 per cent, i.e. £500.
Thus, in the first year the extra interest cost exactly cancels out the acquired profits.

The after-tax debt cost, 5 per cent, is the inverse of Target's P/E ratio of 20. If Bidder could borrow at less than 5 per cent, the deal would be eps-enhancing in year 1. If its borrowing cost exceeded 5 per cent, eps would fall.

Figure 12.2

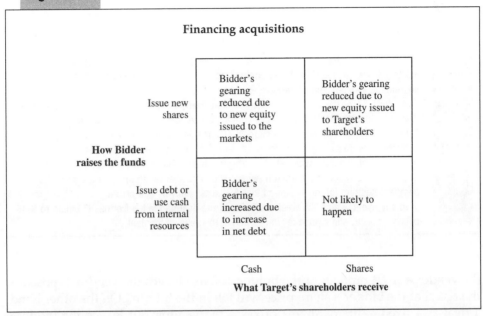

Financing acquisitions

	Cash	Shares
Issue new shares	Bidder's gearing reduced due to new equity issued to the markets	Bidder's gearing reduced due to new equity issued to Target's shareholders
Issue debt or use cash from internal resources	Bidder's gearing increased due to increase in net debt	Not likely to happen

How Bidder raises the funds

What Target's shareholders receive

sale to pay cash for the target company. Figure 12.2 illustrates the different alternatives.

If the target company shareholders receive cash (however raised) for their shares, that is the end of their involvement with the company. However, in deals which pay the target shareholders in shares, they have an ongoing relationship with the company. Thus in share-based deals the vendor shareholders have various matters to consider:

1. Are both companies fairly valued? It is obvious that acquirers always need to understand the value of the target company, but if the target's shareholders are to accept shares in the bidder, they need to know that this currency is not over-valued. Case study 12.1 on AOL/Time Warner illustrates this.
2. What are the prospects for the combined company? Again, this is always a matter of interest to the bidder's shareholders, but in a share-based transaction the target's shareholders are effectively agreeing to accept the risks and rewards of the ongoing company. One of the best pieces of advice given by one of your authors was to a friend who had been offered a large sum (payable in shares) by a quoted dot.com which wished to buy his fledgling internet company. The advice was 'don't see it as selling your company – what you're doing is using your business as a currency to buy a small stake in a larger concern over which you have no control; do you feel comfortable about that?'. A year later his company was thriving...the quoted dot.com had gone into liquidation.

If a transaction is done for shares, the parties have to determine how the price is stated: as a fixed number of shares, or a fixed value. There will inevitably be a delay between announcing a deal and completing it. A deal which offers

CASE STUDY

12.1 AOL/TIME WARNER

In January 2000 it was announced that internet company AOL was to acquire media giant Time Warner. The $163 billion deal, at the time the largest ever, was to be effected by the issue of new shares in AOL Time Warner, with each Time Warner shareholder receiving 1.5 new shares, and each AOL shareholder receiving one new share. This gave Time Warner shareholders 45 per cent of the combined company.

At the time of the deal, AOL's market capitalization was considerably more than Time Warner's, and the deal terms effectively meant that AOL was offering a huge premium to the Time Warner shareholders. It was suggested at the time that this was at least partly because AOL shares were trading on a 'dot.com' valuation, which in early 2000 was at a significant premium to the market, whereas Time Warner shares reflected an 'old economy' company, at a lower P/E ratio. The premium paid to the Time Warner shareholders was perhaps to compensate them for the likelihood that AOL was relatively overpriced.

In any event, within the week the value of the deal had fallen from $163 billion to $145 billion, as AOL's share price fell in reaction to the news of the deal.

the vendor a fixed number of the bidder's shares leaves the vendor exposed to the risk that the bidder's share price will fall in the interim. On the other hand, a deal at a fixed value of shares protects the vendor, but leaves the bidder's shareholders vulnerable to dilution should the share price fall.

EARN OUTS

Another way of structuring an acquisition may be through an earn out, in which the eventual price paid for the business depends in part on its performance in the early years following the transfer of ownership.

Earn outs are often used in the acquisition of private companies, for example in situations where the acquiring company wishes to retain the services and commitment of the director/shareholders of the target company, perhaps because they are crucial to operations. In a business which is very dependent on personal relationships, the bidding company may wish to retain the directors' commitment for long enough to ensure that the goodwill and contact base are secure.

The earn out deal might be that the vendor shareholders receive £X immediately on completion of the deal, and a further £Y if profits of a certain level are achieved within one, two or possibly three years of the deal being done. This gives the key director/shareholders an incentive to perform well during the earn out period.

It should be obvious from the above that earn outs will only be effective in situations in which the vendor shareholders are also the key management of the company, generally in private companies. If the management are not shareholders, an earn out will not benefit them, and management contracts might be a better way to achieve their commitment. If the shareholders are not managers, they may be very reluctant to agree an earn out, leaving their ultimate consideration in the hands of managers over whom they no longer have any sanction.

Earn outs may also be used as a means to resolve differences of opinion as to a company's potential, and thus its value. It often happens that the target

---

Features of an earn out to the acquirer

Advantages

a. Only pay for what is achieved.
b. Defers payment, thus retaining cash resources.
c. Defers payment, thus delaying dilution of eps and control.

Disadvantages

a. Difficult to achieve synergies in combining the businesses, as the continuing management will demand a free hand to run 'their' business.
b. If the bidder's share price falls in the intervening period, it could end up issuing far more shares for the final consideration than was intended.

---

company is small, but with great prospects. Naturally, the vendors wish to receive consideration for the potential that they are selling to the bidder. However, the bidder, quite reasonably, could argue that it will not pay for unrealized potential that cannot yet be proved. An earn out may be used to resolve this situation, with the initial price reflecting the target's current performance, and further payments being made if certain milestones are achieved.

Structuring a deal as an earn out has both advantages and disadvantages to the acquirer, as set out in Working insight 12.5

SELLING A BUSINESS

Having considered acquisitions, it is worth turning briefly to examine matters from the point of view of a vendor selling his/her business. In this section we consider specifically the positions of owner/managers of private companies.

In our opinion, every owner of a private company should consider his/her eventual exit strategy. Do you intend to build the company up quickly and then sell out in five years' time? Is your goal capital growth in the short or long term, or are you seeking a good lifestyle out of the business until your normal retirement age? Even if you intend to 'work until you drop', who will inherit the business from you, and what state will it be in?

There are two main reasons for having your eventual exit strategy in mind. The first one is that owners who seek a lifestyle from the business will run their operations in different ways to those going for aggressive growth leading to an eventual sale. In particular, owners planning to sell out in a few years should be scanning the environment for potential acquirers, and perhaps grooming their companies for that eventual sale, in a similar manner to pre-float grooming discussed in Chapter 11. The second reason for owners to consider their eventual exit strategy is so that they can react more quickly to any out-of-the-blue offer for the business. (Of course, if enough money is offered, it may change your original plans, but it's always useful to have an initial position.)

For a private company, if the out-of-the-blue offer is unwelcome, that is the end of the matter; no-one can force the sale of a private company against the shareholders' wishes. However, often an unwelcome offer is made for a listed company and it is these, hostile, offers which are discussed in the next section.

DEFENCE STRATEGIES

An offer made to acquire a listed company which is rejected by the target company's directors is known as a hostile bid. It is important to realize that the bid is hostile to the directors – the company's shareholders may actually welcome the bid.

Why would the target's directors reject the bid? There are two main reasons:

a. Because they believe that the bid undervalues the company; i.e. they consider that they can create more value for shareholders by continuing to run the company themselves;
b. Because they wish to retain their jobs.

It goes without saying that we see the first reason as totally valid and the second as probably against shareholders' interests. However, an examination of directors' actions in bid situations leads us to believe that reason 'b' often applies in practice.

Directors fending off a hostile bid need a defence strategy (which generally comes courtesy of a host of highly paid advisers). The best defence strategy is to ensure that the company is correctly valued by the markets at all times. Given that quoted company acquisitions generally demand a significant price premium, if the company is fully valued, the potential acquirer is either bringing in synergies or is overpaying. In either of these situations, a bid is likely to generate value for the target shareholders.

As well as continually communicating with the markets to ensure an appropriate valuation, directors of listed companies should maintain a contingency plan of what they will do should an unexpected offer be made. This will help them to react more swiftly and efficiently to the offer. Such reaction will include the preparation of a comprehensive defence document to explain to shareholders why they should not accept the offer, and a concerted effort to woo key shareholders such as major financial institutions.

Within the UK, there are various strategies that can be adopted by the directors of the target company in order to fend off the bid. We list these in Working insight 12.6, but with a health warning – although they might enable the company to remain independent, they may also destroy value for the shareholders.

In other countries, a wider range of defence strategies may be available. For example, 'poison pills' are allowed in the United States and in various European countries. Some examples of poison pills are shown in Working insight 12.7.

Again, we would point out that poison pills may benefit the directors of the target company, but rarely add value for its existing shareholders.

An example of a complex poison pill defence was seen in the attempted takeover of Gucci by LVMH, which commenced in 1999, as set out in case study 12.2.

WORKING 12.6

INSIGHT

Defence strategies available to UK companies

- Make an acquisition, thus making your company larger, and more difficult for the predator to digest.
- Dispose of some key assets which would be particularly attractive to the predator.
- Find a 'white knight' – another company which will acquire the target, and will be more acceptable to the directors.
- Have the bid referred to the competition authorities, which may prevent it, but will almost certainly delay it considerably.

WORKING 12.7

INSIGHT

Some examples of poison pills

- Set up a 'staggered board' such that only a certain number of directors can be made to retire each year. Although this may not prevent the takeover, it means that some of the outgoing directors could retain their jobs for up to three years.
- Issue new shares at a discount to friendly shareholders, thus continually diluting the acquirer's shareholding.
- Set up provisions in the company's internal regulations such that a super-majority (say 80 per cent) is required to agree a takeover rather than the customary 50 per cent.

12.2 A BID DEFENCE – GUCCI, LVMH AND PPR

CASE STUDY

In January 1999 LVMH, the luxury goods company, acquired 34 per cent of the share capital of Gucci, another luxury goods company. LVMH stated that it would not make a full takeover bid, but demanded board representation (which would effectively have given it a great deal of control without the cost of making a bid).

The Gucci directors took the view that this was not in their/the company's interests. Accordingly, their first step (in February 1999) was to issue new shares to an employee share trust, effectively diluting LVMH's stake.

In March that year Gucci issued a further tranche of new shares to Pinault Printemps Redoute (PPR), another luxury goods company, one which the Gucci board viewed more favourably. This gave PPR 42 per cent of the share capital, further diluting LVMH.

In April 1999 LVMH made a bid for the whole company at $91 per share, which the Gucci management rejected. There followed a series of legal actions through the courts.
The situation was eventually resolved in September 2001, as follows:

- PPR would acquire about 20 per cent of LVMH's existing shareholding, thus giving PPR majority control of the company (although, by agreement, not a board majority).
- A special dividend of $7 per share was to be paid to all Gucci shareholders except PPR.
- PPR committed to making an offer, at $101.50, for all of the outstanding shares by March 2004.

It may be argued that by rejecting the original LVMH bid the Gucci management created value for their shareholders. However, based on the opportunity cost of rejecting the 1999 LVMH bid of $91, the IRR receivable by the Gucci minority shareholders to 2004 is less than 4 per cent per year.

In summary, it is very difficult to justify many of the tactics that directors use to defend against hostile bids. However, often the bidder has to raise its original offer in order to overcome their resistance to the deal: this in itself can add considerable value for the target company's shareholders.

ANNEX – 'BOOTSTRAPPING' TO ENHANCE EPS

The following is a mathematical proof of why the purchase of a low P/E company by a high P/E company will lead to an increase in eps for the acquirer.

Bidder company:		Target company:	
Earnings	E_b	Earnings	E_t
Share price	P_b	Share price	P_t
Mkt value	MV_b	Mkt value (value of the bid)	MV_t
P/E	PE_b	P/E	PE_t

Therefore number of Bidder shares in issue $= MV_b/P_b$
Number of Bidder shares needed to acquire Target $= MV_t/P_b$

After the acquisition, the new company will have the combined earnings of Target and Bidder (assuming no synergies). Therefore, the new eps after acquisition will be:

$$eps_{new} = (E_b + E_t) / \text{total new shares}$$
$$eps_{new} = (E_b + E_t) / (MV_b/P_b + MV_t/P_b)$$
$$eps_{new} = (E_b + E_t)P_b / (MV_b + MV_t)$$
$$eps_{new} = (E_b + E_t)P_b / (PE_b \times E_b + PE_t \times E_t)$$

Now, if $PE_b > PE_t$...
Replace PE_t with PE_b in the above equation.
Therefore

$$eps_{new} > (E_b + E_t)P_b / (PE_b \times E_b + PE_b \times E_t)$$
$$\text{i.e. } eps_{new} > (E_b + E_t)P_b / (E_b + E_t)PE_b$$
$$\text{i.e. } eps_{new} > P_b/PE_b \text{ (which is the same as eps old for Bidder)}$$

Therefore $eps_{new} > eps_{old}$ if Bidder P/E is higher than the Target's.

13

Restructuring a company

Companies may need to be restructured to change their financial strategy or to help correct a market underpricing. Changes in financial strategy normally relate to a reduction in gearing. This can be effected by selling assets or raising new funds. In more serious cases, the restructuring might involve re-negotiating terms with creditors, by extending loan repayment dates or by swapping debt into equity. Changes in the market's perception of the company are often managed by demerging units, in order to make the underlying value more transparent to shareholders.

INTRODUCTION

Change is not comfortable; company reorganizations involve change. The implication of this is that company reorganizations are not undertaken lightly, but are done when something is wrong – either with the company, or with the market's perception of it. This chapter considers reorganizations that are done in this context, from re-financings to demergers, and the issues that are faced.

If there is something wrong with the company itself, then the reorganization needs to address the internal issues. If the problem lies with market perceptions, then the focus is on revising how the company is viewed. Although there will be many overlaps in these types of reorganization, it is convenient to discuss them under these headings.

REORGANIZATIONS ADDRESSING INTERNAL ISSUES

Put very simply, companies can face problems due to having the wrong business configuration or the wrong financial strategy. Many, many books have been written about business strategy and change management, and we would do the subject no service by adding our necessarily brief comments to that discussion. Hence, we focus on reorganizations that address situations where a company has the wrong financial strategy.

A company's financial strategy may be wrong because it has too little debt, for example a mature company which has remained equity-financed. To correct this, the company could re-balance its debt/equity ratio, for example by paying out a special dividend or undertaking a share buy back as discussed in Chapter 10. Alternatively, the company could put the money to good use by investing in a value-enhancing investment opportunity. Although the special dividend and buyback may technically be seen as company reorganizations, they hardly present problems, unlike the reorganizations that need to take place because a company is over-borrowed.

A company may have taken on too much gearing for several reasons. It could have been a deliberate, if misguided, financial strategy which has not worked out as expected. Or it could be because the financial strategy suited the company's then business conditions, but changes in circumstances led to a fall in operating profits, and a resulting debt problem. Although the reason for the decline may influence how the company chooses to reorganize, there are several generic strategies that it can follow.

Reorganization strategies can fall into the following categories:

1. Raise cash by selling assets, either outright sale of surplus assets or in a sale-and-leaseback transaction.
2. Raise cash by issuing new equity or another financial instrument.
3. Come to an arrangement with creditors to restructure existing debt.

SELLING ASSETS

The simplest way to manage the company's affairs is by selling surplus assets. If the company clearly has assets which are not necessary for the operations of the business, then realizing the value in them is an appropriate strategy. Issues that may arise here include (a) determining which assets are non core; (b) finding a buyer; and (c) being prepared to take the accounting consequences.

As regards the issue of whether assets are non core, sometimes it takes a fresh perspective on the business to determine this. Companies develop their own internal myths about which assets must be owned in order for them to run their business properly, or which business units are core to their offering. Sometimes a division which has been part of the corporate fabric for many years needs to be sold off to protect the viability of the others. Or, on a more modest scale, attitudes to asset ownership may need to be amended.

Of course, even if a company realizes that it has assets which could be sold, disposing of them at a good price may not be a realistic proposition. If it is known that a company is in financial difficulties, prospective buyers

13.1	ASSET DISPOSALS – MARKS & SPENCER

CASE STUDY

An example of a reorganization occurred in summer 2001 in the UK retailer Marks & Spencer. Facing financial problems due to a trading downturn, Marks & Spencer reversed its long-held strategy of owning its prime High Street sites, and entered into a sale-and-leaseback arrangement. It arranged to sell a portfolio of some of its High Street stores to a financial institution for some £300 m and to lease them back. The stores sold, although raising a significant amount, represented only about 10 per cent of the value of the company's UK property portfolio.

The sale-and-leaseback formed only the first strand of the company's financial reorganization. It was announced that further stages would see the securitization of the income from a portfolio of its stores, and the sale of its head office building to property developers.

may bid low, or may decide not to bid at all, awaiting a possible 'fire sale'. Or, if the company's problems have resulted from poor economic conditions or an industry-wide collapse, there may be a glut of such assets on the market, or indeed no market for them. For example, European telecoms companies took on large amounts of debt during 2000 in order to acquire 3G licences from the various governments. At the time this debt was taken on, the markets were high and the telecoms companies anticipated being able to make asset sales in order to reduce the debt burden. However, the collapse in the value of technology stocks, combined with the many telecoms companies all needing to dispose of assets, meant that sale prices were far lower than originally anticipated, leading to liquidity problems for many of the companies.

And finally, we mentioned that the company has to be prepared for the accounting consequences. This comment arises from the experience of one of the authors who was undertaking a pre-receivership investigation into a building company, on behalf of their bankers. The company was in a very bad situation – a fact not realized by the directors, who were not in the habit of using cash flow forecasts as part of their management information. However, it did own an apartment in London, bought many years ago when times were good in the housing market. It was suggested – strongly – that the directors sell the apartment as soon as possible in order to raise cash for the company. However, they refused on the grounds that the property had cost £400 000 at the height of the property boom; it would now fetch only about £250 000 and they did not want to sell at a loss. It turned out to be difficult to explain to them that they had already made the loss, and the only issue now was whether or not they realized it in the financial statements.

RAISING NEW FINANCE

The company may be able to pull itself out of the financial mess by raising new finance, from existing or new investors. If raising equity from existing shareholders, a deep discount rights issue may be appropriate. Such rights issues were discussed in Chapter 7; a deep discount rights issue is one in which

---

13.2 DEEP DISCOUNT RIGHTS ISSUE BRITISH TELECOMMUNICATIONS (BT)

CASE STUDY

The acquisition of 3G licences in the auctions by Europe's governments meant that by the end of 2000 BT had amassed debt of almost £30 billion (compared to a market capitalization of less than £40 billion). The company was by no means alone in this situation – a combination of 3G licences and expensive acquisitions had led most of Europe's telecoms companies into a similar predicament.

The high debt burden had led to the company's credit rating being downgraded (which increased the cost of its debt), and to financial uncertainty. Accordingly, restructuring strategies needed to be implemented. These included a £5.9 billion deep discounted rights issue; plans to sell and lease back properties; the demerger of the business into two separately quoted public companies; and asset disposals. Further, dividend payments were suspended for the foreseeable future.

The terms of the rights issue were as follows. For every 10 shares held, the shareholder was offered the chance to buy another three shares at a price of 300 p per share. This price was some 47 per cent lower than the price of 568.5 p on the day before the rights issue was announced.

The theoretical ex rights share price based on these parameters would have been about 507 p. (10 shares at 568.5 p plus three shares at 300 p gives a value of £65.85, divided by 13 shares.) However, the news of the deep discounted issue (and of course the situation that had demanded it) caused the company's share price to fall sharply in the first few days of trading after the announcement, dropping some 12 per cent in less than a week.

---

the pricing is at a significant discount to the pre-offer price. The case example of BT, shown in case study 13.2, illustrates a deep discount rights issue.

The BT case also illustrates the fact that a company will rarely reorganize merely by changing one thing. If the crisis is severe, or is likely to become severe, several different restructuring strategies will need to be managed in tandem to achieve the greatest effect.

The new finance that is raised need not be in the form of straight equity. It is sometimes possible for a company to raise the new funds in the form of a convertible, as discussed in Chapter 9. The advantage of a convertible to the investor is that there is some downside protection, but still the upside opportunity that will make the risk worthwhile. The US company Lucent issued a convertible as part of its restructuring, as shown in case study 13.3.

RE-NEGOTIATING EXISTING DEBT

The third type of financial reconstruction relates to restructuring existing debt. If a company can convince its lenders that they will ultimately receive more by waiving interest payments or extending the term of a loan, then debt terms can be eased to aid the company's short term survival. Such renegotiations normally only work in situations in which the creditor banks are owed a significant amount: there is a saying which goes 'if you owe the bank £5 million and can't pay, you have a problem; if you owe the bank £5 billion and can't pay, the bank has a problem'.

13.3 | ISSUE OF NEW SECURITIES – LUCENT TECHNOLOGIES

CASE STUDY

The collapse in the value of technology stocks and changes in global economic conditions badly affected telecoms equipment company Lucent Technologies. Facing a growing debt burden and the possibility of breaching its banking covenants and having its debt status downgraded to 'junk' the company undertook several restructuring strategies. In March 2001 Lucent floated its subsidiary Agere. However, although the IPO was successful, the fall in overall market values meant that it raised only $2.5 billion, only half of the company's original expectations. Accordingly, further funds needed to be raised.

The fundraising carried out in August 2001 was in the form of redeemable convertible preferred stock offered on very favourable terms. The securities carried a coupon of 8 per cent, somewhat higher than the yield on the company's debt, and would convert to equity at a premium of only 22 per cent, giving investors an excellent chance of achieving a significant upside. The issue raised some $1.75 billion, more than originally expected due to the high demand for the generously-priced offer.

One form of debt renegotiation is the debt-for-equity swap, in which existing loans are released in exchange for the creditors taking an equity stake in the company. The argument behind these is that if the creditors insist on their debt being serviced and repaid, the company will be forced into liquidation and they will lose their money anyway. However, if the debt is converted to equity, the creditors – now shareholders – will share in the ultimate upside if this causes the company to recover. Negotiations in debt-for-equity swaps revolve around the proportion of equity which is issued to the creditors; obviously, this new equity will significantly dilute the existing shareholders.

There are likely to be many difficulties involved in debt renegotiation. One fundamental problem is the different interests of the various stakeholders involved. If a company is over-borrowed there is rarely just one creditor; many banks may be owed money, and other stakeholders too may have issues to resolve and have power in the situation. This is illustrated in the case of semiconductor manufacturer Hynix, discussed in case study 13.4.

REORGANIZATIONS TO ADDRESS MARKET PERCEPTIONS

Sometimes the problem is not internal to the company, but relates to the fact that it is trading at a market value considerably below a fair value for its shares (in boxes C or D in the Value Matrix in Figure 1.5). In such cases, if they wish to forestall an opportunistic takeover bid for the company, the company's directors have several different options:

1. Demerger, to demonstrate the value in the group.
2. Blitz on public relations to change market perceptions.
3. Take the company private.

The issue of de-listing a company was discussed in Chapter 11 and will not be revisited here. Similarly, we will spend no time discussing how a

13.4 STAKEHOLDER INTERESTS – HYNIX SEMICONDUCTORS

The South Korean semiconductor manufacturer Hynix experienced major financial difficulties in 2001 due to the economic slowdown and overcapacity in the semiconductor market. In August 2001 it failed to make the due payments on a Won 400 bn ($313 m) bond. At the time it had Won 7100 bn in interest-bearing liabilities.

Hynix was in protracted negotiations with its various stakeholders in order to sort out its financial situation. However, the stakeholders had different interests.

The interested stakeholders included a syndicate of 10 European banks; a syndicate of 19 Korean banks (some state-owned); Korea's investment trust sector which had bought the company's bonds; and Korean and overseas shareholders.

The domestic bank creditors were led by Korea Exchange Bank, which was negotiating a Won 3000 bn debt-for-equity swap together with rolling over some of the debt due for repayment in the short term. The Korean banks were keen to avoid having to make formal write offs of the loans in their financial accounts, as this would have damaged their capital adequacy ratios and credit standing considerably. Had this happened, the Korean government would probably have had to inject further capital into its banks, thus the government was also a key stakeholder in the Hynix reconstruction. However, the many European and American banks who were also Hynix creditors were not in this predicament and were reluctant to forgive the company its debts. This led to considerable dissent amongst the stakeholders.

The terms of a potential debt-for-equity swap also caused dissent amongst the stakeholders. The company's financial situation had led to a massive fall in its share price. Had the swap been carried out at this new share price, shareholder dilution would have been almost total, and they were negotiating to prevent this happening.

Finally, the possibility of a government-supported bail out led to the US administration warning the South Korean government that this would be a breach of international commitments under world trade agreements, which could lead to an international trade dispute.

Source: Financial Times, various dates

---

company may improve perceptions due to a concentrated focus on 'public relations' and explaining its true value to shareholders and analysts. In this section we focus on reorganizations as a way to address the issue of markets undervaluing the company: specifically the process of demerging or spinning off units.

An explanation of some terminology is appropriate here. We will use the term 'demerger' to describe a transaction in which one listed company becomes two or more listed companies, generally with the same shareholders (at least initially). In a demerger, the two resultant companies will be of similar size. This differs from the transaction sometimes referred to as a 'spin off', in which a company divests itself of a division (i.e. a much smaller entity than itself) by distributing the shares of the subsidiary to its own shareholders, generally in the form of a dividend. This differs again from an 'equity carve out', in which the subsidiary company (or generally only a minority stake therein) is sold to the public as an initial public offering. We should point out that the difference between the various transactions and straight sales of subsidiaries is generally one of size. A transaction would not be considered as a reconstruction unless the business disposed of formed a substantial percentage of the overall group value.

WHY DO COMPANIES UNDERTAKE DEMERGERS?

As stated, demergers (in their various forms) are undertaken in order to improve the value attributed to the business by the financial markets. Often, a group includes two or more very different classes of business. This can make it difficult for analysts and shareholders to understand, and such a lack of understanding leads to under-pricing in the markets. Splitting the group into separate companies, each in a defined business sector, clarifies the situation and enables investors to select where to invest their funds.

Research and market sentiment indicate that the post-demerger market value of the separate companies is normally greater than that of the whole group before demerger (an example of the sum of the parts being greater than the whole). Some reasons put forward to explain this are shown in Working insight 13.1.

After the demerger, each separate company can make its own investment and financing decisions and approach the capital markets in a way that is appropriate to its own asset structure, revenue sources and business objectives.

WORKING
13.1
INSIGHT   **Why demergers are seen to add value**

- Separation into clearly defined business segments leads to market transparency and greater understanding.
- The different businesses can follow financial strategies more appropriate to their activities.
- Improvements in corporate governance and efficiencies arise in companies which were subsidiaries but are now separately accountable to the markets.
- Incentive structures can be put in place that link management performance directly to the unit's share price.
- Removal of the 'conglomerate discount'.

CONCLUSION

Company restructuring takes place when the company is in trouble, or is undervalued by the financial markets. Just as there are many reasons why a company may end up in such a situation, there are many ways out of it. This chapter has focused on practical examples rather than underlying theory. It has illustrated that companies' reconstruction plans may of necessity change as market conditions become more or less favourable. It is interesting to note that reconstructions rarely involve just one type of refinancing or realignment: it appears that the more methods that are used to achieve the reconstruction, the more successful it is likely to be.

DEMERGERS

CASE STUDY

British Telecommunications

As discussed earlier, BT undertook an extensive restructuring in order to reduce its debt burden and improve the market's perceptions of it. Over the period between late 2000 and mid 2001 it announced various demerger proposals; the feasibility of some of these strategic options diminished as market conditions changed. At one time the restructuring proposal involved splitting the company into five separate listed companies. However, the final outcome was to split the business into two, with shareholders in the current BT receiving shares (in equal proportions) in the separate businesses to be named BT Group plc (which would hold the network and retail telecoms business) and mmO$_2$ plc (the wireless business). Of the original plans to float off five businesses, some had been combined, and others disposed of in trade sales in the intervening period.

Kingfisher

Kingfisher, the UK retailer, undertook a demerger of its Woolworths general stores in summer 2001. The company had considered various alternatives, including an outright sale, to dispose of the Woolworths business, however, there were no serious buyers for the company and market conditions favoured the demerger instead.

The Kingfisher reorganization also included the sale to a trade buyer of another of its subsidiaries, Superdrug, and the sale of its High Street property portfolio. The effect of the disposals, together with the portion of the group's debt taken over by Woolworths on the demerger, reduced Kingfisher's debt burden by some £1.1 billion. The purpose of the restructuring was to strengthen the balance sheet to enable the group to focus attention on retailing areas in which it saw better prospects for profitable growth.

Source: Financial Times, various issues.

14

Management buyouts and other leveraged transactions

Many private equity deals are structured as highly leveraged transactions. The advantage of this structure is that, as debt is so much cheaper than equity, they provide a great potential upside to the equity investors. This, of course, is predicated on the assumption that the high gearing is sustainable, and does not damage the company's financial position.

Leveraged transactions such as management buyouts (MBOs) involve a series of negotiations between the management, the vendor of the company, and the providers of debt and equity. Each party to the transaction will have different requirements of the deal, and the final structure has to satisfy all of these, providing suitable stability for the debt, a sufficient percentage of the equity for the management, and a satisfactory internal rate of return for the venture capitalists. These conditions are normally met by a transaction which uses both debt and equity gearing.

INTRODUCTION

In previous chapters we have discussed flotations and acquisitions. As companies develop, move into different areas, and occasionally face financial crises, they may also be subject to leveraged transactions such as management buyouts and buyins. These are the subject of this chapter. The matters we will cover include:

WORKING 14.1 INSIGHT

Some types of leveraged private equity transaction

Management buyouts are just one type of leveraged transaction. Venture capitalists and private equity firms may invest in several other, similar types of transaction. These are defined and discussed briefly below.

Management buyout (MBO)	In this transaction, the company's current operating management acquire the business, or purchase a significant shareholding in it, as discussed in the rest of this chapter.
Management buyin (MBI)	A buyin is similar to a buyout, except that the management team comes from outside the company. Sometimes they have worked together previously in another company, but often the management team is put together by a venture capitalist.
Management buyin/buyout (BIMBO)	A BIMBO is a transaction in which some members of the management team acquiring the company come from its existing management, and some of them are outsiders. Quite often the new CEO will be an outsider, but will retain some of the company's existing management team, who will also become equity investors.
Institutional buyout (IBO)	In an IBO, a private equity firm buys the company, following which the incumbent and/or incoming management will be given (or buy) a stake in the business. The deal is driven by the institution(s) rather than the management. Such deals may be quicker to do, because the equity provider is negotiating directly with the vendor, rather than also with the management.
Leveraged build-up (LBU)	Here, a private equity firm acts as principal to buy a company with the intention of developing it into a larger group by making further acquisitions in a specific business area.

Although each type of deal will have its own strategic imperatives, their structures are similar: each involves the purchase of an established business using a financial structure that includes a significant level of debt. Therefore, although in this chapter we discuss how to structure a management buyout, the learning can be applied to the other situations.

- strategic reasons for a management buyout (MBO);
- the process of undertaking an MBO;
- structuring the deal.

However, before we discuss buyouts in particular, we will set them in the context of other, similar types of private equity transaction.

THE IMPETUS FOR A BUYOUT

Management buyouts may be undertaken for a variety of different reasons, reflecting both the holding company's and the management's priorities.

The holding company's reasons might include:

- disposal of a non-core business, to regain focus;
- to release funds to support the rest of the group;
- to pass on a family-owned business from which the owners wish to retire.

The management's reasons could be:

- to run the business autonomously without head office interference;
- fear that the division will be closed down or outsourced unless they buy it;
- prefer to run their own business than to be sold to a trade buyer.

MBOs are sometimes driven by an ambitious management team which sees the potential for high growth of the business once it is outside the control of a bureaucratic parent. In other cases, the parent company might suggest the buyout, either as a means of releasing capital tied up in a division, to use elsewhere in the business, or because the division has become non-core, and the group would be more focussed without it. In some instances, a buyout is undertaken because the management of the division see it as a preferable option to being outsourced or sold on to a trade buyer. The reason driving the MBO will be an important influence on the attitudes of potential financiers and other stakeholders.

THE BUYOUT PROCESS

THE EARLY STAGES

In the early stages, the process of undertaking an MBO will differ dependent on whether the deal is being driven by the management or the owners of the company.

In some ways, the situation is simplest if the owners have expressed a wish that the management team should consider a buyout. Here, the management team is free to pursue the idea as they see fit, and to contact outside parties for financial advice and possible funding, knowing that in principle the transaction will be acceptable to the shareholders.

However, if the impetus for the buyout comes from the management team, then an interesting fiduciary position arises with regard to the owners of the company. To put it simply, management are paid to act in the best interests of the owners, and have a duty so to do. Undertaking a buyout may be in the owners' interests, but it may not: they may object strongly to the proposal. Management thus have two choices: they either investigate the feasibility of a buyout before they approach the owners, or they do so afterwards.

Why should management choose to investigate the feasibility of a buyout before broaching the subject with the owners? Putting it bluntly, if they find that a deal is not feasible, they can quietly drop the idea, and life goes on as usual. The owner need never know that a buyout was being considered. Politically, this might be advantageous for two reasons. If the team were to announce to the owners that they were considering a buyout, and then fail to obtain the finance, their position in the organization could be weakened. However, if the deal is feasible, they can approach the owners secure in the knowledge that their aims are achievable, and in a potentially stronger negotiating position. The second reason for wanting to check out how the land lies is that the owners might react very negatively to any suggestion of a buyout – and it would be a waste of time (and of a potential career!) to ruin the relationship for a deal that might never happen.

The other alternative is for management to respect their fiduciary duties, and approach the owners before determining whether a deal can be done. This has the advantage of being totally 'above-board'. However, should the owners object strongly to the idea, management are in danger of losing their jobs with no fall-back position.

The legal situation will be slightly different in each case. Management teams will probably want to test the lie of the land before approaching the company's owners, but they must be aware of a potential breach of their duties if they release confidential information (for example, management accounts) to outside parties without the owners' approval. Legal advice may need to be taken.

ADVISERS

In order to complete a buyout, the management team will need to make contact with providers of equity and debt finance. They will also need to employ professional advisers: at the very least they will need a lawyer. It is also recommended that they use a financial adviser, an accountant or other professional involved in raising finance.

There are two good reasons for using a financial adviser. Firstly, even if the management team is very experienced in this area, they will have enough to do without project-managing the minutiae of the deal – it is useful to have an experienced agent on whom they can rely. The second reason for employing an adviser is more basic: venture capital houses receive many hundreds of approaches every year from businesses needing finance, and they have to have a filtering system to sort out potentially good proposals from time-wasters. One of the most basic filters is only to consider proposals that come from professional advisers who are respected in the industry – that way the institution can assume that the adviser has done a 'first sort' of the plans, and that only reasonable proposals are reaching them.

This latter point often seems totally unreasonable to entrepreneurs, who do not think the world should work this way, and believe that their plan deserves consideration on its merits. Quite possibly it does, but we live in the real world. Your authors know of a company whose business plan was rejected out of hand by a local venture capital company: the entrepreneur went to a financial adviser who was known in the area, and he re-badged the proposal in his company's binder, without changing a word of it. The business plan was read, and the investment was made. Sometimes you just have to accept that life is not fair – and play by the rules the market sets.

SELECTING FINANCIERS

Different venture capitalists have different investment criteria. For example, some will only invest in deals above £5 m, others might specialize in (or avoid) certain industries. The first point to note in selecting potential financiers is only to approach those who might be interested in your deal: to do otherwise is a waste of both your and their time.

Once a venture capital company is on board for the deal, they will help to make introductions to other sources of finance, including bank and mezzanine lenders, and other venture capital companies with whom they might want to syndicate the deal.

If your investment proposal is very attractive to the venture capital community, for example you are looking to buy a large, profitable, cash-generative company that has just refurbished all of its assets, then you may be in the fortunate position of having venture capital companies vie for your favours. In such cases your advisers would run a 'beauty parade', in which selected venture capital firms would be invited to present to the management team to demonstrate why they should be the ones selected as lead investor.

However, for many 'run of the mill' propositions, the situation is reversed, and the management team has to convince a venture capitalist that they are worth backing. In such cases, it is important to deal only with a few venture capital firms at a time.

Some management teams try to send their business plan out to all of the venture capital market, in the hope that someone will express an interest in their deal. This is a poor strategy. Firstly, if there is a flaw in the business plan, it will have been exposed to the whole market, without the team having a chance to correct it. Sending the plan to just three or four venture capital firms would have given the management and their advisers a chance to understand why it was being rejected, and adjust it accordingly. The second reason that mail-shotting the market is a bad idea is that it makes you seem like a loser – if everyone could have your plan, no-one will want it.

THE STAGES OF THE DEAL

The British Venture Capital Association (BVCA) sets out a list of the stages of a venture capital transaction, as follows:

1. Prepare the business plan.
2. Entrepreneur (management team) approaches venture capitalist(s) with the plan.
3. Venture capitalist(s) make an initial appraisal of the plan.

4. Initial meetings and enquiries.
5. Due diligence is undertaken by the venture capitalist.
6. Final negotiations and completion of the deal.

Much of this is self-explanatory. It is however worth focusing on stages 5 and 6, to see how the transaction progresses once the venture capitalist is committed to it in principle.

The venture capitalists will undertake due diligence on both the company and the management team. However, because the financiers see themselves as investing in the management as much as in the business, a lot of attention will be paid to taking up references on the members of the management team. Such references may be from people suggested by the management team, but will also include trade and other sources, to obtain a good cross-section of views. The results of the due diligence could fall into three categories:

- due diligence shows that the management team is capable of undertaking the transaction and successfully running the business – the transaction can proceed;
- due diligence shows that the management team has a serious flaw(s) – the venture capitalists will probably withdraw; or
- due diligence shows that most of the management team is satisfactory, but there is one (or more) weak member. In such instances, the venture capitalists may demand that a manager be replaced. This can put severe personal pressure on a team of people who have been working together for years, but it may be the only way to get the deal done.

The management team should also do due diligence on the providers of capital (and indeed much of this should have been done before approaching them). How good are they as investors? Are they supportive of their investments? Do they take board positions in their investee companies, or do they manage in a more hands-off way? Do you like these people, and are you prepared to be tied to them for many years? It is a mistake to go into business with people whom you dislike or do not trust – even if they do seem to be the only source of finance.

As regards the negotiation at the final stages of the deal, no management team ever believes that it will take as long as it does, or be as complex as it is!

A typical buyout will involve the following protagonists:

- the management team;
- venture capitalists;
- bankers (and maybe other debt providers);
- the vendor.

Relationships between these parties are complex, and constantly changing. For example

- in negotiating the purchase price of the business, the vendor is pitched against the combined might of the management team, the venture capitalists and the banks;
- in negotiating the banking terms, the venture capitalists and management team are up against the banks;
- in negotiating the equity split, the venture capitalists are now on the opposite side to the management team;

- individual members of the management team may each be defending their own corner when it comes to negotiating equity terms and employment contracts.

The final stages of the deal include finalizing the documentation, for example: the sale and purchase agreement; loan agreements and covenant levels; the new company's articles and memorandum, employment contracts for the directors and key staff, etc. This is generally far more time consuming and difficult than the management team expects.

STRUCTURING AN MBO

Structuring a transaction such as an MBO involves balancing the needs of the various parties, whilst meeting the funding requirements and capacity of the company. Three sets of issues need to be resolved:

- what funding is needed?
- what can the business afford? and
- what do the parties want?

WHAT FUNDING IS NEEDED?

The funding to be raised will primarily comprise the purchase consideration for the business, to be paid to the outgoing shareholders. This will have been determined based on a calculation of the value of the business being acquired. As with all corporate acquisitions, that value will be a matter for negotiation between the parties.

Funding will also be needed to develop the business. Venture capitalists do not normally invest in businesses unless they anticipate growth – and that growth will almost certainly require additional funding. Financial forecasts should demonstrate how much of that funding can be released from internal sources (for example, by better management of working capital) and how much will need to be funded externally.

Finally, the massed ranks of professional advisers would be most upset were we to forget the final funding need – that of paying the deal costs. Accountants, lawyers and other professionals will need to be paid, as will arrangement fees to financiers. As a (very) rough guide, you might expect these to total 5 per cent of the transaction value.

WHAT CAN THE BUSINESS AFFORD?

Here, the main consideration is the cash impact of providing a return on finance. We have established previously that debt is cheaper than equity, and when we discuss funding structures later you will see that MBOs are financed mainly with debt. However, debt finance involves regular interest payments and a repayment schedule: the post-buyout company needs to be able to meet these requirements.

One way to evaluate a company's debt capacity is to select a suitable level of interest cover (operating profit divided by interest charges), and work back to

WORKING
14.2

INSIGHT   **Sustainable level of debt**

BuyOut Ltd is forecasting operating profits of £140 000 in its first year of operation. The directors and the providers of finance have agreed that interest cover of 3.5× is adequate for safety. Interest rates are 7 per cent.

BuyOut has operating profits of £140 000
Therefore, with interest cover of 3.5×, it can afford to pay an interest charge of £40 000.
With interest rates of 7 per cent, this represents a capital sum borrowed of £571 400.

Note: This is the company's debt capacity looking only at interest cover. Ability to make repayments of principal also needs to be considered.

evaluate the level of debt this represents. Working insight 14.2 illustrates such calculations.

Of course, other factors will be considered in determining the company's financing capacity. Interest cover deals only in profit terms: cashflow cover will be equally as important. Furthermore, a company with good asset backing will probably be able to borrow more, at cheaper rates, as the lenders will be more confident of their security.

We should also point out that although in this chapter we will just refer to 'debt', in practice there may be several different financial instruments used, each with different rights and priorities, interest rates and repayment terms. A tranche of senior debt, with low interest cover covenants and strong security, may be supported by senior subordinated debt, junior debt and mezzanine, each with progressively weaker covenants and security, and carrying a greater return for the lender.

WHAT DO THE PARTIES WANT?

The main parties to a buyout or similar transaction are the management team, the providers of institutional equity and the providers of debt funding. Each has a different set of requirements of the deal.

Management generally undertake an MBO in order to become their own bosses and to get rich through an ultimate exit. There may also be an element of doing the deal in order to preserve their jobs – if they don't buy the company it could be sold on, or closed down. Thus management's key requirement is a large share of the equity (for control and for capital gain), and preferably a relatively low cash investment, as they are likely to have other commitments.

The venture capitalists are investing in the deal to make a return. (It is important to remember that venture capital is not a philanthropic exercise, and at the end of the day this is all that will interest them.) They need an IRR (internal rate of return) of more than 30 per cent per annum over the life of the investment, and have to believe that the deal will give them this.

The lenders have a different view again. Lending debt is a low risk activity – which means that they have to be able to protect their downside. Hence the lenders will require strong covenants, and security where available. They will be less interested in the deal's potential upside (in which they do not share) than they will in protecting their position should the downside occur.

STRUCTURING THE DEAL

With these constraints in mind, deal structuring can be simplified to a series of steps, as follows.

1. Determine how much finance is needed. This should be the total finance: sufficient to cover the deal price, working capital requirements, future cash requirements and deal fees.
2. Ascertain how much of that finance can be taken as debt. Debt is a cheaper form of finance than equity, and the gearing of the deal will affect the equity returns, as demonstrated later. The level of debt will depend on the asset backing of the business, and the amount and quality of its cashflow generation.
3. Determine how much funding the management will be able to put in. Investors will generally expect this to be at least one year's salary, often more.
4. Knowing the total funding needed, the level of debt, and management's contribution, the balancing figure normally has to be supplied by the venture capital institutions. This will be split between ordinary and preference shares, as shown below. Factors to consider here are the percentage of equity that management will have in the business, and the prospective IRR on the institutional investment, payment terms, the dividend on ordinary shares, etc.

Working insight 14.3 sets out the deal parameters from which we will build a possible financing structure.

WORKING 14.3 INSIGHT   **Financing structure for an MBO: initial parameters**

The management team of MaMBO is putting together a management buyout from Parent, their holding company. They have approached a venture capital company, VenCo, which has agreed to lead the deal. VenCo has discussed the deal with BestBank, which is leading the debt.
Deal statistics are as follows.

- The parties have agreed a purchase price of £10 m to be paid to Parent.
- A further £2 m is needed to fund working capital requirements and deal costs.
- MaMBO is expected to make operating profit of £1.5 m in the first year of operating after the deal. (This is considerably higher than the company is doing now, but the management will be able to operate more efficiently (and with more enthusiasm) once they are freed of the dead hand of group bureaucracy.)
- BestBank has stated that it will lend at 8 per cent, and has demanded a covenant that interest cover will not fall below 3× for the first year. They have also set a gearing covenant, that debt will never exceed 50 per cent of total funding.
- The management team between them are investing £200 000.

WORKING
14.4
INSIGHT   **Debt capacity in an MBO**

The bank funding is firstly limited by the interest cover covenant:

Forecast operating profit	£1.5 m
Interest cover (min)	3×
Therefore, maximum interest charge	£500 k
At 8 per cent , this equates to borrowing of	£6.25 m

However, the gearing covenant will supersede this, as debt can not exceed
50 per cent of total funding (of £12 m).
This equates to a borrowing of   £6 m

The total financing for MaMBO's deal is £12 million. As stated earlier, the first part of the finance to be evaluated is the new company's debt potential. Working insight 14.4 illustrates this calculation.

Of the £12 million needed for the buyout to go ahead, debt will provide no more than £6 million. This leaves equity sources to provide a further £6 million. We were told that management will put in £200 000; thus the finance from venture capitalists is £5.8 million. The next issue to consider is the form this finance will take.

DETERMINING THE EQUITY SPLIT

In determining how the institutional investment is made, there are several possibilities. The most obvious solution is for management and the institutions to invest on the same terms. Working insight 14.5 illustrates this for MaMBO.

MaMBO has £6 m of equity finance, of which management is putting in £200 k. If shareholdings are split in these proportions, management will obtain 200/6000 of the equity – 3.3 per cent. It is unlikely that they will see 3.3 per cent, split between the members of the team, as sufficient incentive to invest their life savings and work in the business for 25 hours a day for several years.

Therefore a method has to be devised to give management proportionately more of the equity than their money alone would deserve.

WORKING
14.5
INSIGHT   **Institutional investment on management terms**

Investment by management	£200 000 (3.3 per cent)
Investment by institutions	£5 800 000 (96.7 per cent)

> **WORKING 14.6**
>
> **INSIGHT** **Structuring the MBO using differential pricing**
>
> Assume that the management team buy their ordinary shares at £1 each, but the institutions pay £8 per share.
>
> | | Investment | No. of shares |
> |---|---|---|
> | Management @ £1 | £200 000 | 200 000 |
> | Institutions @ £8 | £5 800 000 | 725 000 |
> | | £6 000 000 | 925 000 |
>
> Management now owns 21.6 per cent of the company's equity, which they would probably see as a worthwhile investment for their trouble.

This could be done by differential pricing, by which the different classes of investor pay different prices to invest. Working insight 14.6 sets out a possible solution on this basis.

The position set out in Working insight 14.6 seems to meet the needs of the situation, in that the company has the funding it requires, and management have an acceptable percentage of the equity. However, as with all simple solutions, there is a catch. What if a trade buyer comes along the next day, offering to buy the company for £12.5 m (including the debt)? Once the debt is paid off, that would leave £6.5 m for the equity – a profit of £500 000 in a day! However, £6.5 m for the equity works out at about £7 per share (£6.5 m/925 000 shares). Management will be delighted – they bought in at £1 per share, and can make a huge capital gain. However, the institutions bought in at £8 per share, and would not be prepared to sell out at £7. So immediately we have a conflict of interest, and a very frustrated management team.

Differential pricing can easily lead to such conflicts of interest, which is one reason why it is best avoided. To overcome the problem of giving management sufficient of the equity to make it interesting, the deal can be instead structured using preference shares to 'gear up' their stake. The way that preference gearing works is that the institutions put in their funding in two separate instruments – ordinary shares and preference shares. This is illustrated for MaMBO in Working insight 14.7.

In Working insight 14.7, the institutions invest £800 k in ordinary shares at £1 each, and £5 m in preference shares. Management will own 20 per cent of the company. Any future buyer of the company would have to pay off the preference shares first (at par), with the balance of sales proceeds being split in proportion to the numbers of ordinary shares. This would lead to a situation in which the institutions and management are on the same side. Working insight 14.8 completes the example with the full deal structure and exit calculations.

Based on Working insight 14.8, who has obtained what out of the deal?

Management invested £200 000 and obtained £1 million – an absolute gain of £800 000, which represents an IRR of 124 per cent: an excellent deal!

The institutions put in £5.8 m (£5 million preference capital and £800 000 equity) and obtained £9 million – an absolute gain of £3.2 m, which represents

WORKING
14.7

INSIGHT   **Preference gearing in an MBO structure**

Assume that the institutional investment of £5.8 million is invested as £800 000 in ordinary shares, on the same terms as management, and £5 million as preference shares.

	Investment	*No. of shares*
Equity		
Management @ £1	£200 000	200 000
Institutions @ £1	£800 000	800 000
	£1 000 000	1 000 000
Preference shares		
Institutions	£5 000 000	
	£6 000 000	

an IRR of 24.6 per cent. This IRR would be increased by the fact that they will have received annual dividends on their preference shares. The institutional return is nowhere near as much as management's, but it's quite respectable in terms of their original requirements from the deal.

The decision as to how much of the institutional capital goes in as ordinary shares and how much as preference shares is crucial in the deal structuring, as the preference gearing is what gives the management its excellent return. As

WORKING
14.8

INSIGHT   **Rewards on exit**

Assume that the initial deal is as set out in Working insight 14.7. Two years later, an offer is made to buy the company (including the debt) for £15 million. This reflects the considerable improvements that management has made to the company's trading position. £1 million of the debt has been repaid since the deal was originally done.

	Initial deal	*Exit*
Finance required	£12 000 000	
Sales proceeds		£15 000 000
Less Debt	6 000 000	5 000 000
Management and Institutions	6 000 000	10 000 000
Less Preference capital	5 000 000	5 000 000
Equity funding/return	£1 000 000	£5 000 000
Investment/Return		
Management (20 per cent)	£200 000	£1 000 000
Institutions (80 per cent)	£800 000	£4 000 000

WORKING
14.9

INSIGHT   **Illustration of envy ratio**

For the MaMBO buyout the institutions put in a total of £5.8 m for ordinary and
preference shares, and ended up with 80 per cent of the equity. Management put in
£200 000 and ended up with 20 per cent of the equity. This 'values' the company
as follows:

From the institutions' point of view	5.8 m/80% = 7.25 m	(A)
From management's point of view	0.2 m/20% = 1.0 m	(B)
Envy ratio (A/B)	7.25 times	

with everything, the level of preference gearing is a matter for negotiation:
the more the institutions want to do the deal, the more generous their offer to
management.

One figure which is used to determine how generous, or otherwise, the institutions are being is known as the *envy ratio*. This is most easily explained by
example, as shown in Working insight 14.9.

The higher the envy ratio, the better the deal for management.

TWEAKING THE TERMS

Sometimes it can be difficult to meet the conflicting needs of management, the
institutions and the lenders. For example, if the lenders will only lend a small
proportion of the deal funding, then equity must be found to make up the
balance. If management are putting in relatively little, the institutions have to
make up the balance, and it can be difficult to give management a high
percentage of the equity whilst still obtaining a high IRR for the institutions.
There are two possible ways around this – paying dividends to the institutions,
and using a ratchet.

DIVIDENDS

One way to meet management's desire for a higher percentage of the equity is
for the institutions to increase their potential IRR by taking a dividend return as
well as a capital gain on exit. The ongoing dividend return (normally taken on
the preference shares) will improve the institutions' IRR without, we hope,
restricting the company's ability to grow. Working insight 14.10 illustrates this
for the MaMBO deal.

Dividends can also be used as a tactic to ensure that the institutions do
actually get their exit. In a company which is known to be cash generative, the
dividend terms might be set such that the institutions' ordinary shares (or sometimes all of the ordinary shares) receive an extra dividend that starts at, say, 10
per cent of distributable profits but rises annually by 5 per cent or more. The
payment of such a high dividend can be used to focus management's mind on

Institutional return

In the MaMBO buyout, the preference shares carried a dividend of 7 per cent, payable at the end of each year. The venture capitalists' cash flows (ignoring tax) are as follows:

	Year 0	Year 1	Year 2
	£ k	£ k	£ k
Investment:			
Preference shares	(5000)		
Ordinary shares	(800)		
Preference dividend		350	350
Capital repayment			
Preference shares			5000
Ordinary shares			4000
Annual cash flow	(5800)	350	9350

IRR = 30 per cent

In practice, the venture capital company would calculate a post-tax return, which would depend on its own taxable position.

the possibility of an exit – to realize their potential capital gain before the institutions have taken it all out by way of dividend! Even if there isn't an exit, the institutions still get their high IRR – through the yield.

RATCHETS

There are times when management and the institutions cannot agree about the future prospects of the business. Management want a high percentage of equity, believing that the company will do incredibly well. However, the institutions might argue that there is no guarantee that the company's performance will improve, and so they need a high equity stake to ensure their return. A ratchet can be the answer.

A ratchet is a device that enables the proportion of equity held by management to be altered depending on what profits the company achieves (or depending on any other variable specified). A *positive ratchet* starts management at a low equity percentage with the incentive that should they perform well their percentage will be increased. A *negative ratchet* starts them at a high equity percentage, but they will have to forfeit some shares if the company does not meet its targets.

Warning: Ratchets solve the immediate problem of resolving the conflict between the parties at the commencement of the deal. In many cases they lead to even greater problems in the future when the ratchet is (or is not) triggered.

15

Strategic working capital management

Working capital, the investment in stocks and debtors net of creditors, is a significant investment in many companies' balance sheets. In order to create value for shareholders, this investment needs to be managed down to the minimum levels consistent with the company's business strategy. In order to do this, it is important to understand the reasons why the investment in stocks and debtors is being made, and to deal with areas of inefficiency and inconsistency.

In financing their working capital needs, companies can use short term bank finance such as overdrafts, or can use asset finance such as factoring debtors. Issues to be considered relate to the risk preference of the shareholders and managers, the relative costs of the finance, and the level of flexibility that is desired.

INTRODUCTION

Working capital is the only investment a company makes on which it doesn't expect a defined return. The investment is needed in order to 'oil the wheels' of business rather than to produce something itself. Because of this, many companies have over-invested in working capital, leading to cash flow problems and to a diminution of shareholder value.

For many businesses, the components of working capital represent the largest items on the balance sheet. Despite this, they tend not to be seen as issues demanding strategic consideration or top management attention. Companies which implement detailed procedures for evaluation and approval of even trivial capital expenditure will often leave the management of stocks and debtors to junior employees.

We have already established, in Chapter 1, that reductions in the level of working capital can enhance shareholder value. Accordingly, in this chapter we consider why companies hold working capital; how it can be financed; and how the management of working capital should form part of the overall business and financial strategy.

SHAREHOLDER VALUE MANAGEMENT

In Chapter 1 we considered Rappaport's seven drivers of shareholder value, and established that one of these was a reduction in the incremental need for working capital. Reducing working capital requirements means that a business has less cash outflows (for stocks and debtors) as it expands, and the resultant increase in cash flows adds to the value of the business. Other factors also drive shareholder value – for example increases in profitable sales growth, but for many businesses it is easier to make improvements in the levels of working capital than it is to generate and sustain an improvement in profit. Furthermore, by working on both the profitability and the underlying investment, companies can leverage any improvements they make.

SUSTAINABLE GROWTH

The level of working capital in a business has a direct effect on the amount of growth the company can sustain organically from its own internal resources. Growth in sales requires that the business takes on additional stocks and incurs additional debtors. Even if no further capital expenditure is required to achieve the growth, the underlying capital invested in a business will still need to increase.

The amount of growth that a business can sustain out of its own resources, before issuing new capital, is constrained both by its anticipated rate of profitability and by the underlying asset requirement. Thus, if a company is to grow without borrowing or issuing further capital it needs either to increase its profitability or to make better use of its assets. In Appendix 1 the growth assumptions underlying the dividend growth model are established, so growth can be calculated as:

g = return on investment × retention ratio

Increasing the company's return on investment – for example making the same return on a lower (working capital) investment – will increase the funds available for reinvestment and thus increase the sustainable growth level.

FACTORS AFFECTING THE WORKING CAPITAL CYCLE

The working capital cycle (the time taken to convert orders to cash received, net of creditors) is illustrated in Figure 15.1. The cycle commences when the company receives an order from its customer (or decides to make for stock). Stocks are acquired, which may be converted through the stages of work in progress and finished goods. The stocks are held as current assets until the customer buys them. However, at that point no money has changed hands, and the asset of stock is merely replaced by an asset of trade debtors. It is not until the cash is actually received that the cycle is complete.

The company has to finance the business for the whole of the operating cycle. However, it does not need to do so out of its own resources; some of those stocks will have been bought on credit, and trade creditors finance part of the working capital investment. Thus, the company's cash requirement is limited to the net of stocks and debtors less creditors.

The working capital cycle for any company is a function of several variables: the country; the industry; the company's business strategy and attitude to risk; and the effectiveness of its systems.

COUNTRY IMPACT

Cultural norms and logistical factors impact upon working capital policies. For example, in countries in which the transport system is unreliable, larger stocks have to be held to compensate for possible extended lead times. Also, terms of trade vary considerably between countries; at the time of writing, the countries of southern Europe have a payment norm for debtors substantially more than that for, say, the Scandinavian countries.

Figure 15.1

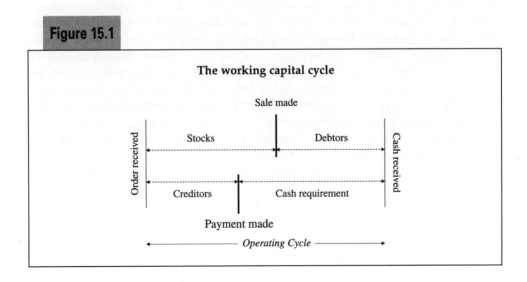

Figure 15.2

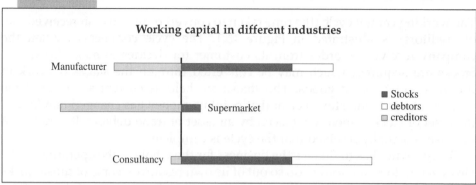

INDUSTRY IMPACT

It is self evident that the investment in working capital will differ across industries. Business-to-business transactions are generally done on credit; manufacturers will have more stocks than will some service industries; professional service firms will have proportionately less reliance on trade creditors than will most other businesses. Figure 15.2 is an illustrative representation of the working capital cycles of some different types of business.

In Figure 15.2, the working capital cycle is displayed in a slightly different manner. Current assets are shown as bars to the right of the vertical line, and creditors to the left. For a manufacturing company, the picture represents a heavy investment in stock and debtors, offset by significant trade credit.

The picture is reversed for supermarkets. These are retail businesses selling to end customers, so there are no debtors; and they operate on minimal stocks. Further, they have the buying power to take long credit periods from their suppliers – accordingly, their net working capital investment is actually negative; the more they grow, the more finance they obtain out of their working capital.

Finally in Figure 15.2 we illustrate the working capital investment for some consultancies and other service firms. Although they have no physical stocks, they often have large sums tied up in work in progress, which cannot be invoiced until milestones are achieved. Once they have invoiced, clients are often slow to pay. But consultancy firms, whose main cost is their people, have no trade creditors against which to offset the working capital investment: they can hardly delay paying staff wages in order to mitigate operating needs.

When moving into an industry it is important to understand why its working capital patterns are as they are. Only with this understanding can the accepted norms start to be changed, for example to reduce stock-holdings or manage debtors more effectively.[1]

---

1. On principle, we never give advice about managing the third element of the working capital cycle: trade creditors. One business's trade creditors are another's debtors, and taking extended credit just moves the problem along the supply chain. Accordingly, when we work with companies in this area we focus on managing the assets down rather than increasing liabilities.

RISK AND RETURN

At an individual company level, which is where financial strategy tends to operate, one of the main factors influencing working capital levels is the business's strategy and its attitude to risk. Each element of the working capital equation can be regarded as taking a particular position on the risk-return continuum, and different companies will adopt differing commercial strategies, putting them in different categories.

The trade off between investing in working capital (reducing returns) and not making the investment (taking risks) is illustrated in Working insight 15.1.

The principles behind the table in Working insight 15.1 can be used to ensure that the chosen working capital strategy ties in with the business strategy. For example:

- A business which sees its competitive advantage as lying in the full service it provides to customers may need to maintain much higher levels of stock than a discount house with limited ranges and service.
- Setting a tight credit policy to control debtors could well counteract other marketing initiatives the company is taking; these activities need to be coordinated and controlled.
- A business which has a policy of working closely with its suppliers may decide to pay far more quickly than one which has determined a more combative stance.

Other working capital issues relating directly to the chosen business strategy include:

- The need to hold additional stocks for each new outlet (retail or manufacturing) opened.
- Synergies created by reducing overall working capital through horizontal or vertical acquisition strategies.
- Credit terms for suppliers and customers will be dependent on the balance of power within the industry.

WORKING 15.1 INSIGHT

Risk and return in working capital

	Risk avoided by holding working capital	Cost of the working capital investment
Stocks	• Stock outs delaying the manufacturing process. • Loss of customers who cannot wait for delivery.	• Cash tied up in stock. • Costs of holding stock.
Debtors	• Loss of customers due to more attractive opportunities elsewhere.	• Credit control costs and bad debts. • Cash tied up in debtors.
Creditors	• Too heavy reliance on bank finance.	• Poor name in the industry. • Charged higher prices.

- The risk of short business cycles resulting in excess stocks of items that are no longer in fashion.
- Decisions to sell into segments with a traditionally poor payment record. (This may be a value-creating strategy if the company can make enough incremental profit out of the customer before the eventual bad debt arises.)

EFFECTIVENESS OF SYSTEMS

The ways in which a particular business processes its transactions can have a significant effect on the levels of working capital maintained. This can be investigated using the components of, for example, the order-to-receipt cycle illustrated in Figure 15.3. This sets out, for a typical company, the processes that are undertaken in order to service the customer and, ultimately, to bank their payment. Analysis of what happens at each stage can help to evaluate where improvements can be made, and the cycle can be shortened. Again, it is worth pointing out that such improvements have to be in line with the business strategy of the unit.

Figure 15.3

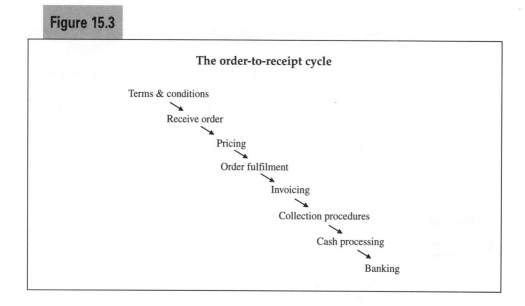

The order-to-receipt cycle

Terms & conditions
Receive order
Pricing
Order fulfilment
Invoicing
Collection procedures
Cash processing
Banking

FINANCING WORKING CAPITAL

The working capital investment, which will vary from day to day as trading progresses, needs to be funded, and companies have several strategic options in managing this financing requirement. Some businesses choose to have sufficient cash funds available to meet their day to day needs; some have overdrafts or borrowing facilities; others use a form of asset finance. Each of these is considered below.

CASH AND OVERDRAFTS

The advantage of holding cash balances (which in some organizations are viewed as part of the working capital investment) is that the business can always meet demands. The disadvantage of holding cash is that cash itself is an investment which generates a very poor return. Funds on deposit with the bank are unlikely, by definition, to produce a return which will satisfy shareholders.

As mentioned in Chapter 3, for private businesses this latter point need not be a consideration. We know of several small private companies in which considerable amounts of money are kept on deposit, instantly available should they be required. As financiers, we understand that this is an inefficient use of funds; as risk-averse individuals we appreciate the attraction of being able to sleep easy at night, knowing that a cash crisis is unlikely to hit. For a private company, in which 'shareholder value' means meeting the needs of the owner/directors, this is a reasonable attitude.

However, companies with a broader shareholder base need to be more focused in their use of funds, and having excessive cash deposits is a poor strategic decision.

As a general rule, a company should finance itself with a mixture of short and long term funds, of which cash plays a part. Figure 15.4 illustrates this.

In Figure 15.4, the business has a mixture of long term debt and equity, determined in accordance with the principles we have been presenting throughout this book. As it grows it needs further cash. However, the cash needs are not uniform – either seasonality or a business cycle could mean that the cash requirement varies. This company has chosen to operate with an initially low proportion of debt, increasing gearing over time. It has increased equity over the period,[2] and has also raised long term loans. The quantum of loans

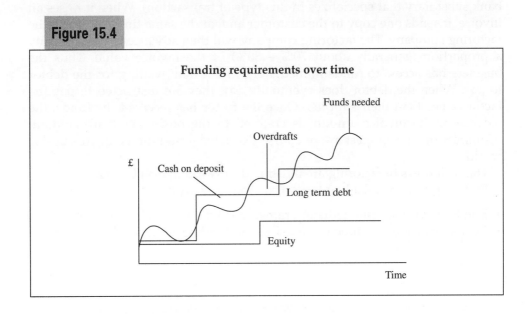

Figure 15.4

Funding requirements over time

£

Funds needed

Overdrafts

Cash on deposit

Long term debt

Equity

Time

---

2. In practice of course, equity will change each period as profits are retained.

raised is such that cash is sometimes on deposit, but that sometimes an over-draft is required.

The decision as to how much short term finance will be used, and how it will be structured, should be made in the light of the business requirements and the preferred attitude to financial risk.

Two final points should be noted as regards the use of short term borrowing facilities. The first is that, in our opinion, it is always useful to have negotiated a borrowing facility even if it is not immediately required, as this gives financial flexibility.[3] The second issue is that, in the UK, overdraft facilities are repayable to the bank on demand. No breach of covenants is needed for the bank to change its mind about the funding, and require repayment. Thus overdraft finance is not nearly as low risk for companies as would be a negotiated loan.

ASSET FINANCE

Banks will lend short term finance against the business generally. However, there are also specialist financial institutions which will advance monies against specific elements of working capital. Stock finance is available from some, but debtor finance is far more common, and so it is this on which we focus.

Debtor finance (invoice finance) has been in common use for many decades. It is interesting to note that accountants and professional advisers tend to fall into two camps about the use of invoice finance: they either hate it and see it as a sign of 'last resort', or they appreciate its flexibility. We own up to falling into the latter camp, having successfully used invoice finance in several growing businesses.

Invoice finance takes two main forms: factoring and invoice discounting.

In factoring, the company effectively sells its debtors to the factor (often a bank subsidiary that specializes in this type of transaction). When it raises an invoice, it sends one copy to the customer and, at the same time, a copy to the factoring company. The factoring company will then advance to the company a proportion (generally about 70% – 80%) of the invoice value. Thus the business has access to funds immediately, rather than waiting for the debtor to pay. When the debtor does eventually pay, they are instructed to pay the factor rather than their supplier. Once the factor has received the funds, the balance of the invoice amount is credited to the business's bank account. (Commission and interest are of course deducted – nothing is for free in this world.)

The cash flows in factoring are illustrated in Working insight 15.2.

Factoring has several advantages as a form of finance:

• Funds are available immediately, rather than waiting until the customer pays.
• Funds available are directly linked to the funding need, as they reflect the level of business.

---

3. Although we should point out that if a company's circumstances change such that it does require the financial facility, this change itself is often sufficient to breach banking covenants so that the funds are no longer available. It's not for nothing that there is a saying about bankers only offering to lend you an umbrella when it's not raining!

**WORKING
15.2**

INSIGHT   **Cash flows in factoring**

Assume that Company factors its debts with FacCo, which advances 80 per cent of
the invoice amount immediately, and the balance when it receives the funds. FacCo
charges commission of 1 per cent of turnover, and charges interest at 2 per cent over
factoring base rate, which is 8 per cent. On 1 January Company sells goods to
Customer for £1000; Customer pays on 31 March.

	Company	FacCo	Customer

1 January
Movement of goods/services
Send invoice for £1000
Send copy invoice

2 January
Commission paid £10
Funds deposited in factoring
account £800

31 March
Payment of invoice £1000
Payment of balance of funds £200
Interest paid on £800 borrowed for
three months at 10 per cent, £20 (actually
charged on a daily basis on the
outstanding balance on the account)

- Factoring companies will advance a higher percentage of the debtor book than would banks which secured overdraft finance on debtors (because they understand the risks better, and have more control).
- Factoring companies often collect debtors earlier than would the trading businesses, as their systems are more efficient.
- The factor manages the company's debtors ledger, effectively outsourcing this operation.
- Factors can advise on the credit-worthiness of potential customers (indeed, they may refuse to take on the debts of some customers).
- A company can choose to factor only part of its debtors, for example those relating to export sales, in which it has little experience of debtor management.
- For an additional fee, the factor will take on the risk of bad debts.

It is also true to say that there are many disadvantages of factoring compared to, say, bank borrowing in a more traditional form:

- Factoring is more expensive, with commission on top of higher interest charges.
- Inserting the factor into the customer–supplier relationship may damage that relationship, particularly if the factor is aggressive in chasing debts.
- The company loses control over its debtors ledger, which some see as a key management and marketing tool.

- Factoring is still trying to get rid of the poor reputation it had in the 1970s as 'lender of last resort' – the use of factors may send unwelcome (and false) signals about the business's financial stability.

Some of the downsides of factoring are addressed in the other main invoice finance technique: confidential invoice discounting. Although similar in effect (the company still obtains a proportion of its debtors ledger instantly), confidential discounting differs from factoring in three ways:

- The debtors remain the legal property of the company, which maintains its own debtors ledger.
- The customer is not aware of the financing transaction, as payment is made direct to the supplier; and
- Costs are lower, because the factor is providing less services.

16

Executive compensation

The way in which directors are paid can influence how they choose to run the business. Thus, it can have a direct impact on both business and financial strategies. Remuneration committees have to devise schemes that will align the directors' interests with those of shareholders, and encourage strategies appropriate to the company's circumstances.

Most UK companies adopt a short term bonus scheme for their executives, together with a longer term scheme which may be based on share options. The performance conditions attached to these schemes generally relate to accounting measures (for annual bonus schemes and share options) or to total shareholder return (for other long term incentive plans). However, accounting measures can bear little relation to the creation of shareholder value; and shareholder return is not necessarily related to management performance. Accordingly, performance measures need to be balanced carefully, to minimize distortion.

Furthermore, even when the performance measures have been selected, the company needs to determine the targets in use. Many of the targets chosen by UK companies, in particular those relating to growth in earnings per share, are flawed in that achievement of the target need not relate to the creation of shareholder value.

Finally, the scheme parameters must set a currency for the payment of the award: in cash, or in shares or options. Each of these methods is discussed, and the advantages and disadvantages are shown.

INTRODUCTION

Worldwide, the issue of corporate governance in general and executive pay in particular has been the focus of much media and regulatory interest, and considerable academic research. Many of the arguments focus around how much executive directors should be paid, and the structure of such pay. In this chapter we examine the issues underlying the debate, and how they relate to the creation of shareholder value.

THE AGENCY DEBATE

In Chapter 1 we introduced agency theory, which discusses the potential for conflict of interest between directors and shareholders.

Shareholders, as diversified owners of the company, wish to see the value of their investment enhanced. In agency theory terms, they are the 'principals' and they employ directors, their 'agents', to run the company on a day-to-day basis. The directors may be motivated to act other than in the shareholders' best interests, for any of the following reasons:

1. They might see advantage in incurring expenses that are not strictly value-adding, otherwise known as 'perks' of the job: the director receives 100 per cent of the benefit of this expenditure, but bears little if any of the cost.
2. They do not have the shareholders' advantage of diversification, and so may not wish to take the risks with the company that shareholders would be prepared to accept; if the company fails, the shareholders have lost only part of their portfolio, but the director has lost his/her job.
3. They might not wish to expend the effort to extract the full potential value from a project or investment, opting instead to 'satisfice' for an easier life.
4. Their time horizons, reflecting individual expectations, may be shorter than those for long term shareholders, implying an unwillingness to take on long term projects.

In summary, agency theory views executives as potentially risk-averse and effort-averse,[1] and sees the need for shareholders somehow to control their actions.

Shareholder control (implemented directly or via the actions of non executive directors) could, in principal, come from two direct sources. Firstly, the shareholders could monitor each one of the director's actions, to determine whether it is designed ultimately to benefit the company or the director. Or secondly, the director's service contract could be drafted so tightly that it would specify the appropriate course of action in every conceivable circumstance. Of course, in practice each of these alternatives is impractical, and so a third method needs to be devised.

---

1. We appreciate that in practice executives may well give 100 per cent effort to the business, and be prepared to take on risk. However, the economic perspectives that drive agency theory see Rational Man in this light, and, as much of the regulation in this area seems implicitly to follow this line of thinking, it is worth setting out its assumptions.

The mechanism used to control directors, by attempting to align their motivation with that of the shareholders, is the design of the remuneration contract. If directors' pay is structured in such a way as to reward directors for creating shareholder value, then, taking an agency theory perspective, they are encouraged to act as if they were shareholders: what is good for the shareholders will be good for the directors. This is the assumption behind most of the regulation underlying directors' remuneration. It leads to the focus on performance-related remuneration discussed in the rest of this chapter.

STRUCTURING DIRECTORS' REMUNERATION CONTRACTS

In listed companies in the UK and USA, directors' remuneration policies are determined by board committees comprising (generally) non-executive directors of the company. These non-executives, often advised by compensation consultants, have to establish the requirements of the remuneration scheme, and determine how these can be achieved.

Most directors' remuneration schemes have three underlying objectives:

1. To attract good executives to the company.
2. To retain them in the company.[2]
3. To align directors' interests with those of the shareholders, in order to promote the company's performance.

In order to achieve the first objective, pay has to be sufficient to meet the executive's needs. The second objective may be met by devising a remuneration package that gives the executive an incentive to remain with the company long term. Received wisdom is that the third objective, aligning directors' and shareholders' interests, is most appropriately managed by using performance-related remuneration and by ensuring that the directors hold an equity stake in the company.

Given these objectives, the basic questions that need to be asked in devising an appropriate remuneration scheme for executives are as follows:

1. How much should be paid for 'expected' performance?
2. Of that, how much should be fixed, and how much performance-related?
3. For the performance-related elements, what performance measures should be used?
4. What targets should be set for these measures?
5. How can we use the scheme to ensure that good executives are retained?

It is the role of the remuneration committee to address these issues in the context of each company's particular circumstances.

---

2. Of course, there may be instances in which it is not to the company's benefit for the director to remain, and buying him/her out of their contract can be costly. Such instances need not relate just to poorly performing executives; situations could arise in which a director's management style, which was ideal for a launch or growth company, is inappropriate as the company approaches maturity and meets different challenges.

THE QUANTUM OF REMUNERATION

The level of directors' pay is, in practice, often based on published pay surveys or on pay levels in specific comparator companies. Although pertinent to the debate, the quantum of pay is not an issue of great relevance to corporate financial strategy; accordingly we do not pursue it here. However, the structure of pay – dealt with in questions 2 to 5 above – is most definitely significant to our deliberations, and is discussed in the following sections.

THE GEARING OF REMUNERATION

In Chapter 1 we argued that the creation of shareholder value is subsequent upon the company having and maintaining a sustainable competitive advantage. Two issues arise here: a strategy has to be devised to create such a competitive advantage, and it has to be implemented successfully. It is for these activities that directors should be rewarded.

Once the quantum of pay for 'average' or 'expected' performance has been determined, companies must decide how much of that should be guaranteed as fixed salary, and how much should be performance-related. Figure 16.1 illustrates some possibilities.

As Figure 16.1 shows, the gearing of pay can take many forms. Companies then have to determine which is most appropriate for their own circumstances.

Figure 16.1

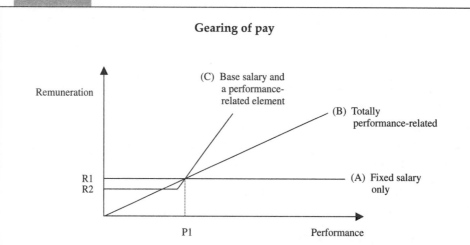

At the expected performance level, P1, the director will be paid R1. However, the three illustrated schemes derive this in different ways. Scheme A has no performance-related pay; the director is guaranteed to receive R1, whatever the level of performance. Alternatively, pay-gearing is total in scheme B – no pay without performance, but higher levels if expected performance is exceeded. Scheme C illustrates a mixture of these: the director is guaranteed to receive at least R2, but can earn R1 (or higher) dependent on performance.

In practice for Scheme B (and perhaps for Scheme C), the level of pay for performing at P1 is likely to exceed R1, as the director should receive additional compensation for the additional risks being taken.

For companies at the launch stage of their lifecycle, when both determining and implementing the strategy are critical, the directors have a huge influence over the short and long term success of the business. Contrast this with the maturity stage, at which the directors' role is more to do with managing the assets in place. At this latter (and later) stage the business has developed momentum and the directors' skill lies in extracting the maximum value out of the existing assets, and in renewing them.

Because different strategies and styles are appropriate at different stages of the lifecycle, it would seem appropriate for different remuneration structures to be applied. For example, in launch and growth stage companies with high volatility, the directors' actions are crucial to the future of the business. It might thus be expected that a large proportion of their pay will be related to an appropriate performance measure. Directors managing mature companies or companies in regulated industries perhaps have less discretion over the company's future, and so might receive proportionately more of their pay as fixed, and less based on performance.

Of course, the exact opposite viewpoint could be argued. As mentioned above, the director is unable to diversify his/her job and, if operating in a risky business environment, may be unwilling to add to his/her personal risk by taking on high pay-risk. It can be argued that in such companies the directors and managers should receive a higher salary-based component, to reduce their personal risk and to encourage them to take business risks that could enhance shareholder value. (However, although this makes sense intellectually, it appears in practice that individuals who take on the job of managing these volatile businesses are in part driven by the opportunity to earn high remuneration due to successful performance, and prefer the high pay gearing.)

SHORT AND LONG TERM SCHEMES

When structuring directors' pay we are seeking to encourage the creation of long term shareholder value. However, it is rare for incentives to relate just to the long term, and in practice incentive pay will represent a mixture of short term and long term elements. Each of these schemes will have its own performance measures and targets.

ANNUAL BONUSES

It is common for directors to be paid annual bonuses based on measures such as: annual profitability; non-financial targets such as sales growth or new product development; or measures related specifically to their individual or team goals for the year. Such bonuses are often capped, as illustrated in Figure 16.2: for example it is common that the level of bonus will not exceed say 50 per cent of the director's base salary.

One reason commonly given for bonuses to be capped is that shareholders (represented in this instance by the remuneration committee) are unwilling for directors to receive large windfall bonuses based on fortuitous market circumstances over which they had no control. Accordingly, once performance exceeds a certain level – P2 in Figure 16.2 – no further bonus will be paid for that year.

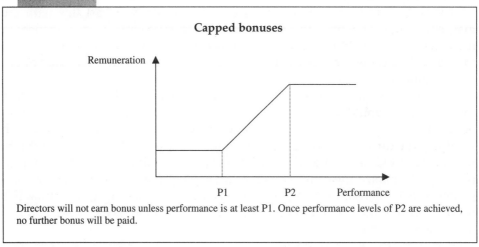

Directors will not earn bonus unless performance is at least P1. Once performance levels of P2 are achieved, no further bonus will be paid.

Although rarely discussed, a second reason for capping directors' bonuses might be that very high bonus levels, even if justified by performance, could be seen as insensitive in the public eye and so damaging to the company's image. An example of this was seen when the UK lottery company Camelot paid large performance bonuses to its directors. Despite the fact that the directors had brought in the National Lottery on time and to budget, there was considerable adverse press and government comment about the level of the bonuses. Some commentators thought that this negative impact on the company's image later damaged its progress in the contest for the award of a further lottery licence.

The capping of bonuses, and the minimum performance level required before a bonus is triggered, can have adverse consequences. The motivational impact on directors and managers of knowing that their superb performance is (in financial terms) unrecognized is significant. Furthermore, research indicates that the cap and floor on bonus levels can lead to manipulation of accounting figures. If a company is falling just short of the profit levels required to trigger the bonus, accounting provisions may be adjusted in order to increase profits to just over the trigger level. Similarly, in cases where performance is well in excess of level P2, so no further bonus is available, provisions may be adjusted to move some of the profits into the following year, building up a 'bank' towards next year's bonus!

LONGER TERM INCENTIVES

Although annual bonuses are seen as a useful tool in ensuring short term performance, companies need to generate shareholder value in the longer term and it is important that directors are rewarded using long term measures. Furthermore, the use of longer term performance measures can be one way to retain good executives in the company, as part of their remuneration is being earned over more than one year.

In the UK, longer term incentives take the form of either long term incentive plans ('ltips') or executive share (stock) option plans.

> WORKING
> 16.1
>
> INSIGHT   **Some features of long term incentive schemes**
>
> - Generally run for three or more years.
> - Incentivize performance over the period, with the executive receiving the reward at the end of the period.
> - Often there is no award if the executive leaves the company during the award period.
> - Remuneration is often paid out in shares in the company.
> - There may be a secondary period during which the executive is required to retain the shares.
> - If there is a secondary period, often the company will award the executive additional shares at the end of that period.

Many different types of ltip have been created, and it would be pointless to describe them all in this chapter, as new schemes are being invented all the time. Accordingly, rather than describe schemes in detail we set out in Working insight 16.1 some of the features common to many schemes.

It should be noted that the three year performance period mentioned in Working insight 16.1 is in common use in the UK. Given that companies have different operating cycles, and are responsive to different economic conditions, it would perhaps be more appropriate for each company to tailor its scheme to the length of its own operating cycle. For example, the scheme in use for a chemicals manufacturer should probably operate over a longer period than that for a developer of software games. However, in practice such diversity is not often evidenced.

Within the wide range of long term incentives, the ubiquity of executive share option schemes and their effect on corporate financial strategy is such that it is worth dealing with them in a separate section, later in this chapter.

APPROPRIATE PERFORMANCE MEASURES

In practice, two main forms of performance measure dominate executive remuneration schemes: those which reward accounting performance, and those which reward market performance. It is common to see annual bonus schemes rewarding the achievement of accounting results, for example profit growth. Share option schemes in the UK often use an accounting measure, growth in earnings per share, as their key goal, whereas ltips will reward both accounting results and shareholder return.

Working insight 16.2 compares accounting and market-based measures, and sets out some of their key features.

Accounting measures are easily manipulated and may drive short term decisions, such as cutting back on discretionary expenditure to boost profits. They can be distorted by inflation and reflect neither risk nor the shareholders' cost of capital. Market measures are also flawed. If the share price rises for reasons unrelated to performance (for example, on the rumour that a poor chief executive is

WORKING
16.2

INSIGHT

Features of performance measures

	Advantages	Disadvantages
Accounting measures Example: profit, return on investment, eps growth	• Simple to use. • Easily understandable by all parties. • Based on audited figures.	• Take no account of the cost of capital, and so do not necessarily reflect shareholder value. • Take no account of risk, and so do not necessarily reflect shareholder value. • Easily manipulable by changes in accounting policies. • May be difficult to compare across companies due to different accounting policies. • May encourage short termism to inflate profits.
Market measures Example: total shareholder return, share price	• Reflects value received by shareholders.	• Share prices reflect market expectations rather than management performance. • Market imperfections may lead to over/under valuation of the shares. • Schemes may be complex and misunderstood by participants.

about to be replaced!), directors could benefit. Alternatively, directors' good performance need not be reflected in the share price, leaving them un-rewarded.

Neither accounting nor market based performance measures have an unequivocal advantage over the other; companies need to judge what measures are appropriate for their circumstances.

SETTING PERFORMANCE TARGETS

As we have seen above, no single performance measure is suitable for all circumstances; each has its flaws. However, even when a remuneration committee has determined which measure(s) it will use, it still has to determine the targets it sets.

Performance targets might be based on internal company figures, or on external benchmarks, or on a mixture of both.

Targets for annual bonuses are often set based on internal company figures, for example the annual budget. Although this has the advantage of simplicity, such practices can lead to 'sandbagging' of budgets (to ensure that targets are low enough to achieve easily), or to a mental attitude that what is important is to beat the budget, rather than to beat the competition.

One step towards externalizing the targets might be to set them based on, say, increasing performance by a certain rate, often a percentage over inflation. This type of measure, based on growth in eps, is most commonly used in executive share option schemes. However, there are serious flaws in the way that most of these schemes set their targets, as discussed later in this chapter, in the section on share option schemes.

Schemes that reward directors for achieving Total Shareholder Return (TSR) most commonly use external benchmarks as their target. TSR represents the percentage return that shareholders receive from the company over the performance period. Methods of calculation of TSR are shown in Working insight 16.3.

Because share prices may rise and fall for reasons which have little to do with company performance, most executive remuneration schemes reward the achievement of TSR compared to an index of comparator companies. In this way, the external 'noise' of price movements in a particular industry sector can be reduced. Schemes may reward executives if their relative TSR is in the top decile or quartile of the comparator index; the rewards would be progressively smaller as performance slipped down the table.

**WORKING
16.3
INSIGHT**

Calculation of total shareholder return

TSR represents the dividend and capital gain on the share, as a percentage of the share price at the start of the period. For example, on 1 January the company's share price is 100 p; on 31 December it is 110 p; and on 1 July the company paid a dividend of 5 p.
Basic TSR calculation:

Increase in share price over the period	10 p
Dividend paid in the period	5 p
Total return to the shareholders	15 p
TSR per cent	15 per cent

In practice, the TSR performance period would be considerably more than one year.

The calculation could be made more sophisticated by assuming that the dividend received in the middle of the year was reinvested in the company's shares at the then-current price.

The calculation may also be adjusted by smoothing share prices to eliminate market distortion, for example by taking a six month average share price rather than that on a single date.

Rewarding comparative out-performance can make it difficult for directors to establish, in the mid-term of a performance period, how they are doing. Quite apart from their own share price data they would need information on the index performance of their comparators. For this reason, some companies prefer not to use this measure.

A second issue in rewarding out-performance of an index is that it can lead to situations in which the directors receive their reward despite the fact that shareholders have lost value. For example, a company whose TSR is minus 3 per cent has done exceptionally well if its comparators have averaged minus 10 per cent. Although shareholders may at times resent this, it is justified as it would be unreasonable to penalize executives for the effects of a bear market. (And by the same token they should not be rewarded merely for having the good luck to ride a bull market.)

EXECUTIVE RETENTION AND ALIGNMENT

Long term incentives are one way to align interests and to encourage directors to stay with the company. Another is to insist that they hold equity, or to reward them in equity which they have to hold for a given period. This payment method has the advantage of encouraging them to take a shareholder perspective.

Broadly, directors' remuneration can be 'paid' by giving the director cash, shares or share options. Each of these payment methods has its own advantages and disadvantages, and the remuneration committee has to balance these in the light of the company's particular situation.

The key features of each of the payment methods are summarized in Working insight 16.4.

Other differentiating factors between cash-, share- and option-based remuneration relate to the directors' and companies' tax positions and the treatment of the remuneration in the financial statements. These issues are country-specific and subject to regular change, and so are not discussed in detail in this book. However, it is worth noting that at the time of writing there is much controversy over companies' use of option-based remuneration, which does not trigger a charge in the profit and loss account and thus flatters profits. International accounting standards regulators are trying to introduce standards that will result in options being charged against profit; companies are arguing strongly that this will reduce reported profits and make them 'uncompetitive'. This discussion mirrors that on pooling reported in Chapter 1; it should be born in mind that the economic effect of the options is the same, regardless of their accounting treatment.

EXECUTIVE SHARE OPTION SCHEMES

The most popular incentive scheme over time has been, and still is, the executive share (stock) option scheme which allows senior managers to buy up to a certain number of shares in the company during a specified period in the future but at a price fixed now. The future price is normally set by reference to today's market price, as is shown in Figure 16.3.

WORKING
16.4
INSIGHT

Features of payment methods

	Advantages	Disadvantages
Cash	• Universally acceptable to executives. • No uncertainty as to the value.	• Depletes company's cash resources. • Provides no alignment or incentive to stay with the company.
Shares	• If the executives retain the shares, provides some alignment of interests. • May encourage executive retention if structured properly. • Does not deplete the company's cash resources.	• Dilutes existing shareholders. • Shares are often not retained for the longer term. • Directors benefit even if the share price falls. • If the director's shareholding forms a very high proportion of his/her personal wealth, this may overly discourage risk-taking.
Share options	• Provides a means to give equity to executives. • Does not deplete the company's cash resources. (In fact, cash is received from the executive when the option is exercised.) • Directors only benefit if the share price rises.	• Dilutes existing shareholders. • Shares are often not retained for the longer term. • May be difficult to value. • If the options are out of the money ('underwater') they may not have an incentive effect. • Alignment of directors' and shareholders' interests is not assured – see section on *options*.

Executive options work in the same manner as any call option, as discussed in Chapter 9. If the managers are successful in achieving capital growth in the price of the shares during the option period, they can make a capital gain by exercising their stock options. If the share price does not rise, or indeed falls, there is no value created for the managers by granting them an option. This is the primary logic behind the use of executive share options, in that it is supposed to create goal congruence between the objectives of the shareholders and the managers; both are rewarded if the share price increases during the stock option period.

Figure 16.3

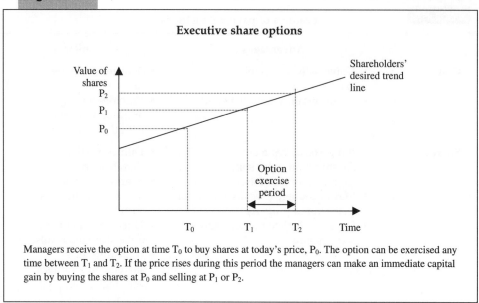

Executive share options

Managers receive the option at time T_0 to buy shares at today's price, P_0. The option can be exercised any time between T_1 and T_2. If the price rises during this period the managers can make an immediate capital gain by buying the shares at P_0 and selling at P_1 or P_2.

Despite the fact that share options are one of the most popular incentive arrangements for directors in the UK and the US, they have certain limitations in their ability to incentivize directors to create shareholder value. These relate to dividend policy; holding costs; and appetite for risk-taking, each of which is discussed below.

EXECUTIVE SHARE OPTIONS AND DIVIDEND POLICY

Shareholders can receive financial returns from their investment either through capital growth or by the payment by the company of dividends. As we have suggested throughout this book, for some companies more value might be created by paying dividends than by retaining profits for growth, as the company might not have available potential reinvestment projects which are expected to generate a return in excess of the shareholders' demanded return on equity. In such companies, shareholder value is created by increasing dividends.

However, there is no incentive for directors to pay increased dividends during the life of any significant share option scheme. If the excess funds are retained within the company, rather than being paid out, the price of the shares should increase to reflect the cash held by the company, even though shareholder value may be being destroyed by such a dividend policy. The problem is that the price at which managers can buy shares (the option exercise price) is rarely adjusted to take account of any changes in the dividend pay-out ratio during the option period; this immediately destroys the aim of total goal congruence.

EXECUTIVE SHARE OPTIONS AND HOLDING COSTS

A second problem with executive share options is that although shareholders have made a material financial investment by buying their shares in the company, in most cases, managers have not. Although it would in theory be possible to require directors to forego part of their salary in order to participate in a share option scheme, this seldom happens. The directors are effectively given their stock options as part of their total remuneration package. This is an important difference because it means that only the shareholder has an opportunity cost of holding the shares. In other words, an increased value of the shares over the three or five years of the option does not automatically create value for the investor, whereas it would translate into a real capital gain for the manager.

The three reasons that shareholders incur a holding cost are liquidity preference, inflation, and risk.

One potentially important factor in this holding cost is clearly inflation because, although the nominal value of the shares may have increased, the shareholder may have lost money in real terms. As managers do not have to pay for their shares unless and until they buy them, there is no such opportunity holding cost. They will still be able to realize an immediate and real gain upon the exercise of their stock options, whatever the rate of inflation; in fact, the higher the rate of inflation, the more certain they can be that the stock option will have value. This problem could easily be overcome by indexing the option exercise price, so that managers only receive financial reward for a real increase in the price of the shares; this is rarely done.

The other main opportunity cost for shareholders arises from their need to be compensated for risk. As has been already made clear, shareholders demand a return which compensates them, *inter alia*, for the specific risk of holding any particular investment. Consequently the mere fact that the real value of the shares has increased over the option period may still represent an unacceptable level of return to the shareholder. It is much more logical that managers should only receive additional compensation (remember that stock options are given on top of their basic salaries, etc.) for generating a more than acceptable level

WORKING
16.5
INSIGHT   **Index linking share options**

A company has a share price of P_0 and a cost of capital K_e, and is due to pay a dividend of D_1.

The shareholders' cost of capital will be met by dividend and capital gain:

K_e = dividend yield plus expected growth in share price.

$\quad = D_1/P_0 + g$

Therefore expected growth in the share price is $K_e - D_1/P_0$.

It would be possible to construct an executive share option for which the exercise price rose at the rate of g per year, thus only rewarding the director if the share price rose above that implicit in the current value.

In practice, the factor of g might be reduced slightly, to compensate the executive for the risks being taken.

of return for their principals. Alternatively, the indexing of the option price suggested above could be adjusted to reflect the full cost of equity to the shareholders (adjusted to reflect the dividends they receive). Working insight 16.5 suggests a hypothetical index-linking scheme for options.

NO DOWNSIDE?

Although the issues raised above are significant, potentially the most damaging concern regarding stock options is that they represent a one-sided bet for the directors. If the share price appreciates, they make potentially large capital gains; but if the share price declines, they do not lose anything, they simply do not make a capital gain. In such an instance, as the option has no economic value it will not be exercised by the managers, whereas the investors in the company will actually have made a loss due to the decline in value of the shares.

As suggested earlier, one mechanism to address this issue would be for directors to be 'charged' for their options, by reducing other elements of remuneration to allow for a calculated cost of the options. However, this is uncommon in practice.

This problem is exacerbated when the main value drivers for any option are considered (this area is considered in more detail in Appendix 2). One such driver is the relationship between the present value of the exercise price and the current price of the asset. In the case of management stock options, this second factor (the asset value ratio) is normally high because the exercise price is fixed at, or near, today's price, so that the present value is already below the current market price. In real terms, the option can be described as being 'in the money' as soon as it is issued. These management stock options are also normally of quite long duration (e.g. three or five years), with a period during which they can be exercised (e.g. six months), all of which increases the value of these share options.

Any option also has value because of its time to expiry (the remaining life of the option) and the expected volatility of the asset price during this period. The latter is vital. It is clearly of no value to have an option to buy something where the price does not move at all; the value of the option is in being able to defer the purchase decision until the actual direction and scale of the movement has been revealed. Thus the greater the volatility, the greater the option value, as illustrated in Figure 16.4.

This is not necessarily in line with the desired objectives of the long-term shareholders in the company. Many institutional shareholders are relatively risk averse and like a boring existence; they want to see the value of their investments increase steadily over time. Watching the price of the shares leap violently along some roller coaster type time chart is not conducive to the good health of a fund manager, but it certainly can increase the returns from a management stock option scheme.

We are not necessarily suggesting that senior managers deliberately go out of their way to increase the volatility of their company's shares during stock option periods (although some researchers have indeed noted such a relationship). However it certainly appears strange to offer managers an incentive where they are effectively penalized for creating stability.

It is also true that these stock option incentive schemes do not turn managers into shareholders. Most of the option gains are realized immediately by selling

Figure 16.4

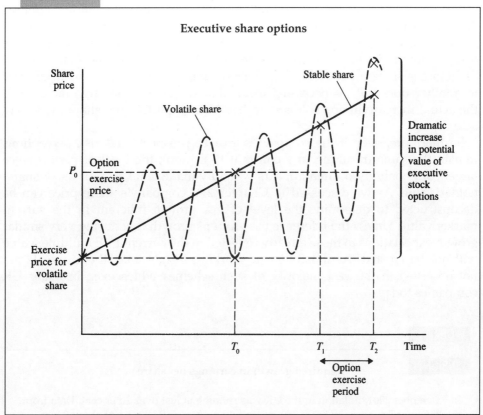

Figure 16.4

Executive share options

these new shares into the market. Clearly this makes the stock option into a deferred bonus plan, triggered by increases in share price.

PERFORMANCE CRITERIA USED IN SHARE OPTION SCHEMES

Many executive share option schemes in the UK attach a condition to the exercise of the options; merely increasing the share price is insufficient. Many different types of condition could be used, but as the majority of UK executive share option schemes grant options based on growth in eps, this measure in particular is examined.

Regular surveys of share option schemes adopted by UK companies show that growth in eps is the major performance measure used to determine whether options are to be granted. Overwhelmingly within companies adopting this measure, the target adopted is based on exceeding the movement in the retail price index (RPI) over a period. And in the category of companies using such a benchmark, the most common target is to grow eps in excess of RPI plus 2 per cent or 3 per cent a year over a multi-year period.

Unfortunately, as we have discussed earlier in this book, growth in eps does not automatically translate into shareholder value. In fact, it does not even necessarily translate into growth in the company's share price.

Share prices are represented by two elements: the eps and the company's P/E ratio. It would be nice to think that increasing eps leads to a price increase, but unfortunately that forgets the fact that the P/E ratio can move independently. As demonstrated mathematically in Chapter 2, the appropriate P/E multiple for any company is derived from the relative risk of the company together with the future growth in earnings per share which is expected by shareholders. Therefore just because earnings per share increase from one financial year to another does not, of necessity, mean that the share price will increase. If the actual increase in eps is less than had been expected, the share price may actually fall.

Furthermore, even if the company's growth prospects and risk perceptions remain the same (resulting in a constant P/E ratio), the level of performance target commonly used often appears woefully inadequate as a driver of shareholder value. As we discussed in Chapter 2, a company's share price can be deconstructed to determine the level of eps growth inherent in the current market value. Unless the reference base for eps growth is set using very similar growth expectations to those already reflected in the current P/E multiple, value will not be created. As illustrated in Working insight 16.6, these caveats are not observed in the vast majority of such schemes which exist in major UK companies today.

WORKING 16.6 INSIGHT

Required growth in earnings per share

In November 2001, inflation in the UK was running at just over 2 per cent. Data from the *Financial Times* for the FTSE 350 indicated an average P/E ratio of about 22; dividend yield of about 2.5 per cent; and dividend cover of just under two times (implying a dividend payout ratio of about 50 per cent). The yield on UK government bonds was about 4.7 per cent.

We can use this data in the Capital Asset Pricing Model to calculate an average cost of equity for FTSE 350 companies. Assuming a market risk premium of 5 per cent and an average beta of 1:

$$K_e = R_f + \beta(R_m - R_f)$$
$$= 4.7\% + 5\%$$
$$= 9.7\%$$

This cost of equity can in turn be used to evaluate the anticipated earnings growth, taking Equation 5 from Chapter 2.

$$\text{P/E ratio} = \text{payout ratio} \times 1/ (K_e - g)$$
$$22 = 50\% \times 1/ (9.7\% - g)$$

Solving this gives an estimated growth expectation of 7.4 per cent.

What this means is that the share price of the average FTSE 350 company implicitly includes an expectation of growth of 7.4 per cent. Even if we ignore any potential reduction in the P/E ratio as discussed in Chapter 2, this represents eps growth of 7.4 per cent as a minimum. This is a shame, as the 'RPI + 3 per cent' performance benchmark would reward growth of only 5 per cent: which is hardly conducive to creating shareholder value.

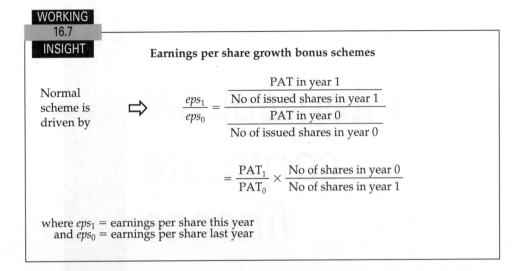

WORKING 16.7

INSIGHT

Earnings per share growth bonus schemes

Normal scheme is driven by

$$\frac{eps_1}{eps_0} = \frac{\dfrac{\text{PAT in year 1}}{\text{No of issued shares in year 1}}}{\dfrac{\text{PAT in year 0}}{\text{No of issued shares in year 0}}}$$

$$= \frac{\text{PAT}_1}{\text{PAT}_0} \times \frac{\text{No of shares in year 0}}{\text{No of shares in year 1}}$$

where eps_1 = earnings per share this year
and eps_0 = earnings per share last year

Working insight 16.6 demonstrates that the performance targets in use for the majority of executive share option schemes are insufficiently demanding to create value for shareholders. Even ignoring this, taking eps growth as the performance requirement is a flawed measure.

By definition, an eps growth bonus scheme is based on an accounting measure; in fact, as shown in Working insight 16.7, it is based on a ratio of two accounting ratios.

It is now fairly well accepted that the level of essential managerial judgements involved in producing a set of published financial statements means that profits can be moved from one accounting period to another. It is important to remember that such discretion – massaging, manipulation or whatever it is called – cannot increase the total profits made over the lifetime of a project or company (these will always be reconcilable to the total cash flows produced in the same overall period), but can only change the timing of when they are recognized. However, if the management bonus scheme is driven by the growth from year to year of a profit-focused ratio, the question of timing can become quite financially significant; particularly, as is often the case, when the bonus scheme has a maximum level built in, as delaying excess profit from a very good year can then be advantageous to the managers.

This still doesn't reflect all the distortions which can be caused by such schemes because, as was previously mentioned and is highlighted in Working insight 16.7, eps-driven bonuses are calculated as a ratio of two financial ratios. These can be restated to show how the bonus can be triggered if profits grow (even if this is primarily caused by a decrease in the effective tax rate) or if the number of shares decrease from year to year. Share repurchase schemes by companies, particularly when offered as an alternative to extra dividend payments, should be carefully reviewed against the incentive schemes in operation for senior executives. It is far more common, however, to find rapidly growing companies which have failed to implement the optimum high growth financial strategy of raising equity because that would, in the short term, have led to a decrease in the earnings per share which were used as the basis for management incentive schemes.

17

International corporate finance

In international corporate finance we face all of the complexities of the domestic variety, together with additional issues relating to dealing with foreign cultures, satisfying different stakeholders, and managing foreign exchange risk.

This chapter briefly discusses the reasons that companies may wish to make overseas acquisitions, and then focuses on the mechanics of how these deals might be found, and the pitfalls involved in completing the transaction, and in running the company thereafter. The method of paying for the business is also considered – which currency should be used, and should the finance be raised in shares or debt?

Within the chapter, the discussions are informed by considering three types of foreign exchange risk – transaction risk, translation risk and economic risk.

INTRODUCTION

As someone once said, the world is becoming more global every day! Certainly, business is increasingly conducted on a global scale, and companies need to understand the implications for their business and financial strategies.

We have already explained that a detailed exposition of business strategy is outside the scope of this book; our remit is to explain financial strategy. Accordingly, in this chapter we will not venture into the 'whys' of investment overseas, but will instead focus on its financial aspects. We will assume that someone else has done the detailed analysis that concludes, for example, that:

- we have exhausted the growth potential of our local market, and international expansion is a more rational strategy than diversification; or
- it is more cost-effective to have operations in [name your country/region] than it is to continue to produce here and export to them; or
- our main competition is coming from this part of the world, and it would be strategically beneficial to move into their territory; or
- we need a presence in this trading bloc in order to be able to compete here without trade restrictions; or
- we need to expand into this territory before our competitors do, to gain first mover advantage in this expanding market.

Or any one of a multiplicity of good strategic reasons for overseas expansion or acquisitions.

In this chapter we will focus mostly on international finance as focused on corporate acquisitions, rather than start-up greenfield sites or joint ventures. However, much of what we say is relevant to all international situations, including instances where a company is seeking foreign investment in itself.

SO, WHY IS 'INTERNATIONAL' DIFFERENT?

Why is 'international corporate finance' different to the domestic variety? Well, other than the fact that it's harder and riskier, the answer is 'it isn't'! All of the principles set out in this book will apply to your international business in the same way as to your domestic business: the financial strategy should be tailored to the business strategy; levels of gearing and dividend payment should reflect the business risks; etc. However, on top of that there are various other issues to consider, such as the currency implications for the deal itself and for ongoing ownership of the subsidiary; different legal and tax regimes; and divergent cultural values which may affect the success of a transaction.

The rest of this chapter sets out these issues in the context of making an overseas acquisition – and making a success of it.

FINDING AN ACQUISITION TARGET

Once a company's strategic priorities are determined, the requirements for an acquisition target are known. But knowing what you want and knowing where to find it are two different matters. In some countries, such as the UK, company information is widely available, and there are many different ways to conduct an acquisition search. However, in different jurisdictions, different norms apply.

When conducting an acquisition search in a foreign territory a company will almost certainly need to find trusted local advisers who understand the market. Publicly available information on targets may be limited, which makes the dynamics of pre-bid due diligence more complex (particularly in a hostile bid situation). There may also be local regulations and cultural norms which would restrict an outsider from outright purchase of a local business, even if one could be found. All these issues need to be addressed by experts who understand the local corporate and market environments.

DOING THE DEAL

Once a target has been identified, the acquisition must be completed. Specific 'international' issues to consider during this process include:

- Negotiation strategies.
- Legal context.
- Availability and interpretation of information.
- Pricing difficulties.
- Competition regulations.

Global deals are inevitably more complex than local ones. Entering into negotiations with someone from a different culture involves understanding their stance on the negotiating process; appreciating their cultural norms; and (preferably) knowing something of their language. It sounds self evident, but business people sometimes overlook the fact that, for example, transactions with North Americans must be handled in a very different way to those with the Japanese, who are different again to Thais or to Chinese business people.

The legal context in which the acquisition takes place must also be fully understood. For example, when buying a business in one's own country one generally understands, to some extent, the issues surrounding intellectual property rights, environmental liabilities, or employee consultation practices. In a foreign environment, each of these – and a thousand other things – could differ widely from pre-conceptions. Furthermore, takeover regulations differ widely among countries, and hostile bids in particular may be difficult or impossible in some parts of the world.

Information sources too could be a problem. As already stated, in some jurisdictions access to public information may be limited. But even if the information is published, or if private access is given, the information needs to be understandable. Just as an example, accounting regulations in Japan are very different to those in the UK: what does the profit reported by your Japanese target actually represent? It is always useful in these circumstances to employ professionals to re-state the target's financial information using the accounting policies acceptable in the acquirer's home territory – to see if the deal is actually worth doing. Case study 17.1 on BMW and Rover illustrates this.

Problems in understanding the financial information will obviously affect the deal pricing, but other issues too will be relevant here. In making local acquisitions, companies generally understand their local market and, in the UK and USA at least, can find a lot of comparative information about previous deals, so that they can price their proposals comparative to the market. In some countries, markets have low liquidity and are not efficient, so market comparisons may be misleading. Furthermore, data on private company deals may not be available, so the potential acquirer is left operating in an information vacuum.

17.1 DIFFERENT ACCOUNTING RULES
BMW AND ROVER

The German car company BMW acquired the UK manufacturer Rover in 1994. After years of heavy financial losses, the German company eventually sold Rover in May 2000. However, was Rover really as bad a company as the headlines reported?

The UK company's results as filed at Companies House under UK accounting regulations differ considerably from those prepared by BMW using German policies, which were the focus of public debate.

	UK result £ m	German result £ m
1995	(51)	(163)
1996	(100)	(109)
1997	19	(91)
Three year total loss	(132)	(363)

Differences in accounting policies include a more aggressive depreciation policy, higher provisions and different rules on stock valuation in Germany.

Source: Accountancy Age, 18 February 1999.

A further issue, of major concern, is the attitude of regulators and competition authorities. Making a major acquisition in their territory may trigger an investigation which could delay the transaction for months or years, or change its form. The *Financial Times* (2 July 2001) quoted a lawyer involved in the merger of Pechiney (a French company) and Algroup (Swiss) as follows: 'Alcan looked at 43 jurisdictions where they had overlaps, filed in 16 of those, in eight different languages, employed 35 different firms of solicitors and had to respond to a variety of different information requests, one of which alone led to the provision of 1 m e-mails from a single office in one agency'.

Of course, we should point out that these problems can occur even in an apparently domestic transaction. In 2001 the acquisition of US company Honeywell by US company GE was terminated when the European Union competition authorities could not be satisfied as to its competitive effects in their jurisdiction.

International transactions will also result in problems for companies in managing the inevitable exposure that arises to a foreign currency(ies). Accordingly, before we discuss how deals can be financed we will consider the sources of foreign exchange risk, and how such risks can be mitigated.

FOREIGN EXCHANGE RISK

Foreign exchange risks relate to the potential for currency movements to impact on the firm. The issues we need to consider are:

- What foreign exchange risks arise due to overseas acquisitions?
- How can these risks be mitigated? and
- Is it worthwhile to mitigate the risks?

Example of transaction risk

UKCo enters into a contract to sell services to FrenchCo for €12 000. The current exchange rate is £1 = €1.50. By the time the debt comes to be paid, the rate has become £1 = €1.60.

The original value of the sale to UKCo was   €12 000/1.5 = £8000

However, the depreciation of the euro means that the sterling amount finally received by UKCo is   €12 000/1.6 = £7500

By pricing its deal in euros the company has accepted the transaction risk, and has lost on the exchange rate movement.

Two matters need to be addressed in dealing with currency issues in an international acquisition: the exposure relating to the deal funding, and the exposure relating to the ongoing operation of a foreign subsidiary. These are both considered in the paragraphs below.

To put it simply,[1] foreign exchange risk can come in one of three flavours: transaction risk, translation risk and economic risk.

Transaction risk is the risk that arises from undertaking transactions in a foreign currency. It is most easily explained by example, as in Working insight 17.1.

Translation risk arises from the need to translate all transactions and balance sheet items into domestic currency for the purpose of preparing the holding company's financial statements. Translation risk, sometimes known as 'accounting risk', does not have an immediate cash effect. However, its impact on the financial statements can be considerable, and, for example, this could affect a company's ability to meet banking covenants. Accordingly, companies may wish to structure transactions so that the balance sheet asset of, say, a dollar investment in a subsidiary, is at least partially 'hedged' by the dollar liability of funds raised to make that investment. In such an instance, any appreciation or depreciation in the £/$ rate would affect each side of the balance sheet, reducing to some extent the impact on the financial statements. (This issue is considered again later in this chapter.)

Economic risk relates to how a company's value (the present value of its future cash flows) might change due to exchange rate movements. This can occur directly or indirectly. An example of a direct risk would be a change in the currency value of sales remittances or a dividend stream receivable from an overseas subsidiary. But indirect economic risks are also relevant. For example, a UK car manufacturer exporting to the USA is obviously exposed to the £/$ exchange rate, but also has economic risk relating to the $/¥ exchange rate – if this changes, their Japanese competitors could undercut prices in this export market.

1. This is a very basic introduction to a complex subject. Readers who wish to know more should invest in one of the specialist books in this area, such as *Multinational Finance*, by Adrian Buckley, published by Prentice Hall (2000).

Foreign currency movements can be hedged in several ways, for example by taking out a forward contract or by using a foreign currency option.

A *forward contract* fixes the rate of exchange for a future delivery of a specified sum of money. Such a contract is binding on both parties, which limits the company's flexibility: as well as removing the downside risk of the exchange rate moving against the company, any upside potential is also lost.

The purchase of a *foreign currency option*, as with any option, gives the buyer the choice as to whether to exercise the option when the actual payment/receipt becomes due. The option contract can be used to establish a minimum rate which will apply to the foreign exchange transaction, so that the option premium (the purchase price of the option contract) should be regarded as a kind of insurance cost. If the actual rate of exchange is better than the option exercise rate, the option can simply be allowed to lapse and the foreign currency can be traded in the normal spot market.

Thus exchange rate movements can be financially managed, but how relevant is this to an overseas acquisition? There are several problems in practically applying the hedging possibilities:

1. The future cash flows which are going to be generated by the foreign acquisition are not known with certainty so that it is not obvious what amounts of hedging cover should be purchased.
2. Some at least of these future cash flows may be reinvested in the acquired business and therefore will not actually be converted into the buyer's local currency. This highlights a real problem because for reporting purposes it is not the cash flows which should be hedged but the profits of the overseas business, since these will be consolidated into the group's home currency-based published financial statements. It is by no means unusual to find that an overseas subsidiary may have increased its local currency denominated profits compared to the previous year but, if exchange rates have moved adversely between the two years, the impact on the group's consolidated results may be to show a decline in performance.
3. Forward exchange rates, at which these fixed future contracts would be agreed, are not designed to be forecasts of where the actual spot rate of exchange will be on that future specified date. Because of the way international financial markets work, the forward rate of exchange is always the current rate of exchange adjusted by the difference in interest rates between the two countries. As illustrated in Working insight 17.2, if this were not the case an arbitrageur could make a guaranteed profit by borrowing in one currency and investing in the other. Such investment actions would force the forward rates of exchange to change in order to close off such arbitrage profit opportunities.

However, the most important problem in trying to manage the currency risk is that it is hoped that the acquisition will continue to produce foreign currency inflows for the foreseeable future and, quite clearly, trying to hedge uncertain amounts of foreign currencies for an unknown period will become both practically difficult and increasingly expensive.

Because it is effectively impossible to hedge operating cash flows using forward or option contracts, companies may consider other forms of hedge. They may examine whether an alternative financing strategy can be used. As suggested

WORKING
17.2
INSIGHT

The arbitrage view of forward exchange rates

Using an extreme example to illustrate the point, suppose that the spot rate of exchange is £1 equals $2 and the annual rate of interest is 15 per cent in £s and 5 per cent in $s. An arbitrageur could borrow funds in US dollars, convert them into £s sterling and deposit them at the higher rate. In order to guarantee the repayment of the US-based loan, the £s sterling receipts could be sold forward at a guaranteed rate to produce US dollars. Unless the forward rate reflects the difference in interest rates, the arbitrageur could generate a guaranteed profit! The forward rate should be $2 \times 1.05 \div 1.15$, i.e. $1.826 : £1.

Arbitrageur borrows $100 million @ 5 per cent for one year.

This is converted into £50 million at spot rate of $2 : £1 and deposited @ 15 per cent for one year

The interest income on the deposit will be £7.5 million

Therefore in one year's time £57.5 million will be held but a liability is also outstanding of $105 million (principal plus interest on the loan)

If the forward rate of exchange is $1.826 : £1, the proceeds of the deposit just repay the loan and no arbitrage profit is available.

earlier, some companies try to reduce the currency risk by using a source of financing for the acquisition in the same currency as the ensuing income stream. For example, if debt funding were appropriate for the particular deal, the borrowings could be raised in the same currency so that only the remaining profit stream of the foreign acquisition would need to be converted into the parent company's own currency. At first glance this would appear to reduce the financial risk associated with the overseas acquisition but this is not so obvious when the driving forces of exchange rate movements are taken into consideration.

Over time, exchange rates must reflect the relative purchasing powers of the respective currencies. If this were not true it would be possible to make long term profits by the physical movement of goods between countries. In the short term, this stable equilibrium position may be disturbed by government interference in interest rates or trade flows, but in the long term this concept, known as *purchasing power parity*, will hold.

Purchasing power parity means that over the long term, exchange rates will move to adjust for differences in inflation rates between any two countries, since this differential inflation will distort the nominal prices of comparable goods. However, interest rates and equity funding costs also include inflation, and so the costs of funding should also be different in these countries if the inflation rates differ. This should result in the source of funding for an international acquisition making no difference to the long-term financial return, as is illustrated in Figure 17.1.

The example in Figure 17.1 shows a UK-based investment opportunity spotted by a USA-based company many years ago (when the rate of exchange was $4 to £l). The investment needed is £250 million and it was expected to

Figure 17.1

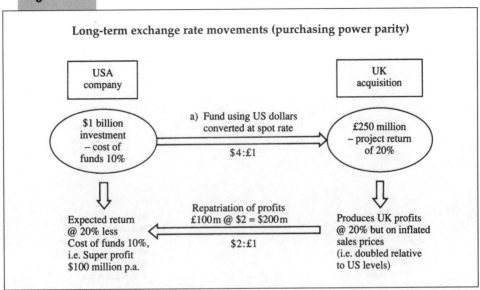

generate a return of 20 per cent, which showed a good super profit as the risk-adjusted cost of funds to the USA-based investor was 10 per cent.

This project could be funded by converting $1 billion into £s sterling at the spot rate of exchange and then repatriating the actual profit streams as dividends. However during the life of the project, the rate of exchange moved steadily to $2 : £1 from its initial point of $4 : £1. If purchasing power parity were performing properly, this would not affect the return to the investor because, as is shown, the UK-based profits should have increased due to the higher inflation which has caused the decline in the rate of exchange. In other words, as the rate of exchange halved, prices should have doubled in the UK, relative to the USA. As long as the company had maintained its UK profit margins, it should have achieved double the expected sterling profits (£100 million rather than £50 million) and this would convert into the originally expected $200 million. Hence the expected super profit is achieved despite the change in exchange rate, as long as the exchange rate movement is caused by inflation differences and the locally based business maintains its profit margins.

However, instead of using US dollars to fund the whole investment, part of the financing could be raised locally. This would hedge some of the translation (accounting) exposure, but would it affect the economic risk? Figure 17.2 illustrates what happens if 50 per cent of the funding is injected locally and the other 50 per cent by converting $500 million at the spot rate of exchange.

In Figure 17.2, the changed source of funding does not affect the operating profits produced by the UK business, but the business now has to bear financing costs on the locally sourced funding. As inflation in the UK is much higher (in this example) than in the USA, these funding costs will also be higher (20 per cent rather than the 10 per cent in the USA). Therefore the £100 million operating profits will be reduced by £25 million (representing a 20 per cent

Figure 17.2

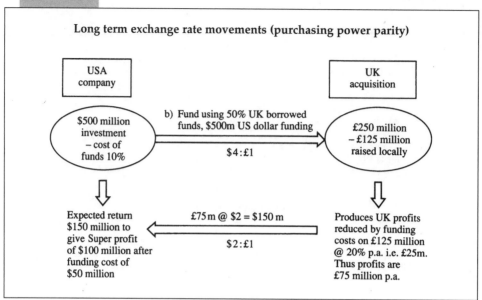

financing cost on the local funding of £125 million). This leaves £75 million which is available for repatriation by converting it at $2 : £1 into $150 million. Since the USA-based funding is now only $500 million this only absorbs $50 million of financing cost, so that there is still a super profit of $100 million on the project even though the financing structure has changed significantly.

The example illustrated in Figures 17.1 and 17.2 shows that if exchange rates do move to reflect differences in inflation rates, which must happen in the long term, the international sourcing of finance does not affect the return achieved on any cross-border investment. However, purchasing power parity is a long term issue. In the real world (the one not inhabited by theoretical economists) there will be long time lags in exchange rate adjustment. As costs of funding and exchange rate movements do not necessarily always reflect differences in inflation rates in the short term, there will be many occasions when the source of financing can make a difference to the performance of the cross-border investment. Thus hedging these potential differences can make sense for a company if it is particularly concerned about its short-term perceived (i.e. accounting) performance.

This helps to explain why many more companies operate sophisticated hedging strategies for their short-term international trading cash flows, but do not take out any hedges relating to the longer-term balance sheet exposures which they create by holding overseas assets.

FINANCING THE DEAL

In Chapter 12 we discussed acquisition finance and stated that there were two basic methods: offer the target's shareholders an equity stake in the acquirer, or offer them cash. In an international transaction, it may not be possible to offer an all share deal, or even a deal for which only part of the consideration is in equity.

There are two potential reasons for equity-based deals to present problems in an international transaction. The first is that regulations may prevent it; in some jurisdictions, nationals are forbidden from owning shares in foreign companies. The second reason is that the shareholders themselves may be uneasy with the idea of changing the 'paper' in a domestic company they know for paper in a company with foreign domicile, whose laws and tax regulations are unclear to them, and in which dealing in the shares, on a foreign stock exchange, will be unfamiliar, and possibly expensive.

Thus the financing for international acquisitions can be carried out by:

1. raising equity on the home market, and using the proceeds to pay cash to acquire the target;
2. raising debt, and using the proceeds to pay cash to acquire the target; or
3. issuing shares tradable in the target's country, which will be an acceptable currency for shareholders.

The first of these possibilities, financing the transaction by raising equity on the home market, has been considered at various times through this book. The decision as to whether to finance the acquisition through raising debt or equity is similar to any investment financing decision, and is not pursued further in this chapter. (Although we would point out that, almost by definition, expansion into a foreign territory will increase business risk, and companies may wish to strengthen their equity base to compensate.)

The second possibility we suggested was to raise debt and use the proceeds to acquire the target. Again, the question of whether or not to raise debt is addressed elsewhere in this book; what is of interest here is *where* to raise the debt. Although companies always have a choice of markets and currencies for their debt finance, the decision becomes more immediate in an international transaction, as discussed earlier in this chapter.

RAISING LOANS IN A FOREIGN CURRENCY

The discussion of foreign exchange risks did, we hope, give you some idea as to why companies might wish to raise acquisition funds in a currency other than their own. Should they choose so to do, it is important to understand that entering into such a transaction itself creates a currency exposure.

For example, if a UK company raises funds in dollars, it will need to make interest and capital repayments in that currency. If the company has a dollar income stream from its subsidiary, that is fine; the currency is available, and any currency movements will affect both its income and outgoings. However, if the income stream is insufficient to meet the debt cash flows, the company will face a transaction risk similar to that described in Working insight 17.1, possibly leading to an unexpectedly high drain on its cashflows. This might be particularly relevant for acquisitions undertaken at a high P/E ratio, for which the finance raised (and thus the servicing charges) will be substantial in relation to the income stream acquired. (Of course, this should only be a problem in the early years after the deal: the whole objective of a high P/E deal is that the target is expected to grow rapidly, and thus generate the required income streams.)

Companies wishing to raise funds in a particular currency will find that today's financial markets provide a variety of mechanisms to effect such transactions, for example the Eurobond markets.

Eurobonds are bonds which are denominated in currencies other than that of the country in which they are sold. For example, a $-denominated bond issued in London, or a ¥ bond sold in the USA are both Eurobonds; the 'Euro' part of the name has nothing to do with the European currency. These international bonds are widely traded on the markets, and give companies access to a more extensive range of financing sources than they would have were they to restrict their activities to their local currency.

We should also remember companies have the ability to enter into currency swaps (which operate in a similar manner to the interest rate swaps discussed in the Annex to Chapter 8), so that the currency in which the loan is first raised need not be the currency finally adopted. For example, it might be the case that an acquisition made in the USA is initially financed in US dollars, but, when the target's main income sources are understood more fully, part of that $ liability is swapped into another more appropriate currency, to hedge trading exposures.

ISSUING SHARES ACCEPTABLE TO FOREIGN SHAREHOLDERS

The third financing possibility we suggested was for the acquirer to issue shares that would be acceptable to the overseas shareholders. This could be done, for example, by listing its shares on the overseas exchange, or by issuing depository receipts.

SECONDARY LISTING

If a company makes a major acquisition in an overseas territory, it may choose to take a secondary listing on one of that country's stock markets. Doing this would mean that shareholders in some jurisdictions would legally be able to own the shares, and all shareholders would more easily be able to deal in them. It would also make it easier to reward overseas nationals using equity-based incentives. Furthermore, the company might benefit in other ways; if a major part of its business is now to be conducted in another country, having wider exposure in their capital markets can be an advantage.

The disadvantages of a secondary listing mostly revolve around its cost; it can prove very expensive to comply with regulatory requirements for two exchanges and, in particular, to prepare full financial statements under two different sets of accounting standards. (At the time of writing, proposals are being discussed to streamline accounting requirements in this area, but these have not yet been put into place.)

A further disadvantage of secondary listing is that shareholders, by and large, just prefer their own territories. When DaimlerChrysler was formed, the company was listed jointly in the USA and Germany, and about 50 per cent of its shareholders were based in the USA. In May 2001 the *Financial Times* reported that only about 20 per cent of the shares remained US-owned, the rest having been sold into the German market (a process known as 'flowback'). It seems that many US shareholders preferred not to invest in what is seen as a 'German' company.

DEPOSITORY RECEIPTS

Should a company choose not to list on another market, it can instead issue depository receipts, which are another means to achieve its aims. The most common form of depository receipts are American Depository Receipts (ADRs), although Global Depository receipts (GDRs) are also available.

Using an ADR facility, a company will deposit some of its shares with a US trust bank which offers this service. The bank will then issue investors with bearer certificates confirming that the bank owns a certain number of shares, and the bearer is entitled to the proceeds of those shares. An ADR might represent an underlying investment of say 10 or 20 shares in the company. The trust bank will pay the underlying dividend entitlement to the bearers, who will be able to trade the ADRs. The market price of ADRs generally follows that of the underlying shares, although supply and demand may at any time lead to a pricing discount or premium.

The advantage to the company of using ADRs is that the administrative burden and cost are considerably lower than those of maintaining a secondary listing. For the investor, ADRs give a chance to invest in an overseas company, making a $ investment which they can easily buy and sell.

POST DEAL MANAGEMENT

In Chapter 12 we pointed out that research indicates that most acquisitions fail. International acquisitions are harder, and the causes of failure more varied. In addition to the 'normal' integration issues, the following should be considered.

- The global structure of the new organization needs to be determined strategically, and issues such as the location of head offices and operating centres must be addressed.
- The management resource required to integrate an international acquisition is considerably greater than for a domestic one. Further, integration managers must be based full time in the acquired company's country, and must have relevant language skills as well as fully understanding the business and strategy of the acquirer.
- Cultural barriers may make integration very difficult. For example, the level of formality between workers and between management levels may differ between countries; employee rights and expectations can be very diverse; ethical issues may be seen in different ways. In a more extreme example, if the takeover was hostile, it may be deeply resented by the target company's employees. See, for example, case study 17.2 on Vodafone/Mannesmann.

- Without full integration of the new subsidiary, it may be impossible to achieve the planned synergies.
- Legal differences may cause problems. For example, at the time of writing the divergence in data protection legislation between the UK and USA may mean that a UK subsidiary could not send certain customer information to its US parent; again reducing the opportunities for synergistic expansion.

Taxation issues and repatriation of profits need also to be considered. These are often linked, and a company should not consider making an overseas acquisition unless it understands how the profits of its acquired subsidiary (and maybe even its worldwide profits from other countries) will be taxed. And the issue of whether, and how, profit can be repatriated, should also be addressed in advance; it is not always automatic that dividend distributions can be made as and when desired.

17.2 CULTURAL BARRIERS
VODAFONE AND MANNESMANN

CASE STUDY

The hostile takeover of Mannesmann by Vodafone in 2000 was unusual, in that the regulatory environment means that successful hostile bids for German companies are very rare (although German companies are very adept at acquiring businesses in other countries). Accordingly, the very fact of the deal came as a culture shock to the employees of the long-established German company.

During the initial period of ownership, Vodafone did the following:

- Sold off the prestigious Mannesmann fine art collection.
- Sold off the century-old wood panels in the board room.
- Stopped the practice of sending employees cards and wine on their birthdays.
- Promoted its charitable donations in order to benefit from the publicity (Mannesmann had always given anonymously).

These actions, which would have been seen as reasonable in shareholder value-based Anglo American cultures, were totally alien to the German employees and caused deep resentment.

Source: Financial Times, 5 June 2001.

CONCLUSION: DOES THE 'GLOBAL COMPANY' EXIST?

International corporate finance is different to the domestic variety, as companies face far more barriers to success at all stages of the transaction and in its ongoing management.

It is interesting that overseas investment risks and foreign currency exposures still take up so much time of senior managers in many multinational or transnational corporations. The development of global brands, global products and, to a lesser extent, global customers, has driven expansion, and yet there is no really global company. A global company would not need to hedge foreign currency exposures because they would not exist.

If a company were truly global, it would have balanced its business exposures (in terms of profits and cash flows) to the relative economic size of the countries and currencies around the world. However it would have gone one stage further and balanced its ownership and funding sources on the same basis as its profits and cash flows so that its investors were not all expecting a return denominated in a particular currency, such as the US dollar. At present, even though investors in very large companies may be located all over the world, they will still view each such investment as being based in a particular currency.

Appendices

Appendix 1:
Review of theories
of finance

This Appendix sets out an explanation of financial theory sufficient to give the reader a background to the issues discussed in the rest of the book. The topics covered are:

- Discounting and calculating the value of bonds.
- The cost of capital:

  - calculating the cost of equity using the Dividend Growth Model;
  - calculating the cost of equity using the Capital Asset Pricing Model;
  - calculating a weighted average cost of capital and designing an appropriate capital structure.

- The efficient market hypothesis.
- Dividend theory.

INTRODUCTION

It would be a very daunting prospect to try to review the mass of developments in the theory of finance in one brief appendix of this book. Not surprisingly therefore, this review is both very selective and very concise on each topic, concentrating only on the key elements of the theories and highlighting, where relevant, the essential underlying assumptions on which the theory or model is based. In writing the book we have assumed that our readers already have some familiarity with financial theory, and seek from us only an aide memoire to remind them of the key points. Accordingly, in this Appendix we cover the theories of finance only insofar as they are necessary to set a context for the rest of the book, and in summary rather than in depth.

In most cases the theories are referred to by their inventors' or discoverers' names but no attempt, due to constraints of space, has been made to be academically rigorous in giving copious references to the derivation of the formulae, etc. This is also partially because the theories are comprehensively covered in most of the basic existing finance textbooks and it was never any intention to try to reproduce that type of book.

DISCOUNTING AND THE VALUE OF BONDS

An appreciation of the time value of money is fundamental to financial theory and practice. Money now is worth more than money in the future; accordingly, if we lend or invest money we expect to receive a return on that investment. This return compensates us for not being able to spend the funds immediately, for the risk of non-return of the funds, and for the fact that inflation might erode the value of the funds over the investment period.

Although in practice the return on an investment means that a greater sum is available at the end of the investment period than the beginning, financial convention dictates that when comparing investments we determine the equivalent sum that they would be worth at the start of the period – the *net present value* (NPV) – rather than the total to be received by the end of the period – the *terminal value*. This facilitates comparisons between investments.

We evaluate the net present value of an investment (be it an investment in financial instruments or in real assets of a business) by discounting the cash flows expected from that investment. *Discounted cash flow* (DCF) analysis applies discounting factors (the inverse of compounding factors) – to each future period's expected cash flows. Working insight A1.1 illustrates an example whereby DCF analysis is used to determine the value of a bond.

In Working insight A1.1, the bond traded at a discount to its face value. This is because the bond only pays an interest rate of 7 per cent, which is lower than the 8 per cent paid by other similar bonds and so the instrument is worth less.

Working insight A1.2 shows what would happen to the value of the same bond if, two years later, market interest rates had fallen to 5 per cent.

**WORKING
A1.1
INSIGHT**

Bond valuation (part 1)

A £1 million 5-year bond offers a 7 per cent rate of interest, payable annually in arrears. The current required market rate of return for this investment is 8 per cent. What is the value of the bond on the market?

Year	Cash flow	Discount factor @ 8%	Present value
1 – 5 (interest)	£70 k p.a.	3.993	£279.5 k
5 (repayment)	£1000 k	0.681	£681.0 k
			£960.5 k

The present value of the cash flows from the bond is £960.5 k, therefore that is what a rational investor would be prepared to pay for it.

> **WORKING**
> **A1.2**
> **INSIGHT**
>
> ### Bond valuation (part 2)
>
> The £1 million bond offers a 7 per cent rate of interest, payable annually in arrears, and has three years to run. The current required market rate of return for this investment is 5 per cent.
>
> | Year | Cash flow | Discount factor @ 5% | Present value |
> |---|---|---|---|
> | 1 – 3 (interest) | £70 k p.a. | 2.723 | £190.6 k |
> | 3 (repayment) | £1000 k | 0.864 | £864.0 k |
> | | | | £1054.6 k |
>
> The present value of the cash flows from the bond is now £1054.6 k.

The fall in market interest rates means that the bond in Working insight A1.2 is relatively more valuable, and so it is trading at a premium to the £1 million face value.

The principles of discounted cash flow underlie much of the theory of finance and are fundamental in understanding the valuation of all types of financial instrument. In order to apply DCF techniques a discount rate is needed, and it is the derivation of this discount rate, based on a company's cost of capital, which is explored in the next section.

THE COST OF CAPITAL

Companies can raise money using two basic forms of instrument – debt and equity. We established in Chapter 1 that the return that the investors demand from their investment is directly related to their perception of the risk of that investment. For the investor, debt is a much lower risk investment than is equity (there is less volatility in the expected returns) and therefore lenders require a lower return than shareholders.

In this section we consider the cost of debt (K_d), two different ways of calculating the cost of equity (K_e), and the calculation of the weighted average cost of capital (WACC), which often forms the basis for the discount factor applied in DCF analysis.

THE COST OF DEBT

We have seen from the example in Working insight A1.1 that the cost of debt is based on the current market rate for debt of that risk level. The fact that a business raised debt at 7 per cent some years ago is irrelevant to its cost of debt; what is significant is that lenders now are demanding an 8 per cent return on their money – that must be the basis for the company's K_d calculations.

However, the cost of debt to the company is actually less than 8 per cent, as governments subsidize debt by allowing interest to be tax deductible. If a company borrows £1 million at 8 per cent, the interest charge of £80 000 is allowable as an expense for tax purposes. Accordingly, if tax rates are 30 per cent, the company's tax liability is reduced by £24 000 (£80 000 × 30%). This means that the net cost to the company is only £56 000. Thus, provided that a company is paying tax, this *tax shield* reduces the cost of the debt.

$$K_d = i(1 - t) \tag{1}$$

where i is the interest rate to be applied, and t is the tax rate.

This means that debt is doubly cheaper than equity: not only is it inherently cheaper as a low-risk financial instrument for the lender, but the additional tax subsidy reduces its cost still further. One begins to see why companies like to use debt as a source of finance.

THE COST OF EQUITY

Two separate ways of calculating the cost of equity will be considered: the Dividend Growth Model and the Capital Asset Pricing Model.

Simple dividend growth model

Shareholders achieve their return through a mixture of dividends and capital gain. Assume an investor, let us call him A, buys a share to hold for three years. At the end of each of those three years he receives a dividend on the share, then he sells it on to investor B. Investor B will only buy the share if she too believes that it will be a good investment, generating dividends and a capital gain. She too holds it for three years, selling on to C. And investor C too...well, you get the picture.

We could run through the whole alphabet with investors receiving dividends and then selling on the share, but the basic principle is clear:

1. investors receive a dividend and capital gain;
2. the reason that they can sell the share to other investors is because those buyers also expect to receive a dividend, and to be able to sell it on at some future point.

We all know of shares which do not pay out dividends (indeed, they are discussed in Chapter 3). However, this in no way invalidates the model: profits reinvested by the company will lead to larger profits and greater dividends in the future. Ultimately, the company has to pay out all of its profits by way of dividend – otherwise there is no point in being an investor.

So, investor A paid price P_0 for the share, and received dividends D_1, D_2 and D_3. He then sold for price P_1.

Investor B bought for price P_1, received dividends D_4, D_5 and D_6 and then sold for price P_2.

Investor C paid price P_2, received dividends D_7, D_8 and D_9 and then sold on for price P_3.

If we eliminate the share prices paid between investors, we are left with a stream of cash flows from the company: D_1, D_2, D_3, ... D_t. It is this stream of cash flows that we can value to value the share.

WORKING A1.3

INSIGHT   **Calculation of growth for the dividend growth model**

Assumptions:

1. Dividend payout ratio is constant over time, and so therefore is the retention ratio.
2. Return on reinvestment is constant over time.

The combination of these assumptions means that profits growth (and therefore dividend growth) is constant over time:

g = retention ratio $\times$ return on reinvestment.

WORKING
A1.4
INSIGHT   **Example of growth calculations**

Company Z started the year with equity of £1000 and made profits after tax of £100. Of this £100, £20 was paid out to shareholders by way of dividend, and £80 was reinvested in the business.

Return on opening equity = 100/1000 = 10 per cent.
Closing equity = £1000 + £80 = £1080

If the return on reinvestment is constant, the company will make profits of 10 per cent of opening capital next year: 10% × £1080 = £108.

This represents a growth rate in profits of 8/100 = 8 per cent.

Which could also be calculated as:

g = Retention ratio × Return on reinvestment
= 80% × 10%
= 8 per cent.

If we assume that the shareholder requires a return of K_e, the cost of equity, then the value to the shareholder of the share (i.e. its price) is

$$P = D_1/(1 + K_e) + D_2/(1 + K_e)^2 + D_3/(1 + K_e)^3 + \cdots + D_t/(1 + K_e)^t \qquad (2)$$

If we assume a compounding relationship[1] between the dividends from each year, with dividends growing at the rate of g per annum such that $D_2 = D_1(1 + g)$ and $D_3 = D_2(1 + g)$, equation 2 can be simplified to give the standard dividend growth model as developed by Gordon and Shapiro:[2]

$$P = D_1/(K_e - g) \qquad (3)$$

This equation sets out the price of the share (or of the company) in terms of its forthcoming dividend, growth assumptions and the cost of equity. It can be re-written to calculate the cost of equity based on a knowledge of the share price, as follows.

$$K_e = D_1/P + g \qquad (4)$$

It is obvious that a key driver of the functions in equations 3 and 4 is the growth assumption. Technically, this represents growth in dividends, and assumes a constant payout ratio over the company's future life (which those of us who have read Chapter 3 will realize is an unlikely situation). We also assume that the amount reinvested (one minus the payout ratio) can be reinvested at a constant rate of return. Thus, we can calculate what g might be, as shown in Working insight A1.3.

The formula in Working insight A1.3 is illustrated numerically in Working insight A1.4.

We must point out that although a formula-based approach to determining g is common, the results can be very misleading, not least because balance sheet values

---

1. We do appreciate the absurdity of the assumption of compound dividend growth to infinity. It is one of the restrictions of the dividend growth model. There are several more complex versions of the model available, which assume linear growth to infinity, or staged growth. However, the basic model is widely used and is essential to financial understanding.
2. M.J. Gordon and E. Shapiro, 'Capital Equipment Analysis: The Required Rate of Profit', Management Science, October 1956.

under current accounting standards may understate the 'true' position. In practice, we often prefer to look at historic trends in growth of profit or dividends, or to take directors' estimates of future growth as a more realistic representation.

Capital Asset Pricing Model (CAPM)

The positive correlation between risk and return has been consistently emphasized in this book; we now examine the theoretical framework for assessing the relevant level of risk. This is one area of finance which has been the subject of massive empirical research because, in the major capital markets at least, there are detailed records of the actual returns achieved by a wide range of alternative financial investments over more than 60 years. Some of these major research studies have compared the levels of average total return (including both dividend, or interest, income and capital gains) for different investment portfolios over almost this entire period. These analyses confirm the intuitive logic that investors receive a higher return on investments which have a higher risk. Whether the historic data indicate what the investors wanted rather than what they received is a separate issue, nevertheless we tend to use these results to predict the future.

Risk is defined as the volatility in the expected return from a financial instrument. An investor buying a government bond can be reasonably assured that the government will be around in the next few years to honour its interest and repayment commitments; consequently the required return is low. An investor in shares is reliant on the directors' intentions to pay a dividend, and on the company's performance and market conditions for her capital gain – this high volatility in expected results translates into a high required return.

The risk of any particular investment can be split into two components – unique risk (also known as company risk or diversifiable risk) and market (systemic) risk.

Unique risk relates to the particular company. It would include the risk of product failures, of the CEO dying, of product-market changes – anything company-specific that affects the operating results. However, because it relates only to that company, bad news (or indeed good news) here should have no impact on the other shares in an investor's portfolio. Market risk on the other hand relates to the market as a whole – for example to the economic cycle which would impact all companies. Market risk cannot be diversified. Figure A1.1 illustrates this.

If I own just one share, then my financial fortune is geared to how well that share performs. If I buy a second share, in a company whose results are not correlated to the first,

Figure A1.1

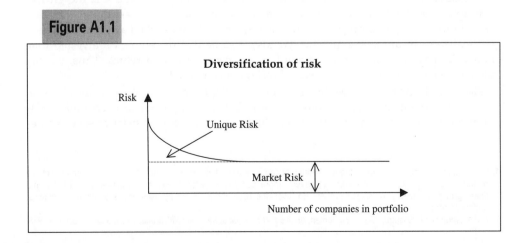

Diversification of risk

then my portfolio is diversified and my overall level of risk is reduced. (This can be shown mathematically, as the average return from the two shares will be the sum of their two average returns, but the volatility of the two, as measured by standard deviation, will be the square root of the sum of their squares, which is lower than merely averaging their individual standard deviations.)

It can be shown that an investor who has a diversified portfolio of about 20 shares can eliminate the unique company risk. However, market risk cannot be eliminated in this way, as all companies, to some extent or another, will be affected by general market movements.

As rational investors can diversify away the unique risk associated with any particular company, they do not need, and should not receive, any additional return to compensate for taking on this unnecessary risk. Therefore shareholders should only be compensated for taking the market risk, which is an inevitable consequence of investing in shares. This is a key principle underlying the Capital Asset Pricing Model (CAPM). In order to use it in practice, we need to understand how individual companies are affected by overall market movements.

The measure we use to determine how sensitive individual shares are to the return of the total stock market is known as beta (β). If, when overall stock market returns increase by 5 per cent, the returns on a particular share rise by 10 per cent, the share is said to have a beta of two. Similarly a less sensitive company may have a beta of 0.75 which means that if returns on the stock market fall by 10 per cent, this company's return will only fall by 7.5 per cent. Clearly the stock market as a whole has a beta of one, because the stock market is a weighted average of all shares.

From this analysis we obtain the Capital Asset Pricing Model developed in the 1960s by Treynor, Sharpe[3] and Lintner.

From Figure A1.2 we can see that if a share has a beta of one, i.e. its movements exactly mirror those of the stock market as a whole, the return that investors require from the share will be the same as the market return. Shares with $\beta > 1$ will demand a higher return than the market; the converse is true for those shares with $\beta < 1$.

The CAPM is elegantly simple, and easy to use. The risk free rate (R_f) can be obtained from the yield to redemption on government bonds. Companies' betas are calculated by investment services, using regression analysis over (say) five years to determine how that company's share price has moved compared to the market as a whole. And the market premium ($R_m - R_f$) has been determined by various academics and practitioners, often by examining 40 or 60 years of data as to how share returns have compared with bond returns.

However, in practice the data are not as straightforward as they may seem. R_f is the yield on government bonds: should this be three month bills, or 30 year bonds – each has a different yield to redemption. Beta is calculated by regression, but selecting different regression periods, or even carrying out the calculations for different days of the week, can give very different results. The market premium has been derived from historic data, but different calculation methods give very different results, and there are also some sources who state that past market returns are no guide to what investors actually require in the future. CAPM, although extensively used in practice, is fraught with problems.

We need to explore one further point on CAPM. As described, the CAPM formula can be used to calculate the cost of equity for a company. The beta we have discussed is the company beta, and reflects the company risk profile. But companies incur two

3. W.F. Sharpe, 'Capital Asset Prices: A Theory of Market Equilibrium Under Conditions of Risk', *Journal of Finance*, September 1964.

Figure A1.2

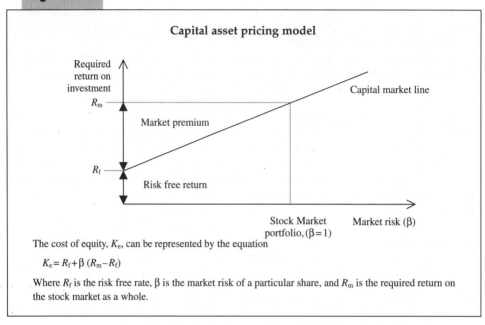

The cost of equity, K_e, can be represented by the equation

$$K_e = R_f + \beta (R_m - R_f)$$

Where R_f is the risk free rate, β is the market risk of a particular share, and R_m is the required return on the stock market as a whole.

main types of risk – business risk and financial risk. The beta of a company, which reflects its historical volatility against the market, incorporates both of these.

It is possible to deconstruct company betas (which are also known as equity betas) in order to establish the beta of the underlying assets – a reflection of the business risk. This can be done using the following equation:

$$\beta_{asset} = \beta_{debt} \times \{Debt/(Debt + Equity)\} + \beta_{equity} \times \{Equity/(Debt + Equity)\} \qquad (5)$$

It is generally assumed that the beta of debt approximates to zero. If we take β_{debt} as zero, then equation 5 simplifies to

$$\beta_{asset} = \beta_{equity} \times Equity/(Debt + Equity) \qquad (6)$$

The difference between the equity beta and the asset beta reflects the financial risk caused by the funding strategy of the company; were the company to be financed totally by equity, the equity beta and the asset beta would be the same.

Asset betas can be used to determine an appropriate discount rate to use on a project which is of a different risk level to the company as a whole, or can be used to determine the appropriate beta to use for evaluating an unquoted business (which, by definition, does not have a share price and so does not have a directly calculated beta).

WEIGHTED AVERAGE COST OF CAPITAL

Companies will be funded with a variety of financial instruments, but for the purpose of this section we will simplify matters so that they have a choice only of debt and equity. As established earlier, debt is a cheaper form of finance, being intrinsically safer for the investor, and subsidized by the tax system. However, it would be unrealistic for a company to finance itself solely by debt; although less risky for the investor, debt carries a significant risk to the company, and too much could drive it into liquidation. Accordingly, we need to establish how to determine an appropriate capital structure for a company, and be able to derive its overall cost of capital at that capital structure.

We should point out that much of financial theory derives from the work of Modigliani and Miller[4] who, in a seminal paper, demonstrated that capital structure is irrelevant to the value of a company. The value of the company is determined by the net present value of its future cash flows, and they argued that this total value is not changed by changing the sources of funding. If the total value is fixed, then an increase to one provider will be counter-balanced by a decrease to another provider. Modigliani and Miller's work, set in the conditions of a 'perfect market' with restrictive assumptions about tax and other variables, provided an important foundation for financial theory, but in practice most companies and analysts believe that capital structure does have an impact on the cost of capital.

It is a simple matter to determine the weighted average cost of capital (WACC) for a company. The costs of the individual capital components are averaged based on their weights in terms of market value. Working insight A1.5 illustrates this.

Based on the above calculation, it might seem that the greater the proportion of debt in the capital structure the lower the WACC of the company. However, this is not the case. As stated earlier, too much debt will increase the company's risk to unacceptable levels, and both the lenders and shareholders will demand increased returns to compensate for this risk. Further, at very high levels of debt the company may suffer the loss of its tax shield (if interest charges turn profits into losses there is no further tax advantage) and business may experience loss of confidence due to bankruptcy risk.

The trend in the WACC as debt levels change is illustrated in Figure A1.3.

In Figure A1.3, at a gearing level of zero the company is totally equity financed, so the average finance cost is the same as the cost of equity. As the company begins to substitute cheap debt for expensive equity, the WACC reduces. However, this substitution,

---

WORKING INSIGHT A1.5

Determining the weighted average cost of capital

Company W has established (using CAPM or the DGM) that its cost of equity is 11 per cent. Its pre-tax cost of debt is 6 per cent, and tax rates are 30 per cent. The market capitalization of W's equity is £1 million, and its debt is valued at £300 000.
  The weighted average cost of capital is calculated as:

$$\text{WACC} = \{K_e \times E/(E + D)\} + \{K_d \times D/(E + D)\}$$

where E and D are the market values of debt and equity respectively.

For Company W

$$\text{WACC} = 0.11 \times 1/1.3 + (0.06 \times 0.7) \times 0.3/1.3$$
$$= 9.4\%$$

Note: If market values are unavailable, or unrepresentative, the weights can be based on the company's target capital structure if it has one.

---

4. F. Modigliani and M.H. Miller, 'The Cost of Capital, Corporation Finance and the Theory of Investment', *American Economic Review*, June 1958.

Figure A1.3

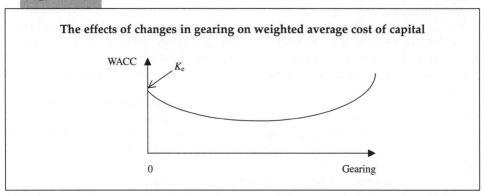

The effects of changes in gearing on weighted average cost of capital

Figure A1.4

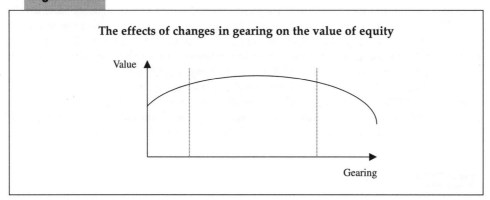

The effects of changes in gearing on the value of equity

increasing the gearing of the company, makes both debt and equity more expensive. Accordingly, although the debt is still cheaper than the equity, both rise in cost and the curve flattens. At the extreme right of the curve, investors and lenders realize their somewhat precarious position and demand very high returns to compensate for the risk.

As we use the company's cost of capital as a discount factor to apply to its future cash flows, Figure A1.3 can be mirrored in Figure A1.4, which reflects how the value of equity changes with gearing.

It can be seen from Figure A1.4 that ideally a company would wish to position its capital structure somewhere between the dotted lines – minimizing the cost of capital in order to maximize company value. Alas, this theoretical model gives little mathematical indication of where the 'correct' capital structure would lie for any company – hence Chapter 3 of this book, which sets out factors to consider.

THE EFFICIENT MARKET HYPOTHESIS

This one sub-section of this appendix has, itself, been the subject of innumerable books, journal articles and other academic treatises; consequently only some of the key elements of the continuing debate can even be alluded to. An initial assumption is one already used right at the beginning of the book but in different words. It is much more difficult to find sources of finance (often referred to as financing decisions so as to separate them from the investment decisions made by the company) which by themselves generate positive net present values than it is to find similarly attractive investment opportunities.

Indeed, if capital markets are truly efficient, it should be impossible for financing transactions to generate consistent positive net present values; such a transaction represents a zero sum game so that any gain to one party (the issuer or seller of the financial instrument) must equal a loss to the other party (the purchaser of the same investment). It is important immediately to be precise about what is meant by the word 'efficient'. This is not intended to mean that asset prices are always 'right' in the sense that expectations are always exactly, but only exactly, fulfilled. It simply means that today's prices incorporate all the information which is currently available to potential buyers and sellers. If this is true then price movements are caused by new information and as the nature of this new information is, by definition, unknown the impact on prices cannot be predicted. Logically this would suggest no correlation between the direction and size of tomorrow's price movement and today's.

The theory of efficient markets was quite neatly broken down into three stages by Roberts in 1967[5] so that interested parties can now select how efficient they think markets are.

- The *weak form* of the efficient market hypothesis is that all historical price information is incorporated into current share prices. This means that price movements are random and are not controlled by past trends. Commonly referred to as the 'random walk' theory, this implies that technical analysis of past price movements (such as is done by 'chartists') cannot give investors a competitive advantage.
- The *semi-strong form* argues that all published financial information is already included in the current share price; consequently detailed analysis of a company's published financial statements should not give a consistently superior return.
- The *strong form* of efficient markets says that current prices reflect all the available information which could be known; in other words, even insider and privileged information would not enable investors regularly to make a better than normal return.

These hypotheses have been tested extensively and most research studies have been unable to demonstrate consistently superior performance by investors, which would disprove the theory. However it is much more difficult to prove such a theory than it is to disprove it and other researchers have argued that most of the large studies have been flawed, pointing to particular studies which indicate consistent superior performance for certain investor groups (such as managers of the companies) or classes of investment (such as small companies in the 1980s and low P/E multiple large companies). In other words, despite massive research efforts there is not universal agreement on whether financial markets are efficient; even among those who believe they are, there is disagreement as to how efficient!

It is also important to remember that these arguments must be applied to specific financial markets. Just because the intense level of analysis and high degree of competition among research brokers, fund managers and other professional investors may make the stock markets of New York and London quite efficient, say at the semi-strong level, this does not mean that all the other stock markets around the world automatically function in the same way.

---

5. H.V. Roberts, '*Statistical Versus Clinical Prediction of the Stock Market*'. Paper presented at the Seminar on the Analysis of Security Prices, May 1967, University of Chicago.

The implications of an efficient market are quite substantial. If future price movements are random, it is fair to say that share prices have no memory; thus talk of the market reaching record levels is irrelevant: share prices merely move to reflect the new information which has become available. Also if markets are efficient so that current prices are always 'as right as they can be', the most logical investment portfolio is the stock market index. No consistent gain can be achieved by active trading, i.e. moving from one share to another, and increased costs will be incurred.

However, another implication for this book is that the theory, even if true, is always applied statistically, i.e. to large samples or to the market 'on average'. Thus it may be impossible to identify superior returns for a significant 'group' of investors but such returns may be achieved by a particular investor. All such specific illustrations of excess return or consistently good financing decisions by particular companies are dismissed by efficient market advocates as 'anecdotal and statistically irrelevant'. Perhaps this book can help to make the reader and/or your company such an anecdotal irrelevance.

Another fundamental conclusion of the efficient market hypothesis is that all financially viable projects (those generating a positive net present value using an appropriately risk-adjusted discount rate) will be able to raise the required funding. This is because investors are intelligent, rational and objective and can use the available information which is known to the promoters of the project to assess properly its expected risk; thus their views of the project's financial viability should coincide given this same information which is the essential assumption of an efficient market. Years of anecdotal experience of trying to raise venture capital for many new businesses tend to make this statement debatable, at least.

DIVIDEND THEORY

Earlier in this Appendix, share values were established as being driven by the present value of future dividends. Yet a fundamental theory of finance argues that dividend policy is irrelevant to share values; an apparent contradiction which requires resolution. Dividends form one part of the total return expected by investors; consequently, if a change in dividend policy is to have no effect on share value this change must cause an equal but opposite change in the expected capital gain component of total return. The only other alternative explanation would be that although the change in dividend policy did alter the return, it also affected the investors' perceived risk by a corresponding amount so that share values were still constant.

The theoretical framework was laid out in 1961 by Modigliani and Miller[6] when they demonstrated that, under the conditions of perfect competition (including no taxes and no transaction costs), dividend policy is irrelevant. Not only do they require the conditions of perfect competition but dividends are defined as being the residual cash flow item after the company has decided on its investment and borrowing plans. In other words investment and capital structure decisions are completely independent of the decision of whether or not to pay dividends.

Clearly if dividends are to be increased but investment and borrowing plans are kept constant, there is a financing gap. This financing gap can only be filled by raising equity (issuing new shares). Those new shares must be worth their issue price (under perfect competition, if this were not true no-one would buy them) but, in total, this is equal to the total additional dividends being paid. However the total value of the company has

---

6. F. Modigliani and M.H. Miller, 'Dividend Policy, Growth and the Valuation of Shares', *The Journal of Business*, October 1961.

not been altered because its investment policy is still the same, so that the expected present value of its future cash flow has not changed. The value of these new shares can only be produced from a reduction in the value of the existing shares, on which the extra dividend is being declared. The reduction in value of the existing shares is, therefore, exactly equal to the extra dividend being paid to the holders of these existing shares. Hence they should be indifferent as to whether they receive the extra dividend or not; the first alternative condition outlined above has been satisfied. The extra dividends do, of course, provide a cash inflow to the shareholders but, in a perfectly competitive market, they could generate the same cash flow by selling the appropriate proportion of their existing shares in the market. Their remaining fewer shares, which have not been reduced in value by the issue of new shares, will have the same value as the larger number of lower priced shares held following the increased dividend declaration.

The logic of this analysis is self-evident but it does, of course, hinge on some very restrictive assumptions regarding the external market environment and investors' reactions to changes in the mix of their returns. However the most critical restriction is caused by the total separation of dividend policy from investment and financing policies. Clearly in an environment of no taxes and transaction costs there will be no value change in paying a dividend if the amount of the dividend has to be reinvested, either by the existing investors or by new investors with the same risk perception. This same risk perception is also a key assumption of perfectly competitive and even efficient markets. Indeed this argument of dividend irrelevance holds for efficient rather than perfectly competitive markets (the key difference being that perfectly competitive markets require perfect foresight, i.e. no risk regarding future cash flows) as long as the investment and financing policies are kept totally independent of the dividend policy.

This does not contradict the logic of Chapter 3 because an increasing dividend policy was driven by the reducing opportunities for profitable reinvestment during a period of increasing positive cash flow. In other words the financial strategy is interrelated rather than compartmentalized and abstracted.

There are, as usual, many differing views regarding the relevance of dividend policies to share values in the real world where not only taxes and transaction costs exist but dividends may also provide information signals to investors. Although investors are actually interested in future cash flows, they receive primarily historic accounting based earnings information from the company. If increased current accounting earnings are followed by an increased dividend payment, investors may become more confident that these earnings are both real in that they represent current or future increases in cash inflows (i.e. they are not achieved by 'Mickey Mouse' creative accounting) and are expected by the company's managers to be maintained or further improved in the future. This increased confidence reduces the investors' perceived risk and can therefore increase the share price; but, of course, advocates of the efficient market theory argue that this information is already built into the existing share price. If it is not already incorporated, the counter-argument is that this information flow represents a one-off movement in the share price caused by a change in the dividend payment, hence the actual level of dividends is still irrelevant.

Taxation policies in many economies treat dividends differently to capital gains and hence may create distorted incentives for companies either to pay out or retain profits purely due to the particular taxation environment. Normally dividends are taxed heavily for the average individual investor, thus giving companies an incentive to pay lower dividends. However in many cases different classes of investors are also taxed differently with some being completely tax-exempt, some being more highly taxed on dividends (high income individuals) and some more highly taxed on capital gains (companies). This further complicates the picture because it makes high dividend paying stocks less attractive to some investors but more attractive to others.

The good news is that many governments do seem to be trying to reduce some of the distortions but, if capital markets are functioning efficiently, these different groups of investors will buy and sell shares as their attractiveness changes. Thus, as mentioned in Chapter 3, the composition of the shareholder body of a company may change as the financial strategy unfolds; the more predictable this strategy is, the easier it is for the investors to buy and sell at a fair price. Such distortions also encourage companies to find ways around the tax disincentives of paying cash dividends; this may be achieved by offering stock (or scrip) dividends, where instead of cash the investor receives extra free shares in the company, or by repurchasing an equivalent value of existing shares from shareholders. These methods are considered in more detail in Chapter 10.

A very important issue in assessing the theory on dividend policy is to see how companies actually set their dividend policies. Based on the evidence, the most common policies seem to be to pay out a constant proportion of post-tax profits ('to give the shareholders their share of the returns achieved by the company'), to attempt to maintain, or grow at a steady rate, the value (sometimes in nominal and sometimes in real terms) of the dividend stream, or preferably to do both of these.

Research by Lintner in 1956[7] indicated that companies have a target dividend payout ratio, but that they never actually pay that full amount. He suggested that companies determine their annual dividend based on the following formula:

$$DIV_1 - DIV_0 = a \times \{(r \times eps_1) - DIV_0\} \tag{7}$$

where
  DIV_0 is the dividend paid last year
  DIV_1 is the dividend to be paid this year
  eps_1 is the earnings per share this year
  r is the target dividend payout ratio
  a is an adjustment factor.

Equation 7 shows how the dividend changes from one year to the next. With a target payout ratio of r, the company would pay a dividend of $(r \times eps_1)$. However, it does not pay this full amount, as the directors try to 'smooth' the trend in dividend payments over time. Accordingly, the 'ideal' payout is adjusted based on how different it is from the dividend in the previous year. The adjustment factor of 'a' is company-specific, and would depend, *inter alia*, on the directors' confidence in the sustainability of future profits.

7. J. Lintner, 'Distribution of Incomes of Corporations Among Dividends, Retained Earnings and Taxes', *American Economic Review*, May 1956, pp97–113

Appendix 2: Valuing options and convertibles

INTRODUCTION

In this Appendix we explain the different types of option and the terminology used in discussing options, and review the principles behind option valuation. Because convertible financial instruments, as discussed in Chapter 9, include an option component, we then go on to examine the valuation of convertibles.

OPTIONS TERMINOLOGY

An option is a contractual right to buy or sell something at a particular time in the future, or during a given future period, at a fixed or specified price. Options can be divided into two basic types; a *call option* gives its owner the future right to buy, while a *put option* provides the future right to sell. The key to the value of options is that ownership conveys the 'right' to do something, i.e. the choice of whether to exercise the option is left to the owner, who can instead choose to do nothing, letting the option lapse.

Sellers of options have to meet their contractual obligations. The seller of a call option must deliver the asset in exchange for the agreed payment (known as the exercise or strike price) if required to do so by the buyer of the call option. The seller of a put option must pay the agreed price to the buyer of the put option if the asset is offered (put) to the seller.

All options contracts are made for a specified time period but there are two ways in which the contract may be determined. Under what is known as an *American option*, the owner can exercise the option at any time during the period of the contract; whereas under a *European option* exercise is only allowed at the maturity of the contract. In most cases, because remaining time to expiry has a positive impact on the value of an option, the differences do not have a major impact on the prices of option contracts but, theoretically, European options are much easier to value.

VALUING OPTIONS

The factors relevant to option pricing are: the exercise price, the volatility of the underlying asset, the current price of that asset, interest rates and the time to expiry. Each of these terms will now be explained, together with a discussion of how and why they affect the option value. All of the explanations of value that follow relate to call options, the right to buy an asset. A moment's reflection will tell you how put options – the right to sell – would differ.

The *exercise price*, also known as the strike price is the price that will be paid to exercise the option to acquire the asset. Working insight A2.1 illustrates this.

Volatility is the variability in the asset price. Its impact on option valuation is illustrated in Working insight A2.2.

The *asset price* is the current price of the asset over which the option has been granted. Working insight A2.3 illustrates how this impacts the price of a call option.

Later in this section we will introduce the Black–Scholes formula for valuing options. However, at this point it is worth noting another piece of terminology relating to

---

WORKING
A2.1
INSIGHT   **Impact of the exercise price on call option valuation**

Shares in Company X are trading at £10 per share.

1. You are offered the option to buy the share two years in the future at £11
2. You are offered the option to buy the share two years in the future at £15.

Option 1 is obviously more valuable. So, the exercise price is an influence on the value of the call option – the lower it is, the more the option is worth.

WORKING
A2.2
INSIGHT   **Impact of volatility on call option valuation**

Shares in Company X and Company Y are both trading at £10 per share, and you are offered an option to buy them at some point in the future at £11.

1. In the past three years Company X shares have traded between £5 and £15.
2. In the past three years Company Y shares have traded between £9.90 and £10.10.

The option over Company X is more valuable. There's little point in buying an option to buy an asset if the volatility is so low that its price is unlikely ever to reach that level. With Company X, there's a good chance that you'll be able to make a profit on exercise.

So, the greater the volatility, the more the option is worth.

**WORKING
A2.3
INSIGHT**

Impact of the asset price on call option valuation

You are offered the option to buy a share in Company P or Company Q at £11.

1. The current share price of Company P is £6
2. The current share price of Q is £10

The option over Company Q is more valuable – you have the option to buy a more valuable asset. So, the price of the underlying asset is a factor in valuing the option.

option values. The *intrinsic value* is the difference between the asset price and the exercise price. This could be at one of three states. If the intrinsic value is positive (for example, a call option at £10 to buy an asset currently trading at £11) then the option is said to be *in the money*. If option price and asset price are the same, the intrinsic value is nil and the option is referred to as *at the money*. Finally, the asset price could be lower than the option price – you would not wish to exercise the call option at £10 if you could buy the share for say £8. Such options are known as *out of the money* or colloquially as *underwater*.

Continuing with our discussion of factors that affect value, the level of the *risk free interest rate* also needs to be taken into account in option valuation, as shown in Working insight A2.4.

One final factor affects option valuation – the *time to expiry*. This is illustrated in Working insight A2.5.

Working insight A2.6 summarizes the five factors affecting call option valuation, and also demonstrates how these same factors affect the value of put options.

One further factor affects the value of options over shares. Shares pay dividends, so the shareholder will receive the dividend, but the owner of a call option over the share will not. So, the higher the dividends a company is paying, the less the value of a call option over its shares (and obviously the opposite applies to a put option).

**WORKING
A2.4
INSIGHT**

Impact of interest rates on call option valuation

For some unspecified reason, you know that you are going to need to own a share in Company M in two years' time. You have the funds available to buy it now, but if you delay the purchase you will invest the funds in government gilts. You are offered the option to buy a share in Company M for £11 in two years' time.

1. If interest rates are currently 6 per cent, then you could set aside £9.79 now, which will attract interest to compound to £11 in two years' time, when you need to buy the share.
2. If interest rates are currently 10 per cent then you could set aside £9.09 now, and the compounded interest will take this to the required £11 in two years' time.

Accordingly, the interest rate is an important factor in valuing call options – the higher it is, the more the option is worth. (Many people find this counter-intuitive, but it does make sense once you follow the logic through.)

WORKING
A2.5
INSIGHT
Impact of time to expiry on call option valuation

Shares in Company T are trading at £10 per share.

1. You are offered the option to buy the share a month in the future at £11.
2. You are offered the option to buy the share two years in the future at £11.

Obviously the two year option is more valuable – there's more chance that the share price will exceed £11 in two years than in one month. So, time to expiry is another influence on option price: the longer the time to expiry, the greater the value.

WORKING
A2.6
INSIGHT
Factors increasing option valuation

	Call options	Put options
Exercise price	Lower	Higher
Volatility	Higher	Higher
Asset price	Higher	Lower
Interest rates	Higher	Lower
Time to expiry	Longer	Longer

OPTION PRICING MODELS

These valuation characteristics were brought together in the famous option pricing model developed by Fischer Black and Myron Scholes in 1973.[1] They used some sophisticated mathematics which is deliberately not reproduced in detail here. They produced a continuous time (i.e. using integration calculus rather than discrete binomial models) option pricing valuation model which showed:

Call option value $= P_0 N(d_1) - E e^{-K_f t} N(d_2)$

where P_0 = asset price now
E = option exercise price
K_f = risk-free discount rate (continuously compounded)
σ = standard deviation of the return on the asset
t = time to maturity of option

and $d_1 = \dfrac{\ln(P_0/E) + K_f t}{\sigma \sqrt{t}} + \frac{1}{2} \sigma \sqrt{t}$

and $d_2 = d_1 - \sigma \sqrt{t}$

1. F. Black and M. Scholes, 'The Pricing of Options and Corporate Liabilities', *Journal of Political Economy*, May 1973.

and $N(d_1)$ and $N(d_2)$ are cumulative probabilities for a unit normal distribution, which is defined as having a mean of zero and a standard deviation of 1. Mathematically this can be shown for

$$f(y) \text{ as } N(d_1) = \int_{-\infty}^{d_1} f(y) dy$$

(the area under a normal distribution curve).

This formula looks fairly mind-blowing and yet its application is relatively straight-forward, particularly using tailored computer software. It is even easier when using sets of call option valuation tables (as set out on p. 298 of this book); these give the call option value as a percentage of the current asset price. Not surprisingly given the earlier discussions, the tables utilize two factors; the time value represented by $\sigma \sqrt{t}$ and the asset value ratio, which is the current asset value divided by the present value of the option exercise price.

The problem with the Black–Scholes formula is not that it is complicated but that it is, as with many financial formulae, based on a series of restrictive assumptions. It represents the value of a simple call option on an asset which produces no income stream during the life of the option (such as a non-dividend paying share in an equity-financed company). However many real-life options are actually complex options on options; for example a share in a leveraged company could be described as a call option on the underlying assets and future cash flows of the business, so that an option on a share is really an option on an option. The Black–Scholes model does not handle complex options.

A further complication is that the standard deviation of the return on the asset can itself change over time and can only really be measured historically, when it is the *expected* future volatility that is required. Empirically it has been found that this model tends to price options wrongly where the exercise price is a long way away (either way) from the current asset price, undervaluing deep in the money options and overvaluing deep out of the money options.

(It should be noted that another model has been subsequently developed in 1979 by Cox, Ross and Rubinstein[2] and independently by Rendleman and Bartter,[3] which encompasses the Black–Scholes model as a particular continuous time case. This is known as the binomial option pricing model, not surprisingly because it uses multi-period binomial distributions to drive the option valuation.)

STRUCTURING AND VALUING CONVERTIBLES

As explained in Chapter 9, convertibles are financial instruments that start out as debt (or preference shares) but give the holder the option to convert into ordinary shares of the company. Because of this, we value convertibles based on both their bond value and their option value. In this section we show how the variables of yield and potential capital gain can be combined to produce a convertible bond that is attractive to the markets.

2. J. Cox, S. Ross and M. Rubinstein, 'Option Pricing: A Simplified Approach', *Journal of Financial Economics*, September 1979.
3. R.J Rendleman Jr. and B.J Bartter, 'Two-State Option Pricing', *The Journal of Finance*, December 1979.

WORKING
A2.7
INSIGHT

Star plc – using a convertible

STAR plc wants to raise £100 million in long-term financing for a project which will take some time to become significantly profitable and cash positive. Accordingly the company prefers not to raise either debt or equity and is considering using a convertible.

   The current post-tax cost of debt for STAR is 8 per cent compared to the risk-free rate of interest at 6 per cent. At present STAR has a total of 1000 million issued shares with a market price of 50 p per share. Its forthcoming results are expected to show eps of 4 p and dividends per share of 1 p; in addition to the current dividend yield it is known that shareholders expect capital growth of 15 per cent p.a.

   Using Gordon's dividend growth model, the company's cost of equity capital can be calculated as 17 per cent as follows:

$$K_e = \frac{D_1}{P} + g$$

$$= \frac{1\,p}{50\,p} + 15\% = 17\%$$

In Working insight A2.7 we set out the parameters for STAR plc, a growth company which seeks to raise £100 million using convertible debt.

It can be seen from Working insight A2.7 that the majority of the investors' expected return in STAR plc comes from the capital growth of 15 per cent p.a. This implies that current shareholders expect the price of the shares to have doubled to 100 p in five years time $(1.15^5 = 2)$, provided that the current 75 per cent retention policy is maintained during this period.

The future expected share price is important as it determines, from the existing shareholders' perspective, the level at which the conversion price should be set. Any conversion price below 100 p in five years time should represent an expected gain to the option holder, because that level of increase in value is already effectively expected by current investors.

The company is considering issuing a 5-year convertible and the first alternative is to issue £100 million of a 10 per cent 5-year convertible unsecured loan stock. At the end of the 5-year period, the loan stock can either be redeemed at par or it can be converted into ordinary shares at a price per share of 90 p; i.e. a total of 111.11 million new shares will be issued.

The company has an effective tax rate of 30 per cent which is the same as its major investors, so that for both parties the post-tax return on the debt portion of the convertible is 7 per cent. However, from Working insight A2.7 we know that investors require an 8 per cent yield on debt issued by STAR plc. This enables the present value of the debt component to be valued by applying this rate of discount to the expected cash flows from the potentially redeemable bond, as is done in Working insight A2.8.

From Working insight A2.8 we can see that the bond portion of the convertible should be valued by the market at £96 million. However, the company wishes to raise £100 million. Thus the conversion option must be designed to have a present value of at least £4 million in order to fill the gap.

INSIGHT

Valuing the bond part of a convertible

The redeemable bond portion is simply valued at the present value of its expected future cash flows, assuming redemption at maturity, but using the appropriate full cost of debt as the discount rate rather than the yield actually offered on the bond. For STAR plc this gives:

K_d = 8 per cent

Year	Cash flow	Discount factor	Present value
1–5	£7 m	3.993	£27.9 m
5	£100 m	0.681	£68.1 m
		Net present value	£96.0 m

The equity option can be valued by the investors in a number of different ways but its exercise has an opportunity cost of £100 million in total because, by exercising their conversion option, the investors forgo their right to redeem their bonds at par. Thus the option will not be exercised unless the share price increases above 90 p. Remember however that the share price is expected to increase to 100 p during this period; this would leave the convertible holder with a capital gain upon conversion into equity.

Technically the Black–Scholes option pricing formula does not work properly for options on options, which is what a convertible is (remember that a share represents a call option on the assets of the company), particularly when dividends are paid on the shares. However, developments and variations of the formula are widely used in financial markets so that this practice will be followed here. The option valuation can be simplified by employing the key value drivers and call option valuation tables; this requires calculating the intrinsic value of the option and the time value.

The time value of the option depends on the time to maturity (note that this is a simple European option as it can only be exercised at maturity) and the expected volatility of the share price during the option period. We will assume that the standard deviation of the return of STAR plc is 0.25. Based on these parameters, the calculation of the option value is shown in Working insight A2.9. This demonstrates that the option value should have a present value of £6.6 million which can be added to the bond's present value of £96 million.

If we add the £6.6 m option value calculated in Working insight A2.9 to the £96 m bond value shown in Working insight A2.8, we arrive at a total value for the convertible of £102.6 million. In practice, this would enable the company to raise its required £100 million and pay the expenses of the issue.

By now, it should be clear that in corporate finance there are, at best, usually only zero sum games, so where does the extra value of £2.6 million come from?

Looked at from the current investors' point of view there is a saving created by the reduced rate of interest for the 5-year life of the bond element of the convertible; this has a present value of £4 million. Therefore the current investor can afford to give away an equity option with a present value of £4 million and be made no worse off as a result of this financing structure.

In order to keep the rational convertible investor happy, this £4 m present value of the option has to increase by at least 17 per cent per annum (the full cost of equity must be used because no dividends are received on the option). As shown in Working insight A2.10, this

Valuing the option part of a convertible

Time value

Standard deviation (σ) of STAR plc	$= 0.25$ p.a.
Time to maturity	$= 5$ years
Time value factor	$= \sigma \sqrt{t}$
	$= 0.25 \times \sqrt{5}$
	$= 0.56$

Intrinsic value

Risk free rate of interest (post tax) from Working insight A2.7	$= 6\%$
Present value of exercise price	$= 90 \text{ p} \div (1.06)^5$
	$= 67.25$
Asset value ratio (current price $\div$ PV of exercise price)	$= 50/67.25$
	$= 74.35\%$

Using the call option tables (p. 298 of this book), the closest we can come to these parameters is an asset value ratio of 0.75 and $\sigma \sqrt{t}$ of 0.55, which gives a factor of 11.9 per cent.

Thus the value of each option is 11.9 per cent of the current share price

	$= 11.9\% \times 50$ p
	$= 5.95$ p

In total, 111.11 million options are created at an exercise price of 90 p per share.

The present value of these options is	$= 111.11 \text{ m} \times 5.95$ p
	$= 6.6$ m

gives a required year 5 value of £8.77 million for the equity option. This can be added to the redemption value of the bond which is the convertible investor's opportunity cost, i.e. if the value of the equity offered at the time of conversion is less than £100 million, redemption will take place in preference to conversion.

From the shareholders' perspective, this can all be achieved by offering to issue 108.77 million new shares in year 5, which implies a conversion exercise price of 91.9 p per share. This price would leave current investors indifferent, and should make the convertible bond just attractive to the new investor.

If more attractive investment terms than 91.9 p are offered, the transaction becomes less than break-even from the current shareholders' viewpoint unless the issue generates greater proceeds. In other words the £2.6 million in the first structure has been achieved at the expense of existing shareholders, as the equity conversion option has been made more attractive (90 p rather than 91.9 p) but only £100 million has been received by the company. However, this is not unreasonable – the shareholders always end up paying the effective cost of new fund raising.

The basic valuation model has made a number of simplifying assumptions, several of which have been mentioned in the above discussion. However, one important issue has not yet been considered. The equity conversion option, if exercised, automatically will lead to an increase in the total issued shares of the company in five years' time, but no new funding will be made available to the company at that time. It has been assumed that the exercise of the equity option does not lead to a decline in the value of all the existing shares; such a decline would also decrease the capital gain achieved by the con-

WORKING
A2.10
INSIGHT

Break-even equity option value – viewed from existing shareholders' perspective

Saving from lower interest rate on bond portion of convertible – present value of £4 million

This present value can be given away in the equity option without making current shareholders worse off; it also keeps convertible holders at break-even.

However, the option will be exercised in year 5 so, in order to have a present value of £4 million, it should have a year 5 expected value of £4 m $\times (1.17)^5$ or £8.77 million.

(*Note*: The expected return on options may be slightly higher than the normal cost of equity to allow for the higher risk perception of investors in the option.)

Desired equity total value at end of year 5

Redemption value of bond	£100.00 million
Expected value of equity option	£8.77 million
Equity value to be issued	£108.77 million

Current shareholders expect share price to be 100 p in year 5. So, from their perspective, £108.77 m of equity value in year 5 can be satisfied by offering to issue 108.77 million shares. This gives an option exercise price of

$$\frac{£100 \text{ m}}{108.77 \text{ m}} = 91.9 \text{ p}$$

from the perspective of the convertible holder.

Note: Strictly speaking existing shareholders could still be marginally worse off after granting this option; they want the share price after the option exercise to be kept at the 100 p which they are currently expecting in year 5. Allowing 108.77 million new shares to be issued at 91.9 p would reduce the average share price below this desired level; however, in an efficient market the earlier saving in financing costs should have boosted share prices above their expected levels.

version. If the financial market can properly value the convertible (through its component parts) prior to its conversion, there should be no such change – but this is a big 'if'. Remember, the valuation of traded equity options is different to the situation of a convertible, as the exercise of a traded option does not result in an increase in the total number of shares in existence; the shares required under the option contract are either already owned or must be bought in the market.

ANOTHER WAY TO VALUE CONVERTIBLES

In the above discussion, the convertible in the example was kept very simple and restrictive; a 5-year fixed term with the exercise of the conversion option only being allowed at the end of the term. In practice companies issuing convertibles like to offer potential investors more alternatives, as they see this as making the investment more attractive. One way of making any investment involving an option more attractive is to extend the life of the option: for example, a 15-year convertible might appear better than a 5-year time period. However, the other part of the convertible is a bond which carries a below-market rate of interest; thus the longer the life of the bond, the lower its present value.

Normally it is uneconomic for the company to increase the value of the option at the expense of an equal decline in the bond value, due to the different effective costs of capital used by investors to value each element. Therefore companies are constantly looking for ways to increase the value of the option without an offsetting decline in the value of the bond, or vice versa. One common way of increasing investor flexibility is to allow conversion of the bond into equity within the life of the convertible; an American option, of course, has this ability to exercise the option at any time already built in. In many UK convertible issues, conversion is allowed on a specified date each year or for a stated number of years prior to the expiry of the convertible when, if conversion has not been requested, redemption takes place.

In theory for a normal option, this extra flexibility should have no real impact because an unexpired option always has a time value; thus it should be financially more attractive to sell the option rather than to exercise it before maturity date. However, convertibles have a complication because shares can receive a dividend yield, while the unexercised options do not. This means that there may be an opportunity cost associated with not exercising the option within its lifetime. There is an offsetting cost associated with exercising the option because the yield on the convertible bond or preference share will be lost once the conversion option is exercised.

This trade-off has led to the development of a different method of valuing certain convertibles, which is commonly described as the 'dividend cross-over model'. The model basically assumes that, as long as the market price of the share is above the exercise price of the option, conversion will take place when the opportunity cost of the foregone dividend exceeds the yield on the bond or preference share. Thus the value of the convertible can be calculated as the present value of the equivalent equity investment made now plus differential cash flows received in this period up to conversion plus the value of the put redemption option should conversion never take place.

This is at first sight a complex issue, but can be made much clearer using an example. The case of STAR plc is not appropriate to this situation, as it would not be expected that the dividend in that high growth company would exceed the interest yield during its 5-year life. Accordingly a new, more appropriate example is given in Working insight A2.11.

The logic of the cross-over valuation model is to consider the investment in the convertible as an investment in a deferred equity, in that the investor could, as an alternative investment, buy an equivalent number of shares today. If the shares are bought now, the investors receive dividends and make capital gains from 100 p (or make losses if the value falls). These dividends are discretionary and should therefore be discounted to their present values using the equity cost of capital. Once these equity dividends exceed the convertible preference yield, which is fixed, investors will exercise their right to convert (the option should be 'in the money' from year 3 onwards using a 10 per cent p.a. rate of capital growth); this conversion is expected to occur at the end of year 6. After conversion, the two investments are exactly the same so there is no need to continue the comparison.

During the life of the convertible, the fixed preference dividend would be received and its present value can be assessed using the debt-based rate of discount (8 per cent) due to its non-discretionary nature. The convertible also has the added attraction that the bond can be redeemed at the end of its 10-year life if the share price has not risen above 125 p. This shows how this method of valuation looks at the convertible in the opposite way to the earlier method; the convertible is regarded as being equivalent to buying the shares today and having a put option on the bond back to the company.

WORKING
A2.11
INSIGHT

Example of use of a dividend cross-over model

The current share price of Slowing Growth Inc is 100 p. Its expected dividend yield is 5 per cent; the dividend and capital value are expected to grow at 10 per cent per annum. The company has recently issued a 10-year convertible redeemable preference share which has a 7 per cent fixed dividend yield and the right to convert into ordinary shares at any time at a price of 125 p per share.

Thus £100 of convertible preference shares can convert into 80 ordinary shares. The company wishes to use a dividend cross-over model to value these convertible preference shares. The full company rate for debt is 8 per cent and for equity 15 per cent. (Tax is ignored in this example.)

Assuming conversion of £100 of convertibles into 80 shares, the equivalent alternative equity investment today is to buy 80 shares (i.e. an investment of £80).

Year	Equivalent 80 shares investment				£100 nominal convertible investment		
	Expected dividend payment per share	Dividend yield on 80 shares	Discount factor @ 15%	Present value	Preference dividend yield	Discount factor @ 8%	Present value
1	5 p	400 p	.870	348.0 p	700 p	.926	648.2 p
2	5.5 p	440 p	.756	332.6 p	700 p	.857	599.9 p
3	6.1 p	488 p	.658	321.1 p	700 p	.794	555.8 p
4	6.6 p	528 p	.572	302.0 p	700 p	.735	514.5 p
5	7.3 p	584 p	.497	290.2 p	700 p	.681	476.7 p
6	8.1 p	648 p	.432	279.9 p	700 p	.630	441.0 p
*7	8.9 p	*712 p	N/A	N/A	*700 p	N/A	N/A
8	9.7 p	776 p	N/A	N/A	700 p	N/A	N/A
9	10.7 p	856 p	N/A	N/A	700 p	N/A	N/A
10	11.8 p	944 p	N/A	N/A	700 p	N/A	N/A
		Total present value		1873.8 p		Total present value	3236.1 p

*Shows where conversion becomes logical.

Difference in present value	= £13.62
Plus equivalent investment cost at present value	= £80.00
	93.62
Deemed minimum value of redemption put option	6.38
Total value of convertibles	£100.00

Glossary
of selected
financial terms

ADR. American Depository Receipt – a bearer security issued in the United States which represents a block of securities of a non-US company.

Agency theory. A theory which considers ways to limit the divergence of goals between shareholders (principals of the company) and directors (their agents, who run the company).

Annuity. The receipt or payment of the same sum of money each year for a given number of years.

Annuity value of a share. The value justified by the current level of earnings per share.

Basis point. 0.01 percent.

Beta. A measure of risk compared to the market. The equity beta is the beta of the company's share. The asset beta reflects the business risk.

Bond. A long term debt.

Bonus issue. An issue of shares to existing shareholders made by capitalizing retained profits. No cash is transferred, and shareholders end up holding the same proportions of the company as they did before the issue.

Buyback. Also known as a share repurchase, this is where the company acquires its own shares.

CAPM. The Capital Asset Pricing Model, a method of calculating a company's cost of equity by using the risk free rate, the company's beta and the market premium.

Convertible. A financial instrument that starts as a debt or preference security, but gives the holder an option to convert into ordinary shares instead of being repaid.

Cost of capital. An average of a company's costs of equity and debt (and other forms of finance such as preference shares), weighted in accordance with their relative values in the capital structure.

Covenant. A clause in a loan agreement giving the lender the right to call in the loan if conditions are breached.

Deep discount rights issue. A rights issue at a share price considerably below the current market price.

Delisting. The opposite of flotation – when a listed company goes private.

Discount rate. The rate used to discount future cash flows. Often a company's cost of capital, suitably risk-adjusted, is used as the discount rate.

Dividend growth model (DGM). A method of calculating a company's cost of equity capital by taking the dividend yield and the expected future growth in dividends.

Due diligence. The investigatory work undertaken by a prospective acquirer or lender prior to an investment being made.

Envy ratio. In a leveraged transaction, the ratio of the venture capitalist's capitalization to the management's capitalization of the company. Capitalizations are calculated as the amount invested by each party, divided by their percentage share of the equity.

Eps. Earnings per share, the profits available to the ordinary shareholders divided by the number of ordinary shares outstanding.

Exercise price. The price at which an option may be exercised.

Flotation. The act of listing a company on a public stock market. Also known as an Initial Public Offering.

Fundamental value. The value of a company (or a share) calculated by discounting its forecast future cash flows.

Gearing. The relationship between a company's debt and equity. Also known as Leverage.

High yield debt. Previously known as 'junk bonds' this is debt which is rated below investment grade.

Intrinsic value. The difference between an option's exercise price and the price of the underlying security. Could be 'in the money', 'at the money' or 'out of the money' depending on whether the exercise price is below, the same as, or above the asset price.

IPO. Initial Public Offering – another term for flotation.

IRR. Internal Rate of Return. The discount rate which, when applied to all of the cash flows to be generated by a project, results in a net present value of zero. If the IRR exceeds the company's criterion discount rate, this is an indication that the company is returning greater than its target rate.

Junk bonds. High yield bonds, with a credit rating lower than BBB- (Standard and Poor's rating) or Baa (Moody's rating).

Leverage. Gearing.

LIBOR. London Inter Bank Offered Rate. A benchmark rate used in determining corporate interest rates.

Ltip. Long term incentive plan, normally for executive remuneration.

Market capitalization. The market value of a company's equity, calculated as the current share price multiplied by the number of shares outstanding.

MBO. Management Buy Out. A transaction in which the company's management acquire the company, often financed by private equity.

Merger. Combination of two or more companies of approximately equal size.

Narrow discount rights issue. A rights issue for which the rights price is only slightly lower than the market price. (See also Deep discount rights issue).

NPV. Net Present Value, the sum of the present values of all positive and negative cash flows associated with a project. A positive NPV implies that the project is making a return in excess of the discount rate used.

Option. The right, but not the obligation, to do something. A call option gives the holder the right to buy a given security at an agreed price at a specific time; a put option gives the right to sell. Options which have a specific date on which they can be exercised are known as European options; those which can be exercised over a given period are known as American options.

P/E. The Price/Earnings ratio is the company's current share price divided by its earnings per share.

Payout ratio. The dividend paid to ordinary shareholders as a proportion of the profits available for ordinary shareholders. (Payout ratio = 1 − retention ratio.)

Perpetuity. The receipt or payment of the same sum every year in perpetuity.

Poison pill. A specific bid defence tactic which makes the target company less attractive to the bidder.

Preference gearing. The use of preference shares in a private equity transaction in order to increase management's proportion of the equity.

PVGO. Present Value of Growth Opportunities – the amount of the current share price that is not supported by existing earnings.

Ratchet. A means to increase or decrease management's proportion of the equity in a private equity transaction based on the achievement of certain results.

Retention (plowback) ratio. The retained profits of a company as a proportion of the profits earned for ordinary shareholders. (Retention ratio = 1 − payout ratio.)

Return on equity (RoE). Profits available for ordinary shareholders divided by the company's equity.

Return on investment. Profits before financing charges (and often before tax) divided by the total funds (debt and equity) invested in the business.

Rights issue. An issue of shares to existing shareholders, generally at a price below current market value.

Risk. Volatility in the expected return.

Security (1). A financial instrument.

Security (2). Lenders can gain security by taking a charge over assets such that the assets can be used to repay their loan if the company fails.

Steady state. A company in steady state is neither growing nor contracting. This is a theoretical construction, unlikely ever to occur in practice.

Tax shield. The reduction in the company's tax burden due to debt interest being tax deductible. Calculated as the interest charge multiplied by the tax rate.

Underwriting. An arrangement whereby a financial services company agrees to acquire the shares in a listing if they are not taken up by other shareholders.

WACC. Weighted average cost of capital – see Cost of Capital.

Discount table: present value of £1

Years	1%	2%	4%	5%	6%	8%	10%	12%	14%	15%	Discount rate 16%	18%	20%	22%	24%	25%	26%	28%	30%	35%	40%
1	0.990	0.980	0.962	0.952	0.943	0.926	0.909	0.893	0.877	0.870	0.862	0.847	0.833	0.820	0.806	0.800	0.794	0.781	0.769	0.741	0.714
2	0.980	0.961	0.925	0.907	0.890	0.857	0.826	0.797	0.769	0.756	0.743	0.718	0.694	0.672	0.650	0.640	0.630	0.610	0.592	0.549	0.510
3	0.971	0.942	0.889	0.864	0.840	0.794	0.751	0.712	0.675	0.658	0.641	0.609	0.579	0.551	0.524	0.512	0.500	0.477	0.455	0.406	0.364
4	0.961	0.924	0.855	0.823	0.792	0.735	0.683	0.636	0.592	0.572	0.552	0.516	0.482	0.451	0.423	0.410	0.397	0.373	0.350	0.301	0.260
5	0.951	0.906	0.822	0.784	0.747	0.681	0.621	0.567	0.519	0.497	0.476	0.437	0.402	0.370	0.341	0.328	0.315	0.291	0.269	0.223	0.186
6	0.942	0.888	0.790	0.746	0.705	0.630	0.564	0.507	0.456	0.432	0.410	0.370	0.335	0.303	0.275	0.262	0.250	0.227	0.207	0.165	0.133
7	0.933	0.871	0.760	0.711	0.665	0.583	0.513	0.452	0.400	0.376	0.354	0.314	0.279	0.249	0.222	0.210	0.198	0.178	0.159	0.122	0.095
8	0.923	0.853	0.731	0.677	0.627	0.540	0.467	0.404	0.351	0.327	0.305	0.266	0.233	0.204	0.179	0.168	0.157	0.139	0.123	0.091	0.068
9	0.914	0.837	0.703	0.645	0.592	0.500	0.424	0.361	0.308	0.284	0.263	0.225	0.194	0.167	0.144	0.134	0.125	0.108	0.094	0.067	0.048
10	0.905	0.820	0.676	0.614	0.558	0.463	0.386	0.322	0.270	0.247	0.227	0.191	0.162	0.137	0.116	0.107	0.099	0.085	0.073	0.050	0.035
11	0.896	0.804	0.650	0.585	0.527	0.429	0.350	0.287	0.237	0.215	0.195	0.162	0.135	0.112	0.094	0.086	0.079	0.066	0.056	0.037	0.025
12	0.887	0.788	0.625	0.557	0.497	0.397	0.319	0.257	0.208	0.187	0.168	0.137	0.112	0.092	0.076	0.069	0.062	0.052	0.043	0.027	0.018
13	0.879	0.773	0.601	0.530	0.469	0.368	0.290	0.229	0.182	0.163	0.145	0.116	0.093	0.075	0.061	0.055	0.050	0.040	0.033	0.020	0.013
14	0.870	0.758	0.577	0.505	0.442	0.340	0.263	0.205	0.160	0.141	0.125	0.099	0.078	0.062	0.049	0.044	0.039	0.032	0.025	0.015	0.009
15	0.861	0.743	0.555	0.481	0.417	0.315	0.239	0.183	0.140	0.123	0.108	0.084	0.065	0.051	0.040	0.035	0.031	0.025	0.020	0.011	0.006
16	0.853	0.728	0.534	0.458	0.394	0.292	0.218	0.163	0.123	0.107	0.093	0.071	0.054	0.042	0.032	0.028	0.025	0.019	0.015	0.008	0.005
17	0.844	0.714	0.513	0.436	0.371	0.270	0.198	0.146	0.108	0.093	0.080	0.060	0.045	0.034	0.026	0.023	0.020	0.015	0.012	0.006	0.003
18	0.836	0.700	0.494	0.416	0.350	0.250	0.180	0.130	0.095	0.081	0.069	0.051	0.038	0.028	0.021	0.018	0.016	0.012	0.009	0.005	0.002
19	0.828	0.686	0.475	0.396	0.331	0.232	0.164	0.116	0.083	0.070	0.060	0.043	0.031	0.023	0.017	0.014	0.012	0.009	0.007	0.003	0.002
20	0.820	0.673	0.456	0.377	0.312	0.215	0.149	0.104	0.073	0.061	0.051	0.037	0.026	0.019	0.014	0.012	0.010	0.007	0.005	0.002	0.001

Years	1%	2%	4%	5%	6%	8%	10%	12%	14%	15%	16%	18%	20%	22%	24%	25%	26%	28%	30%	35%	40%
21	0.811	0.660	0.439	0.359	0.294	0.199	0.135	0.093	0.064	0.053	0.044	0.031	0.022	0.015	0.011	0.009	0.008	0.006	0.004	0.002	0.001
22	0.803	0.647	0.422	0.342	0.278	0.184	0.123	0.083	0.056	0.046	0.038	0.026	0.018	0.013	0.009	0.007	0.006	0.004	0.003	0.001	0.001
23	0.795	0.634	0.406	0.326	0.262	0.170	0.112	0.074	0.049	0.040	0.033	0.022	0.015	0.010	0.007	0.006	0.005	0.003	0.002	0.001	
24	0.788	0.622	0.390	0.310	0.247	0.158	0.102	0.066	0.043	0.035	0.028	0.019	0.013	0.008	0.006	0.005	0.004	0.003	0.002	0.001	
25	0.780	0.610	0.375	0.295	0.233	0.146	0.092	0.059	0.038	0.030	0.024	0.016	0.010	0.007	0.005	0.004	0.003	0.002	0.001	0.001	
26	0.772	0.598	0.361	0.281	0.220	0.135	0.084	0.053	0.033	0.026	0.021	0.014	0.009	0.006	0.004	0.003	0.002	0.002	0.001		
27	0.764	0.586	0.347	0.268	0.207	0.125	0.076	0.047	0.029	0.023	0.018	0.011	0.007	0.005	0.003	0.002	0.002	0.001	0.001		
28	0.757	0.574	0.333	0.255	0.196	0.116	0.069	0.042	0.026	0.020	0.016	0.010	0.006	0.004	0.002	0.002	0.002	0.001	0.001		
29	0.749	0.563	0.321	0.243	0.185	0.107	0.063	0.037	0.022	0.017	0.014	0.008	0.005	0.003	0.002	0.002	0.001	0.001			
30	0.742	0.552	0.308	0.231	0.174	0.099	0.057	0.033	0.020	0.015	0.012	0.007	0.004	0.003	0.002	0.001	0.001	0.001			
35	0.706	0.500	0.253	0.181	0.130	0.068	0.036	0.019	0.010	0.008	0.006	0.003	0.002	0.001	0.001						
40	0.672	0.453	0.208	0.142	0.097	0.046	0.022	0.011	0.005	0.004	0.003	0.001	0.001								
45	0.639	0.410	0.171	0.111	0.073	0.031	0.014	0.006	0.003	0.002	0.001	0.001									
50	0.608	0.372	0.141	0.087	0.054	0.021	0.009	0.003	0.001	0.001	0.001										

Discount table: present value of £1 received annually for N years

<table>
<thead>
<tr><th rowspan="2">Years</th><th colspan="21">Discount rate</th></tr>
<tr><th>1%</th><th>2%</th><th>4%</th><th>5%</th><th>6%</th><th>8%</th><th>10%</th><th>12%</th><th>14%</th><th>15%</th><th>16%</th><th>18%</th><th>20%</th><th>22%</th><th>24%</th><th>25%</th><th>26%</th><th>28%</th><th>30%</th><th>35%</th><th>40%</th></tr>
</thead>
<tbody>
<tr><td>1</td><td>0.990</td><td>0.980</td><td>0.962</td><td>0.952</td><td>0.943</td><td>0.926</td><td>0.909</td><td>0.893</td><td>0.877</td><td>0.870</td><td>0.862</td><td>0.847</td><td>0.833</td><td>0.820</td><td>0.806</td><td>0.800</td><td>0.794</td><td>0.781</td><td>0.769</td><td>0.741</td><td>0.714</td></tr>
<tr><td>2</td><td>1.970</td><td>1.942</td><td>1.886</td><td>1.859</td><td>1.833</td><td>1.783</td><td>1.736</td><td>1.690</td><td>1.647</td><td>1.626</td><td>1.605</td><td>1.566</td><td>1.528</td><td>1.492</td><td>1.457</td><td>1.440</td><td>1.424</td><td>1.392</td><td>1.361</td><td>1.289</td><td>1.224</td></tr>
<tr><td>3</td><td>2.941</td><td>2.884</td><td>2.775</td><td>2.723</td><td>2.673</td><td>2.577</td><td>2.487</td><td>2.402</td><td>2.322</td><td>2.283</td><td>2.246</td><td>2.174</td><td>2.106</td><td>2.042</td><td>1.981</td><td>1.952</td><td>1.923</td><td>1.868</td><td>1.816</td><td>1.696</td><td>1.589</td></tr>
<tr><td>4</td><td>3.902</td><td>3.808</td><td>3.630</td><td>3.546</td><td>3.465</td><td>3.312</td><td>3.170</td><td>3.037</td><td>2.914</td><td>2.855</td><td>2.798</td><td>2.690</td><td>2.589</td><td>2.494</td><td>2.404</td><td>2.362</td><td>2.320</td><td>2.241</td><td>2.166</td><td>1.997</td><td>1.849</td></tr>
<tr><td>5</td><td>4.853</td><td>4.713</td><td>4.452</td><td>4.329</td><td>4.212</td><td>3.993</td><td>3.791</td><td>3.605</td><td>3.433</td><td>3.352</td><td>3.274</td><td>3.127</td><td>2.991</td><td>2.864</td><td>2.745</td><td>2.689</td><td>2.635</td><td>2.532</td><td>2.436</td><td>2.220</td><td>2.035</td></tr>
<tr><td>6</td><td>5.795</td><td>5.601</td><td>5.242</td><td>5.076</td><td>4.917</td><td>4.623</td><td>4.355</td><td>4.111</td><td>3.889</td><td>3.784</td><td>3.685</td><td>3.498</td><td>3.326</td><td>3.167</td><td>3.020</td><td>2.951</td><td>2.885</td><td>2.759</td><td>2.643</td><td>2.385</td><td>2.168</td></tr>
<tr><td>7</td><td>6.728</td><td>6.472</td><td>6.002</td><td>5.786</td><td>5.582</td><td>5.206</td><td>4.868</td><td>4.564</td><td>4.288</td><td>4.160</td><td>4.039</td><td>3.812</td><td>3.605</td><td>3.416</td><td>3.242</td><td>3.161</td><td>3.083</td><td>2.937</td><td>2.802</td><td>2.508</td><td>2.263</td></tr>
<tr><td>8</td><td>7.652</td><td>7.325</td><td>6.733</td><td>6.463</td><td>6.210</td><td>5.747</td><td>5.335</td><td>4.968</td><td>4.639</td><td>4.487</td><td>4.344</td><td>4.078</td><td>3.837</td><td>3.619</td><td>3.421</td><td>3.329</td><td>3.241</td><td>3.076</td><td>2.925</td><td>2.598</td><td>2.331</td></tr>
<tr><td>9</td><td>8.566</td><td>8.162</td><td>7.435</td><td>7.108</td><td>6.802</td><td>6.247</td><td>5.759</td><td>5.328</td><td>4.946</td><td>4.772</td><td>4.607</td><td>4.303</td><td>4.031</td><td>3.786</td><td>3.566</td><td>3.463</td><td>3.366</td><td>3.184</td><td>3.019</td><td>2.665</td><td>2.379</td></tr>
<tr><td>10</td><td>9.471</td><td>8.983</td><td>8.111</td><td>7.722</td><td>7.360</td><td>6.710</td><td>6.145</td><td>5.650</td><td>5.216</td><td>5.019</td><td>4.833</td><td>4.494</td><td>4.192</td><td>3.923</td><td>3.682</td><td>3.571</td><td>3.465</td><td>3.269</td><td>3.092</td><td>2.715</td><td>2.414</td></tr>
<tr><td>11</td><td>10.368</td><td>9.787</td><td>8.760</td><td>8.306</td><td>7.887</td><td>7.139</td><td>6.495</td><td>5.938</td><td>5.453</td><td>5.234</td><td>5.029</td><td>4.656</td><td>4.327</td><td>4.035</td><td>3.776</td><td>3.656</td><td>3.544</td><td>3.335</td><td>3.147</td><td>2.752</td><td>2.438</td></tr>
<tr><td>12</td><td>11.255</td><td>10.575</td><td>9.385</td><td>8.863</td><td>8.384</td><td>7.536</td><td>6.814</td><td>6.194</td><td>5.660</td><td>5.421</td><td>5.197</td><td>4.793</td><td>4.439</td><td>4.127</td><td>3.851</td><td>3.725</td><td>3.606</td><td>3.387</td><td>3.190</td><td>2.779</td><td>2.456</td></tr>
<tr><td>13</td><td>12.134</td><td>11.348</td><td>9.986</td><td>9.394</td><td>8.853</td><td>7.904</td><td>7.103</td><td>6.424</td><td>5.842</td><td>5.583</td><td>5.342</td><td>4.910</td><td>4.533</td><td>4.203</td><td>3.912</td><td>3.780</td><td>3.656</td><td>3.427</td><td>3.223</td><td>2.799</td><td>2.468</td></tr>
<tr><td>14</td><td>13.004</td><td>12.106</td><td>10.563</td><td>9.899</td><td>9.295</td><td>8.244</td><td>7.367</td><td>6.628</td><td>6.002</td><td>5.724</td><td>5.468</td><td>5.008</td><td>4.611</td><td>4.265</td><td>3.962</td><td>3.824</td><td>3.695</td><td>3.459</td><td>3.249</td><td>2.814</td><td>2.477</td></tr>
<tr><td>15</td><td>13.865</td><td>12.849</td><td>11.118</td><td>10.380</td><td>9.712</td><td>8.559</td><td>7.606</td><td>6.811</td><td>6.142</td><td>5.847</td><td>5.575</td><td>5.092</td><td>4.675</td><td>4.315</td><td>4.001</td><td>3.859</td><td>3.726</td><td>3.483</td><td>3.268</td><td>2.825</td><td>2.484</td></tr>
<tr><td>16</td><td>14.718</td><td>13.578</td><td>11.652</td><td>10.838</td><td>10.106</td><td>8.851</td><td>7.824</td><td>6.974</td><td>6.265</td><td>5.954</td><td>5.669</td><td>5.162</td><td>4.730</td><td>4.357</td><td>4.033</td><td>3.887</td><td>3.751</td><td>3.503</td><td>3.283</td><td>2.834</td><td>2.489</td></tr>
<tr><td>17</td><td>15.562</td><td>14.292</td><td>12.166</td><td>11.274</td><td>10.477</td><td>9.122</td><td>8.022</td><td>7.120</td><td>6.373</td><td>6.047</td><td>5.749</td><td>5.222</td><td>4.775</td><td>4.391</td><td>4.059</td><td>3.910</td><td>3.771</td><td>3.518</td><td>3.295</td><td>2.840</td><td>2.492</td></tr>
<tr><td>18</td><td>16.398</td><td>14.992</td><td>12.659</td><td>11.690</td><td>10.828</td><td>9.372</td><td>8.201</td><td>7.250</td><td>6.467</td><td>6.128</td><td>5.818</td><td>5.273</td><td>4.812</td><td>4.419</td><td>4.080</td><td>3.928</td><td>3.786</td><td>3.529</td><td>3.304</td><td>2.844</td><td>2.494</td></tr>
<tr><td>19</td><td>17.226</td><td>15.678</td><td>13.134</td><td>12.085</td><td>11.158</td><td>9.604</td><td>8.365</td><td>7.366</td><td>6.550</td><td>6.198</td><td>5.877</td><td>5.316</td><td>4.844</td><td>4.442</td><td>4.097</td><td>3.942</td><td>3.799</td><td>3.539</td><td>3.311</td><td>2.848</td><td>2.496</td></tr>
<tr><td>20</td><td>18.046</td><td>16.351</td><td>13.590</td><td>12.462</td><td>11.470</td><td>9.818</td><td>8.514</td><td>7.469</td><td>6.623</td><td>6.259</td><td>5.929</td><td>5.353</td><td>4.870</td><td>4.460</td><td>4.110</td><td>3.954</td><td>3.808</td><td>3.546</td><td>3.316</td><td>2.850</td><td>2.497</td></tr>
</tbody>
</table>

Years	1%	2%	4%	5%	6%	8%	10%	12%	14%	15%	16%	18%	20%	22%	24%	25%	26%	28%	30%	35%	40%
21	18.857	17.011	14.029	12.821	11.764	10.017	8.649	7.562	6.687	6.313	5.973	5.384	4.891	4.476	4.121	3.963	3.816	3.551	3.320	2.852	2.498
22	19.660	17.658	14.451	13.163	12.042	10.201	8.772	7.645	6.743	6.359	6.011	5.410	4.909	4.488	4.130	3.970	3.822	3.556	3.323	2.853	2.498
23	20.456	18.292	14.857	13.489	12.303	10.371	8.883	7.718	6.792	6.399	6.044	5.432	4.925	4.499	4.137	3.976	3.827	3.559	3.325	2.854	2.499
24	21.243	18.914	15.247	13.799	12.550	10.529	8.985	7.784	6.835	6.434	6.073	5.451	4.937	4.507	4.143	3.981	3.831	3.562	3.327	2.855	2.499
25	22.023	19.523	15.622	14.094	12.783	10.675	9.077	7.843	6.873	6.464	6.097	5.467	4.948	4.514	4.147	3.985	3.834	3.564	3.329	2.856	2.499
26	22.795	20.121	15.983	14.375	13.003	10.810	9.161	7.896	6.906	6.491	6.118	5.480	4.956	4.520	4.151	3.988	3.837	3.566	3.330	2.856	2.500
27	23.560	20.707	16.330	14.643	13.211	10.935	9.237	7.943	6.935	6.514	6.136	5.492	4.964	4.524	4.154	3.990	3.839	3.567	3.331	2.856	2.500
28	24.316	21.281	16.663	14.898	13.406	11.051	9.307	7.984	6.961	6.534	6.152	5.502	4.970	4.528	4.157	3.992	3.840	3.568	3.331	2.857	2.500
29	25.066	21.844	16.984	15.141	13.591	11.158	9.370	8.022	6.983	6.551	6.166	5.510	4.975	4.531	4.159	3.994	3.841	3.569	3.332	2.857	2.500
30	25.808	22.396	17.292	15.372	13.765	11.258	9.427	8.055	7.003	6.566	6.177	5.517	4.979	4.534	4.160	3.995	3.842	3.569	3.332	2.857	2.500
35	29.409	24.999	18.665	16.374	14.498	11.655	9.644	8.176	7.070	6.617	6.215	5.539	4.992	4.541	4.164	3.998	3.845	3.571	3.333	2.857	2.500
40	32.835	27.356	19.793	17.159	15.046	11.925	9.779	8.244	7.105	6.642	6.234	5.548	4.997	4.544	4.166	3.999	3.846	3.571	3.333	2.857	2.500
45	36.095	29.490	20.720	17.774	15.456	12.108	9.863	8.283	7.123	6.654	6.242	5.552	4.999	4.545	4.166	4.000	3.846	3.571	3.333	2.857	2.500
50	39.196	31.424	21.482	18.256	15.762	12.234	9.915	8.305	7.133	6.661	6.246	5.554	4.999	4.545	4.167	4.000	3.846	3.571	3.333	2.857	2.500

Black–Scholes value of call option expressed as a percentage of the share price

Share price divided by present value of exercise price, that is S/PV(E)

σ√t	0.30	0.35	0.40	0.45	0.50	0.55	0.60	0.65	0.70	0.75	0.80	0.82	0.84	0.86	0.88	0.90	0.92	0.94	0.96	0.98	1.00	1.02	1.04	1.06	1.08	1.10	1.12	1.14	1.16	1.18	1.20	1.25	1.30	1.35	1.40	1.45	1.50	1.75	2.00	2.50	σ√t
0.05	0.0	0.0	0.0	0.0	0.0	0.0	0.0	0.0	0.0	0.0	0.0	0.0	0.0	0.0	0.0	0.0	0.1	0.3	0.6	1.2	2.0	3.1	4.5	6.0	7.5	9.1	10.7	12.3	13.8	15.3	16.7	20.0	23.1	25.9	28.6	31.0	33.3	42.9	50.0	60.0	0.05
0.10	0.0	0.0	0.0	0.0	0.0	0.0	0.0	0.0	0.0	0.0	0.0	0.0	0.0	0.3	0.5	0.8	1.2	1.7	2.3	3.1	4.0	5.0	6.1	7.3	8.6	10.0	11.3	12.7	14.1	15.4	16.8	20.0	23.1	25.9	28.6	31.0	33.3	42.9	50.0	60.0	0.10
0.15	0.0	0.0	0.0	0.0	0.0	0.0	0.0	0.0	0.1	0.2	0.5	0.7	1.0	1.3	1.7	2.2	2.8	3.5	4.2	5.2	6.0	7.0	8.0	9.1	10.2	11.4	12.6	13.8	15.0	16.2	17.4	20.4	23.3	26.0	28.6	31.0	33.3	42.9	50.0	60.0	0.15
0.20	0.0	0.0	0.0	0.0	0.0	0.0	0.0	0.1	0.4	0.8	1.5	1.9	2.3	2.8	3.4	4.0	4.7	5.4	6.2	7.1	8.0	8.9	9.9	10.9	11.9	13.0	14.1	15.2	16.3	17.4	18.5	21.2	23.9	26.4	28.9	31.2	33.5	42.9	50.0	60.0	0.20
0.25	0.0	0.0	0.0	0.0	0.0	0.1	0.2	0.5	1.0	1.8	2.8	3.3	3.9	4.5	5.2	5.9	6.6	7.4	8.2	9.1	9.9	10.9	11.8	12.8	13.7	14.7	15.7	16.7	17.7	18.7	19.8	22.3	24.7	27.1	29.4	31.7	33.8	42.9	50.0	60.0	0.25
0.30	0.0	0.0	0.0	0.1	0.1	0.3	0.7	1.2	2.0	3.1	4.4	5.0	5.7	6.3	7.0	7.8	8.6	9.4	10.2	11.1	11.9	12.8	13.7	14.6	15.6	16.5	17.4	18.4	19.3	20.3	21.2	23.5	25.8	28.1	30.2	32.3	34.3	43.1	50.1	60.0	0.30
0.35	0.0	0.0	0.1	0.2	0.4	0.8	1.4	2.3	3.3	4.6	6.2	6.8	7.5	8.2	9.0	9.8	10.6	11.4	12.2	13.0	13.9	14.8	15.6	16.5	17.4	18.3	19.2	20.1	21.0	21.9	22.7	24.9	27.1	29.2	31.2	33.2	35.1	43.5	50.2	60.0	0.35
0.40	0.0	0.1	0.2	0.5	0.9	1.6	2.4	3.5	4.8	6.3	8.0	8.7	9.4	10.2	11.0	11.9	12.5	13.4	14.2	15.0	15.9	16.7	17.5	18.4	19.2	20.1	20.9	21.8	22.6	23.5	24.3	26.4	28.4	30.4	32.3	34.2	36.0	44.0	50.5	60.1	0.40
0.45	0.1	0.2	0.5	1.0	1.7	2.6	3.7	5.0	6.5	8.1	9.9	10.6	11.4	12.2	12.9	13.7	14.5	15.3	16.2	17.0	17.8	18.6	19.4	20.3	21.1	21.9	22.7	23.5	24.3	25.1	25.9	27.9	29.8	31.7	33.5	35.3	37.0	44.6	50.8	60.2	0.45
0.50	0.2	0.5	1.0	1.7	2.6	3.7	5.1	6.6	8.2	10.0	11.8	12.6	13.4	14.2	14.9	15.7	16.5	17.3	18.1	18.9	19.7	20.5	21.3	22.1	22.9	23.7	24.5	25.3	26.1	26.8	27.6	29.5	31.3	33.1	34.8	36.4	38.1	45.3	51.3	60.4	0.50
0.55	0.5	1.0	1.7	2.6	3.8	5.1	6.6	8.3	10.0	11.9	13.8	14.6	15.4	16.1	16.9	17.7	18.5	19.3	20.1	20.9	21.7	22.4	23.2	24.0	24.8	25.5	26.3	27.0	27.8	28.5	29.2	31.0	32.8	34.5	36.1	37.7	39.2	46.1	51.9	60.7	0.55
0.60	0.9	1.6	2.5	3.7	5.1	6.6	8.3	10.1	11.9	13.8	15.8	16.6	17.4	18.1	18.9	19.7	20.5	21.3	22.0	22.8	23.6	24.3	25.1	25.8	26.6	27.3	28.1	28.8	29.5	30.2	30.9	32.6	34.3	35.9	37.5	39.0	40.4	47.0	52.5	61.0	0.60
0.65	1.4	2.4	3.6	4.9	6.5	8.2	10.0	11.9	13.8	15.8	17.8	18.6	19.3	20.1	20.9	21.7	22.5	23.2	24.0	24.7	25.5	26.2	27.0	27.7	28.4	29.1	29.8	30.5	31.2	31.9	32.6	34.3	35.8	37.4	38.9	40.3	41.7	48.0	53.3	61.4	0.65
0.70	2.1	3.3	4.7	6.3	8.1	9.9	11.9	13.8	15.8	17.8	19.8	20.6	21.3	22.1	22.9	23.6	24.4	25.2	25.9	26.6	27.4	28.1	28.8	29.5	30.2	30.9	31.6	32.3	32.9	33.6	34.2	35.8	37.3	38.8	40.3	41.6	43.0	49.0	54.0	61.9	0.70
0.75	3.0	4.4	6.1	7.9	9.8	11.7	13.7	15.8	17.8	19.8	21.8	22.5	23.3	24.1	24.8	25.6	26.3	27.1	27.8	28.5	29.2	29.9	30.6	31.3	32.0	32.7	33.3	34.0	34.6	35.3	35.9	37.4	38.9	40.3	41.7	43.0	44.3	50.0	54.9	62.4	0.75
0.80	4.0	5.7	7.5	9.5	11.5	13.6	15.7	17.7	19.8	21.8	23.7	24.5	25.3	26.0	26.8	27.5	28.3	29.0	29.7	30.4	31.1	31.8	32.4	33.1	33.8	34.4	35.1	35.7	36.3	36.9	37.5	39.0	40.4	41.8	43.1	44.4	45.6	51.1	55.8	63.0	0.80
0.85	5.1	7.1	9.1	11.2	13.3	15.5	17.6	19.7	21.8	23.8	25.7	26.5	27.2	28.0	28.7	29.4	30.2	30.9	31.6	32.2	32.9	33.6	34.2	34.9	35.5	36.2	36.8	37.4	38.0	38.6	39.2	40.6	41.9	43.3	44.5	45.8	46.9	52.2	56.7	63.6	0.85
0.90	6.4	8.5	10.7	13.0	15.2	17.4	19.6	21.7	23.8	25.8	27.7	28.4	29.2	29.9	30.6	31.3	32.0	32.7	33.4	34.1	34.7	35.4	36.0	36.6	37.3	37.9	38.5	39.1	39.6	40.2	40.8	42.1	43.5	44.7	46.0	47.1	48.3	53.3	57.6	64.3	0.90
0.95	7.8	10.1	12.5	14.8	17.1	19.4	21.6	23.7	25.7	27.7	29.6	30.4	31.1	31.8	32.5	33.1	33.9	34.6	35.2	35.9	36.5	37.2	37.8	38.4	39.0	39.6	40.1	40.7	41.3	41.8	42.4	43.7	45.0	46.2	47.4	48.5	49.6	54.5	58.6	65.0	0.95
1.00	9.3	11.8	14.3	16.7	19.1	21.4	23.6	25.7	27.7	29.7	31.6	32.3	33.0	33.7	34.4	35.1	35.7	36.4	37.0	37.7	38.3	38.9	39.5	40.1	40.7	41.2	41.8	42.4	42.9	43.4	44.0	45.2	46.5	47.6	48.8	49.9	50.9	55.6	59.5	65.7	1.00
1.05	10.9	13.6	16.1	18.6	21.0	23.3	25.6	27.7	29.7	31.6	33.5	34.2	34.9	35.6	36.2	36.9	37.6	38.2	38.8	39.4	40.0	40.6	41.2	41.8	42.4	42.9	43.5	44.0	44.5	45.0	45.5	46.8	48.0	49.1	50.2	51.2	52.2	56.7	60.5	66.5	1.05
1.10	12.6	15.4	18.0	20.6	23.0	25.3	27.5	29.6	31.6	33.5	35.4	36.1	36.7	37.4	38.1	38.7	39.3	40.0	40.6	41.2	41.8	42.3	42.9	43.5	44.0	44.5	45.1	45.6	46.1	46.6	47.1	48.3	49.4	50.5	51.6	52.6	53.5	57.9	61.5	67.2	1.10
1.15	14.4	17.2	20.0	22.5	25.0	27.3	29.5	31.6	33.6	35.4	37.2	37.9	38.6	39.2	39.9	40.5	41.1	41.7	42.3	42.9	43.5	44.0	44.6	45.1	45.6	46.2	46.7	47.2	47.7	48.2	48.6	49.8	50.9	51.9	52.9	53.9	54.9	59.0	62.5	68.0	1.15
1.20	16.2	19.1	21.9	24.5	27.0	29.3	31.5	33.6	35.5	37.3	39.1	39.7	40.4	41.0	41.7	42.3	42.9	43.5	44.0	44.6	45.1	45.7	46.2	46.7	47.3	47.8	48.3	48.7	49.2	49.7	50.1	51.3	52.3	53.4	54.3	55.2	56.1	60.2	63.5	68.8	1.20
1.25	18.1	21.1	23.9	26.5	29.0	31.3	33.5	35.5	37.4	39.2	40.9	41.5	42.2	42.8	43.4	44.0	44.6	45.2	45.7	46.3	46.8	47.3	47.8	48.4	48.8	49.3	49.8	50.3	50.7	51.2	51.6	52.7	53.7	54.7	55.7	56.6	57.4	61.3	64.5	69.6	1.25

Square root of cumulative variance, that is σ√t

	0.30	0.35	0.40	0.45	0.50	0.55	0.60	0.65	0.70	0.75	0.80	0.82	0.84	0.86	0.88	0.90	0.92	0.94	0.96	0.98	1.00	1.02	1.04	1.06	1.08	1.10	1.12	1.14	1.16	1.18	1.20	1.25	1.30	1.35	1.40	1.45	1.50	1.75	2.00	2.50	
1.30	20.0	23.0	25.9	28.5	31.0	33.3	35.4	37.4	39.3	41.0	42.7	43.3	43.9	44.5	45.1	45.7	46.3	46.8	47.4	47.9	48.4	48.9	49.4	49.9	50.4	50.9	51.3	51.8	52.2	52.7	53.1	54.1	55.1	56.1	57.0	57.9	58.7	62.4	65.5	70.4	1.30
1.35	21.9	25.0	27.9	30.5	33.0	35.2	37.3	39.3	41.1	42.8	44.4	45.1	45.7	46.3	46.8	47.4	47.9	48.5	49.0	49.5	50.0	50.5	51.0	51.5	52.0	52.4	52.9	53.3	53.7	54.1	54.6	55.6	56.5	57.4	58.3	59.1	59.9	63.5	66.5	71.1	1.35
1.40	23.9	27.0	29.9	32.5	34.9	37.1	39.2	41.1	42.9	44.6	46.2	46.8	47.4	47.9	48.5	49.0	49.6	50.1	50.6	51.1	51.6	52.1	52.6	53.0	53.5	53.9	54.3	54.8	55.2	55.6	56.0	56.9	57.9	58.7	59.6	60.4	61.2	64.6	67.5	71.9	1.40
1.45	25.8	29.0	31.9	34.5	36.9	39.1	41.1	43.0	44.7	46.4	47.9	48.5	49.0	49.6	50.1	50.7	51.2	51.7	52.2	52.7	53.2	53.6	54.1	54.5	55.0	55.4	55.8	56.2	56.6	57.0	57.4	58.3	59.2	60.0	60.9	61.6	62.4	65.7	68.4	72.7	1.45
1.50	27.8	31.0	33.8	36.4	38.8	40.9	42.9	44.8	46.5	48.1	49.6	50.1	50.7	51.2	51.8	52.3	52.8	53.3	53.7	54.2	54.7	55.1	55.6	56.0	56.4	56.8	57.2	57.6	58.0	58.4	58.8	59.7	60.5	61.3	62.1	62.9	63.6	66.8	69.4	73.5	1.50
1.55	29.8	33.0	35.8	38.4	40.7	42.8	44.8	46.6	48.2	49.8	51.2	51.8	52.3	52.8	53.3	53.8	54.3	54.8	55.3	55.7	56.2	56.6	57.0	57.4	57.8	58.2	58.6	59.0	59.4	59.7	60.1	61.0	61.8	62.6	63.3	64.1	64.7	67.8	70.3	74.3	1.55
1.60	31.8	35.0	37.8	40.3	42.6	44.6	46.5	48.3	49.9	51.4	52.8	53.4	53.9	54.4	54.9	55.4	55.9	56.3	56.8	57.2	57.6	58.0	58.5	58.9	59.2	59.6	60.0	60.4	60.7	61.1	61.4	62.3	63.1	63.8	64.5	65.2	65.9	68.8	71.3	75.1	1.60
1.65	33.8	36.9	39.7	42.2	44.4	46.4	48.3	50.0	51.6	53.1	54.4	54.9	55.4	55.9	56.4	56.9	57.3	57.8	58.2	58.6	59.1	59.5	59.9	60.2	60.6	61.0	61.4	61.7	62.1	62.4	62.7	63.5	64.3	65.0	65.7	66.4	67.0	69.9	72.2	75.9	1.65
1.70	35.8	38.9	41.6	44.0	46.2	48.2	50.0	51.7	53.2	54.7	56.0	56.5	57.0	57.5	57.9	58.4	58.8	59.2	59.7	60.1	60.5	60.9	61.2	61.6	62.0	62.3	62.7	63.0	63.4	63.7	64.0	64.8	65.5	66.2	66.9	67.5	68.2	70.9	73.1	76.6	1.70
1.75	37.7	40.8	43.5	45.9	48.0	50.0	51.7	53.4	54.8	56.2	57.5	58.0	58.5	58.9	59.4	59.8	60.2	60.7	61.1	61.5	61.9	62.2	62.6	62.9	63.3	63.6	64.0	64.3	64.6	64.9	65.3	66.0	66.7	67.4	68.0	68.7	69.2	71.9	74.0	77.4	1.75
2.00	47.3	50.1	52.5	54.6	56.5	58.2	59.7	61.1	62.4	63.6	64.6	65.0	65.4	65.8	66.2	66.6	66.9	67.3	67.6	67.9	68.3	68.6	68.9	69.2	69.5	69.8	70.0	70.3	70.6	70.8	71.1	71.7	72.3	72.9	73.4	73.9	74.4	76.5	78.3	81.0	2.00
2.25	56.1	58.6	60.7	62.5	64.1	65.6	66.8	68.0	69.1	70.0	70.9	71.5	71.6	71.9	72.2	72.5	72.8	73.1	73.4	73.7	73.9	74.2	74.4	74.7	74.9	75.2	75.4	75.6	75.8	76.0	76.3	76.8	77.2	77.7	78.1	78.5	78.9	80.6	82.1	84.3	2.25
2.50	64.0	66.1	67.9	69.4	70.8	72.0	73.1	74.0	74.9	75.7	76.4	76.7	77.0	77.2	77.5	77.7	78.0	78.2	78.4	78.7	78.9	79.1	79.3	79.5	79.7	79.9	80.0	80.2	80.4	80.6	80.7	81.1	81.5	81.9	82.2	82.6	82.9	84.3	85.4	87.2	2.50
2.75	70.9	72.7	74.2	75.4	76.6	77.5	78.4	79.2	79.9	80.5	81.1	81.4	81.6	81.8	82.0	82.2	82.4	82.6	82.7	82.9	83.1	83.3	83.4	83.6	83.7	83.9	84.0	84.2	84.3	84.4	84.6	84.9	85.2	85.5	85.8	86.0	86.3	87.4	88.3	89.7	2.75
3.00	76.9	78.3	79.5	80.5	81.4	82.2	82.9	83.5	84.1	84.6	85.1	85.3	85.4	85.6	85.8	85.9	86.1	86.2	86.4	86.5	86.6	86.8	86.9	87.0	87.1	87.3	87.4	87.5	87.6	87.7	87.8	88.1	88.3	88.5	88.8	89.0	89.2	90.0	90.7	91.8	3.00
3.50	86.0	86.9	87.6	88.3	88.8	89.3	89.7	90.1	90.5	90.8	91.1	91.2	91.3	91.4	91.5	91.6	91.6	91.7	91.8	91.9	92.0	92.1	92.1	92.2	92.3	92.4	92.4	92.5	92.6	92.6	92.7	92.8	93.0	93.1	93.3	93.4	93.5	94.0	94.4	95.1	3.50
4.00	92.0	92.5	92.9	93.3	93.6	93.9	94.2	94.4	94.6	94.8	94.9	95.0	95.0	95.1	95.2	95.2	95.3	95.3	95.4	95.4	95.5	95.5	95.5	95.6	95.6	95.7	95.7	95.7	95.8	95.8	95.9	96.0	96.0	96.1	96.2	96.2	96.3	96.6	96.8	97.2	4.00
4.50	95.7	96.0	96.2	96.4	96.6	96.7	96.9	97.0	97.1	97.2	97.3	97.3	97.3	97.4	97.4	97.4	97.5	97.5	97.5	97.5	97.6	97.6	97.6	97.6	97.6	97.7	97.7	97.7	97.7	97.8	97.8	97.8	97.9	97.9	97.9	98.0	98.0	98.2	98.3	98.5	4.50
5.00	97.8	97.9	98.1	98.2	98.3	98.3	98.4	98.5	98.5	98.6	98.6	98.6	98.6	98.7	98.7	98.7	98.7	98.7	98.7	98.7	98.8	98.8	98.8	98.8	98.8	98.8	98.8	98.8	98.8	98.9	98.9	98.9	98.9	98.9	99.0	99.0	99.0	99.1	99.1	99.2	5.00
6.00	99.5	99.5	99.6	99.6	99.6	99.6	99.7	99.7	99.7	99.7	99.7	99.7	99.7	99.7	99.7	99.7	99.7	99.7	99.7	99.7	99.7	99.7	99.7	99.7	99.7	99.7	99.7	99.7	99.7	99.8	99.8	99.8	99.8	99.8	99.8	99.8	99.8	99.8	99.8	99.8	6.00

Note: Values in the table represent percentages of the underlying share price: for example, 40.4 denotes a call option worth 40.4 per cent of the underlying share price.

Values in the table were computed from the Black–Scholes option pricing model

Reprinted with permission from *Corporate Finance Europe* by Buckley, Ross, Westerfield and Jaffe. McGraw–Hill, 1998.

Index